FATAL JUSTICE

Jerry Allen Potter and Fred Bost

FATAL
JUSTICE

Reinvestigating

the

MacDonald

Murders

W· W· Norton & Company

New York

London

The text of this book is composed in 11/13.5 Berkeley Old Style Book with the display set in Lucian Bold. Composition by Crane Typesetting Service, Inc. Manufacturing by The Haddon Craftsmen, Inc. Book design by Margaret Wagner.

Library of Congress Cataloging-in-Publication Data

Potter, Jerry Allen.
    Fatal justice : reinvestigating the MacDonald murders / by Jerry
Allen Potter and Fred Bost.
       p.   cm.
    Includes index.
    ISBN 0-393-03000-8
    1. MacDonald, Jeffrey R., 1943–   2. Murder—North Carolina—
Case studies.   3. Trials (Murder)—North Carolina—Case studies.
I. Bost, Fred. II. Title.
HV6533.N8P68   1995
364.1′523′092—dc20   94-20537

ISBN 0-393-03000-8

W. W. Norton & Company, Inc., 500 Fifth Avenue, New York, NY. 10110
W. W. Norton & Company Ltd., 10 Coptic Street, London WC1A 1PU

2 3 4 5 6 7 8 9 0

Dedicated to
Inge Bost
and
Prebble Potter

Contents

"Let the jury consider their verdict," the King said, for about the twentieth time that day.

"No, no!" said the Queen. "Sentence first—verdict afterwards."

"Stuff and nonsense!" said Alice loudly. "The idea of having the sentence first!"

Alice in Wonderland, by Lewis Carroll

PART
ONE

The Army
Investigation

1

The Murders
on Castle Drive

At the end of a rainy Monday afternoon, February 16, 1970, Green Beret physician Jeffrey R. MacDonald left his office at Fort Bragg, North Carolina. For a while, he played basketball with friends, then he stopped by his apartment to pick up his two little daughters. As they had done nearly every day for six weeks, they drove out to a farm where he had rented space for Trooper, the Shetland pony he had bought them for Christmas.

As he approached the small barn he had built, Captain MacDonald saw that the drizzle had turned the barnyard to mud, so the children didn't ride that day. Two-year-old Kristen, as usual, held a carrot while the horse's big teeth munched down toward her tiny fingers. Finally, her father told her it was time to turn the carrot loose. She did, reluctantly, and reached for another.

Kimberly, delicate and already ladylike at age five, hadn't responded as eagerly to the horse, so MacDonald and the girls' mother, Colette, added a bunny to their little "farm." When they had fed and watered both animals, MacDonald drove his daughters home for dinner.

Within hours, at 3:33 the next morning, telephone operator Carolyn Landen in Fayetteville, North Carolina, took a strange call. A man's faint voice gasped, "My name is Captain MacDonald . . . stabbings . . . need a doctor . . . MPs and an ambulance at 544 Castle Drive. . . . Hurry!"[1]

"Is this on post or off post?" she asked.[2]

"Damn it, lady . . . my family . . . it's on post!"

"In that case I'm sorry, sir, but you'll have to call the military police yourself. You see. . . ." Landen heard a clatter as MacDonald dropped the phone. She kept the line open and dialed the military police at Fort Bragg, gave the desk sergeant the address, then waited about three minutes until she finally heard a noise in her receiver. "Is this Captain MacDonald?" she asked.

"Yes. Don't you understand, I need—"

"Just a minute, sir." She connected the relays and listened to the conversation.

She heard a man's voice ask, "Can I help you?"

"Thank God," MacDonald said. "We've been stabbed . . . people are dying . . . I may be dying . . . we need a doctor and ambulance . . . 544 Castle Drive. . . ."

"They'll be right there!" the man said. The operator heard the desk sergeant yell to someone, "Get me Womack ASAP!"

But Womack Army Hospital was not sending help. The noncommissioned officer on duty at the hospital had told the MP desk sergeant that an ambulance would not be dispatched until the military police first went out to the MacDonald residence and checked things out.

First Lieutenant Joseph Loy Paulk was the officer in charge of the military police patrol on duty that night. He and his driver, David Dickerson, departed the operations building to personally check out the call. As Paulk left he instructed the radio dispatcher to send support from patrolling units. But the dispatcher didn't express a sense of urgency, nor did he inform the MPs that Captain MacDonald had mentioned stabbings. Instead, at 3:42 A.M., the dispatcher issued a domestic disturbance call to all cruising MPs: "A DD in progress at 544 Castle Drive." He told his MPs he would keep the MacDonald phone line open, adding that they should pick up the telephone at the residence and make an immediate report of the situation.

The Corregidor Courts area of Fort Bragg consisted of single-family and large, brick, multi-family buildings on grassy yards amid meandering tree-lined streets. All the units were reserved for warrant and commissioned officers. Military policemen Kenneth Mica and Dennis Morris, assigned to patrol there that night, responded to the radio call. But they understood this was a "domestic disturbance" so they didn't hurry. The rain had stopped, but the canvas side curtains remained on their jeep as they eased through a red light on Honeycutt Road at Lucas Drive, about three blocks from the MacDonald home.

Mica, in the passenger seat, was surprised to see a woman standing alone on the corner. Although the plastic window of the side curtain was still wet with mist, he saw she wore a wide, floppy-brimmed hat and a dark raincoat hemmed above her knees. Mica wondered aloud to his partner what the woman might be doing there at 3:55 A.M. in such bad weather. He later said that if he hadn't been responding to a call he would have stopped to check her out.

As the pair braked their jeep in front of 544 Castle Drive, they found a half dozen other MPs already gathered at that end of the four-family building. White lettering centered on the front door read:

CPT J. R. MacDONALD

Lieutenant Paulk pounded on the door, but got no response. The apartment was silent. Paulk told his men to check the back.

Sergeant Richard Tevere found the rear screen door closed but the back door itself open. He entered through a small utility room into a master bedroom to see two motionless bodies lying tangled together on the floor. The room was splattered with blood, and the unsettling stench of fresh blood stung his nostrils. He turned around, raced back through the door, charged into the open backyard, and yelled, "They've been stabbed!"

Other MPs rushed through the rear door and into the master bedroom to find a woman's battered, bloody body, heavy around the middle. She lay face up and unmoving, one sightless eye open, the bloody soles of her feet toward the door. At her left side a man lay on his belly, his head cradled on her left shoulder, his face turned away from hers, his left arm stretched across her still body. The man wore only blue pajama trousers.

Mica moved forward and knelt beside the pair. The man stirred, and moaned, "Check my kids. How are my kids? I heard my kids crying."

Mica darted through the doorway into the hall. In the unlighted room to the left, the sweep of his flashlight revealed the motionless body of a small brown-haired girl in bed, almost invisible beneath the covers. His flashlight beam revealed that her head had been smashed. Mica left the room to encounter MP Williams standing in the hall, his face pale.[3] Moving on, Mica passed a lighted bathroom on his right. In the room beyond it he spotted the body of a younger girl on a small bed. Blood dripped off the bed into a dark puddle on the floor. The child lay still as stone, and she wasn't breathing. Mica quickly checked the rest of the house, then hurried back to the master bedroom where he found his fellow MPs standing dumbstruck, doing nothing to help the injured MacDonald who was now trying to sit up.

Mica forced his way between the two bodies and pushed MacDonald onto his back. The injured man was trembling and his teeth chattered. "I can't breathe, I need a chest tube," he gasped. Then he appeared to lose consciousness. Mica began applying mouth-to-mouth resuscitation as other MPs looked on.

Tevere picked up the telephone handset from the dresser to report the situation. Unknown to him, however, the desk sergeant, William Boulware, had already received a report by radio and had hung up his own phone, thereby closing the connection. Landen, the telephone operator, had also left the line when she heard the MPs arrive. Tevere heard no dial tone. Not knowing another phone in the kitchen remained off the hook, he believed the line was still open. He spoke into it, but received no response. He said he replaced the handset where he had found it on the dresser.

Under Mica's ministrations the injured man revived, only to collapse again. Mica again performed mouth-to-mouth until his patient began to struggle. "Fuck *me*, man, look to my *wife!*" MacDonald gasped, pushing Mica away. "I tried to find a pulse," MacDonald said. "Check the pulse in her leg."

"Who did this?" Mica asked.

"Check my wife—check my kids," the man pleaded, then groaned, "Why did they do this to me?"

"Who did it?"

The man's teeth were still chattering, but he was breathing better. He told Mica, "Three men—a woman—one man was colored, he wore a field jacket, sergeant's stripes—the woman, blond hair, floppy hat, short skirt, muddy boots—she carried a light, I think a candle—"

Mica looked up at Lieutenant Paulk and told him about the floppy-hatted woman he and Morris had passed only minutes earlier a few blocks back. He asked Paulk, "Don't you think we ought to send out a patrol?"

But Lieutenant Paulk ignored Mica's suggestion. He continued writing on his clipboard as the injured man began a bizarre story. "I heard Colette scream. . . ."

The Question

Because of the book *Fatal Vision* and the television movie based upon it, many know that the young captain, Jeffrey Robert MacDonald, still struggling to breathe, told the MPs a story about drug-crazed assailants who stabbed him and beat him unconscious. He related his story in an abbreviated version to MP Mica who had revived him through mouth-to-mouth resuscitation. Later that day, to CID and FBI agents at the hospital, MacDonald went into more detail. FBI agent Robert Caverly reported that MacDonald attempted to tell him what had occurred in his home before the attack. He and Colette had shared an orange liqueur, MacDonald said, then she had retired for the evening. MacDonald continued to watch the *Tonight Show* until Kristen began crying. He went to her room, then prepared her a bottle. He watched the rest of Johnny Carson's show, washed the dishes, and checked the windows in the children's rooms to be sure they weren't open too wide. When he started to retire, he saw that baby Kristen had crawled into bed next to Colette in the master bedroom and had wet his side of the bed. He carried the sleeping baby to her own bed, then moved the covers on his and Colette's bed back from the wet spot so it would dry. He said he then returned to the living room sofa and slept there.

When Caverly asked him to talk about his children, MacDonald began to cry uncontrollably. The agent summoned MacDonald's doctor, who helped to calm him. Then MacDonald explained that he had struggled with three intruders as he tried to get off the sofa in response to screams from his family. He said he had to fight not only the black man's baseball bat, but the fists and blades of the two white assailants. Somehow his faded blue pajama top had gotten pulled over his head, trapping his hands. He then used the garment between his wrists as a kind of shield to try to ward off the blows. He was ultimately knocked down by blows to the head. As he fell to the floor, just before losing consciousness, he saw a bare leg and a woman's boot.

He said he awoke to sharp pains in his head, and experienced difficulty breathing. He went to his wife and tried to revive her with mouth-to-mouth resuscitation, but without success. Frantic and unbelieving, he went to his daughters and tried to revive them, then made another round before phoning for help.

The story was widely publicized. MacDonald was a Green Beret captain, a Princeton man, a physician and group surgeon for his army unit. He was well liked, held impressive credentials, and had an impeccable college, medical school, and army record. What's more, according to his neighbors and his in-laws, he had loved his family very much. On the surface, at least, Jeffrey MacDonald didn't seem the type to have committed these monstrous crimes.

Yet, William Ivory, the young army investigator who arrived at the crime scene about fifteen minutes after the MPs, said he found things which suggested that MacDonald's story wasn't true. That very morning the CID command at Fort Bragg agreed with the investigator's assessment—the physical evidence at the crime scene seemed to prove that Captain MacDonald lied about what had happened in the murder apartment that morning.

MacDonald's in-laws, Alfred and Mildred Kassab, at first offered zealous support of him. But based upon the army's evidence and upon MacDonald's own behavior, they said, they eventually lost their faith in him and joined the army's efforts to bring the popular and highly successful physician to trial. For the brutal murders of his wife, Colette, and his little daughters, Kimberly and Kristen, a federal court in 1979, nine years after the crimes, sentenced Jeffrey MacDonald to three consecutive life terms.

MacDonald's appeals to reverse the verdict, including those based upon his claims of suppressed evidence, ultimately failed. But his lawyers say that MacDonald is truly factually innocent. They claim that evidence long suppressed by the government proves that the assailants were actually in the murder apartment that night, as MacDonald claimed, and that MacDonald was later dealt a new gang of assailants—some incompetent and untruthful army investigators, and an army lawyer who turned Justice Department prosecutor expressly to convict Jeffrey MacDonald.

Surprisingly, given the government's charges and the hard evidence they presented to prove them, a number of people in law enforcement and criminal justice have come to believe that, despite the failure of his multiple court appeals, MacDonald's claims are true, that he is, in fact, innocent. These MacDonald supporters have been vocal, and they have continually stirred national media interest. Ted L. Gunderson, a colorful former chief of the FBI's Los Angeles Bureau, continues to swear that his own reinvestigations show that MacDonald was framed. Others echoed similar sentiments, many of them calling to question various aspects of the government's forensic methods. Raymond Shedlick, Jr., a retired New York City homicide detective, made extensive inquiries in the MacDonald neighborhood and in nearby Fayetteville and, after also studying the forensic evidence, insisted, literally to his dying day, that there was absolutely no evidence against MacDonald, and that he had been cheated out of a fair trial. Aspects of the MacDonald prosecution were also questioned by the findings of Dr. Ronald Wright, Broward County medical examiner; former L.A. County coroner Dr. Thomas Noguchi; Dr. David Raskin, a leading polygrapher, and professor at the University of Utah; Dr. Emanuel Tanay, an expert on the psychiatric aspects of homicide; and many other forensic experts and attorneys.

Much of the work by these supporters and interested parties has been gratis, or for expenses only, a practice emulated in 1989 and which continues to this writing by chief MacDonald defense attorneys Harvey Silverglate and Alan Dershowitz. These two lawyers made the public claim in 1991 that the mass of evidence the government posits against MacDonald is "an absolute myth," and is "the product of prosecutorial chicanery at its worst."

In a videotaped interview, MacDonald's father-in-law, Alfred "Freddie" Kassab, was asked why MacDonald generated such support. "That's the sixty-four-thousand-dollar question," Kassab remarked, then suggested that MacDonald possesses a sociopathic ability to sway people to believe in him despite the evidence.

Not so, say various defense team investigators and researchers, each of whom insists the claims are based upon the government's own reports, upon thousands of documents heretofore held secret. The MacDonald defenders say these papers were released only when MacDonald's lawyers persuaded senators and congressmen to force the prosecutors finally to respond to the lawyers' requests for disclosure through FOIA, the Freedom of Information Act. Not until 1983 did the prosecutors provide some, but not all, of the requested information—fully thirteen years after MacDonald was charged by the army and those charges were dismissed, and four years after his federal conviction and incarceration. Many documents specifically requested have yet to be provided fully twenty-three years after the murders and more than thirteen years after MacDonald was sentenced.

Hence, the questions: Do these government files, finally released by FOIA, really corroborate the defense allegations? Did Jeffrey MacDonald murder his wife and daughters, or were they actually the victims of a group of drug users, as MacDonald had claimed from the beginning? And, if MacDonald is innocent, how has the government managed to keep him in prison thirteen years? And why?

Gunderson

When I met retired FBI agent Ted L. Gunderson in December of 1985, before I teamed up with co-author Fred Bost, Gunderson was a relic dating from the glory days of J. Edgar Hoover. The zenith of his career found him serving as chief of the Los Angeles Bureau of the FBI. He managed 800 people and a $23 million annual budget. He had supervised investigations into kidnapping, armed robbery, murder, and many other crimes. He had been especially successful in hostage negotiations with skyjackers and bank robbers. After retiring from the FBI he supervised security arrangements for the American team at the troubled 1968 Olympics in Mexico City. Following that assignment he set up his own security and investigations business in Los Angeles. When I met him he was looking into the possible ritual murders of children by a satanic cult in the Seattle area. Therein lay our mutual interest, for I had co-authored an article with psychologist Dr. Joel Norris about ritual murder. Joel told me Gunderson had read our piece and he had a case he wanted to tell me about.

"What case?"

"It involves witchcraft," Joel said, smiling.

"More witchcraft." I wasn't smiling. Joel and I both had interviewed serial killer Henry Lee Lucas. He was the one-eyed emotionally retarded handyman who had been convicted of killing a dozen women, including his mother, his girlfriend, and a sweet old woman Henry and his girlfriend had lived with in Texas. During my interviews with this killer, the very memory of ritual murder and dismemberment caused his one good eye to shine with an unholy light. I wanted no more sordid tales about bestiality and necrophilia. "I don't think I can handle any more witchcraft," I told Joel.

"This one is interesting," he said. "But I'll let Gunderson tell you about it."

So Gunderson set up a meeting in Chinatown. He asked Dr. Norris not to spread the fact around because Gunderson was currently a bit shy about exposure. He had helped convict a man of arranging contract killings eight years earlier. Now the man was paroled, and word was out that he had contracted to have Gunderson gutted and dropped into the L.A. harbor.

I would soon learn that Ted wasn't beyond setting a dramatic stage, but he couldn't have had anything to do with the cold fog rising out of Chavez Ravine that night to pour over the freeway like a wet ghost slithering through the Asian business district. Most of the buildings in the area were dark as I drove around the neighborhood craning my neck straining to see addresses. As I passed a little mall near the China Gate, the fog danced quickly upward in a wispy swirl to reveal the restaurant I was seeking. I parked and walked across the mall, pulling up my jacket collar against the wet night air. A small, possibly feminine figure shuffled by, head down, arms folded in a dark coat, socked feet in flip-flops softly slapping the ground.

A naked yellow bulb cast an orange tint on a red door and lighted a sculpted golden dragon which guarded the place against evil spirits. I entered and moved on back through a smoky bar where a handful of Asian men leaned over drinks and watched a flickering television set. At a scraggly, underdressed Christmas tree I ducked through an archway into a sparsely occupied dining area.

A man in the rear stood and waved at me—Ted Gunderson, a broad-shouldered linebacker type, maybe six feet tall. He didn't appear to have given up much since his football days at Nebraska thirty-five years earlier. With his ruddy chipmunk cheeks and busy eyes, he could have passed for George C. Scott on a foggy night.

"I'm Gunderson," he said, offering his hand. "You must be Potter." I found myself believing his Hollywood smile as he shook my hand firmly and motioned me into a chair across from him.

To get acquainted we drank green tea and bragged a bit about our best days, sparring, as it were, each perhaps looking for the real person. Gunderson sat hunched over his tea bowl, as if ready to spring. From time to time he cast appreciative glances toward the door, and I realized the old cop had situated himself, no doubt intentionally, with his back to the wall.

After a while Gunderson began to talk about the MacDonald murders. "You need to write a book about it," he said in a gravelly voice.

"Joe McGinniss already did that."

"Joe didn't write about this case."

"Well, of course he did," I said. I named Joe's book.

Gunderson smiled coldly. "He didn't write about *this* case. He wrote about the *government's* side and left out all the good stuff on the *MacDonald* side."

"Which is?"

"Which is MacDonald didn't do it," Gunderson said, watching my eyes.

I didn't say anything.

"The guy didn't get a fair trial," Gunderson said.

"Nobody in prison ever got a fair trial," I told him.

"That's true enough," Gunderson said.

"McGinniss lived with MacDonald throughout the entire trial," I reminded him. "He found out MacDonald's not a nice guy."

"*Joe McGinniss* isn't a nice guy, which you'll see soon enough. And MacDonald *isn't* the asshole McGinniss made him out to be."

"You're asking me to believe that you think that the United States Army, the FBI, the Justice Department, MacDonald's in-laws, and Joe McGinniss are all mistaken about this guy?"

"Now, you've got it," Ted said happily.

"So, what you're telling me," I said, "is that you've got a major conspiracy here."

"No. What we've got is a case gone wrong from the very first moments. As to any conspiracy, it simply happened that other law enforcement officers, being on the same team, believed their fellow investigator who misdiagnosed the crime scene and fed them reports which were less than candid. So the investigator's teammates, thinking MacDonald's really guilty, join the fray with a vengeance. 'This guy MacDonald really killed his kids, you say? Okay, let's get the bastard.'"

I looked at Gunderson's face. Sometimes you can tell people are crazy just by looking.

"Listen," he said. "You don't need a major conspiracy to make something like that work. All you need to do is convince your superiors that this guy's getting away with murder. All the real evidence is either still at the crime scene or back in the lab. If some of the evidence is confusing, that evidence just disappears or gets interpreted in the government's favor. Maybe your boss will even help. The judge and jury then see a rigged case, and sometimes the judge even closes one eye and fails to make the government adhere to the rules. It happens more than any of us would like to admit."

"And you really believe this is what happened?"

"I *know* this is what happened," Gunderson said. "I'm staking my professional reputation on it."

Ted's steady eyes and easy smile told me he believed it like he believed the floor would still hold him when he stood up. With Gunderson, I perceived, you either give up, or get the hell out of Dodge. I finally leaned back and said, "Okay. What have you got?"

He raised his hands palms up as if the whole thing were quite simple. "My guys kept back evidence," he said.

"Your guys?"

"My team, or the team I was on for years, the FBI and the prosecutor. The Justice Department. Army CID, too, far as that goes, the good guys."

I thought about that a minute.

"I'm dead serious," Ted said.

"You're out of the Bureau now."

"Retired. I went back into the field for the MacDonald defense team and I found some stuff."

"What stuff?"

"Come to my office on Saturday. You take it home and read it and if you still think MacDonald got a fair trial, you walk away."

I thought about it. MacDonald already had been in prison for almost five years when I met Gunderson. The idea that he might be innocent was unnerving. That somebody in the government could make him look so guilty on purpose was even more so. Realizing I had nothing more to go on than Ted's word, I nevertheless told him I'd give it a look. "Deal," I said.

Gunderson rose so suddenly that I flinched. But as he moved quickly toward the door of the restaurant I realized there was no danger, he was greeting an elderly lady helped along by a younger gray-haired woman and a smiling round-faced man. The older woman's expression brightened and she threw her arms around Gunderson, who hugged the old girl and planted a kiss on the top of her head. Laughing, he shook hands with the man and kissed the other woman on the cheek.

"Come on back," he told his newly arrived guests. He introduced them as old friends, and we were soon joined by others. An investment banker from Fort Worth, a television producer, a computer importer. We ordered family style—a huge steamed fish, a mountain of lemon chicken and rice—and we drank gallons of tea and white wine. I got to know some of Ted's friends. Joel Norris said they were just people passing through Ted's aura. And I watched Gunderson.

The man did have a certain charm. He seemed genuinely interested in whatever anyone was saying at the moment. That's hard to fake for more than a little while unless you're an absolute sociopath. He was enjoying himself, and I found myself liking the guy in spite of an apparently skewed judgment about MacDonald.

If ever there was an evil man in the world, I mused, Jeffrey MacDonald had to be a prime candidate. The crimes for which he was convicted were unspeakable, even unthinkable, except by a madman. I talked myself out of the trip to Gunderson's office and back into it a half dozen times before we finished dinner that night.

Gunderson said his goodbyes to the others, then walked with me through the fog. "You're still wondering how it could happen," he said, "how an innocent man gets convicted."

"That's part of it."

"The way the system works," Gunderson said, "and I know it better than most, is that the government controls the evidence."

"Okay."

"And they're supposed to turn everything over to the defense team so the defense lawyers can use anything helpful to get their guy off."

"Right."

"Well, as I said earlier, the cops or the prosecutors don't always turn everything over. And, sometimes when they do, the judge, who is really part of the prosecution—no matter what anybody says—won't let the defense use a lot of it. The idea is to get *convictions*. When you even *think* a guy's guilty, you keep anything away from the jury that might confuse them. It's a kind of game, with the defendant putting up the big stakes. They hardly ever send a prosecutor to jail for holding back evidence."

"And that's what happened here, suppressed evidence?"

"I think so."

"You think so?"

"It's complicated," Ted said, grinning broadly, pulling his Sam Spade raincoat together in front. "Trust me." He walked away quickly, head down. He put his hand up and waved goodbye without looking back. The fog wrapped around him and he was gone, leaving only the intrigue of a big case that might have gone wrong. Driving home I asked myself, could Gunderson possibly be right?

For a year I had investigated the Lucas case in Texas before it turned into a political football during an election campaign. One group of law enforcement officers said Lucas had killed hundreds of people. Another group said Lucas and the first group were lying. I watched as each side in that case told its own version lavishly, giving short shrift to any fact which seemed to support the other team's claims. Was that happening here? Perhaps there were some things in the MacDonald case that caused some confusion and Gunderson was taking advantage of them. That didn't make MacDonald innocent. In fact, it would be unusual in a triple homicide if everything *did* fit together perfectly. So, I asked, as I drove home, were both sides playing mind games with the evidence? Undoubtedly. To some extent that always happens in anything involving humans.

But, if so, where was the middle? And in that middle, where was the truth?

The Government Case against Jeffrey MacDonald

Before visiting Gunderson's office I reread Joe McGinniss's book, *Fatal Vision*, and I dipped into old newspaper reports. And what I found there made me feel as though Ted Gunderson were either a damn fool, or he really knew something no one else did.

The MPs who responded to MacDonald's urgent telephone call for help that February morning fifteen years earlier had found Kimberly and Kristen MacDonald both dead in their beds in separate small bedrooms in the small, on-post apartment. Both had suffered multiple stab wounds. Kimberly's head had been crushed, actually misshapen, by powerful blows with a club.

On the floor of the master bedroom Colette MacDonald, twenty-six, lay on her back in a pool of her own blood. She was dead from stab wounds and blows from a club which was found in the backyard where it might have been tossed from the apartment. The two types of blood on the club matched Colette's and Kimberly's. Both of Colette's arms were broken. Her torn fingernails further indicated she'd been in a fight. Her swollen middle and the subsequent autopsy revealed she was well into pregnancy.

The husband and father of the victims, Green Beret captain Jeffrey MacDonald, also twenty-six, was the only survivor. Once revived by mouth-to-mouth resuscitation, MacDonald, apparently unable to breathe well due to a chest wound which had collapsed his right lung, told the MPs, and later told the army and FBI agents, that he had been asleep on the living room sofa because baby Kristen had wet his side of the bed. He was awakened by screams from his wife and older daughter in the back of the apartment.

He claimed he tried to get up to go to his family's defense, but found himself under attack by a black man and two white men. The black attacker was wearing an army field jacket with E-6 stripes.[4] He struck at MacDonald with a baseball bat. The two white men seemed to be hitting MacDonald with fists, until he felt sharp pain in his chest, at which time he realized he was being stabbed.

MacDonald insisted that he had tried to fight off the assailants, but the black man continued striking at him with the club. The other two intruders punched at him using bladed weapons as he again attempted to rise from the sofa, and free his hands of the Afghan blanket he had been sleeping under. He said he struggled to get his feet under him so he could effectively fight back, but one of the assailants pulled MacDonald's pajama top over his head and the garment got around MacDonald's wrists, binding his hands and restricting his ability to strike blows in return. While he was being stabbed repeatedly and hit on the head with the club, he caught a brief glimpse of a blond woman carrying a flickering light. She chanted, "Acid is groovy. Kill the pigs." He also heard her say, "Acid is rain." She wore a floppy hat, and, as MacDonald fell unconscious at her feet, he saw that she wore wet boots.

He says he awoke to sharp pains in his head, and had difficulty breathing. He was face down at the living room end of the hallway leading to the bedrooms, his legs extended over the two steps into the living room, his arms bound up in his pajama top as if by a rope. His teeth chattered in the cold, and he distinctly remembered the smell of Johnson's floorwax.

From where he fell he could see Colette in the master bedroom at the end of the hallway. She was on the floor, partially sitting with her upper body lying back against a green chair. He went to her, saw the terrible wounds she had suffered, and moved her downward so that she lay on her back.

He has always claimed he possesses only dazed, disjointed recollections of what immediately followed—fighting his arms out of the pajama top, pulling a knife from her chest and throwing it to the side, trying desperately to breathe life back into her, knowing he was failing and his wife was dead.

Realizing suddenly that the house was completely silent, he went to his daughters, finding them bloodied, broken, unmoving. He recalls the surge of sick disbelief, his frantic efforts during another round through the house to try to help each family member again, using the bedroom phone to call for help, getting questions from a telephone operator, finding himself in the hallway on his hands and knees, gasping for breath, wondering if he himself were going to die, examining his wounds hastily in the hall bathroom before trying the kitchen phone, moving once more to his wife, then awakening to a ring of military helmets shimmering above him.

He says he has never been certain about other things. He has a vague recollection of placing his pajama top on his wife's chest, but he's not certain when he did it. He thinks it's possible that he also placed a bathmat on her abdomen, for he might have wanted to keep her warm, but he has no recollection of it. He would say later that many of his movements were suggested to him by investigators and, since their conclusions seemed reasonable, he had agreed, without knowing whether he was agreeing to fact or to conjecture.[5]

The nation's news media carried MacDonald's disturbing story to doorsteps and living rooms all over the country. Editions of local papers sold out. The next day at Fort Bragg and nearby Fayetteville families installed deadbolts and put heavy locks on their windows, and the sale of handguns and other weaponry greatly increased. People were careful of strangers, especially hippie types. Fewer children played outdoors. It was chilling news that a family could be wiped out in their beds, on an army post, and the murderers simply walk away, unseen, unheard, perhaps to kill again.

But did these so-called hippies really exist? The army's Criminal Investigative Division (CID) at Fort Bragg said they found no debris evidence on the floors which would have indicated intruders had come into the house from the wet yard. They also said that queries in the surrounding neighborhood revealed that no one except MacDonald claimed to have seen or heard intruders in the area, and that nothing unusual had occurred in the neighborhood that night. The lead army investigator, William Ivory, told his bosses that the arrangements of certain items at the crime scene caused him to suspect that the murders did not happen in the manner MacDonald claimed. Things in the living room, especially, seemed to have been artificially placed, apparently by MacDonald, to make the investigators believe an attack really had occurred there. MacDonald claimed he had taken off his pajama top before going to the children's bedrooms, yet fibers from that ripped pajama top, the agents said, were found in those bedrooms. How did those fibers get there if he had removed the ripped pajama top before going to his daughters' rooms?

The CID agents said they encountered evidence that the stab wound into MacDonald's right lung was self-inflicted, no doubt to make the "attack" on him seem more real. The agents believed that crime-scene evidence proved that the other, more superficial wounds must have come from a fight between Jeffrey and Colette, not in a fight with drug-crazed intruders.

Even though the army soon found that MacDonald had apparently loved his family and had possessed no motive for the murders, Ivory and his team of CID agents stuck by their guns. Also, the weapons, two knives, an ice pick, and a bloodied, crude wooden club, were said by investigators to have originated from inside the MacDonald home—they weren't brought in from outside. And, the CID said, it seemed that the alleged intruders hadn't stolen anything. Jewelry, guns, drugs from MacDonald's medicine chest, including some valuable amphetamines which MacDonald had used in a weight loss program for the troops, all remained untouched, according to lead investigator Ivory. Everything the investigators looked at, it seemed, pointed toward MacDonald, not toward outside intruders.

Acid and Rain

The news media weren't the only source of information about the case. Joe McGinniss's book, *Fatal Vision*, also fascinated me. I respected the author's ability to turn a phrase, but even more impressive, under McGinniss's sharp pen the dark character of MacDonald took brilliant and frightening shape. John Steinbeck once told his editor that today he was going to sit down and create Cathy in *East of Eden*, and that she would be a monster. Such people do exist, Steinbeck insisted.

McGinniss, too, fashioned his monster. But instead of building the character out of whole cloth, as Steinbeck had done, it appeared that McGinniss simply stepped back and let the reader listen to MacDonald's own words from tapes he made for McGinniss from prison. In this way the author cleverly appeared to allow a villainous MacDonald to create himself, and MacDonald seemed to rise out of the pages as the very specter of evil incarnate.

Whether or not he actually had murdered his family, I found I did not like this Jekyll-and-Hyde Dr. MacDonald, and well into my reading I decided Ted Gunderson had to be unsound, completely mistaken, or otherwise motivated.

But, as I read McGinniss's book, something gnawed at the edges of my memory. It was the vague recollection of a tale Dr. Joel Norris had related a few months earlier when he and I were crossing the East River in New York on the aerial gondola from Roosevelt Island to Manhattan. I had been watching tugboats working the river barges, and didn't have any reason to be interested in Joe McGinniss, but Joel was talking at the time about having the same literary agent as McGinniss. Remembering this, I put down *Fatal Vision* and phoned Joel. I asked him to recount the story he had told me while we crossed the river in New York City earlier in the year.

"Sure," he said. "McGinniss and I both used Sterling Lord."

"But you were telling me something about the MacDonald book."

"Oh, yes," Joel said in a soft and comfy Georgia accent, "at this party, Sterling was bragging that he made *Fatal Vision*."

"What do you mean *made*?" I asked.

"Joe's book was in trouble," Joel said. "McGinniss had signed with a publisher, and they were going to call the book *Acid and Rain*, I guess to tie their title to the flipped-out woman MacDonald said he saw in the house that rainy morning, and, I guess, the woman the MP saw a few blocks away a few minutes later, but after MacDonald was convicted, Joe couldn't very well complete the book with the theme he'd started with—"

"That MacDonald was innocent," I said.

"Sure. So when McGinniss changed his mind about MacDonald, the first publisher was suing, or threatening suit, for the two hundred thousand and some odd dollars they had earlier advanced to McGinniss."

"Okay."

"Now comes the interesting part. Sterling also became Alfred Kassab's agent."

"MacDonald's father-in-law?"

"Right. And the father-in-law was trying to find a writer to do a book about MacDonald being guilty, not innocent the way McGinniss had started out. I think Kassab actually found someone to write it, but I'm not sure they had a publishing deal yet. That's when Sterling had this flash of brilliance. He bragged that he brought McGinniss and Kassab together. McGinniss then rewrote his story, went with MacDonald being guilty, got a new publisher, and the rest is history."

"And you were there when Sterling Lord said this?"

"Sitting right there. He was damn proud of what he'd done," Joel said. "He was talking about it being his idea to make MacDonald the guy in the black hat and Kassab the guy in the white hat." Joel laughed. "There *was* a kind of literary elegance about it, you have to admit."

"How could you prove this?" I asked. "About Sterling being the agent for both, and bringing the two together?"

"You don't have to," Joel said. "MacDonald's lawyers are right now trying to get McGinniss into court. If that happens it'll all come out. I heard it with my own ears from Lord himself, and I'm sure it'll be covered when MacDonald sues McGinniss. If I remember correctly, Sterling also got Kassab a hunk of change from the movie deal."

Joel's story cast a shadow over McGinniss's book as I continued to read about the murder trial and the conviction. At every turn, however, it seemed McGinniss had encountered evidence which condemned Mac-Donald. So, how in the world, I asked myself, could MacDonald still be innocent, as Gunderson claimed? And if the man was guilty, he was a monster of diabolical proportions. What, then, did it matter if McGinniss had teamed up with Kassab to expose him? I continued reading McGinniss's book.

I learned that no one from the army or the Justice Department could provide a motive for MacDonald until Joe McGinniss himself turned sleuth. He told his readers he discovered that before the murders MacDonald had lost a lot of sleep from working every night in his moonlighting jobs as an emergency physician, and that he had probably ingested a large dose of amphetamines taken during a weight loss program. McGinniss said his investigations uncovered evidence that MacDonald actually exhibited personality changes which, according to doctors who treated him after the murders, indicated amphetamine psychosis. McGinniss painted a harrowing picture of a wild, strung-out MacDonald, in a psychotic state, rampaging through his home murdering everyone in his family.

So, I thought, if MacDonald is innocent, where did McGinniss's amphetamine theory come from?

In Gunderson's Boxes

As I drove to Gunderson's office in Westwood, an upscale community just west of Beverly Hills, I told myself that, like McGinniss, I didn't believe MacDonald's story, and Gunderson, who did seem to believe it, was either mistaken or there was something in it for him. At that moment I was determined not to get involved. I had a novel in mind and I wanted to wallow around in it awhile, unfettered, unowned, like a rich man in his own green garden, breathing clean air.

Clean air I got, by Los Angeles standards, that Saturday morning, and even before I left the San Diego freeway I could clearly see the huge "Monty's" steakhouse sign atop an office tower a few blocks south of the UCLA campus and medical center.

I parked in the basement of that building, rode the elevator up, and pushed open the door to Gunderson's office. I found myself in a room with two paper-strewn desks and cardboard file boxes stacked on the floor, but no Gunderson. I peeked into the next room, found it vacant also, and walked over to the window. I visually followed Wilshire Boulevard eastward to the emerald sweep of golf greens and the expansive fairways of the posh Los Angeles Country Club. High rent. North of Wilshire I spied the little churchyard where the remains of Marilyn Monroe lay in a wall crypt. The graves of Natalie Wood and Darryl Zanuck were there, too, as were the bones and ashes of other lesser lights of this privileged paradise.

Stepping back from the window, I saw that Gunderson had attained his own fair measure of fame. The walls displayed photos aplenty of the smiling detective shaking hands with Olympic champions, with Los Angeles Rams, Dodgers, Lakers, and with F. Lee Bailey, J. Edgar Hoover, and President Gerald Ford. There was a picture of Judge William Webster when he was director of the FBI.

"Hey, sorry I'm late," Gunderson said from behind me. "Had to step out for a minute."

"Nice family," I said, pointing toward the wall.

"Lots of turkeys, too," Gunderson said. "People get some limelight—" He tossed his head as to dismiss them. "I like Ford," he said. "Good man. And Lee Bailey. He's interested in the case, too."

"The MacDonald case."

"Right. He wants MacDonald to take a lie detector test."

"Why won't he?"

Gunderson's face darkened almost imperceptibly, then he smiled. "He will."

"So, he's going to take one? A polygraph?"

"I don't know. I think he will."

"If he's innocent, why didn't he at least take a sodium amytal test when the grand jurors asked him to?"

"That's a pretty rough test," Gunderson said. "You relive the whole murder attack over again. People go nuts from it."

"Better that than go to jail forever."

"Maybe he got bad advice," Gunderson said. He didn't seem to want to talk about it.

"If he's innocent, why wouldn't he have taken a lie detector test when the army investigators asked him to?"

"That one's easy. He believed they had lied to him about the evidence in the crime scene and he didn't trust them."

"Okay," I said. "Fair enough. But now, after his appeals have all failed, why doesn't he take a polygraph to at least corroborate his own claims of innocence?"

"He will when the time's right."

"Seems to me the time's past right," I said.

"I agree. I sent MacDonald a letter I got from F. Lee Bailey urging him to do it and clear the air. He's talking with his lawyers about it right now."

Gunderson motioned for me to sit down. Then he pointed toward one of three boxes of documents in file folders and notebooks. He sat beside me and picked up a big blue binder and thumbed through it, and stopped at a picture of a young woman. "Helena Stoeckley," he said. "She was just a kid at the time of the murders. Seventeen. Self-styled witch. Also the best drug informant the local police had at the time. Worked for the army, too, *and* the State Bureau of Investigation through a multi-departmental narcotics squad—even though they knew the kid was dealing drugs. You didn't know that, did you?" Gunderson said, a grin on his face.

"No," I admitted.

"She wore a blond wig the murder night, floppy hat, boots. Just like MacDonald saw in his living room. You didn't know that either, did you?"

Gunderson showed me several photos of Stoeckley's boyfriend at the time. He was a lean man with light brown hair. In each picture his eyes were dark and piercing. "This guy's important," Gunderson said. "Greg Mitchell. Get this. When Beasley and I found her, Stoeckley confessed to me, took a lie detector test, and passed it when she said she was in the murder apartment that morning and could name the murderers. Government was saying she's crazy, so I asked her to take a battery of psychological examinations here at UCLA. She wasn't crazy. And Greg Mitchell confessed, too, to murders at Fort Bragg. So then the government conveniently said he must be talking about something that happened in Vietnam—not the MacDonald murders."

I found myself wondering, uncomfortably, what were the chances of two people in the same small group confessing to murdering two little girls and a pregnant mother. Then Gunderson told me, "Still another member of their witchcraft coven confessed, too. That made three members of that unhappy little family of dope heads that had implicated themselves in the murders. You didn't know about any of that, did you?

"No," he answered for me. "And neither does anybody else, even though McGinniss could have told you, but chose to leave most of it out of his tidy little book."

Gunderson showed me another picture, of the third confessor, a thin girl named Cathy Perry sitting at a kitchen table with two other people. She appeared to be small, with straight brown hair, plain features except for heavy eyebrows. "Ten months after the murders," Gunderson continued, "she stabbed her boyfriend. She stabbed him in the back with a butcher knife while he slept. And she stabbed her puppy dog till he was flat, the police report said."

"Nice girl," I said.

"The government said Perry got too many things wrong when she described the murders." Gunderson laughed and said, "There's a second verse to that song, too. You'll see."

"If these three confessions were good," I asked, "then why didn't the government just reopen the case?"

"They don't like to lose. They like to win."

"That's too easy, Ted."

"Okay. Remember, the trial that convicted MacDonald was held nine years after the murders. Things change. The judge said that all this stuff is interesting, but MacDonald's still gotta be guilty because they've got all this evidence against him, hard evidence."

"And you're saying they really don't have that kind of evidence."

"They've got evidence that MacDonald was in the home," Ted said. "Of course he was. He lived there. But you'll find that's all they've really got. They manufactured evidence against him, and they kept back other evidence that showed he wasn't the only one there that morning."

"You're sure of that."

"You wouldn't be here if I wasn't," he said, smiling. He closed the binder with a *whop* and said, "Start with this. Then we'll get the lawyers to get you the stuff we got from the Freedom of Information Act. You'll need a U-Haul trailer for it, though, and stuff's still coming in."

So far I had Gunderson's word against McGinniss's book and a handful of newspaper clippings. I spent a week in Gunderson's boxes, and when I had finished my pulse was racing from excitement. If only half the stuff in his files was true, then something incredible had happened.

In Gunderson's boxes I saw actual government documentation that evidence MacDonald could have used at trial had really existed, then had disappeared. MacDonald's lawyers had filed post-trial appeals on several of these items in 1983, but the judge ruled they didn't matter, that these things wouldn't have changed the 1979 jury verdict even if the jurors had known about them. On the very surface this seemed self-serving of the judge. And the thing that bothered me the most was that Gunderson's box also held documents which showed that this judge, Franklin T. Dupree, Jr., the same one who had presided at the MacDonald grand jury, presided over his trial, and heard his appeals at the district level, had been the father-in-law of James Proctor, the Assistant U.S. Attorney into whose hands the MacDonald case was passed after the army dropped its charges. That young prosecutor, Gunderson's paperwork said, had clamored for MacDonald's indictment and even had threatened to resign his post if he were not allowed to charge MacDonald in the criminal courts. That same judge, Proctor's father-in-law, Gunderson's report claimed, then ruled with the subsequent prosecutors' motions to keep key evidence from the jurors.

Gunderson's claims were beginning to sound as farfetched as MacDonald's story about drug-crazed intruders. I had wanted to write another mystery novel—now, I had found myself a true mystery to investigate. While I tried to grasp the meaning of it all, the detective called my home at 6:30 one morning. He said he had been out all night on a surveillance and was "in the neighborhood." I invited him over for breakfast and asked him, "If all this stuff's real, why didn't the appeals work?"

Gunderson smiled forgivingly the way a grown-up will when a child asks why things are the way they are. "Appeals aren't really about innocence," he said. "They are about mistakes in the trial. Judge Dupree ruled he didn't make any mistakes, and the appeals court ruled he didn't either. They don't like to make each other look bad, you see."

That sounded a little simplistic, and I guess my face said I didn't quite buy it. So, Gunderson drove it home. "Same way the judge said he didn't talk with his prosecutor son-in-law about the case, and the appeals judges, in turn, said they didn't think good old Judge Frankie Dupree would lie to them about a thing like that. So they let a judge who was related to an earlier prosecutor on the same case remain the judge of record." Gunderson let me think about that for a moment, then said, "This is just a bad, bad case."

There was no doubt in my mind that Gunderson, at least, believed what he was saying. He might have been dead wrong, but he had bought into it as if it were religion. And that bothered me, too.

■

As I continued to examine Gunderson's report and McGinniss's book, the case troubled me day and night. I had witnessed behind-the-scenes political machinations in the Lucas case, the likes of which I could before that time only have imagined; so Gunderson's claims, incredible as they seemed on the surface, intrigued me precisely because they *were* so extreme. Why would Gunderson put himself out on the edge for a child killer, if the detective didn't sincerely feel something was terribly wrong with the conviction? He was setting himself against his old outfit, the FBI, and aligning himself with a cruel, sick individual. Why would Gunderson do this for a case that didn't appear to have a chance in hell of being overturned?

And, if Joe McGinniss had fully researched the story, as he claimed, why didn't he deal with the questions I encountered in the Gunderson report, a report which the detective insisted had been given to McGinniss while the author was writing *Fatal Vision*?

Meanwhile, I heard about a retired reporter who had followed the MacDonald case closely and had expressed his own concerns that something had gone awry. His name was Fred Bost and he happened to live in Fayetteville, only a few miles from the scene of the crime. Knowing a reinvestigation would be a mammoth undertaking, I considered flying to North Carolina, to see if Bost might be someone I could work with.

I phoned ahead, set up a meeting, and asked him if he'd show me the murder apartment at Fort Bragg. I wanted to start at the beginning. And, since Joe McGinniss's book hadn't told me much about the crime scene, the first question that had to be asked was: Why didn't the book tell more about what was found in the apartment at 544 Castle Drive, for this was the alleged source of the government's entire case? And, I wanted to know, what did the first MPs and CID agents on the scene really find there?

2

■

The Crime Scene

Upon Fred Bost's retirement from the army, he launched a second career as a news reporter. He proved to have a knack for it, for he soon won North Carolina statewide awards in three consecutive years. The last two were for his skill at investigative journalism. Intrigued by the MacDonald case, Bost sought out Helena Stoeckley after the conviction and was the first to publish an interview about the young woman's confessions in the MacDonald murders. When I phoned Bost, he didn't press MacDonald's innocence as Gunderson had, but he clearly believed that the army and the government had prevented full disclosure of some key facts. I suggested we talk about teaming up for a complete reinvestigation using the FOIA documents as source material. Luckily, he proved to possess as little restraint as I. He readily agreed to join the quest.

I met this pleasant, silver-haired man in person at the Holiday Inn coffee shop in Fayetteville where I learned he possessed a ferocious penchant for details. "And details," he assured me, "is where the real case is, not in the broad claims—from either side. What was the evidence claimed at trial, specifically? Did someone change it between the army hearing in 1970 and the trial nine years later, as Gunderson said? And if so, in what specific way did it change? Was some evidence held back, and if so, was it something that might have benefited the defense?"

Fred insisted that a thorough study wouldn't be simple or smooth going. "The defense team doesn't just say that something is wrong here," he said. "They say *most everything* of importance is wrong, right down to their claim that the FBI filed false affidavits to win in the 1984 and 1985 appeals hearings."

"Well, Gunderson at least says that."

"You won't find many on the defense team who wouldn't agree with Gunderson on most of his charges."

"What do you think?"

"We can't afford to think anything. We have to look."

I found myself liking Bost. I had already read some of his magazine and newspaper articles, and knew a bit about him. Before retiring from the army to begin a career as a writer he had served as a sergeant major in the Green Berets. As an intelligence/operations sergeant he saw considerable action in Vietnam, and was wounded in combat in July of 1966. After returning to Fort Bragg late in his military career, Bost was selected by General George I. Forsythe to serve at the Pentagon in the office of General William Westmoreland, army chief of staff. His duties included travel to military posts around the country to determine whether specific ideas might work in the newly proposed volunteer army. For his service in the chief of staff's office Fred received the Legion of Merit.

Also at the invitation of the army, Fred gave a speech at the U.S. Capitol Building before an assemblage of Gold Star Mothers, women who had lost sons and daughters in American wars. In that 1971 Veterans Day address, he spoke of his experiences in Vietnam during the army's early involvement there, and related the poignant story of the combat death of a young soldier Bost had grown to respect and admire.

I appreciated that Fred Bost was a decorated army man, that he had no axe to grind, and that he was willing to examine what the army might have done. In time I also would learn to value his dry wit, his naturally buoyant nature, and his ability to dig, for years, in boxes of old paper.

"The defense lawyers," Bost said, "are claiming, in effect, that if we look closely enough at each piece of evidence against MacDonald it will disappear like a ghost in the sunshine, that there is no such evidence, that it's a major hoax. To answer the defense complaints, then, we have to weigh the public declarations of the army and the government on each contested issue. And we must compare each piece of evidence against their own official documents, the documents they refused to turn over during trial. If there are discrepancies between what they claimed in court and what their withheld documents said, that's where they'll show up." In short, from the beginning, we knew that a new book on this case could not be "our" book; it had to be written from the government's own files—what did the government say they found in the murder apartment, and were the prosecutors' and investigators' public words supported by the source documents they refused to allow the jurors to see?

To provide those documents was the purpose of the Freedom of Information Act, of course, but Fred's plan meant analyzing more than 10,000 pages of badly copied material—investigative reports, witness statements, affidavits, handwritten lab notes, transcripts, official letters, and other documents. In addition, we decided we'd have to interview scores of witnesses and try to find new ones who hadn't yet come forward. It was a formidable course. "But," Fred said happily, "I just retired from my second career. Why not a third?" We settled our business arrangements over another cup of coffee, then decided two things: We'd concentrate on the key topics the defense and the prosecution had fought over in the trial; and, even though true-crime writers are notorious for changing events for dramatic purposes, we could not succumb to the temptation to do that. We wouldn't write the book for titillation or for sheer entertainment value. No matter what we found, whether for or against MacDonald, Fred and I agreed we wouldn't dramatize anything beyond the documentable facts. Aristotle had written in his *Rhetoric*, "We ought in fairness to fight our case with no help beyond the bare facts." It was a simple plan, but the only thing easy about it was the initial decision—fools rush in, and all that.

Our business completed, Fred and I were suddenly new friends of a common mind. I asked him to show me where the murders happened. "Strictly speaking," Fred remarked as we drove toward Fort Bragg, "the crime scene doesn't exist."

"They tear it down?"

"The building is still there, but the apartment has been gutted, expanded, and reconfigured into two dwellings. Walls were moved so the rooms aren't the same. All the stuff they took out, wall surfaces, flooring, carpeting, cabinets, nearly everything, was destroyed."

"Even while appeals are still going on?"

Fred grinned and gave me the army answer. "They got tired of keeping the quarters vacant."

Fort Bragg is an open post with a state highway running through it.

Armed MPs don't guard the entrances, so anybody can come in, drive around, and drive out, as we did, unchallenged. The post was much more accessible to the general public than I had imagined, and Fred assured me it was that way in 1970.

Once on post, we stopped at the traffic light at Honeycutt and Lucas which had momentarily halted one team of responding MPs on that rainy morning. Fred pointed at the corner where MP Kenneth Mica saw a woman in a floppy hat just after the murders had occurred.

"There's a phone there where she stood," I pointed out.

"It was there at the time of the murders, too," Fred said. "Stoeckley said she freaked out at the sight of all the blood when things got out of hand, and ran out of the apartment."

"But was it Stoeckley?"

"Your guess is as good as mine," he said. "Apparently several of the kids in that group had floppy hats. But then again," Fred said, "maybe the woman wasn't anybody connected with the group at all."

We headed for nearby Corregidor Courts and turned onto Castle Drive, a wide and pleasant tree-lined street. Kids' bikes and wagons and colorful plastic push toys decorated the lawns and sidewalks.

"So, someone lives here now," I said, looking at the front door to 544.

"Right. And the Kalin family lived there." Fred pointed at the door to the left. "The Edwards there," he said, motioning farther left. Stepping around to his right, he showed me a smaller building offset behind 544 and told me the Pendlyshoks had lived there. "Almost all of them heard or saw things the army never reported, or never asked about," Fred said, "or the official version was somehow skewed in the army's favor.

"For instance," Fred said, pointing down the street, "over there a neighbor unloaded his U-Haul trailer on what the army called the night of the murders. He hadn't seen anything out of the ordinary, so they added that to their proof that MacDonald was lying about intruders."

"What time was it?" I asked. "He wouldn't have been unloading a trailer at 4 A.M."

"The time doesn't matter," Fred said. "The army messed up. It was really the wrong night, but that didn't keep them from using it."

Fred turned and pointed toward another apartment unit across the intersection catty-corner from 544. "That's where some of the assailant group might have come from," he said, "between those units. One neighbor said he saw three robed figures carrying candles walking across there toward the MacDonald house earlier that night, maybe midnight or later, too early for the murder group unless they were just checking things out, or," Fred said, "maybe they saw MacDonald still hadn't gone to bed."

"There were other sightings of the Stoeckley group just before and just after the murders," I said, remembering Gunderson's report.

"Many others," Fred said. "But."

"Lotsa buts," I said.

"Yeah," Fred said. "That's the trouble."

As we walked toward the back, he pointed at a front window in the former MacDonald apartment. "Kimberly died there," he said. "Kristen was killed in her bedroom across the hall from Kimberly. Colette was found in the back bedroom. That would have been right about there in the original configuration." He pointed to the front corner of the building.

Unsettled, I stood behind the MacDonald apartment on that warm, sunny day and realized that even after seeing the crime-scene photos in Gunderson's reports, I found it impossible to make it all real. This small, grassy backyard had given up a knife, an ice pick, and a bloody club that morning, and I wondered again, did this popular and talented young physician, as the government claimed, lose his temper when the baby wet the bed? Was it that horribly simple? Had he, as in Joe McGinniss's dramatic scenario, ingested so many diet pills that a dark alchemy transformed a loving father into a raging maniac?

Surely the MPs and army agents knew the same sick indignation that invaded my insides as I stood outside those silent walls and listened to the screams. But the MPs and investigators must have experienced it a hundredfold once they got inside to find blood everywhere, pools of it— on the floors near the bodies, splashes of blood on the walls and ceilings, the bedding and carpets soaked with it, the bodies red with it, the air thick with the smell of it. Observers at any murder scene are force-fed an overdose of this kind of kick-in-the-gut reality, and it's far worse when the bodies are children.

In the Government Files

From the very beginning the army claimed that the crime scene those unsuspecting medics and MPs walked into was well protected, that the evidence was not contaminated, and that it was professionally and competently collected and analyzed. This adamant claim became the foundation of the army's case against MacDonald, but his lawyers insist that the evidence was botched, that the evidence handlers were incompetent, that the CID investigators were amateurs and ill equipped. Further, the defense team believed that all of the most critical evidence, in fact almost anything in MacDonald's favor, disappeared or was ignored and covered up.

Without doubt, this is a fundamental ingredient in the case, for if the crime scene at 544 Castle Drive was not well handled, then the evidence collected there cannot be considered reliable. If the evidence in MacDonald's favor was slighted in any significant measure, then the army official reports on this evidence also cannot be trusted. A foundational question, then, is: What really happened to the evidence during the first days and weeks of the MacDonald case?

WILLIAM IVORY'S STAGED-SCENE THEORY

Case records tell us that just about the time the medics were loading the injured MacDonald into the ambulance, which was approximately 4:15 A.M., investigator William Ivory arrived.[1] Ivory was the Criminal Investigative Division (CID) agent on duty that night and the case would come under his personal, official responsibility.

On that dreadful morning, Ivory stepped into the house and listened to Lieutenant Paulk relate MacDonald's story about intruders. Paulk told Ivory about the bodies still lying in the three bedrooms only a few steps away; then the detective began looking things over. Ivory was tall and good-looking, and wore a dark, well-oiled curl down the middle of his forehead. He was twenty-six years old, and had never conducted a homicide probe. Only once had he participated in a murder case, and that was as a military policeman interviewing witnesses. He was a high school dropout turned career soldier, and had attained the rank of Specialist E-7. He had completed the basic CID investigation course the year before, and until then, as an MP, he had worked traffic, made accident queries, and asked questions in drug cases. He had been placed on special duty with the CID to help ease the workload in the manpower shortage caused by the war in Vietnam. But, inexperienced as he was, in this, his first murder case, he would earn a reputation for brilliance—whether or not it was deserved.

Ivory walked through the house slowly, his eyes taking in everything the way he was taught in the CID course the previous year. He viewed the bodies, taking care not to touch anything in the bedrooms, not even the light switches, which he turned on and off with his ballpoint pen.[2]

Then he returned to carefully examine the living room again. According to his subsequent testimony, a flowerpot sitting upright on its base on the living room floor immediately bothered him. The white plastic pot, separated from the dirt and the green plant strewn outward from the coffee table, seemed unnaturally positioned, for if the flowerpot had toppled off the overturned coffee table in the fight MacDonald had described, logic ruled that it should not have landed upright—as it now stood.

The small living room didn't seem as disarranged as it might have been had a fight really occurred there. MacDonald's eyeglasses lay on the floor near the bottom of a curtain. The coffee table lay on its side opposite the couch where MacDonald said he had been sleeping when he heard screams. Ivory studied the coffee table and found it especially top heavy, yet it had fallen over on its side and had remained there. This was curious, Ivory reasoned, for if the top-heavy table had been kicked or knocked over in a fight, then it would have fallen all the way over onto its heavy face.[3] Also, the magazines trapped under the edge of the table seemed stacked too neatly. If they had been knocked off the table when it was toppled they should have been strewn outward from the force of the blow. Ivory also noticed that the throw rug between the living and dining rooms wasn't rumpled. It lay flat and incongruously undisturbed.

Ivory looked further. He found numerous blue cotton pajama fibers in the master bedroom, and he reasoned these had come from the ripped blue pajama top which lay atop the dead woman's chest. He found a fiber under the headboard of the bed in the master bedroom. On that headboard someone had written the word "PIG" in blood.

Then, he later reported, came the clincher—when MPs and medics lifted Colette's body from the floor, Ivory squatted down and spied a tiny blue cotton fiber protruding from a clot of drying blood under her head. This troubled him because he reasoned that this fiber, too, had come from MacDonald's torn pajama top. It presented a tantalizing mystery. For if MacDonald had been struggling with intruders in the living room when his wife was killed, as he claimed, and if his pajama top wasn't torn before her death, and if it wasn't torn in this very bedroom, how did that fiber get under her head—or, to put it another way, how did her head come to be placed over that fiber? Ivory thought he knew the answer.

By 5:30 A.M. the authorities were in consensus—Ivory, his boss, CID chief Franz Joseph Grebner (whom the agents called "Joe"), and Fort Bragg's provost marshal,[4] Colonel Robert J. Kriwanek, all agreed. MacDonald was saying one thing, but the crime scene suggested another, that MacDonald, not four mythical strangers, had slaughtered his family. With this supposition a critical, perhaps fatal, juncture in the case had been reached. Had civilians been involved, as MacDonald claimed, the case would have come under the jurisdiction of the FBI. Yet, at 5:30 A.M., as a result of the CID consensus of MacDonald's guilt, and a conscious decision to exclude the Bureau from the case, Colonel Kriwanek called the CID laboratory in Fort Gordon, Georgia, and asked for a team of army laboratory technicians.

Never before had military authorities asked for analysts and evidence gatherers to be flown to a distant crime scene from the Fort Gordon CID laboratory. Two hours after this call, when a Fort Bragg spokesman finally alerted the local FBI in Fayetteville that the murders had occurred, a makeshift army laboratory team had already gathered equipment and was arranging for the use of an aircraft.

TURF WAR

But the FBI moved fast, too, knowing that most overworked local officials welcome their assistance and their superior laboratory facilities. Special Agent Jim Lothspeich of the Fayetteville FBI received news of the murders by telephone at about 7:30 A.M. He rushed to Fort Bragg and met with Kriwanek in the colonel's office. Colonel Kriwanek told Lothspeich that the FBI had no jurisdiction in the case. Lothspeich reminded him about the FBI's responsibility for investigating crimes by civilians, but Colonel Kriwanek assured the FBI agent that his people already had determined that Captain MacDonald, not civilians, had committed the murders.

Federal law requires that the FBI assume control of any felony investigation on a military post when the crime involves civilian suspects. MacDonald had described people who might be civilians, particularly the woman in the floppy hat. So to Lothspeich, the army's assumption of MacDonald's guilt was premature. No one had yet conducted evidence collection, lab tests, and neighborhood queries, and no one had yet searched for persons matching the descriptions given by MacDonald. Not surprisingly, agent Lothspeich didn't accept Colonel Kriwanek's judgment. Lothspeich made a report to FBI headquarters in Washington, D.C. FBI director J. Edgar Hoover immediately issued instructions to Robert M. Murphy, his lead agent in the state, to take charge of the probe at the MacDonald apartment, and also to investigate the local drug community. Hoover reminded Murphy that MacDonald's duties included counseling drug addicts. The director's teletype stated flatly, "Preliminary investigation indicates civilians are involved."

Army authorities ignored Hoover's opinion and forged ahead as if they couldn't be wrong. Yet despite Kriwanek's insistence to Lothspeich that it was a cut-and-dried case, records show that the army failed to make this known to MacDonald. Investigators questioned him not once but twice on that first day in the hospital as well as on two subsequent days, and at each of these occasions they masked the fact that he was their key suspect.

The FBI and the CID immediately entered a four-day turf war over control of the crime scene and the evidence, and documents reveal that Colonel Kriwanek continued to bar FBI control of the case. When lead FBI agent Murphy pressed him again, Kriwanek told the FBI man that what they were looking at here was a family dispute which ended in murders and a botched suicide. Murphy's offer of the better-equipped FBI labs to process the evidence held no sway. Kriwanek decided that the FBI would not be allowed to take charge of or examine any of the crime-scene evidence.

The FBI knew that such a determination cannot logically be made until the crime-scene evidence is actually lab tested to see whether any of it was brought in from the outside. Especially important would be any hair or other fibers, blood, semen, or weapons. The FBI men know that foreign items, that is, items that could not be matched to known family members, especially to Jeffrey MacDonald, should be considered suspicious.

The argument continued, and came to a head on Friday, February 20, just three days after the murders. Murphy had learned through his agent monitoring the crime scene that the CID had found wax drippings on the coffee table in the living room, on an upholstered chair in Kimberly's room, and on Kimberly's bedspread. Considering these critical locations, Murphy cited MacDonald's description of a woman carrying a "flickering light, perhaps a candle." Based upon this finding and MacDonald's story, Murphy again challenged the CID jurisdictional claim. At the very least, he suggested, the FBI laboratory should analyze this undoubtedly important candle wax and the other evidence for the army. But Kriwanek and Grebner still would not yield; and Kriwanek adamantly repeated that no civilians were involved.[5] By not revealing the remainder of the evidence they were holding, including challenges to their staged-scene theory, the army averted further argument and maintained control of the crime scene.

EVIDENCE COLLECTION AT THE CRIME SCENE

Case records show that the chief CID lab tech, Hilyard O. Medlin, had been working with the CID laboratory for the past seven years, but at no time had he run into the miserable luck that seemed to plague him in the MacDonald apartment. Howard Page, his photographer, hadn't brought a fingerprint camera with him. He arrived at the scene with an unstable tripod and no lighting equipment. He ended up taking fingerprint pictures while Ralph Turbyfill, another lab technician, held an apartment table lamp at his shoulder. The result was a large number of shaky, out-of-focus, poorly lighted photographs. But that wasn't all. Before their work was done, Medlin and Page had managed to destroy nine good fingerprints and three good palm prints.[6]

William Ivory was certain that two bloody footprints in the entrance to the baby's room would prove significant, so Medlin sent Turbyfill to the hospital to get inked impressions of the feet of Jeffrey and Colette MacDonald for comparison purposes. He also told Turbyfill to get inked fingerprints from all the victims. But Medlin told him, inexplicably, "Don't worry about getting the little girls' prints."

Turbyfill, therefore, took no fingerprints or footprints from the children. Also, he didn't know to massage a corpse's hands to soften rigor mortis long enough to get good prints. Consequently, his attempt to fingerprint Colette's stiffened fingers yielded only partial prints of the balls of her fingertips. A later effort to get full fingerprints from the corpses, at the funeral home after the bodies were embalmed, also resulted in failure.

A major error also occurred in the collection of the two bloody footprints found in Kristen's room near the hall doorway and the one footprint found just outside in the hall. Page claims he couldn't photograph the prints well enough to discern the ridges, so Medlin attempted to cut out the wooden flooring to remove one to the lab. But the floorboards fell apart in his hands and permanently destroyed crucial ridgelines needed for identification. The CID later reported that Medlin had looked at the prints before they fell apart, however, and he was sure they were the footprints of Captain Jeffrey MacDonald.

Instead of immediately processing the all-important hallway floor, where MacDonald said he fell wounded and unconscious near the living room steps, the agents waited three more days to collect evidence in that location. But by this time scores of persons wearing wet shoes and boots had moved back and forth through the area. At the spot where MacDonald said he had lain unconscious, nothing remained on that third day but two pajama fibers, a hair, and a small spot of blood, even though many blue fibers had been seen there earlier by CID agent Robert Shaw, who had documented them in his notes.[7]

Long before their investigations were complete in the apartment, the CID agents used the toilet, made coffee in the kitchen, washed dishes in the sink, sat on the furniture, read the magazines, and played the stereo—all this before evidence collection was completed.

Late that first week, a friend of Jeffrey MacDonald's, Lieutenant Ron Harrison, unwittingly handed Ivory another item which, to Ivory, further indicated MacDonald's guilt, but which also indicates CID procedural error in evidence handling. During an interview, Harrison mentioned to the CID that MacDonald and he had recently discussed an *Esquire* magazine article about cult murders, devil worship, and the Manson murders, which were currently in the news.

CID statements show that for the first three days after the murders, investigators working in the bloody apartment leafed through the *Esquire* magazine during their breaks. Yet not until that third day did lab tech Ralph Turbyfill discover a bloody smear on the cover as if a soiled fingertip had been wiped across its edge. This discovery seemed to have significance to the investigators, but an argument broke out among the detectives. They knew from Harrison's story that MacDonald's fingerprints could be expected on pages of the magazine, because, after all, he lived there. This made the prints worthless as proof that he handled the magazine at the time of the murders. The investigators' own fingerprints were probably there as well, since they handled the magazine for days after the murder, which would be an embarrassment if admitted publicly. They asked whether the magazine at this late date truly could be used as evidence. Those who said yes won the argument. Despite its being frequently handled by CID agents for several days, the magazine was collected, listed, and made part of the fragile evidence to be protected from further contamination. The laboratory technicians could not determine when the smear was placed on the magazine, or even whether it was from one of their own people, yet the CID, ignoring their own mishandling of the item, said it was MacDonald's finger smudge. And

William Ivory soon began using this stain as an explanation for the "over-kill" of Colette and Kimberly and Kristen. He theorized that MacDonald used the *Esquire* article as a manual, copycatting the Manson murders. Ivory thought MacDonald had referred to the story, using it as a guide to faking mayhem even while arranging the crime scene to make it appear there had been intruders.

Initial tests and observations by the lab personnel gathering evidence gave Ivory even more reason to blame MacDonald for staging the scene. The knife in the master bedroom, the one MacDonald said he had taken out of his wife's chest, contained only a tiny speck of blood. It contained no fingerprints and may have been wiped off on a white Hilton bathmat, found in the master bedroom, which showed bloody streaks on it. The baby bottle in Kristen's bed yielded no fingerprints, and both telephones also were free of prints, further proof to Ivory that the scene didn't match occurrences as voiced by MacDonald.

Ivory's superiors agreed with his ideas; and they continued to insist that sound crime-scene procedures had been scrupulously followed at 544 Castle Drive. They swore that the analysts from Fort Gordon collected evidence that was entirely uncontaminated.[8] The government lawyers later presented this theory as true. But was it?

EARLY CRIME-SCENE PROTECTION

The army based its claims of MacDonald's guilt upon Ivory's staged-scene theory. Ivory had based his theory upon the crime scene as *he* found it, but without checking whether anything had been moved, touched, or otherwise altered before he arrived. However, case records prove there had been people in the apartment, many people, for approximately fifteen minutes before Ivory arrived—and Ivory's own later admissions reveal that he ignored the activities of MPs, medics, neighbors, and strangers in the home during that critical period. He didn't factor in their movements in the home as he developed his theory.

Testimony and statements by MPs and medics leave no doubt that some of the men whose job it was to protect the apartment were clearly stunned by the grisly murder scene they entered. For instance, MP Mica saw Williams standing in a state of shock in the hallway; and Morris was told to go outside because he looked as if he were going to be physically sick. And MP statements show that the MPs who were watching Mica's attempts to revive MacDonald failed to block further entrance to the yard and the apartment. Large numbers of late-arriving military policemen, medics, and gawkers loitered in the yard and entered the home, not as investigators, but as unsupervised spectators wandering through the fragile crime scene.

In the MacDonald backyard, even before three murder weapons were found, military police, ostensibly standing guard, allowed neighbors to walk across the grass. Janice Pendlyshok stood in the unprotected, yet unprocessed, backyard and talked to a military policeman,[9] as did Captain Jim Williams, a man who worked with MacDonald. James Paulsen, one of the ambulance drivers, walked out of the rear of the house, looked around the yard, and returned inside without being challenged.[10] Later that morning, Dick Blount, from the *Fayetteville Observer*, crossed the yard to take a picture through the window of Kristen's bedroom, and he and other newsmen continued to roam the grounds freely. And still later, military police in the backyard allowed garbage collectors to walk across the yard and empty the MacDonald trash cans before they had been examined for possible evidence by lab technicians.[11] Such actions are precisely the reasons crime scenes are immediately roped off, something which was not done in the MacDonald case.

When military policeman Richard Tevere had first approached the apartment early that dark morning he noticed that the front windows had been open. Yet crime-scene photographs taken later that morning, and described by the CID as "the crime scene as found," show the windows all closed. When military policeman Robert Duffy first entered the master bedroom, he noticed a bureau drawer was open and the contents appeared to have been rifled. By the time photographs were made later in the morning, that drawer was closed. Records reveal no attempt by the CID to determine who had been looking through the drawer or who had closed it.

The first military policemen on the scene had used flashlights to scan the girls' rooms. Yet the medic Paulsen reported that the light was on in Kimberly's room when he arrived minutes later. Then, when William Ivory later examined that room, probably only moments after Paulsen examined the child's body, the light was off again.

According to CID chief Grebner, shortly after he arrived he observed footprints in the kitchen "with blood contamination,"[12] but when the kitchen floor was processed later that week, no such footprints were found.

The confusion during the first hours at the crime scene was most graphically illustrated by what happened to Jeffrey MacDonald's billfold.

Shortly after the arrival of the MPs, Mica saw the wallet on the living room floor, but someone in the crowd of people in the house soon moved it to the top of a desk near the front entrance. It lay on a corner of the desk when Major Joe Parson and CID chief Grebner first became aware of it around 5:15 A.M. But at about 5:30, a military policeman in the living room noticed that the wallet was no longer there. Grebner and Parson first performed embarrassed searches of each other, then they searched the MPs and medics. Finally, they had the vehicles searched, including Paulsen's ambulance, but to no avail. The wallet was gone.

When questioned ten months later as part of the army's reinvestigation of the case, ambulance attendant Paulsen freely admitted that it was he who stole the billfold.[13] He took the money, six dollars, and tossed the wallet out of the ambulance window on his way to the hospital later that morning.[14]

But even more theft occurred after the apartment came under the control of the CID agents. A large bottle of Eskatrol diet tablets, used in a weight control program MacDonald had set up for his troops, disappeared from the hall closet where Jeffrey MacDonald kept his medical supplies. Both Dr. William P. Neal, who examined the bodies, and lead CID investigator William Ivory had seen the bottle there.[15] Since the theft of the highly valued amphetamines occurred *after* the CID was on the scene, after Ivory and Dr. Neal had seen them, they were not taken by intruders but by crime-scene personnel or unsupervised visitors. Yet two rings that disappeared from Colette MacDonald's jewelry box might have been taken by outside persons.

If the rings weren't stolen by someone controlling the crime scene (as the wallet, and apparently the amphetamines, had been), then who took them? Ivory, by his own admission, had dumped the contents of the jewelry box into a plastic bag without inventorying the items. That bag was placed in a bureau drawer in the apartment, all but forgotten. When Colette's mother, Mildred Kassab, asked specifically for two of Colette's rings weeks later, the bag was checked, but the rings weren't present.[16]

Did the CID or MPs take the rings, or were they taken by intruders? The latter possibility was never officially considered. Ivory came under blame on the matter, and claimed another investigator had already given the rings to MacDonald. But the other agent was never identified, and CID paperwork necessary for turning over property[17] has never surfaced. When MacDonald made a formal claim on November 23, 1970, alleging that the rings were lost due to army negligence, the CID didn't challenge it. The army paid MacDonald for the rings.

Chaplain Kenneth Edwards and his wife, Rosalie, who lived two doors away in the same building as the MacDonalds, complained that nothing was done on the murder morning to seal off the apartment or the area around it. The Edwards had been awakened by loud voices under their second-story window and by the flashing of red and blue lights on emergency vehicles. They looked down to see MPs in MacDonald's front yard and military vehicles, emergency lights flashing, parked at the curb.

Chaplain Edwards put on a robe and went out to see if he could be of assistance. From her upstairs bedroom window two apartments away, Rosalie watched him cross the grass to the MacDonald apartment and enter it. She said she saw "a lot of people milling about, people from the neighborhood as well as military policemen." According to Mrs. Edwards, all the people going in and out of the house were not military police. "No," she said. "Neighbors. People just going in to see—the curious crowd went in to see. They were not stopped."[18]

At the 1979 trial William Ivory told the jurors he had seen only four MPs, but CID agent Robert Shaw had already secretly addressed this issue back in 1970 in an official statement. "Prior to the arrival of Mister Ivory, who was the first investigator on the scene, there were approximately eighteen military policemen who went through the quarters." Shaw himself judged this as "incompetent."[19] In like manner, one of the first military policemen on the scene, Richard Tevere, named twelve patrol members who he was certain had been in the apartment or on the grounds.[20]

Chaplain Edwards says he entered the murder house unchallenged and walked down the hallway to the back bedroom and saw Colette's body. Another neighbor, Donald Kalin, also entered the apartment and looked around.[21] Captain Jim Williams was allowed into the murder apartment without challenge.[22] Dr. William Neal, called to the scene shortly after 5 A.M. to confirm the deaths, saw about fifteen people crowded into the apartment at that time, some of them "appearing to be spectators."[23] And later Master Sergeant Medlin, chief technician in charge of laboratory analysts sent from Fort Gordon, Georgia, said the local army CID investigators conducted at least one VIP tour through the crime scene for some of the ranking officers on post. Medlin recalled that while dusting the important flowerpot in the living room for fingerprints the day after the murders he became aware of this group of officers watching over his shoulder. He said it made him so uncomfortable that he put the pot down and went to another room. Medlin never got back to dusting the flowerpot. He forgot it. And any prints on it were lost forever.

Fred Bost and I agreed, after reading the MP and CID statements, that the prosecutors' claims of a protected crime scene were overstated, to say the least. In those first fifteen minutes, major errors had occurred. We then addressed a more crucial question: Did the failure to guard the scene during that fifteen minutes lead to contamination of any key pieces of evidence, items which, specifically, led to Ivory's theory, and to the army's accusation?

THE FLOWERPOT

If Hilyard Medlin had finished dusting the flowerpot after being interrupted by the VIPs touring the murder scene, he might have been able to pick up the prints of the man who had actually moved the pot, for, according to MP Kenneth Mica, it was not Jeffrey MacDonald. While testifying at the army hearing six months after the crimes, Mica said that early on the murder morning, just moments after Captain MacDonald had been wheeled from the apartment, he saw in the living room a man with "longish" hair. This man wore an army field jacket and jeans. That unknown man picked up the overturned flowerpot and set it upright on its base. Mica said the man then sat down on the very couch where Jeffrey MacDonald had allegedly been attacked. This act, without doubt, compromised the quality of any evidence not yet collected in that area. Who the man might have been is still not known, except that he was one of the up to four strangers seen in the living room that morning by military personnel.[24] It is evident that during the fifteen-minute period before Ivory arrived items on or around the couch could have been moved. Yet Ivory immediately blamed MacDonald for the flowerpot's strange position while at the same time assuming that the couch had also remained untouched.[25]

FINGERPRINTS WIPED OFF KEY ITEMS

Case records reveal major problems with the other items in Ivory's staged-scene theory as well. Lab reports show that, as Ivory claimed, the army laboratory techs found no fingerprints or print smudges on the baby bottle, the bedroom knife, or the telephones, and MacDonald was blamed for wiping them off to remove his own prints.

MacDonald told of giving the bottle to Kristen early on the morning of February 17, so he must have handled the bottle, as did Kristen. And Dr. Neal said that as he was examining the baby's body, to make the official pronouncement of death, his weight on the bed caused the bottle to begin to move. He said he saw someone take it and put it somewhere else on the bed.[26] Neal didn't know who the man was who moved the bottle, but, since MacDonald was already at the hospital by this time, whoever wiped the bottle clean did so after Neal saw it moved, for that mover's fingerprints were also missing from the flat surfaces of the bottle.

The lack of prints on the knife found in the master bedroom also poses a mystery. MacDonald said he pulled a knife from his wife's chest. If so, his fingerprints should have been on the weapon, along with Colette's blood. But the lab techs found no fingerprints on it.[27] And three witnesses, MPs Mica and Tevere and CID chief Grebner, all said they saw blood on the bedroom knife at a time after MacDonald was under the care of the MPs and medics. Not only did they see blood on the blade, but also on the handle. Tevere told the grand jury, "There was blood on the knife that was next to the dresser. There was blood on it."[28] So, why did the CID laboratory techs report only a minuscule trace of blood on the blade and none on the handle?[29] Clearly, the knife must have been wiped not only after MacDonald left the apartment, but after three of the new arrivals saw blood on it. Who among the personnel in the house that morning wiped the knife?[30]

Strangely enough, the phones, too, had been wiped off. Missing were the bloody fingerprints made by Jeffrey MacDonald when he telephoned for help; missing were the prints of Tevere, the military policeman who had attempted to call his desk sergeant using the bedroom phone[31]; and missing were all those prints put on the phones by the MacDonald family before the crime.[32] But, as in the cases of the bedroom knife and the baby bottle, someone else, *not MacDonald*, had to have wiped prints off the phones, since Tevere's prints had also disappeared.

TELLTALE PAJAMA FIBERS

Ivory said he found no blue fibers in the area where MacDonald said he had fought with his attackers, and where MacDonald said the pajama top had been pulled over his head in that struggle. But, again, the case records now reveal Ivory was in error, an error that was consistently presented by the prosecutors at the 1979 trial and one that continually weakened MacDonald's defense case. The CID had found fibers there. A sworn statement by CID agent Shaw reveals that when Shaw got to the apartment early that morning, he saw blue fibers at the very spot where MacDonald claimed to have fallen unconscious—"in the west entrance to the hallway on the floor," Shaw said, "near the south wall, just a pile laying there."[33] But by the time laboratory technicians got around to collecting evidence from the hallway floor three days later, the "pile" of fibers had been reduced to a mere two fibers analyzed as pajama fibers. The failure to collect and catalog these witnessed fibers where MacDonald said he fell became a significant loss for the MacDonald defense as the government continued to use Ivory's claim as if it were true.

Ivory also cited the blue cotton pajama fibers in the children's bedrooms, and a fiber on Kristen's fingernail, as proof MacDonald had murdered them, yet Ivory did not account for MacDonald's pajama bottoms, which had been ripped from knee to knee through the crotch, according to three medics who gave aid to MacDonald.[34] Unlike the pajama top, MacDonald said he was wearing his pajama bottoms as he made his rounds to try to resuscitate his wife and his children. And he had been wearing the bottoms when the MPs found him unconscious lying next to Colette. These shredded pajama bottoms, which might have been considered the source of the suspicious fibers as easily as the top, were discarded at the hospital in the presence of a CID agent who didn't think to save the garment as evidence. Yet the CID team continued to operate as if the only source of fibers had to be MacDonald's pajama top.

Investigators insist that the fibers found under Colette's head and body were on the floor and that her body was placed upon them. But case records provide two other ways these "telltale" fibers may have gotten there. MacDonald said that when he found his wife dead, she was leaning against a green chair in the master bedroom. He said he moved her downward to a supine position to give her mouth-to-mouth resuscitation. There is crime-scene evidence that corroborates his story—a downward swipe of blood was found on the lower front panel of that green chair, lending support to MacDonald's claim. Another crime-scene photo also shows a throw rug flipped up at her foot as it might have been had she been moved downward. Further support for MacDonald's claim comes from fibers gathered under Colette's crotch area as they might be if they had been scooped ahead of her body as she was moved downward onto the floor.

Still further support for the claim that MacDonald moved her was developed by private investigator Raymond Shedlick, Jr., who pointed out that the largest number of fibers near and on her body were found in precisely the location where they would have been had MacDonald ripped his trousers upon first kneeling or squatting down at Colette's body.

The physician who examined her for signs of life, Dr. William Neal, insists that he, too, moved her body. He says he actually turned her over to check her back area. He thought he might have placed her in a position different than that in which he had found her, and he might have placed her over fibers. Ivory says this didn't happen, that Neal never moved Colette. Agent Shaw supports Ivory, saying he, too, watched Neal, and that the doctor didn't move Colette's body. But the statements of Shaw's boss, Joe Grebner, and three MPs place Shaw outside the apartment conducting a search for weapons in the backyard at the time of Dr. Neal's work in the house.[35] The assistant provost marshal, Major Joe Parson, has also confirmed that Dr. Neal rolled the bodies.[36]

When Neal left the crime scene that morning, the agents realized they hadn't yet drawn lines around the bodies, so they finally accomplished that necessary chore, but too late to determine in what way Neal might have changed the positions of the victims.[37]

Ivory made much of a cotton fiber on Kristen's fingernail. He insisted that Kristen had clutched at her father when he was stabbing her. Dr. Neal, however, thought that he might have transferred a pajama fiber to Kristen's finger, since he noticed his hands were bloody after examining her.[38] Apparently Neal thought a fiber might have stuck to his bloody hands, then was dropped on Kristen.

Another "telltale" fiber under the headboard of the bed where the word "PIG" was written might have been deposited as easily by medic John Nuchereno as by MacDonald. Case records reveal that Nuchereno, while preparing to move the wounded MacDonald from the bedroom, became fearful his patient was going into shock, so he maneuvered through the crowded room by crawling across the bed to get a pillow at the headboard near the word "PIG" written in blood. William Ivory wasn't in the house when this movement happened, and he never learned of the bed-crawling incident while on the case.[39]

A PIECE OF SKIN

The MacDonald defense team claimed that the crime-scene search was "botched." One consultant, Richard Fox, an independent criminalist and crime-scene analyst who had managed major government crime labs, studied the way the army had handled the scene and reported that "it looked like a paraplegic marching band went through the place before the evidence was even collected." Fox added that "nothing collected there should ever be trusted by any court."

Fred Bost and I spent more than a year reading every available FOIA document about the crime scene, and it is apparent that army personnel who were at the apartment that morning reveal that most key items which affected Ivory's staged-scene theory had been touched, moved, changed, wiped, or used by persons other than Jeffrey MacDonald. The official documents leave virtually nothing of importance unassailable in this regard. The documents reveal that most of the changes occurred within that crucial first fifteen minutes in which the apartment and the evidence were unprotected. Yet, even as the MP and medic statements were being taken, and as the extent of the crime-scene damage was being learned, the CID continued to claim that the scene had been well protected, that MacDonald and no one else had staged the scene, and that he had killed his family. In spite of all the various challenging statements by army personnel, Ivory's course was set.

The CID and Provost Marshal Kriwanek told the FBI and Fort Bragg army brass that they had found nothing in the apartment to indicate the presence of intruders. That statement would be challenged by their own documents. Certainly, something important was found in the autopsy room. CID agent Paul Connolly spied something on one of Colette MacDonald's fingernails. Upon closer inspection, it appeared to be a piece of skin. Dr. George Gammel, the pathologist who performed the autopsy, removed the item, which he also identified as skin, placed it in a vial, and personally handed the vial to CID agent Bennie Hawkins for safekeeping.[40] A competent investigator might suspect that it had been scraped from the person who killed Colette, and it should have been carefully protected. The skin did arrive at the lab, for lead agent William Ivory, who traveled to Fort Gordon the following week, found the vial containing the skin. He even viewed it through a microscope.[41] He went so far as to verify with laboratory technician Dillard Browning that it was, in fact, skin. Ivory labeled it as "oily skin" when questioned about it years later. However, when the lab experts later prepared to analyze the materials in the "fingernail scrapings" exhibit, the piece of skin was missing. This crucial evidence had somehow disappeared from the vial Ivory had recently examined.

There was more to the story about the skin than appears in the documents. Fred Bost and I interviewed Paul Connolly, William Ivory's CID partner at the time of the crimes. Connolly was the agent who first alerted the pathologist to the skin. "Of course it existed," he said. "They even took pictures of it." If photos ever existed, they have never surfaced, not in releases to the defense team by the army, or in any FOIA offerings. When the defense team learned, via FOIA documents after the 1979 trial, that the item taken from Colette's nail was really skin, and the army hadn't reported its loss, MacDonald's lawyers were shocked.

The skin might have provided a signature of the killer, whether Mac-Donald or an intruder. Yet it is curious that the CID didn't even photograph MacDonald's wounds or examine him in any way for fingernail scratch marks. CID agent Peter Kearns, on December 15, 1970, had questioned William Ivory on this very subject. Ivory excused this oversight by claiming that no photos were taken of MacDonald's wounds "because at the time that Captain MacDonald was admitted to the hospital, he was not a suspect in the case." This, of course, was not true, but even if it were, it would not have been an adequate explanation, for correct investigative procedures call for wounds of all victims to be photographed.

While still trying to understand the disappearance of the piece of skin found on Colette's fingernail, Fred Bost and I learned that thirteen months after the murders Paul Connolly suddenly remembered that when he had visited MacDonald in the hospital on the day of the murders he saw "a five inch diagonal scratch mark down MacDonald's chest."[42] Defense lawyers point out that, considering the timing, this is suspiciously convenient, since Connolly's earlier, 1970, written statements contain no such claim. It is also interesting that Connolly, the discoverer of the skin in the first place, was the CID agent first sent to interview the injured MacDonald in the hospital, and he did not immediately draw Ivory's attention to an alleged scratch mark on MacDonald's chest. This was during the time Ivory was building his case against MacDonald, and while the army was trying to keep the FBI out of the picture. If Connolly indeed had seen such a scratch mark, then he had discovered the perfect proof of MacDonald's guilt, proof that his partner Ivory was desperately seeking. Yet Connolly had remained silent.

Did MacDonald have such an incriminating scratch as testified to by

Connolly nine years later under oath at trial? Fred Bost and I interviewed Dr. Severt Jacobson, the emergency physician who treated MacDonald's wounds on the murder morning. "Were there fingernail scratch marks on his chest?" Fred asked.

Jacobson told us about multiple *ice pick* wounds, seen as puncture marks on MacDonald's chest where Connolly said he saw a scratch. But Jacobson said, "I saw no fingernail scratches on Jeffrey MacDonald."

"And no long, diagonal scratch mark down his chest?"

"No. I made notes and I drew diagrams. There were no fingernail scratches on MacDonald."[43] And so the question of whose skin was found on Colette's fingernail will perhaps never be answered, but medical records and Jacobson's statement regarding the absence of fingernail scratches on MacDonald create grave doubt that it was MacDonald's skin, as the army claimed.

UNIDENTIFIED FINGERPRINTS

Interestingly, more than three dozen finger or palm prints taken from the murder apartment were never identified. And all of them couldn't have been "old" prints made by former tenants of the apartment, as maintained by investigators. Documents reveal that a solitary unmatched print had been recovered from a drinking glass found on an end table near the living room sofa.[44] This was the same sofa where MacDonald said he fought the intruders. And MacDonald says he doesn't remember a drinking glass being there. Also, the evidence shows that MacDonald washed the glasses he and Colette used that night when they enjoyed a liqueur nightcap. Yet the glass found in the living room contained dregs of chocolate milk, the same kind of chocolate milk that was in the refrigerator, the same refrigerator that bore bloodstains. It's also noteworthy that the chocolate milk had been purchased by Colette that very evening as she returned from school. Since the children were in bed at that time, and since she and her husband chose an alcoholic beverage to drink, and since the fingerprint on the glass was neither hers nor her husband's, who poured and drank the chocolate milk?

AN UNIDENTIFIED HAIR IN COLETTE'S HAND

As Fred Bost and I considered the forensic evidence mentioned in the laboratory notes we were especially troubled by the unreported hair evidence in the case. Hairs unmatched to MacDonald or any other known person were found at every suspected area of struggle in the murder apartment. One of these was a "pubic or body hair" found close to baby Kristen's body on her bedspread. Another was a "pubic or body hair" found near Kimberly on her bedspread. Both of these hairs were compared to the hairs of MacDonald and to samples from other persons, yet they remained unmatched and were kept secret by the authorities.

There were many other such fibers and hairs,[45] but perhaps the most important, and without doubt the most troubling, was a hair which would become one of the key points of contention between the MacDonald lawyers and the government. It was a short brown hair found clutched in Colette's left hand.

A hair in the hand of a murder victim may be significant. If that hair is from someone other than the suspect, it is crucial. Given the defensive nature of Colette MacDonald's wounds, and the wooden club splinters found in her grasp, it was obvious that Colette had fought someone in hand-to-hand battle. Therefore, extraneous materials found on her body which could not be matched to her or to items in the apartment should be regarded as critical evidence. After all, MacDonald said he saw three male assailants and a female standing by. Could this hair have been from one of these assailants? The hair in question had turned up among other longer hairs found in Colette MacDonald's left hand, and, if the hairs did not belong to members of her family, it is inescapable that they may have belonged to her assailant or assailants. Was it Jeffrey MacDonald's hair?

The army case handlers conceded that the longer hairs belonged to Colette herself, but they didn't know who was the source of the shorter brown hair, for MacDonald was blond, and the CID, not wishing to alert MacDonald that they were trying to build a case against him, apparently made no immediate attempt to match MacDonald's hairs against this still secret mystery hair. Dillard Browning first cataloged this troublesome hair on March 11, 1970, as an "arm or body hair—no known for comparison." Janice Glisson, Browning's CID laboratory associate, later would draw a picture in her notes of the mystery hair showing its pertinent characteristics.[46] Government laboratory reports misled the defense as to the findings about this hair, and Glisson's crucial drawing was never revealed until the FOIA forced its release years after trial.

When Bost and I became aware of this hair, we harked back to what Gunderson had told me, that he and others had collected numerous statements from witnesses who said they had seen in the vicinity people who loosely matched the descriptions of MacDonald's alleged intruders.

Was this hair physical proof of these assailants? Whatever its source, that single hair had been effectively masked by the government, and months later would become the focal point of one of the more dramatic incidents of the entire MacDonald affair.

UNIDENTIFIED BLOND WIG FIBERS

Another item the CID kept very quiet about was a clear-handled hairbrush found on a stool a few feet from the place where MacDonald said he saw the blond female intruder. The hairbrush contained long blond tresses, but these blond fibers weren't mentioned in the typed CID reports turned over to the defense. And they continued to be ignored by the CID even though MacDonald had specifically described seeing a woman with long blond hair.[47] Also, during the time the CID agents were telling their superiors and the FBI agents that they'd found nothing in the home pointing to civilian intruders, they again ignored the blond fibers in the hairbrush.

A BURNT MATCH

A page from the CID evidence log, released through FOIA in 1983, shows another item that was kept from the defense. A CID lab technician found a burnt match near the base of the radiator in Kristen's room, two feet from the bed. Yet there was nothing in the room requiring the use of flame, the MacDonald children weren't allowed to play with matches, and neither Jeffrey nor Colette MacDonald smoked.[48] Again, it seems that the CID ignored key evidence, for MacDonald had reported that the female intruder was carrying a flickering light, "perhaps a candle."

A BLOODY SYRINGE

Still another item the CID kept from the defense was a bloody syringe found by Hilyard Medlin, the senior lab tech from Fort Gordon. A page from an FBI report,[49] only released in 1983, states that at 8 A.M. on February 21, 1970, during a debriefing session of laboratory personnel as they prepared to depart Fort Bragg, "Mr. Medlin also advised that a half filled syringe that contained an as yet unknown fluid was located in a hall closet, which also contained some evidence of blood. In this connection, Medlin said that it appeared that someone with a bloody hand had reached into this cabinet containing medical supplies for some purpose." This item was never tested in the lab. Like the piece of skin, it disappeared; and its loss, like its very existence, was kept from the defense.[50]

MULTIPLE BLOODY GLOVES

The CID also had found in the murder apartment snippets of thin, stretchy rubber from gloves like surgeons wear. The army thought that MacDonald must have worn the gloves to write the word "PIG" in blood on the headboard of his bed to further throw the investigators off his trail, and that he had ripped them trying to take them off. But documents prove that five other gloves also were found in the kitchen. There were three cloth gloves and two rubber. Both rubber gloves and two of the cloth gloves were bloodstained. The laboratory reported that the stains were too sparse to analyze, other than to determine that the blood was human.[51]

As Ivory constructed his theory, he apparently didn't consider these bloodstained gloves, a fact whose significance increases given the presence of multiple weapons, multiple unidentified fingerprints, and when measured against MacDonald's story of multiple assailants. Were those multiple bloody gloves worn by intruders? And if there were intruders, who might they have been?

3

The Woman
in the Floppy Hat

Jeffrey MacDonald said the faces of his assailants seemed "wasted," as if they were drug users. Yet the CID ridiculed the very idea that such people could get on post, actually get as far as an officer's apartment, murder the family, and simply leave without being detected. But to arrive at this conclusion, the CID agents had to ignore MP Kenneth Mica's sighting of a woman in a floppy hat and boots, forget about the multiple bloody gloves, the bloody syringe, the unmatched fingerprints, foreign candle wax, unmatched blond fibers in a hairbrush, and other things found in the murder apartment. To flatly rule out the presence of "hippies," the agents also had to deny their own knowledge about conditions in the drug community around Fort Bragg at the time of the murders.

Fayetteville, 1969–1970

To people who lived on post at the time, the idea of marauding crazies wasn't farfetched, and the CID agents themselves, trusted with fighting drug crime on post, knew this personally. At the time of the murders, Fort Bragg was involved in a deteriorating conflict in Vietnam and bogged down in an equally hopeless effort against drug crimes at home. In 1970, the year the murders occurred, the census takers counted more than 53,000 people in the small city of Fayetteville.

It was an old city, named after the French general Lafayette, and it had long hosted the military, and served, sometimes reluctantly, as the civilian consort of nearby Fort Bragg. Although the post housed only about 52,000 troops, the turnover was so great that some 200,000 soldiers shipped out annually. Those headed for Vietnam left Fayetteville full of hope, fear, patriotism, courage. Many returned bled of innocence, disillusioned. They had witnessed horrors. Some were injured, some mentally undone.

Many of these troubled young people sought solace in marijuana, LSD, amphetamines, and heroin. By 1968, two years before the MacDonald murders, drug abuse and its residue of crime gave this anteroom to Southeast Asia a new name—Fayettenam. In 1969 surrounding Cumberland County estimated that 25,000, or 11 percent, of its 225,000 residents were drug offenders; 1,000 of these were considered hardcore heroin addicts. Another thousand people addicted to heroin lived among many other drug users on the military reservation.

Dealers pipelined the drugs in from New York, Miami, and directly from the Far East. Hookers and pimps and pushers thrived, but at high cost. In the fall of 1969 a soldier under the influence of LSD leaped to his death from an upper story of the post hospital. On a single day in the following January two twenty-year-old soldiers died in unrelated drug overdoses in their own units on post, four miles apart.

According to the post newspaper, the *Paraglide*, complaints on Fort Bragg itself were so numerous in 1969 that the military police "blotter" (the official logbook, using thirteen-inch paper) averaged twenty-two pages of incidents daily.[1] So many prisoners packed the post stockade on Armstead Street that many slept on cots in the halls. In 1969 thieves stole the CID's own evidence safe. Many soldiers carried weapons because of so many armed robberies on the post itself; in one instance a gunman walked into a barracks on a payday evening and held up five soldiers at once.[2] Concealed weapons had become such a hazard on post that the provost marshal had written a paper on the subject. The month before the murders, someone broke into the building adjacent to the MacDonald apartment. Nothing was stolen, but Janice Pendlyshok, the tenant, found her underwear scattered and obscenities written on a mirror.[3] Aviator James Milne, a MacDonald neighbor, had seen robed, candle-carrying figures headed for MacDonald's house the night of the murders.[4] Milne said someone had broken into his car not long before the murders. Drug users had been caught after breaking into the police car of Fayetteville police detective Sergeant Prince Beasley. They had been looking for narcotics.

On May 28, 1970, two soldiers died after overdosing on uncut heroin in a Laundromat restroom in Fayetteville. So strong was the heroin product being marketed on post that a CID agent interviewed years later remembered finding "stiffs with the needles still in their arms, the syringes just dangling there."[5]

By June 7, 1970, the Fort Bragg commander, Lieutenant General John Tolson, offered amnesty to any drug abuser on post who would step forward to seek help.[6] Army medics began caring for admitted drug addicts in a hippie-decorated "halfway house," a clapboard building in the post's old hospital area.[7] In an effort to gain financial backing for this experiment, dubbed Operation Awareness, Tolson invited Senator Harold Hughes of Iowa to visit Fort Bragg. Hughes reported to his fellow senators on September 1, 1970, that drug addiction at Fort Bragg was heavy among some 9,000 soldiers.[8] In substantiation of Hughes's assessment, the Washington Post–Los Angeles Times News Service circulated a September story by reporter Bernard N. Nossiter saying that 2 to 3 percent of Bragg's troops "are 'strung out' on heroin, amphetamines, and other hard drugs."[9] General Tolson himself, on November 27, 1970, would appear before a congressional subcommittee, called there to explain the disturbing situation at Fort Bragg.

But before that meeting would occur the drug problems had escalated. On July 9, three days after the army began its Article 32 hearing into the MacDonald case, a Fayetteville drug dealer was found dead slumped over the steering wheel of his 1967 Cadillac, two bullets in the back of his head, bundles of heroin hidden in his socks.[10] And it happened on a Fort Bragg street.

The following week three soldiers and a Fayetteville youth were charged with kidnapping a young couple, tying the male to a tree and beating him to death, then raping his fourteen-year-old female companion.

Fayetteville's Rowan Park, a local recreational area, was overrun with young people buying, selling, and using drugs. It became commonly known as "Skag Park." In desperation, on July 6, 1970, the Fayetteville City Council announced an evening curfew at city parks. Narcotics agents, police officers, deputies, and army CID men prowled the surrounding neighborhoods, watching for activity, setting up clandestine meetings with informants, making sudden, sometimes violent arrests. By August the drug traders became so resentful of the park curfew that riots occurred. The confrontations with police resulted in the use of tear gas. Gunshots were fired, multiple arrests were made, and trials ensued.[11]

Helena Stoeckley

The CID agents well knew that the area, on Bragg and off, was rife with drugs, drug users, dealers, death, and violence. To say otherwise is to, again, ignore the evidence. In fact, to fight the plague of crime and drug-sponsored deaths the army in 1968 had cooperated with other law enforcement authorities to form an Inter-Agency Narcotics Bureau. Officers from the army CID, the Fayetteville police, the Cumberland County Sheriff's Department, and the State Bureau of Investigation teamed up to move in pairs amongst the drug community, prowling, watching, and working with young people who lived with the drug crowd and risked exposure to inform on dealers. One such young informant was Helena Stoeckley.

An enigmatic teenager, Stoeckley was a daughter of a career army officer. She attended grammar school in France and high school in Fayetteville, where her father had retired as a lieutenant colonel. According to her yearbook she played intramural basketball and volleyball, acted with the school Drama Club, held membership in the French Club and Latin Club, and sang with the Senior High Singers and the Mixed Chorus. She was even a volunteer candy striper at E. E. Smith Memorial Hospital. That's where her apparent normalcy ends.

By her own admission, Helena began running with drug users during her school days, all older youths. Her parents were alarmed at her behavior and her "hippie" appearance, but they were unable to curb her activities. By the time she was fifteen she was hooked on heroin.[12] At first she bartered syringes stolen from the hospital where she worked, then traded sexual favors for the drug.

When Stoeckley was sixteen, Sergeant Rudy Studer, a Fayetteville policeman and member of the Inter-Agency Narcotics Bureau, arrested her and immediately recognized her intelligence and stoic absence of fear. He gave her a choice: She could serve as his informant, or face charges for narcotics possession. Despite the danger of snitching on users and dealers, she chose to become his informant and, as such, was free to continue feeding her own addiction with little fear of the police.

Even in the disruptive atmosphere of her new life she graduated high school ahead of her age class a week shy of her seventeenth birthday. She moved into a flat in the Haymount District where she served Sergeant Studer as an informant. Then when Studer made lieutenant, he passed her to Sergeant Prince Beasley, also an officer of the Inter-Agency Narcotics Bureau.

Beasley said she was the best informant he ever had, "crafty," he said, "sneaky smart and bold." She worked in perilous situations and once even placed herself in jeopardy to yell a warning to Sergeant Beasley that a dealer he had just arrested, one she secretly had fingered for Beasley, was about to hit him.[13] With characteristic cleverness, she told the dealer on the way to jail that the reason she'd yelled to warn Beasley was to keep the dealer out of deeper trouble for slugging a cop. The dealer, who had just seen Helena swallow a sealed packet of LSD "to keep from getting caught with it as the arrest was going down," seemed to believe her, at least for the moment. In little more than a year's time, she provided tips that led to dozens of arrests.

Even with the Inter-Agency Narcotics Bureau working day and night, the drug and crime situation seemed no better. The authorities were losing the battle. Of the thirty-one murders being tried or prepared for trial in and around Fayetteville in 1970, the bulk were drug related, and the narcotics officers, on post and off, could do little to stem the tide.

This is the world Captain Jeffrey MacDonald and his family came into during the late summer of 1969 when they moved to Fort Bragg. As group surgeon for his unit, he also was assigned to provide medical counsel for Green Beret heroin addicts. Another Green Beret physician, Dr. Jerry Hughes, invited MacDonald to moonlight as an emergency physician at nearby Cape Fear Valley Hospital. A night or two of civilian doctoring per week offered MacDonald an opportunity to pay off his medical school bills, and it gave him experience in a variety of medical emergency situations, including drug overdoses.

Not long after MacDonald assumed his duties at Fort Bragg and at the civilian hospital in the fall of 1969, the Fort Bragg commanders suddenly changed the long-standing rules of physician-patient privilege. Because of the drug problem, soldiers were informed that their doctors would now be required to report the names of drug users. Not surprisingly, given the drug problem on post, the decision wasn't popular. The number of soldiers seeking counseling from these army doctors soon dwindled. Like most medical personnel, MacDonald thought the new move unwise because it turned physicians into policemen, and it encouraged addicts to seek medical assistance off post.

MacDonald insists that he did not adhere to the new regulation with any kind of vigor. He says he did talk with one addict's commanding officer, and, instead of disciplining the soldier, MacDonald and the officer worked out a way to get the man some help.

In another case, MacDonald says, in lieu of being reported, a soldier brought in his wife and the two agreed to work together to get the man off drugs. Yet things were not always that smooth between MacDonald and drug users. In an incident at Cape Fear Valley Hospital, MacDonald, as the doctor on duty, was called upon to clear the emergency room when a group of young people became rowdy. But this was nothing unusual. Aberrant, angry activity was an unhappy norm in his everyday work with drug abusers.

Sergeant Prince Beasley was well aware that his best informant lived with a group of young people like those MacDonald had encountered at his emergency room. Stoeckley's roommates and fellow travelers were military and civilian and they were using and selling drugs. But, a few months before the murders, in the fall of 1969, Beasley learned they had gotten into something else.

One crisp autumn evening he was asked to make a run to the Haymount District, a once plush area gone to seed. A woman on Clark Street had called the police because she was alarmed at something up in a tree. Beasley knew the address well, for his key informant, Helena Stoeckley, lived next door.

When he arrived, the troubled caller pointed up into a tree. There was Helena sitting on a limb, silhouetted by the light of a full moon. Two others sat with her, a woman Beasley knew and a man he didn't. "What are you doin' sittin' up there like fools," he called. "Come down from there."

"We're witches," Helena told him, giggling. "This is how we just sit." Presuming she was high on something, he talked her and her friends down and they disappeared, still giggling, into her apartment.

Another neighbor had been concerned about the aberrant behavior of the same group. William Archbell had moved away because he said that automobiles and taxis arrived at all hours apparently indicating a brisk business in drugs. Archbell said Helena's companions were "weird people," who urinated outside and sometimes "had sex in the yard."[14]

Soon after the incident in the tree, Helena called the station and told the dispatcher that "Blackjack" wanted to see Beasley. She gave the code word for the Presbyterian church in her neighborhood, and that night Beasley met her there. After giving him leads, she told him that her group was changing, and not for the better. A man named Candy had assumed control from Greg Mitchell. Candy was teaching them about black witchcraft. This new leader was a charismatic sort, she said, and the others would do anything he wanted them to. Beasley didn't worry much about this news, at first.

According to Beasley, Helena enjoyed the power her informant duties gave her. She could point her finger and, *poof!*, a "friend" would be picked up, jailed, and sent away for a long time. One day she pointed her finger toward Candy. Beasley, happy for a chance to nail this guy, got a warrant and he and his men went in. But they found no drugs. Instead, they found Candy in a room painted black. On a stairwell wall was a painted rendition of Christ with his robe pulled up and a hippie on his knees fellating him. Upon Beasley's expression of disgust, Candy simply laughed. "Jesus is a man, too," he said, "if there is a Jesus, and he likes the same things we do."

In the backyard behind the building with the black room, one of Beasley's men found the mutilated carcass of a cat. Beasley began to worry about Helena's attachment to this new breed of drug user.

Beasley soon confronted Helena with the failure to find drugs in Candy's Hay Street apartment. She explained, simply, "I changed my mind. Candy's our man." Soon she told Beasley that the group members were using the sacrifice of cats in their rituals. "They'd hang a cat up in the room, slit its throat, and have sex on the floor in the warm blood, men on women, men on men, women on women, it didn't matter," Beasley said. Now really concerned, Beasley said he tried to get her to get out of the group and the weird behavior. He said he asked her to just leave them, but she wouldn't listen to him.

MacDonald's Conflicts with Drug Users

MacDonald did little to endear himself to the drug addicts on post. He complained that when he assumed his position as group surgeon of his unit he found medical equipment stacked on the back steps of the medical area. He asked about it and was told it was going to be taken to the dump. Upon further examination he found drugs and syringes that he feared would be salvaged by scavenging addicts. He asked for the policies and procedures manual, and no one could find it. Master Sergeant Leo Violette, a combat veteran of Korea and Vietnam, testified at the army hearing that MacDonald's work, which included restricting access to drug materials, had improved their unit's performance. But Jim Williams later remarked that due to MacDonald's hard-nosed stance on drugs the young doctor became known, sarcastically, as "wonderboy."

On January 16, 1970, a month before the murders, a soldier named Robert Wallack overdosed on heroin.[15] Instead of taking him to Womack Army Hospital where his drug habit might be reported to his superior officer, two of Wallack's friends took him to the Cape Fear Valley Hospital emergency room in Fayetteville. Dr. Jeffrey MacDonald was on duty that night and performed a tracheostomy to save Wallack's life. A nurse, learning heroin was involved, called the police. The officers who reported to the hospital escorted Wallack's two friends downtown where the men identified their heroin supplier, a "black man" who reportedly dealt drugs in a certain pool hall. The black man was subsequently arrested.[16]

Soon after the arrest of the heroin dealer, Captain Williams warned MacDonald that the enlisted medics working in the field now were being told that Dr. MacDonald was a "fink." But MacDonald had dealt with the almost daily threats of drug addicts during his internship in New York. He shrugged off William's cautionary remarks.

On the morning of February 16, 1970, the day before the murders, a young corporal visited MacDonald's office on post and demanded that the doctor discharge him from the army because of his heroin habit. When MacDonald informed him that he had no power to do this, the man flared up and began yelling at MacDonald. Captain Jim Williams, who worked in the same building, heard the man and rushed to help. Williams said it took three men to remove the wildly agitated soldier from the premises.[17]

Again, Williams, knowing many of the drug users had just come from Vietnam, cautioned MacDonald about his deteriorating reputation among users. These people were angry and unstable, Williams told MacDonald, and they were armed. This was something every officer of experience knew. But MacDonald replied that he wasn't all that concerned about it.

In less than a day, his wife and daughters were dead.

At about 6:30 A.M., mere hours after the murders, Captain Jim Williams told MPs about the young addict who had become angry at MacDonald in his office the day before. And he told them that due to the new army regulation revoking physician-patient confidentiality, MacDonald had been labeled as a fink. MP Richard Tevere picked up the soldier, but learned he had a sound alibi for the time of the murders.

No such effort was made in the case of another suspect who matched, to an uncanny degree, MacDonald's description of the female intruder. Even though military policeman Kenneth Mica told the provost marshal, Colonel Kriwanek, about the woman with the floppy hat and boots he had seen standing on the street corner, Kriwanek and the CID investigators told the FBI there were no civilians involved. But agents at CID headquarters had other ideas. In particular, the CID agent[18] and drug investigator who had worked with Stoeckley and Beasley in town on the Inter-Agency Narcotics Bureau wasn't convinced. He says he and other agents discussed the descriptions MacDonald had furnished and they immediately came up with a name for the woman MacDonald had described. That name was Helena Stoeckley.[19] "Her name was on a lot of tongues that morning," the former CID agent said.[20]

The CID agents weren't the only law officers thinking about Helena Stoeckley and her friends on the murder morning.

At 7 A.M. on February 17, 1970, Sergeant Prince Beasley awakened to the ring of his telephone. Captain J. E. Melvin of the Fayetteville Police Department apologized for calling at this hour since Beasley had worked late the night before and hadn't gotten to bed till 4 A.M.

"What've we got?" Beasley asked him.

Melvin told him about the murders, then Beasley asked him what they knew about the assailants.

"Three men, two white, one Negro. The Negro was wearing an Army field jacket with sergeant's stripes, Prince. And, something else—there was a blond girl with a floppy hat and boots egging them on."

"You say it was a Negro with a field jacket?"

"That's how the doctor described them," the captain told Beasley.

"Captain, this sticks in my throat, but that description of the woman matches your neighbor on Valley Road, the Stoeckley kid. She was dressed that way last night, wearing a blond wig. I saw her. And one of the guys she was with last night was a black wearing a field jacket with stripes. That's not a combination you see just everywhere."

"How soon can you move?" Melvin asked.

Within fifteen minutes Beasley was in his car. He drove to Stoeckley's usual habitats, the apartment she had taken on Clark Street, Candy's pad a few blocks away on Hay Street, and he checked out the Village Shoppe where he had seen her the night before, only hours before the murders. It troubled him that she had been dressed in boots, her floppy hat, and the blond wig. Failing to find her, he headed for police headquarters to arrange for a warrant to search a house trailer where Stoeckley had told him drugs would soon be stashed. If the group was on the move, Beasley hoped, they might try to get their drugs out of town, too.

Corroboration Around Town

THE AVERITT SIGHTING
On that same murder morning various people in the community saw interesting things. At about 8 A.M., Mrs. Dorothy Averitt entered Mrs. Johnson's grocery store on Murchison Road and found a black man and a girl as the only customers inside, and Mrs. Johnson was clearly nervous. Averitt immediately understood why. She had seen this pair before, and the memory wasn't a happy one. At that previous time the girl wasn't wearing a blond wig as she was now. But it was the same girl, and the same man. Averitt delivered newspapers for a living, and on that day a week or so before, she had been delivering in the rear of the Hickory Trailer Court when the black man swung a baseball bat and deliberately hit a ball at her.[21] She remembered that the brown-haired girl had apparently been high on drugs because she laughed and screamed at the baseball's near miss.[22]

The grocery store they were in was only two blocks away from that trailer court. The girl was dressed differently now, with a plastic raincoat and go-go boots, but the man wore the same army field jacket he had worn the day of the bat-and-ball incident. When the man walked to a refrigerator in the back of the store, Mrs. Johnson whispered to Averitt, "Don't leave me alone with them."

Mrs. Averitt tried to engage the girl in small talk, but she appeared to be drugged. "Where'd you get all that mud on your boots?" Dorothy Averitt asked. "I've lived in this country all my life and I've not seen mud that looked like that." Although Averitt had been a newspaper carrier for twenty-seven years, she had also once worked as a nurse's aide and her father had butchered hogs on the farm where she had grown up.

She thought the girl projected a familiar stench of blood. When the black man returned from the back of the store, he saw Averitt talking with the girl. He put a milk carton on the counter and said, "Let's get out of here."

The girl held out some candy. "I want these."

"Let's get out of here," he said again, pushing her toward the door.

"No. I want these." The man threw a wad of money down on the counter and they left.

Under oath Dorothy Averitt would later identify a 1970 photograph of Helena Stoeckley as the girl she had seen with the black man and baseball bat at the trailer park, the same girl she had seen wearing the wig in the grocery store.[23]

THE SONDERSON SIGHTING

The next known sighting of such a group occurred a little later on the morning of the murders. While the bodies of Colette, Kimberly, and Kristen were being autopsied, and while MacDonald was undergoing surgery for his collapsed lung, only a few miles away Joan Sonderson, a carhop at the Chute Drive Inn restaurant on Fort Bragg, reported early for her 9 A.M. shift. She noticed an automobile parked under the overhang in her service area. She thought it was empty, but about an hour later she saw a pair of "white or beige" muddy boots of someone who appeared to be sleeping in the front seat. The boots belonged to a girl with blond hair and a floppy hat.

When the girl got up and got out of the car, Sonderson asked her if she wanted some coffee. "No," the girl replied. "The MacDonalds were murdered last night. Did you know that?" Sonderson said she didn't. "And that MacDonald is in the hospital and his wife and children are dead?"

The right rear passenger door opened and a black male stepped out of the car. He wore an army fatigue jacket and dark civilian pants. He told Sonderson he was just going to use the men's room. She noticed another white male slumped down in the seat behind the wheel, but she couldn't see him well. The girl and the black man used the restrooms, then returned to the car and they all drove away.[24]

In the Sonderson sighting, as in that of Dorothy Averitt, the blond-haired girl exhibited curious behavior, as if she were drugged, but the black man, in each case, seemed in control. MacDonald, too, in describing the female intruder and the black man, said that the female was chanting in a monotonous voice, "Acid is groovy; kill the pigs," as if she were drugged, but the black man who used the baseball bat did not appear to be so influenced.

THE STOECKLEY TIP

By the early afternoon of the murders, detective Beasley had acquired a warrant for a drug raid on the trailer in the Hickory Trailer Court where he thought Stoeckley and her friends might be hiding. This was the same small trailer park where the black man hit the baseball at Dorothy Averitt. It was located down the street near Mrs. Johnson's grocery store where Averitt saw Stoeckley and a black man that same murder morning.

Stoeckley's earlier tip, that Beasley would find drugs stashed in the trailer, proved characteristically fruitful. Beasley and his fellow officers broke in the trailer door at about 2 P.M. on Tuesday, February 17, the same day of the murders. And they found the drugs in cellophane packets, hidden behind a wall panel in the trailer. Neither Stoeckley nor her friends were present.[25]

The small trailer house had been rented by two white men and a black man who wore an army field jacket with sergeant's stripes.[26] A resident living in an adjacent trailer, Bill Guin, recalled seeing the men come to the trailer in the company of a girl at about 5:30 A.M. on the morning of the murders.[27] After hearing the descriptions given by MacDonald, Guin realized that his neighbors matched those descriptions.[28] He recalled that the neighbors usually traveled in a light-colored car and a small foreign sports car.

OTHER SIGHTINGS

Over the years the MacDonald defense team has compiled a file on other sightings, most of them having occurred in the hours before the murders, most of them involving a group of people like Stoeckley and her friends. On Monday night, well before the murders occurred, a teacher, Edith Boushey, said she saw Colette MacDonald being harassed by several young people at night school on Fort Bragg. Mrs. Boushey had to pass the group as she was leaving the North Carolina University Extension Campus, and noticed how Colette had been backed defensively against a wall in the ground-floor hallway by a young man speaking to her.

In 1983 Ray Shedlick showed Mrs. Boushey a large collection of photos and the teacher pointed to the picture of Greg Mitchell (Stoeckley's boyfriend at the time of the murders) as the man who had been intimidating Mrs. MacDonald that evening.[29]

Detective Beasley had seen Stoeckley and the black man in a blue Mustang fastback the night before. Shortly after Beasley's sighting, and approximately three hours after the incident at the university extension building described by Mrs. Boushey, a group of young people who fit the MacDonald descriptions in dress, hair color, and racial mix was seen at about midnight at Dunkin' Donuts on Bragg Boulevard in Fayetteville. The young woman with the group appeared to be high on drugs.[30]

James Milne's sighting of three people wearing sheets and carrying candles occurred at about 12:30 A.M. on the morning of the murders. At Dunkin' Donuts about an hour after the Milne incident, another woman, Marion L. Campbell, saw a group of young people. The young woman was blond and wore a floppy hat. The white man appeared to be "in another world. He was just staring vacantly out the window as if there was absolutely nothing around. It didn't even look as if he was blinking his eyelids."

Campbell observed that the black man, who wore "an olive drab field or fatigue[31] jacket," was standing there not saying a word to either of them. "He acted more aware, more like he was in charge." Campbell says the black man glared at her angrily when he saw her staring at the group. The black man walked "very erect" as the group left.[32]

At an undetermined time in that early morning near the MacDonald residence, First Lieutenant Edwin Casper II and his wife, Winnie, were awakened by people giggling outside as they apparently splashed through rain puddles. There was at least one female and at least two males. The group seemed to be moving through the yard from Bragg Boulevard, which ran behind the building, toward the MacDonald building, about 200 yards away. Neither of the Caspers could fix the time precisely, but they knew it was sometime between 11:45 P.M., when Mrs. Casper joined her husband in bed, and 3:45 A.M., a time she noted when she was awakened by her two-year-old daughter.[33]

Another resident in the same building as the Caspers was able to place the time more precisely. Captain James Shortill and his wife, Rita, who lived two doors down from the Casper residence, were also sleeping with their bedroom window open. Mrs. Shortill heard the same group go by and noted her clock said 2:10 A.M. She said she heard "at least three people speaking and laughing. I heard a female voice and at least two male voices. I also heard footsteps." The Caspers and Shortills were never aware of each other's information.[34]

Several hundred yards from the MacDonald home, Green Beret captain Kenneth Lamb and his wife were awakened by someone fumbling at their back door. By the time Lamb got to the door, whoever had been there had vanished.[35]

Also early on the murder morning of February 17, half a block from the MacDonald residence, Jan Snyder had been asleep in her second-floor apartment at 308 Castle Drive (the MacDonalds lived at 544) when she was awakened by the sound of a loud muffler.[36] She went to the window to see a light-colored car, its headlights on, standing next to the curb directly in front of the building. The muffler was not just loud, it was impertinent. Because it might awaken her child, she watched with relief as it pulled away. But when she returned to her bed, she heard the car returning. This time she flicked on her bedroom light before going to the window. The noisy car and a jeep beyond it were side by side facing up the hill, their lights on a Mustang in the nearest parking slot. People got into the Mustang and the vehicles' occupants were talking back and forth.

She remained at the window and watched as the three vehicles disappeared from sight up the hill. She was trying to make up her mind whether to return to bed or stay up for the baby's feeding when the Mustang came back down the street and drove slowly past the Snyder apartment again before it headed down the hill toward North Lucas Drive.

Was this coincidence? Beasley had seen Stoeckley and the black man in a Mustang that night. Two days after the murders, on February 19, a Fayetteville police officer cited Greg Mitchell, Helena Stoeckley's sometime boyfriend, for having a loud muffler on his faded pale yellow 1964 Plymouth.

Upon learning of the murders, Mrs. Snyder immediately told her neighbors about the loud car that had awakened her and of what she had seen in those darkened morning hours. She later said she told an investigator about it and he told her someone would come back and take a statement, but no one did.

At sometime between 2:05 and 2:15 A.M. on the morning of the murders, military policeman Carlos Torres had just left work at the NCO Club at Fort Bragg. He stopped for a traffic light on Honeycutt at Bragg Boulevard in the MacDonald neighborhood. While waiting for the light to change he observed a dark blue van, which he believed was a Volkswagen, parked on Bragg Boulevard about 60 to 75 yards from the intersection. (Marion Campbell, who saw a group at Dunkin' Donuts, said some of the kids left in a blue van.) Torres made a left turn onto Bragg Boulevard toward his home at Spring Lake. At that moment he saw three white males running out of the trees toward the van. Two of the men had long hair; one had a military-type haircut and wore a dark brownish jacket.[37]

Also early that morning, at a time between 1:30 and 2:30 A.M., Martha Evers,[38] driving on Bragg Boulevard, saw a blue Mustang parked on the shoulder of the road approximately 200 feet west of Honeycutt Road in the MacDonald neighborhood. The trunk of the vehicle was open. A white female wearing a wide-brim white hat stood toward the rear of the vehicle. A white male squatted nearby facing the bushes. Another stood near him also facing the bushes.

In an apartment across the walkway next to the MacDonald residence, Janice Pendlyshok was awakened early on the murder morning by the barking of her German shepherd dog, then she heard a woman screaming and two children crying. The screams soon stopped and she drifted back to sleep.[39]

In the apartment next to the MacDonald residence, in the bedroom directly over the MacDonald living room, sixteen-year-old Pamela Kalin was awakened momentarily by the sounds of laughing, sobbing, or conversation, she couldn't be sure, apparently coming from the MacDonald residence, but the noises didn't seem important. She went back to sleep.[40] She and her family would initially tell the CID agents that they heard nothing.

Cumberland County sheriff's detective John DeCarter had been alerted by phone of the murders at Fort Bragg and was on his way from his home to the sheriff's department early that morning when he stopped for a red light at Stamper Road and Bragg Boulevard. While waiting for the light to change, a small foreign sports car jammed with people crossed his headlights on the otherwise deserted Bragg Boulevard, headed toward town. This type of little two-seater sports car was rarely seen in the Fayetteville area. Years later, MacDonald's defense team would learn that Raymond Cazares, a member of the Stoeckley group, owned a small foreign sports car at the time of the murders, and, of course, Mr. Guin at the trailer park had said the men who lived there had a small sports car.

On that same murder morning, pre-dawn, a night man at Dunkin' Donuts claimed to have seen a black man and white woman enter his establishment.[41] He said they came in to wash their hands in the restrooms. He said they had something on them which he thought was blood.

William Posey, a next-door neighbor of Helena Stoeckley (whom he knew as "Helen"), also saw something on the morning of the murders that made him wonder whether the girl and her friends were involved in the murders.[42] Posey's story of seeing "Helen" coming home that morning would soon become a focal point in the case.

The First Stoeckley Admissions

After the drug raid on the house trailer on the day of the murders, Beasley went home to get some sleep for the rest of the afternoon. That night while eating supper, he read the story of the murders in the afternoon edition of the *Fayetteville Observer*. Under the subhead "Victims of a Hippie Cult?" the front-page headline was big and bold: "Officer's Wife, Children Found Slain At Ft. Bragg." The opening paragraph in the story by Pat Reese stated, "An Army doctor's wife and their two young children were stabbed to death in their Ft. Bragg home early today, apparently victims of a 'ritualistic' hippie cult."

Beasley read the story, paying particular attention to the woman assailant described by MacDonald. The description matched the one given to Beasley by Captain Melvin on the phone, but there was one additional item. According to the paper the female intruder was said by MacDonald to be carrying a candle. Melvin either had forgotten to mention that or hadn't known it.

Beasley knew Helena's apartment to be full of candles. He read further. If the paper was accurate, the victims had been stabbed "over and over again." But the only possible weapon mentioned by the paper was an ice pick found with a club outside the home. Another informant had told Beasley that Helena carried an ice pick in her clutch bag.

Beasley arrived back at his office at about 7:30 P.M. Tuesday night approximately sixteen hours after the murders had occurred. He asked about the stakeout at the trailer on Murchison Road. No one had shown up there.

Cuyler Windham, boss of the Inter-Agency Narcotics Bureau, had left a verbal message for Beasley and the other members. "Cooperate with the army," Windham had ordered, "but otherwise don't get sidetracked from your own drug job." Beasley understood his point. The city council had told Windham they intended to close Rowan Park if drug activities there weren't curtailed. The army and FBI would handle the MacDonald murders.

But Stoeckley was his drug informant, Beasley reasoned, and he had a right to talk with her. When he went back to work he made a quick cruise through Rowan Park, observing nothing unusual, then, a little after 8 P.M., he headed for Helena's pad on Clark Street. After checking to see that no one was in the apartment, he parked his Ford in a dark spot up the street where he could watch the old house in relative comfort. He relaxed as best he could, his police radio on the seat beside him. The vigil developed into a long wait in the darkness as he watched Stoeckley's apartment.

According to Beasley, he had already gotten his first look at the inside of Stoeckley's pad. A month earlier he had entered the one-room apartment with a warrant to arrest an AWOL soldier (for which he received a reward). He found his soldier, lying naked with two nude women, all basking in the glow of a circle of lighted candles on a coffee table near the bed. All the furniture in the room, including the refrigerator, was painted bright green. "Hippie" pictures of dubious religious significance were everywhere, and a zodiac circle dominated one wall. All the light bulbs had been painted blue, adding an unearthly cast to the flickering candlelight. Many unused candles were stacked in a wicker basket near the zodiac wall.

Now as Beasley watched the house, he lay his head back, his eyes still open. He was stretching his arms about 2:30 A.M. when he heard a loud car approaching. He knew that sound; it was Greg Mitchell's light yellow Plymouth with the blaring muffler. Helena had told him to watch out for Mitchell, that he was "mean as a snake." Headlights approached Beasley from the corner down the block, and, as he expected, they turned into Helena's driveway. Beasley hit the starter on his Ford and brought the engine to life. He surged forward and braked across the driveway.

Beasley saw occupants unloading from both sides of the automobile. He realized that there were more people than he had anticipated. One of them, a female, was already disappearing into Helena's apartment. Beasley hastily scanned the silhouettes of the others milling in the driveway as they looked warily in his direction. He spotted Helena and quickly counted five males, including the nervous, lean Greg Mitchell. The black man with the field jacket wasn't among them.[43]

"Hey, you've got to move that car," one of them yelled at him. "You're blocking us."

"I want to talk to Helena," Beasley yelled back. He stepped around the Ford, his radio in his left hand, his right hand free to reach for his pistol.

"That's a pig," he heard someone grumble.

"I only want to talk to Helena Stoeckley."

"Get lost!" one of the shadowed men shouted at him just as he saw Helena step forward, separating herself from the group. Some of the others began following menacingly behind her. Beasley says he then placed his hand on the pistol at his hip, gripping the butt loosely, slowly, making sure the motion was seen. Helena turned and waved her arm drunkenly at the others. "Hey, guys, everything's cool," she giggled. Beasley realized she was high.

She ambled out to the street while the others held their distance. "I know what you're looking for, Mister Beasley," she said nervously, the giggle still in her voice, her eyes barely focusing on his face. "You wanta see my ice pick."

"Stop it, Helena!" he growled. He moved to keep the men in view behind her. "Those children aren't anything to joke about!"

Beasley said her lopsided smile disappeared. Tears formed. She lowered her head, but he put a finger under her chin and forced her to look up at him. "Have you heard the descriptions they're broadcasting?" he asked her.

She nodded, looking at him through tears. Her lips trembled and her shoulders shook.

"I saw you last night, Helena—you and the black guy." Beasley pointed at the loafers on her feet. "You were wearing boots last night, and your wig and hat. The descriptions fit you and your black friend to a tee."

She didn't reply. She hung her head again.

"Helena, tell me the truth," he said, quietly, trying to get through her stupor. "You've never lied to me before. Were you involved in those killings?" He looked over her head toward the angry group, milling ever nearer.

Helena stood unmoving until he began to think she intended to ignore the question. Again he glanced toward the men near the other car.

"Helena," Beasley insisted. "Were you involved?"

She wiped a hand across her eyes without looking up. "I don't know, Mister Beasley—" She began to cry. "I was spaced out last night—so spaced out—but my mind—in my mind I may have been there. I see things happening—awful things." Beasley realized that something had shaken this usually cool and deliberate informant, and he worried that she might actually have seen the murders.

"Now listen to me carefully, Helena. Be sure of what you're saying. This is serious. It won't end here."

She nodded her head without looking up, swaying a bit as she moved again to brush her eyes with her arm.

Beasley lifted his radio to his mouth and called for the police dispatcher. The voice of Faddis Davis answered almost immediately.

"Get in touch with the CID at Fort Bragg," Beasley told Davis. "Tell them to send someone to 1108 Clark Street. I'm holding people for questioning who may have been involved in the murders out there. Got that?"[44]

Helena looked up at Beasley as Davis acknowledged the instructions. "A bad trip—bad trip," she wept.

"Don't say anymore now," he says he cautioned her. "Wait until the army guys come. It's a federal case. I don't have any jurisdiction in it. It'll be better if you wait and tell them."

Helena nodded, and continued to cry softly.

Beasley says he left Helena leaning against the fender of his car as he moved toward the group of angry men in the driveway. "I have backup officers on the way," he told them. "Cooperate with me and there won't be any problems."

They obeyed his instructions as he moved from one to another demanding identification. He began listing their names in his notebook, writing in large block letters to compensate for the near darkness. According to Beasley, he wanted the names for his report, knowing that once the CID arrived he might never have an opportunity to gather identifications.[45]

He says that the first man he braced, a man he knew as Don Harris, was stoned. The man was nervous, slightly incoherent, but fully cooperative. As Beasley spoke to a second man, he noticed another member of the group moving impatiently, edging closer. It was Greg Mitchell, his eyes angry, his face hard. Another informant had told Beasley that Mitchell was dangerous and unpredictable, "not playing with a full deck." And Helena had once told him, "Always keep an eye on Greg Mitchell. He considers himself a protector of the group. Never turn your back on him."

Beasley stepped around to face Mitchell as he continued to list names. "What's the hassle for?" Mitchell demanded. "This is gestapo stuff. We haven't done anything. This is private property and nobody's made a complaint here!"

Beasley says he ignored the words as he stepped up to the last man. "Let's see some identification."

"I ain't got any!" the man retorted belligerently. Mitchell moved to the left, which forced Beasley to reposition himself to keep the man he was addressing between them. The move hadn't gone unnoticed. According to Beasley, at that moment he felt he had lost the psychological advantage.

"Stay here," he ordered. He placed his right hand on his pistol and stepped backward toward his car and to Helena, who hadn't moved from her position at the fender. He pulled her to the other side of the car and placed her near the door where she would be better shielded if he were fired upon.

He lifted his radio again and called impatiently for the dispatcher. When Davis responded, Beasley says he asked angrily, "What's with the CID?"

"Bragg's been notified," Davis answered. "They're probably halfway there now."

Beasley grunted acknowledgment and put the radio down on the car hood, his eyes intent on the group of men bunched in the alley. Minutes dragged by as everyone waited tensely. Beasley said the men seemed to be gathering resolve. Some of them went into Helena's apartment, slamming the door violently. Beasley said he wondered if they had a gun in the house.

More time passed. Still no sign of the CID agents.

The men came out of the apartment again and joined the others in an irate, murmuring huddle. Beasley raised his radio to his lips and complained to his dispatcher.

"They're not there yet?" Davis asked.

"No, they're not." Beasley says by this time he was very angry. "And I can't hold this thing together much longer. I got half a dozen people here. If the CID doesn't show soon, I'm going to have to drop it."

Cursing quietly, he lowered the radio. Mitchell had sidled closer and Beasley was certain the man had overheard him. Mitchell went back and began talking quickly with his friends, occasionally gesturing toward Beasley.

"Listen," Beasley told Helena, "this is bad stuff. You've got to keep from getting in any deeper. If the CID doesn't get here, and if I have to leave, I want you to call Fort Bragg in the morning and tell them everything you know. Understand? I can't afford to take you with me when I leave. They'll know you've been working for me. If I have to go, tell them I picked on you because somebody saw you in your wig last night. Now call the CID in the morning. Understand? It's for your own good, Helena. It's the only way. Do you understand me? Tell me you understand."

He says he saw real fear in the girl's eyes. "Mister Beasley—I'm so—. It was such a bad trip."

At that moment men began to move out of their huddle. They fanned out across the driveway, facing Beasley, moving toward him, obviously no longer cowed by the threat of his pistol. "We're not staying here any longer, pig," Mitchell called. "We're driving out. So get that fucking car out of our way!"

Beasley backed off. His orders were that if he found anything, he was to notify the CID. He had done that. He gave Helena's arm a reassuring squeeze; then he slipped into his car, tossed his radio on the seat in disgust, and started the engine. As he pulled away, taunts and jeers followed from the driveway behind him.

When Beasley again reported for duty late that afternoon, on Wednesday, February 18, he immediately called CID headquarters to determine if Helena Stoeckley had contacted their agents or if they had contacted her.

"I'm sorry," said the person who answered, "but all of our agents are busy right now."[46]

William Ivory, though, had received Beasley's insistent message about Stoeckley,[47] a woman he apparently knew well according to later testimony.[48] According to an agent who worked with Ivory,[49] he and Ivory picked up Helena Stoeckley two nights later and escorted her to a safehouse where, according to this agent, Ivory interviewed her.[50] Ivory made no report of the interview and the CID didn't let Beasley know they had interviewed her.

STOECKLEY AND THE FBI

According to an army report,[51] soon after Ivory's alleged interview with Helena Stoeckley some unknown person apparently recommended her to the FBI, who at that time was searching for suspects amongst the hippie community. But Stoeckley wasn't given to them as a suspect. The FBI had asked for help and, incredibly, Stoeckley was offered under another name, as a trusted informant, this even though some CID agents and local police believed she might be connected with the murders.[52]

So it happened, in a case in which she was already a key figure and would remain so for many years, that Helena Stoeckley helped the FBI search for a woman in a floppy hat, blond hair, and boots—a description of herself on the murder night.

While she "aided" the FBI,[53] Stoeckley was placed "off limits" to local police officers. They were told by a superior in the Fayetteville Police Department that only "the government man" was to talk with her.[54] Nevertheless, Beasley saw her again that week after Ivory and a partner picked her up, and, now apparently to prove to Beasley that her earlier admissions were groundless, she showed Beasley her wig and hat. She insisted that he'd find nothing on them tying her to the murders. He told her he couldn't see the objects in the dark car and would have to take them with him. The next day he phoned the CID and asked them to lab-test the items. He says they refused, there was no need. He then asked his boss, Rudy Studer, to have them tested in the police lab. Studer also refused. Beasley returned to his office and immediately got a phone call from an angry Stoeckley demanding that he return the items to her. He did so, and she later reported that she burned them. Studer then specifically ordered Beasley to stay out of the case unless he was asked in.

But the FBI agents, under orders from Hoover to investigate local drug users, were not yet convinced. For the next few days the Bureau remained busy taking statements from young "hippie types" in the local area, some of whose names were given them by Stoeckley. The FBI agents photographed the potential suspects she gave them, and they sometimes had the females speak into a tape recorder, saying, "Acid is groovy; kill the pigs."[55]

According to Ivory's later statement during the army hearing, Stoeckley herself was among those "hippies" interviewed by the FBI. Yet, strangely, Jeffrey MacDonald was never shown a single such photograph, nor was he ever asked to listen to a tape recording.

The FBI at Cape Fear Valley Hospital

During this hectic week of FBI activity the agents went to the places MacDonald had frequented in an effort to find someone who had a grudge against him. They soon learned about the overdosed soldier MacDonald had treated at Cape Fear Valley Hospital a month before the murders, and they found out about the police interrogation of that soldier's two friends and the arrest of their heroin dealer. Agent Vernon Spessert of the CID interviewed the nurse who had phoned the police the night of the incident. An FBI report detailing Spessert's interview says:

> Emergency Room, Cape Fear Valley Hospital, advised that in regard to (BLACKED OUT) who was received in that hospital on January 16, 1970, from an overdose of heroin, that she personally called the Fayetteville, North Carolina, Police Department and reported same. She advised that (BLACKED OUT) was treated by Doctor JEFFREY MC DONALD [sic] and was brought into the Emergency Room by two white males whom she described as hippie types, who told her that they had given him mouth to mouth resuscitation. She further advised that (BLACKED OUT) had on his arm a lot of scars from injecting himself with heroin and that Doctor MC DONALD saved his life by performing a tracheotomy. She stated that Doctor MC DONALD, to the best of her judgment, had no hostility or sympathy for these drug users and was in her opinion a good doctor.[56]

This report posed a tantalizing mystery for MacDonald's defense team when they learned about it through FOIA releases many years later. They reasoned that if the drug users involved had jumped to a conclusion that it was MacDonald who had called the police, the arrest could have served as a motive for revenge. Yet the team was stymied in their efforts to follow the idea any further; the FBI documents which attested to the essential facts of the event showed the names of the officers and suspects blacked out, and there was nothing in the local newspaper concerning the arrest of the black drug dealer. It wasn't until mid-1990 that Fred Bost was able to see an unmarked copy of that same FBI report,[57] and discovered that the overdosed patient was Robert Wallack and that the two friends were named Larry Cook and Thomas Vincent Brown.

If the FBI had continued a coordinated probe, it is probable that the federal agents would have learned a number of interesting facts. For instance, Larry Cook was either a part of, or very tight with, the Stoeckley crowd. An item in a CID case file quoted army chaplain John P. McCullagh as saying that Cook and Greg Mitchell were close friends and had been in the drug program Operation Awareness together.[58] Mitchell, who had been Helena Stoeckley's boyfriend, would later say he met Cook after the murders[59]; however, the stories offered to the FBI by Cook and Brown suggest otherwise.

Brown told the FBI agents that he spent the night of the murders in a house on Haymount Street. There is no Haymount Street in Fayetteville, but there is a Hay Street, which runs through the center of the then drug-plagued Haymount District. According to Helena Stoeckley, her group conducted ceremonies in Candy's black-painted pad at 908 Hay Street near Stoeckley's pad on Clark. That is the place where Beasley's fellow officer found the carcass of the dead cat in the weeds behind the house.

Larry Cook, on the other hand, told the FBI agents that he spent the night of the murders with friends at a trailer on Murchison Road near a foreign car garage. Hickory Trailer Court, the home of the black man with the field jacket, and the location of the drugs Beasley found in the raid, was on Murchison Road near the only foreign car garage in the area, and across the street from Johnson's store where Averitt saw Stoeckley and a black man the morning after the murders.[60]

These statements meant nothing to the FBI at the time. Yet if they had been allowed to continue their investigation in depth, they might have discovered that Cook was connected with the Stoeckley group through yet another close friendship, one suggesting equal significance—a friendship with Richard Fortner. Helena Stoeckley is on audiotape describing how her group got angry with Fortner one day when he spilled their liquid opium during a group "shoot-up" at 1108 Clark Street.[61] William Posey, Stoeckley's neighbor, also knew Fortner and had seen him with the Stoeckley circle. Another documented fact ties Cook to the Stoeckley group. He and Fortner were arrested together with two other men for group possession of eighty-seven capsules of heroin on May 11, 1970.[62]

So there is some indication that those in the Stoeckley crowd were aware of the hospital incident of January 16, 1970. Two men—one of them being a group friend or compatriot, Larry Cook—took a sick friend to MacDonald at the hospital and were immediately taken into custody where they revealed their drug dealer.[63] Their black drug dealer was arrested, and he no doubt wondered who had called in the police.[64] A month later Jeffrey MacDonald told of being attacked by a black man wielding a baseball bat.

The MacDonald defense team could locate no document which gave them the name of the black drug dealer who had been arrested as a result of the emergency room incident, but the FBI report said the man was "a Negro male who hangs around the Action Poolroom and Bar and who is described as being five feet nine inches tall, weighing 160 pounds, and age twenty-nine to thirty."

Interestingly, the description given by MacDonald that would run in a newspaper ad published by Bernard Segal that summer, seeking help in finding the assailants, shows a sketch of a full-cheeked, thick-necked black man, described by MacDonald as five feet eight inches tall and weighing about 165 pounds.

■

It seems that CID agents knew much more about Stoeckley, about her admission to Beasley, about her mode of dress on the night of the murders, and about her drug-dealing friends than they were admitting. And they were well acquainted with MacDonald's own troubles with the drug community. Yet this Helena Stoeckley, even though she matched the descriptions given by MacDonald and Mica, even though she had no alibi for precisely the hours in question on the murder morning, and even though she said she might have been in the home and saw "awful things," this strange girl was allowed to continue her travel within the circles of law enforcement and the underworld at will, as if she enjoyed a special brand of immunity.

On April 6, 1970, seven weeks after the murders, the CID finally revealed that Jeffrey MacDonald, and only Jeffrey MacDonald, remained their target.

4

The Army Hearing

After Fred Bost and I had examined the laboratory reports and statements of army personnel, which represented information Ivory had immediate access to, we came to suspect that the army detectives had ample reason, from their own investigations and lab findings, to revise their initial assessment of MacDonald's guilt or innocence during the weeks following the murders. They knew of MacDonald's eyewitness account, Mica's sighting, blond tresses in a hairbrush, unmatched candle wax at key locations, and a burnt match. They had found a bloody syringe, and they had discovered a piece of skin on Colette's fingernail, and this was in the absence of fingernail scratches on Jeffrey MacDonald. Thus, if Ivory had consolidated the evidentiary facts, not to mention what was known about Stoeckley and her friends, he would have possessed strong reason to question his own staged-scene theory. Yet MacDonald remained his suspect. And, based upon Ivory's facile staged-scene theory, CID chief Joe Grebner subjected Captain MacDonald to a tense and tearful interview on April 6, 1970.

On February 17, after having been removed to the hospital, MacDonald had received treatment for multiple ice pick wounds into his chest and stomach area, a knife wound reaching his stomach muscle, cuts on his left hand and arm, a stab wound in and out at the edge of his left bicep, and multiple contusions of the head. Two surgical procedures were necessary to correct a collapsed lung caused by a knife wound into his right chest.[1] When he was released from the hospital a week and a half later, he moved into the Bachelor Officers' Quarters (BOQ) on post. This would be temporary housing until he found an apartment in Fayetteville. On April 6, seven weeks after the murders, he visited Chief Grebner at CID headquarters to ask about case progress, and to inquire about some personal items to use in a new apartment. When he entered Grebner's office, agents Ivory and Shaw fell into step behind him. One of them closed the door, and Grebner told him to sit down.

The CID Accusation

Grebner asked him if he'd be willing to tell his story again.[2] MacDonald, who had been badgering the CID office about their lack of progress, assured the investigator that he would do anything he could to help find the killers. The agent turned on a tape recorder and MacDonald repeated his story. When he was done, Grebner told the young captain they believed that he, not intruders, had murdered his family. The agents insisted that an unnamed witness had said that one of the knives came from his kitchen; they said the club was also from his home; they told him that the scene seemed staged because of the standing flowerpot and the on-edge coffee table. They told him about the blue fibers under Colette's body and in the rest of the house, and that the presence of such fibers looked ominous since MacDonald had supposedly brought the pajama top into the master bedroom *after* Colette had fallen to the floor. If that were true, they asked, how could she have fallen onto its fibers? They also told him they had found a piece of pajama top fiber under Kristen's fingernail.

They pressed MacDonald to submit to a lie detector test. He, in turn, asked them to explain the accuracy of the polygraph. Grebner assured him that it was virtually foolproof, and MacDonald agreed to take it. They told him to go to lunch and come back to the office; they would arrange for a polygraph that afternoon.

MacDonald drove back to his office. In a notebook made for his attorney a few weeks later he wrote that he didn't eat lunch. Instead, he sat looking out the window, thinking about the accusation, wondering what to do about it. He also told his friend and co-worker Captain Jim Williams about Grebner's accusation of him, and Williams expressed astonishment that MacDonald would trust the CID to administer a polygraph test under the circumstances. Nevertheless, MacDonald decided that the polygraph would be the best way to relieve the CID suspicions of him, because, he wrote, he still believed he was dealing with "simple incompetence."

But when he returned to CID headquarters that afternoon, the polygraph arrangements Grebner had promised him had not been made. Even though Grebner had told MacDonald the test could be taken immediately, he now said it would take several days to set it up. MacDonald wrote that he became suspicious of the agents because he felt they had lied to him about having a polygrapher standing by. Now thinking he might be facing something more sinister than incompetence, he went on the offensive, and verbally attacked the agents' reasoning.

In this taped interview, he asked them to consider, logically, that the pajama *bottoms*, instead of the top, might have been the source of the fibers found in the bedrooms. At the time he made this suggestion, he had no way of knowing that the CID possessed sworn statements from medical personnel that, indeed, his pajamas had been ripped through the crotch from knee to knee.

He hadn't worn his ripped pajama top throughout the house, but he *had* worn the bottoms. He asked the agents also to consider that the fibers, whether from the pajama top or the bottoms, might have been tracked into the children's bedrooms by wet MP boots, given the number of MPs surrounding him when he regained consciousness in the master bedroom. He asked them to consider that while he attempted to revive Kristen, a fiber from his pajama trousers might have come in contact with her fingernail. He suggested that the top-heavy coffee table, so important to their staged-scene theory, might have struck one of the intruders' legs, and for that reason, perhaps, landed on its edge and not on its top.

The agents studiously ignored his arguments, offering little or no response to each one, then they told him, untruthfully, that they had found "absolutely no evidence" of any intruders in his house.

"What do you want me to say?" MacDonald asked, his crying now audible on the tape. "You're telling me that I staged the scene and that's it? It's ridiculous!"

"Notice the rug right there?" Grebner asked, suddenly pointing to a photograph of the throw rug between the living room and dining area. "It slips and slides and rolls up very easily. In the position it is in, that's where you would have been having this struggle, pushing against three men." MacDonald acknowledged the point, and Grebner added, "The rug was undisturbed."

MacDonald asked whether the dozens of boots that had hurried across that same rug that morning wouldn't also have disturbed it. He asked why the wheels of the medics' gurney hadn't also disturbed it. He asked if it might not have been disturbed to the extent that it had to be straightened by the ambulance attendants so they could roll the gurney across it. But MacDonald's explanations did not dispel the agents' deadly stares. Finally he said, "Well, what do you want me to say? I don't—I'm not an investigator and you are telling me that—that I staged that scene and I—I'm telling you that things happened the way I told you!"

Grebner asked MacDonald why the pile of clothing seen at the living room end of the hallway wouldn't have been kicked around in the struggle. But MacDonald challenged the statement because the photo Grebner was holding showed the clothing not on the floor, but on the sofa.[3]

"That particular shot there," Grebner said, "was taken—"

MacDonald angrily finished it for him, "—after some things changed position."

"No," the detective said.

"Yeah? Bullshit! You just told me everything was in the hallway."

"Yes," the investigator admitted, "that clothing changed position."

"Oh, I see," MacDonald said, sarcastically, "that's the only thing in here that's changed position? Uh-huh, who's going to swear to that?"

"This was moved so we wouldn't step on it," Grebner said. "But it was photographed in place."

"Good! What else was moved so you wouldn't step on it? Maybe this? Maybe the coffee table. This gets more unprofessional every minute, I tell you that."

"That's not true," Grebner said, defensively. In notes made for his attorneys a few days later, MacDonald reported that Grebner's hands were shaking. MacDonald posed the question in his notes, characteristically for a physician, whether such shaking might be from stress, drinking, or some kind of palsy.

"How can you show me a photograph and make a big point out of a flowerpot's position," MacDonald challenged, "when something else in that photograph has changed position?" The CID photographers had, in fact, failed to follow regulations requiring a written record of photo sequences, so it was difficult or impossible to determine the original positions of some items which had been moved between the times of two photographs. MacDonald reached across the table to Grebner's stack of photos and showed Grebner two of the CID photographs which had both been marked number "one," even though one of them was taken during darkness and the other during daylight.

Then MacDonald cut to the heart of the case and first broached the issue that would characterize bitter defense complaints for the next twenty-three years. "You mean to tell me you found no other fingerprints of any aliens on any weapons or anything in that house?"

Of course, the CID laboratory had informed Grebner about three samples of foreign candle wax, a missing bloody syringe, a missing piece of skin, unidentified blond hair in an unidentified hairbrush, four bloody gloves, another unmatched glove, Mica's sighting of a woman with a floppy hat, and an unidentified brown hair in Colette's left hand. And the laboratory knew, if Grebner did not, about many unmatched fingerprints. But, instead of answering MacDonald's question, Grebner reminded the young captain that his bloody fingerprints should have been on the telephone and weren't. And that brought the agents back to Ivory's key theory, that MacDonald, and no one else, had moved or wiped down the items that led Ivory to suspect him in the first place.

Grebner demanded that MacDonald explain why the arrangement of items in the house didn't match his story. MacDonald, unaware of the activity in the house during that fifteen minutes before the CID agents arrived that morning, could not explain why the flowerpot was upright or why the rug had appeared straight, among other things. That very day, April 6, 1970, the CID used MacDonald's inability to explain the changes in the crime scene as justification to place him under house arrest for the murder of his family.

They put guards on his room, and assigned him Green Beret escort officers to see that when he left his quarters, he remained on post in designated areas. Three weeks later, on May 1, he was officially charged with the murders of Colette, Kimberly, and Kristen. Two months after that, the army opened an Article 32 hearing to see whether MacDonald would be held for a full court-martial.

The Evidence at the Army Hearing

The officer chosen to weigh the case was Colonel Warren V. Rock, a lean-jawed, graying paratrooper, and the commander of the 4th Psychological Operations Battalion at Fort Bragg's John F. Kennedy Institute of Military Assistance. With thirty years of army experience behind him, Rock was known as a tough, but not unreasonable, no-nonsense officer. His chief duty would be to examine the army's claims and recommend to Major General Edward "Fly" Flanagan whether MacDonald should be held for a court-martial. Advising Rock in matters of law and procedure was army attorney Captain Hammond A. Beale. Two other army attorneys, Clifford Somers and William F. Thompson, accepted the duty of prosecuting the army's case against MacDonald.

MacDonald had secured civilian attorney Bernard Segal of Philadelphia, assisted by his associate, Dennis Eisman. Segal and Eisman would work directly with MacDonald's army attorneys James Douthat and Michael Malley. Douthat was a tall, Virginia-bred and -educated lawyer fulfilling his military obligations. Malley had been a MacDonald roommate at Princeton University, and had gone on to Harvard Law School.

On Monday morning, July 6, 1970, the hearing was called to order in a small frame building that had once been a post schoolhouse. Both sides presented their cases in six weeks of actual hearings spread over a two-month period, the longest such hearing in army history to that time.

Captain Somers's opening prosecution statements centered upon the crime scene itself, and the arrangement of the items which comprised Ivory's staged-scene theory. Not surprisingly, Somers opened with the witnesses he thought could best corroborate the genesis of Ivory's theory. And the ploy blew up on him with his very first witness. Lieutenant Joseph Paulk, the MP duty officer who had taken charge of the crime scene that morning, revealed that he didn't even know how many MPs were in the apartment. He could not furnish their names, and had little control over their movements. This was immediately destructive to the CID claims of a well-controlled crime scene.

Paulk's memory was fuzzy about many additional things, but he did recall MP requests that he set up roadblocks, which Paulk admitted he ignored, damaging the widespread belief that the agents had acted quickly to block the escape of any intruders. His testimony did not give the army good marks in crime-scene control.

When Segal and MacDonald returned from lunch that first day of the hearing they were informed by a sheepish Colonel Rock that Major General Edward Flanagan had ordered him to close the hearing to the press and to all outsiders. Segal, of course, objected. He believed the closed-hearing order had been engendered by Paulk's crippling admissions, and the army wanted no more reporters telling the world such things as the MPs having dawdled on their way to a triple homicide, or that Paulk didn't keep track of the number or identities of people he allowed in the house. Segal insisted that MacDonald, under the Uniform Code of Military Justice, had an undeniable right to an open hearing. But despite his arguments and further pressure by congressmen, whose help was sought by Segal that very day, his attempts to get the hearings opened again to the press were in vain.

As the six-week hearing continued, it seemed that all parties concerned, the defense team, the prosecutors, and Colonel Rock, exhibited a keen interest in understanding just who Jeffrey MacDonald really was. This was a subject that had confounded the CID agents early on. Segal looked at the hospital report on MacDonald's blood and urine tests, and learned that laboratory tests made immediately after the murders had found no dangerous drugs. Although the doctor had possessed a minuscule amount of ethyl alcohol in his blood, the report dismissed its significance, saying, "this generally means that the subject was not under the influence of alcohol."[4] The report served to corroborate MacDonald's statement that he had shared a liqueur with Colette the evening before, and it ruled out drug usage.

When Segal learned that MacDonald wasn't under the influence of drugs or alcohol that night, he thought that the only other possibility, if MacDonald had actually committed the crimes, was that he was somehow unbalanced. So he had him examined by a defense psychiatric team. Colonel Rock also ordered MacDonald to undergo psychiatric scrutiny at the army's Walter Reed Hospital. Neither team found any pathology in MacDonald, and both found him normal and sane and not likely to have committed such a crime.

The CID had learned that MacDonald's reputation at his moonlighting jobs off post was excellent. During his first night on duty as a moonlighting emergency physician at Cape Fear Valley Hospital in Fayetteville he saved the life of a patient by performing a difficult emergency tracheostomy, his first such operation. Dr. Jerry Hughes, another Green Beret and MacDonald's superior at the hospital, felt that the twenty-six-year-old MacDonald was already a great natural physician, not only because he was smart and had good hands, but because he cared about people.

After getting such positive reports about their suspect, CID agents had tried to imagine what diverse circumstances might have driven MacDonald to kill his family. In the absence of drugs or alcohol or any evidence of psychiatric imbalance, they considered whether he had a violent nature. No one had seen any indication of violence or lack of control in him. So they looked to see if he might have been influenced by a love interest outside his marriage.

In this area of MacDonald's life the investigators did manage to find an incident which revealed a blemish in MacDonald's character. They made it part of the hearing testimony, but it had nothing to do with violence or psychotic pathology. During a 1969 army training trip to Fort Sam Houston, Texas, MacDonald had gone to bed with an army WAC. Interviewed independently, both the woman and MacDonald admitted spending the night together, but both said that she felt ill with a bad cold that night, and they hadn't had sexual relations. MacDonald admitted to other meaningless one-night affairs during his lifetime, but agents found no evidence that Colette ever learned of her husband's infrequent interludes.

As the army hearing proceeded, the defense called character witnesses who shed further light, or, some say, more confusion, on the question of MacDonald's true identity. Freddie Kassab, then a steadfast supporter of MacDonald, talked under oath about his earliest memories of his son-in-law. "Captain MacDonald used to come and see my daughter and there was a period when they were on the outs, and Captain MacDonald still used to come to our house, and he used to mow the lawn in the summer time and shovel the driveway in the winter time, regardless of the fact that they weren't going together, and he'd stop by every once in a while and leave a gift on the back steps and leave."[5] Kassab had never seen any violent arguments between Jeff and Colette. They were as happy as "pigs on ice." He said they seemed considerably happier at Fort Bragg than they ever had been because their financial burden had eased. He assured the hearing officer, "If I had another daughter, I'd still want the same son-in-law."

Also during the hearing a family friend read a note Colette had written in the MacDonald Christmas card that year. It said, in part, "We're having a great, all-expense paid vacation in the Army. . . . Life has never been so normal nor so happy. . . . been having such a good time lately that we're expecting a son in July. . . ."

This note wasn't unusual, for other friends when questioned at Fort Bragg made it clear that Colette's pregnancy came as no surprise to her or her husband. She had mentioned during the prior fall that Jeff had agreed she would stop taking her birth control pills. The friends told investigators that Colette loved children, that when her pregnancy was confirmed she seemed to be even more fulfilled.

There was evidence, too, that Jeffrey MacDonald enjoyed children. Captain Kenneth Edwards, the chaplain who lived near MacDonald, remembered him taking the Edwards children and his own daughters to town from time to time for hamburgers and ice cream. In 1969–1970, it was still unusual in the South for white and black families to mix socially, and Reverend Edwards, a black man, would later remark about how well his family was treated by Captain MacDonald.

Early in their investigation, well before the Article 32 hearing, the army prosecution team had to accept that, in the face of MacDonald's character and reputation, they weren't going to win by concentrating on MacDonald's extramarital transgressions. They would have to engage the defense on the subject of the crime-scene evidence. Knowing this, Segal's defense team had done considerable research into events at the crime scene. And they pressed the issue of crime-scene control.

On the witness stand, MP Kenneth Mica recalled seeing the stranger move the critical flowerpot. Mica did not mention that he had seen a woman in a floppy hat, and that the woman was standing a few blocks away from the murder apartment. MP Richard Tevere admitted he had handled one of the telephones. MP Dennis Morris testified that the crime-scene photos of the weapons in the backyard showed that they, too, had been moved from their original positions. When an emergency room attendant, Michael Newman, revealed to the defense that MacDonald's pajama bottoms were badly ripped when he arrived at the hospital, Segal insisted that the fibers Ivory had attributed to the pajama top might as easily have come from the pajama bottoms. Dr. William Neal, in turn, said he definitely had moved Colette's body, and might have returned her to a position other than that in which he found her. Neal's testimony included the possibility that he, not MacDonald, might have transferred a fiber to little Kristen's fingernail.

Yet when lead agent William Ivory eventually appeared as a witness at the army hearing room he again presented his staged-scene theory. Segal, concerned about that initial fifteen minutes prior to Ivory's arrival, asked him, "Did you ever make any efforts to determine whether the crime scene had in any way been altered or changed prior to your arrival there?"

"Yes," Ivory said, "I did."

"How did you do that?"

"I asked Lieutenant Paulk."

"Did you ever question any of the MPs who were in the house before you got there as to what they may have done to the crime scene, if anything?"

"No, I did not."

"Did you ask any of the MPs who were there before you arrived at the crime scene as to whether they saw any other persons touch anything or alter the crime scene?"

"No, I did not."

Eventually, after establishing that Ivory knew that an unidentified man wearing jeans was in the MacDonald living room, Segal asked, "What investigation, if any, did you make to determine whether that person touched any part of the crime scene?"

To Segal's pleasure, the lead investigator replied, "I did not, personally."

"Did you ever learn that Specialist Four Mica, a Military Policeman, observed an individual dressed as I have described touch certain items in the living room prior to your arrival?"

"I have heard that or read accounts of it in the newspaper."

"Having learned that information in the newspaper, what if anything, did you do to check that out further?"

"I personally did nothing."

With this line of questioning Segal easily established that the author of the staged-scene theory upon which this entire hearing had been based had not interviewed a single individual to establish whether his theory was sound, even though more than a dozen men had arrived before him, and even after becoming aware of evidence to the contrary.

While Ivory had admitted learning about key aspects of the case from newspapers instead of the MPs who were there, he still had not revealed to Segal the discovery of the bloody syringe, or the blond hairs in the hairbrush, or even the crucial loss of the piece of skin. Yet he insisted that there had been no intruders because, he reasoned, if intruders had come into the house they would have tracked in grass and debris from outside, and they had not. Ivory said he had personally verified that the grass he saw on the floor had been tracked in by the MPs, not by intruders. Segal asked him how he had done this. Ivory said he went outside and looked at the grass in the yard.

"There are in excess of 1,200 varieties of relatively common lawn grasses in the United States," Segal said. "How many leaves of grass did you have in your hands from inside the house when you were outside on the lawn making the check?"

"None in my hands."

"None at all. In other words, all you did was look at the grass on the floor in the house, then walked outside and looked at the grass outside?"

"Correct."

THE HAIR INCIDENT

With MacDonald's attorneys clearly pleased at their progress regarding the staged-scene theory, the CID needed solid evidence against MacDonald. They finally turned their attention to the unmatched hair from Colette MacDonald's left hand, a short brown arm or body hair. The CID had not asked earlier for MacDonald's hair samples because they hadn't wanted to alert him that he was a suspect. And, apparently, they had taken conscious measures to conceal that this hair existed. Indeed, in a hand-written laboratory note not released to the defense team until fourteen years later, someone in the CID laboratory had listed "hair & debris from hand of Collette [sic]." Below this handwritten note were the words "Not Listed in Report." Accordingly, looking for a source for the hairs in Colette's hand, the CID had secretly taken hairs from one of MacDonald's sweatshirts a month after the murders and labeled the samples as "known hair of Jeffrey MacDonald." They were disappointed, however, for in the laboratory the samples were discovered to be horse hair. The donor was probably Trooper, the Shetland pony MacDonald had bought his daughters for Christmas. With the army hearing now already in progress, it suddenly became imperative that the investigators actually possess hair confirmed to be from MacDonald, so they informed MacDonald of arrangements to take hair from him.

But Segal had been resisting the army's attempt to force hair from MacDonald. Despite the fact that William Ivory disclosed in a deposition that a mystery hair was found in Colette's hand, Segal felt the government was playing fishing games. The defense had been told that the hairs found in Colette's hand were long and blond, which automatically pre-cluded Jeffrey MacDonald as the source. Segal convinced a federal court to look at the issue, insisting that it was illegal to force a person already charged with a crime to surrender his hair, this being tantamount to forcing that person to testify against himself. The defense argued that the evidence should be gathered and then followed by a charge, not vice versa. Segal already possessed evidence which led him to believe that investigators had illegally searched MacDonald's rooms at the BOQ, and he felt this new move was merely another form of harassment. So early on the morning that MacDonald's hair was to be plucked, Segal sent Malley to seek a federal court injunction against the army's effort. At the same time, he sent Douthat and Eisman to request intervention by Fort Bragg's commanding general.

When CID agents and MPs approached MacDonald's quarters that morning to take hair samples, MacDonald's escort officer, Green Beret captain Jim Williams, told them that the defense was pursuing a legal solution to the hair question. But the agents refused to wait for further instructions. They attempted to force their way into MacDonald's quarters, only to be blocked by Williams, who told the men he wouldn't allow their entry because their names weren't on the official access list. Physical violence was narrowly averted when Eisman arrived from headquarters to say that Lieutenant General Tolson had agreed to await a verdict from the federal court. Federal Judge Algernon Butler in Clinton, North Carolina, that day set a hearing date for July 1.

Upon learning of Judge Butler's reaction, James C. Proctor, the Assistant U.S. Attorney in Fayetteville, telephoned Michael Malley and made an angry effort to forgo the court appearance. He told Malley that if MacDonald wasn't guilty he had nothing to lose by peacefully surrendering hair samples. Malley told Proctor to save his arguments for the courtroom.

It turned out that Proctor argued well. On Friday, July 17, Judge Butler ruled that the civilian court had no jurisdiction in the matter, and once again the prosecutors set a time and date to take hair from MacDonald. The judge had not ordered MacDonald to surrender his hair, so Segal used a legal method to thwart the army—just before the time set for the hair to be taken, Segal required MacDonald to attend an "attorney's conference," making him, for the moment at least, legally unavailable to others.

Once the watching CID agents grew weary of the standoff and drove away from the hearing building where Segal was holding his conference, the lawyers and MacDonald felt safe to leave. As MacDonald and attorneys Bernard Segal and Dennis Eisman got into MacDonald's white Chevrolet convertible, a group of reporters asked for an interview and were invited to follow along to MacDonald's quarters where the questions could be answered in comfort. But as the convertible approached the quarters, Segal spotted a group of military policemen apparently awaiting MacDonald's arrival, so he instructed the driver, escort officer Captain Sal Ranieri, to head for the coffee shop at the post exchange.

As their car entered the fashionable area of Fort Bragg known as "Colonel's Row," an unmarked car driven by MP Captain Carl Chase roared abreast of them and darted forward to cut off the MacDonald vehicle. Chase was immediately joined by an MP jeep and another car. Captain Ranieri pulled the MacDonald car over and stopped.

The reporters following the convertible toward the post exchange coffee shop witnessed the entire incident, including Associated Press writer Bill McKeithan and reporter Jim Carr of the *Fayetteville Observer*. Carr wrote in that afternoon's paper, "Military police converged on the car from two directions as did CID agents. An MP went to the car and ordered MacDonald out. At that point, Dennis Eisman, one of MacDonald's attorneys, got out and demanded an explanation."

According to Carr's report, "The MP then called for one of the CID agents, who came to the car and, without a word, grabbed Eisman and threw him to the ground. Bernard Segal, MacDonald's other attorney, was pushed aside moments later and the CID agent grabbed MacDonald and pulled him from the car. The captain was forced into the agent's car and taken from the scene."[6] The Associated Press release by McKeithan stated that it was an MP who threw Eisman face down and appeared to knock him unconscious.

The official army report, prepared for the press late that same day, was contrary to all civilian eyewitness reports. It said that Eisman "stood as to block the military police from reaching MacDonald. One of the agents moved forward to move Mr. Eisman out of the way. Before any force could be exerted, Mr. Eisman wrenched himself violently aside and either fell or threw himself to the ground."

Eisman's glasses had been shattered; he was bleeding from his lip, and holding his head very still. Rushed to Fort Bragg's Womack Army Hospital, Eisman was refused admission.[7] Segal, now furious, had Eisman moved to a local civilian hospital where he was treated for a minor aggravation, for which Eisman donned a neck brace in ceremonious defiance.

MacDonald, kicking and struggling, had been forced into an MP car which sped away to the provost marshal's office. He was held there while arrangements were once again made for a doctor to take hair from him at his quarters. Although his attorneys were invited to observe, they declined the invitation, choosing instead to accompany Eisman for treatment at Cape Fear Valley Hospital.

At his bachelor quarters, in front of a group of CID witnesses, MacDonald, stripped naked of clothing, stood stiffly in embarrassment as hair samples were plucked from every part of his body, including head, chest, groin, arms, and legs. Then he was released from "protective custody."

The army lab at Fort Gordon then analyzed the multiple hairs from MacDonald, only to discover in consternation that none resembled the mystery hair found in Colette's left hand. In a face-saving effort to identify that hair as extraneous, lab technicians, unbeknownst to Segal, quickly tested it against samples from MacDonald family members and army friends, and even against samples taken from CID agents and others known to have come close to the body. They found no match.

The Fort Gordon CID lab dutifully and properly reported to the CID at Fort Bragg that the samples taken from MacDonald didn't match the mystery hair.[8] Grebner received the report on July 30, yet he didn't give the report to Colonel Rock. Grebner and his fellow agents had found themselves in the unenviable position of prosecuting a man for murder when a hair found clutched in his supposed victim's hand came not from their suspect, MacDonald, but from someone else.

Grebner, however, didn't move to drop the charges. Army prosecutor Clifford A. Somers did see the report, and learned that it ruled out MacDonald as the donor of the hair in Colette's hand. Now, not only did the CID possess a piece of skin, a bloody syringe, long blond hair fibers from a hairbrush, candle wax, multiple bloody gloves, and an eyewitness account of intruders, it also had a foreign hair from a murder victim's hand, and not only Grebner but also the prosecuting attorneys knew that hair's owner was not Jeffrey MacDonald.

Yet, all was not lost for the prosecution team. The defense didn't know about the syringe, the skin, the blond fibers in the brush. And they didn't yet know about the failure to match the mystery hair to MacDonald. On

August 25, Somers sent a written request to the laboratory asking for "clarification."

The following week, on September 8, prosecutor Somers submitted a "clarified" report to Colonel Rock, saying the original report seemed to be "ambiguous." When Rock learned that the report had been kept from him for weeks, he recalled Grebner to the stand and demanded an explanation, which Grebner was unable to supply adequately. This new report, signed by laboratory technician Janice Glisson, and not by the man who had made the original finding, now said that the hair found in Colette's hand "probably didn't originate from the same point sources as the hairs taken from Captain MacDonald. However," Glisson now added, "it must be pointed out that the requested opinion regarding positively eliminating the subject as a possible source of the hair cannot be given without first examining numerous other points of body hair from the subject."[9]

But the CID "damage control" was too late. Colonel Rock knew that hair samples already had been taken from every part of MacDonald's body and they didn't match the mystery hair. Rock didn't order MacDonald to submit to further plucking. He concluded that the original lab report was correct—the hair found in Colette's hand was not Jeffrey MacDonald's.

The Wax Analysis

The CID embarrassment continued. An analysis report on the three wax drippings found at the crime scene was also slow in coming to Colonel Rock. The CID initially had reported finding the wax, and had gathered all the candles in the apartment for comparison, but six months later the report on their comparisons still hadn't arrived at Fort Bragg. Finally, an apparently angry Colonel Rock asked Grebner sternly "to make a good effort" to find the wax report and get it to him.

Grebner, under fire for the various misuses of lab results, did so immediately. The analysis revealed that Dillard Browning, forensic chemist from the Fort Gordon laboratory, had compared the wax drippings with all fourteen wax candles found in the MacDonald apartment. The three wax drippings were all different in chemical composition and were different from any of the candles found in the MacDonald home. It wasn't lost on Colonel Rock that the CID had ignored the existence of foreign candle wax even when they knew that MacDonald claimed to have seen a flickering light on the face of the female intruder, and they had held that critical information back from the defense team and even from their own field investigators.

THE TOP-HEAVY COFFEE TABLE

As the hearing progressed, Segal had so far succeeded in convincing Colonel Rock that evidence existed in the house which suggested the presence of intruders, and the hearing witnesses had, by this time, revealed that Ivory's staged-scene theory had been based upon contaminated evidence. But one aspect of that theory remained intact. That was the top-heavy coffee table which fell onto its edge instead of its top, and the magazines trapped unnaturally in a neat stack beneath it.

Ivory had insisted that the magazines couldn't have been under the edge of the table if they had been knocked off the table in a struggle. However, he failed to consider that they might have been stacked on the floor earlier, before the table toppled. Years later, when MacDonald was finally asked about this during the grand jury investigation in 1974, he explained that he had stacked the magazines on the floor so Kimberly would have a clear table for her games. In support of this claim, crime-scene photos show a box of children's games and a box of Play-Doh on the floor near the overturned table.

Of course, Ivory, in 1970, never having asked MacDonald about the magazines, was unaware of this explanation. He insisted that the top-heavy coffee table could not have landed on its edge if knocked over. He maintained that he and others on his team had kicked the coffee table over "at least thirty times." Each time, he said, it had fallen all the way over on its face, proof, he insisted, that MacDonald had turned it onto its edge to create false evidence of a struggle at that location. In fact, this oft-performed demonstration was a key ingredient in Ivory's ability to convince army brass that MacDonald had staged the scene.

To test Ivory's table-kicking theory before closing the hearing, Colonel Rock went to the crime scene himself and, in the presence of witnesses, gave the coffee table a kick. It fell over onto its edge, struck the rocking chair, and remained there—on its edge. Colonel Rock went back to the hearing room and, in laconic tones, placed in the case record that his one kick, contrary to Ivory's claims, had resulted in the table coming to rest exactly as seen in the crime-scene photos, exactly as Ivory had claimed it would never do.

Immediately after the murders the CID had convinced the commanders of Fort Bragg that they had collected hard evidence which would convict MacDonald of triple homicide. With that promise they were allowed to accuse MacDonald, charge him with murdering his family, and bring him to a pre—court-martial hearing. But upon completion of the army's forensic case in that hearing, Colonel Rock had seen nothing that would convince him of MacDonald's guilt. Before Rock could bring the hearing to an end, however, something happened.

At 3:55 on the morning of the murders, not far from the MacDonald apartment, MP Kenneth Mica had seen a woman wearing a floppy hat. The MP had told Colonel Kriwanek and Lieutenant Paulk about his sighting, and he had filed an official, but still secret, signed statement about what he'd seen. But when Mica testified at the Article 32 hearing, he didn't mention it and the CID had not given Segal the statement. To Mica, his failure to share this information represented a lapse of honor, and it ate at him. He told his wife that he had been ordered not to volunteer the fact of his sighting to the defense team. Together, the two weighed the issue—should Mica tell about seeing the woman in the floppy hat, or should he keep quiet, as ordered?

The Stoeckley Issue at the Army Hearing

At the army Article 32 hearing the army prosecutors and CID agents presented their claims against MacDonald as if they had encountered nothing, either at the murder scene or out of it, to support his story. Besides failing to mention a great deal of physical evidence found in the apartment, they also kept quiet about Mica's sighting and about CID and police suspicions regarding Helena Stoeckley. One would never know from their presentations at that hearing that Sergeant Beasley had elicited self-implicating admissions from Stoeckley, or that Beasley himself had attempted to get the CID to pick up Stoeckley and her friends for questioning.[10]

MICA COMES FORWARD

MP Kenneth Mica had gone on the witness stand at the hearing to tell about finding the bodies in the MacDonald home, and about helping the injured MacDonald. But he says he was ordered not to volunteer any information about seeing the woman wearing a floppy hat that morning. So when he testified, he left that part out.

Mica later said, "I knew something that might have saved a guy from going to jail on a murder charge. I was ordered not to volunteer anything, you know, we're the prosecution and you just don't give up everything you know. I was told that if they ask you a direct question about it, you have to answer it, but other than that, don't tell, but I couldn't play games with something like this."[11] Mica's conscience bothered him. He approached Jeffrey MacDonald's mother, Dorothy, in the Fort Bragg post exchange and told her he knew something, and he and his wife were troubled that he'd been asked not to tell it. She insisted that the young man see Bernard Segal. Mica did, and Segal immediately put him back on the stand before the hearing closed.

Mica, well aware that he had disobeyed his superiors to come forward, nevertheless told Colonel Rock he had seen the floppy-hatted woman on the street corner at 3:55 the morning of the murders.[12]

THE POSEY REVELATIONS

Then on August 13, Segal called a second surprise witness. William Posey, a dark-haired, stocky man, told Colonel Rock that at the time of the murders he had lived at 1106 Clark Street in the Haymount area of Fayetteville, next door to a "hippie" woman he knew as Helen. At sometime between 3:45 and 4:30 A.M. on the morning of the MacDonald murders, he awakened to go to the bathroom. "All of a sudden I heard a car whip in. There was a lot of laughing and carrying on, so I walked around to my front door to see what was going on," Posey said. "I noticed that the lights were on in their apartment. Two of the girls were in there painting, and then I saw the car that had pulled in. It was a Mustang."

Posey said he knew the girl only as "Helen." She was a "friendly girl," he said. She wore purple a lot, wore a floppy hat, and sometimes a blond wig. At the term "blond wig," prosecutor Somers said quickly, "I object to the testimony about the blond wig since that's obviously not normal wearing apparel."

"I *agree* it is not normal wearing apparel," Segal said. "That's *exactly* why it is relevant testimony." Segal turned back to Posey and asked him how often Helen wore the floppy hat.

"Just about every time she went out the door she had it," he said.

Posey said that a week or two after the murders he observed a friend, Paul Bowman, talking with Helen in the backyard. Posey approached them and Bowman told Posey that Helen needed an alibi for the morning of the murders. She admitted she indeed had been questioned three or four times. Posey then said to her, "I could be your alibi, because I saw your girl friends painting [the] apartment, and I saw you when you got out of the car that morning." Upon hearing that, Posey said, Helen beat a hasty retreat.

Posey described the group that gathered in Helen's apartment as self-styled witches who engaged in séances, had a lot of candles, and used love potions they made from things they found in the woods. Posey said Helena also had one black friend. Segal showed Posey the artist's sketches of MacDonald's assailants. Posey said that the female looked very much like Helen when she was wearing her wig, although he thought her chin came up a little more. And he identified one of the males pictured as a good representation of one of Helen's frequent companions.

He then told the hearing officer how he had learned her name was Helena Stoeckley.[13] He said when he approached the defense team to tell about Helen on Monday of that week, they wanted to know her last name. So on Tuesday he went back to the neighborhood and found her. While talking with her they were joined for a few minutes by a boyfriend she introduced as "Jim."[14] Jim asked Posey if he wanted to "tab out on acid," and he talked about cutting the throat of a man if the man didn't pay him two hundred dollars. Posey said that when the person known as Jim had gone, he resumed his conversation with Helen, learning her correct name, finally talking about the "MacDonald thing."

"She told me she was stoned out. She didn't remember what she had done. And I said, 'Well, did you do it? Were you a part of it?' and she says she doesn't know, she just drew a blank, but she said that she didn't think she could kill anyone because she wasn't that type of person. And I said, 'Well, you could have just been holding the light,' and she kind of just nodded her head and let it go at that."

The Posey testimony was still hanging heavy on the prosecution when Jeffrey MacDonald took the stand later that day to testify on his own behalf. He was shown a police photo of a young girl by prosecutor Somers. It was a picture of a brunette with bangs almost to her eyebrows, her petulant mouth accenting a rather bloated face. MacDonald failed to recognize her as anyone he had seen before. MacDonald wasn't told who the woman was.

IVORY AND STOECKLEY

Almost four weeks later, on September 8, the prosecution sought to counter Posey's testimony about Helena Stoeckley. Somers called William Ivory back to the witness chair, prepared to prove that Helena Stoeckley could not have been the young woman MacDonald alleged to have seen in his home. To begin, Somers asked Ivory to identify the photograph of the young woman that Somers had shown to MacDonald some four weeks before. Ivory identified the photo as that of Helena Stoeckey. There is no doubt it really was Stoeckley. What wasn't being revealed was that she had been hospitalized through most of the summer and had gained approximately forty pounds between the day of the murders and the day the picture was made, giving her face a less gaunt look. MacDonald, of course, hadn't known this, nor was he informed of the weight gain by the prosecutors or by Ivory. Therefore, if he had seen Helena Stoeckley in his home on the murder morning, her appearance would have been significantly different by the time the photo was made.

Ivory then told hearing officer Colonel Rock that he had interviewed Stoeckley and had dismissed her as a possible suspect. Somers asked him when he had interviewed her. Ivory at first said it was two weeks earlier, then said, "It may have been further than that in time." It actually might have been much further back than that. An agent who worked with Ivory places the first Ivory interview at two days after the crimes.[15] Grebner, in his December 15, 1970, statement, says Stoeckley was interviewed within a few days of the crimes. Both of these statements place Ivory's first Helena Stoeckley interview six months earlier than did Ivory himself.

Under Somers's questioning, Ivory said that Helena Stoeckley told him that on the night of the murders she had borrowed a blue Mustang from a friend, and that when Posey saw her return that morning she was alone in the car. This, of course, refuted Posey's testimony of hearing "laughing and carrying on." Under Segal's cross-examination, Ivory said that Helena knew only the first name of the owner of the car, a man named "Bruce."

"Did you make notes of your interview with Miss Stoeckley?" Segal asked.

"No, I did not."

"Is there any reason why you didn't make any notes of your interview with this lady?"

"No particular reason, no."

"Isn't it standard operating procedure, when you are conducting an interview that's related to an Article 32 inquiry into a triple homicide, to make notes?"

"I did have a notebook with me," Ivory said, "and I started to take notes and she got very nervous and shied away, and I put my pen and notebook away. She said something to the effect of, 'What are you doing? What are you writing?'"

"And what did you say?"

"I said, 'Nothing, I'm not writing anything' and I just put it down."

Segal asked Ivory how the photo of Stoeckley had been acquired. Ivory explained that he had caused the picture of Helena Stoeckley to be made as a result of Posey's testimony. He said he had arranged for Helena to be brought into the police station and that he had been present when the picture was made.

But facts contradict Ivory's words. Under oath, Ivory swore that he arranged for the picture of Helena Stoeckley only *after* Posey brought her name into the case, on August 13, at the army hearing. Yet next to the serial number in the police photo's identifying data was the date "8–10–70"—August 10, 1970. The date is confirmed by a newspaper story identifying Margie H. Raynor (Helena Stoeckley's favorite alias) as one of a group picked up that very day in a drug raid.

This indicates, of course, that Ivory's subterfuge "arrest" of Stoeckley for the purposes of the photograph could not have resulted from Posey's testimony, as Ivory claimed, because Posey didn't testify until three days *after* the "arrest" photograph was made. So Ivory hadn't been candid about the reason he was motivated to pick Stoeckley up or about the date the event occurred. The reason for interviewing her certainly hadn't been, as he said, because Posey talked about her, for Segal had arranged things so that Posey's testimony was to be a complete surprise to everyone including his own client, Jeffrey MacDonald. Yet despite Segal's precautions, the prosecution had the photo of Helena Stoeckley *in hand* on the afternoon of the day that Posey testified.

How, then, had Ivory known that the photo would be necessary? One thing is certain, Ivory didn't tell Segal all he knew about why Stoeckley's photograph was made.

Segal bore down hard on Ivory during this second appearance in the hearing. On the subject of Stoeckley's apparent truthfulness, Ivory told Segal that she "struck me as being frank."

"Candid and open," Segal added.

"Right."

"And you thought a person who did not know the names of the persons she lived with was being frank, candid, and open?"

"Yes."

"And you thought that her inability to tell you the last name of the owner of the automobile that she used for the evening was also frank, candid, and open?"

"Yes."

"And you thought that her telling you that she could not remember where she was for approximately four hours, because she was smoking marijuana, was frank, candid, and open?"

"That's the answer she gave me and I couldn't get anything else," Ivory said.

Segal, now visibly angry, reminded Ivory that marijuana doesn't cause memory loss. Ivory agreed that he knew this, but he didn't know what else to do. Segal then insisted, "You might have called her a liar!"

But Ivory said he had not.

Segal asked, "What made her a suspect in your mind as a potential connection with the MacDonald case?"

"It came to my attention that she was the one that Mr. Posey had testified about," Ivory said, once again being less than open about why and when he first interviewed her.

Incredibly, Ivory revealed to Segal and to Colonel Rock that Stoeckley had admitted to having a blond wig, and boots, that she was on drugs that night, and that she actually had no alibi. Ivory also admitted that he knew that Stoeckley had been among those young people the FBI had questioned, photographed, and audiotaped saying "Acid is groovy; kill the pigs."

When Somers took up the questioning of Ivory on redirect, he asked, "Do you know, sir, whether Miss Stoeckley was cooperating with and working for the local police?"

"Yes, she was," Ivory replied.

Somers then requested Colonel Rock to instruct everyone present to keep the girl's name and her relationship with the police in confidence.

Ivory added, "If her position with the police were known, her life would be in jeopardy." Before leaving the stand, Ivory told Colonel Rock again, "Sir, may I just make a statement in regard to my testimony about Helena Stoeckley? I'd like to restate, most emphatically, that if it is publicized in the newspapers or in any other way . . . she is . . . most assuredly a dead woman, and I just want to make that perfectly clear."

Colonel Rock asked, "How can you assure this hearing that she is a dead woman?"

"Just knowing the type of people, and the people in particular that she deals with," Ivory said.

Again, Ivory was fudging. The term "people in particular" didn't match his testimony of only moments before when he had said he hadn't bothered to learn the names of her friends. Segal now asked Ivory if he knew "specifically, individuals whom Helena Stoeckley is associated with or has dealt with who are persons you believe might try and kill her if her involvement with the police were known?"

"Yes," Ivory now said.

Indeed, William Ivory had good reason to suspect that Stoeckley's friends were dangerous. One of her companions, Richard Fortner, had been kidnapped by other friends intending murder, and the subsequent criminal trials were being publicized in the daily newspaper. As a CID investigator of drug cases in the area, Ivory would have known who Fortner was. In fact, two of the accused in the Fortner case had already been convicted of kidnapping and attempted murder, with sentences ranging up to fifteen years in prison.[16] The man currently on trial, Terry Ingland, was also a friend of Helena Stoeckley's. He resided at 908 Hay Street, where Stoeckley said she attended cult meetings and where Beasley had searched the black room that at the time had been the domain of the man known as Candy.[17] Therefore, Ivory had good reason to know who, specifically, made up the group Stoeckley was informing about, and he had reason to know these people were dangerous.

That is how William Ivory, the army's lead agent, became perhaps the most valuable witness for the defense at the army hearing in the summer of 1970. He substantiated the existence of the woman in the floppy hat, her involvement with drug dealing, her mode of dress on the very night of the murders, her lack of alibi, and the fact that she traveled with people who would not hesitate to commit murder. And his testimony proved that Ivory hadn't taken notes on his interview, hadn't investigated Stoeckley or her friends Ivory knew as capable of murder, and hadn't come forward with critical knowledge that would challenge the central tenets of his case.

In the end, Colonel Warren Rock learned that the CID's lead agent knew Helena Stoeckley as an informant, had worked with her, and had found many reasons to suspect her. Yet, for whatever reasons, William Ivory actually took measures to keep her name out of the case.

The Rock Report

After hearing six weeks of testimony, including character testimony and psychiatrists for both the army and the defense, Colonel Rock closed the

Article 32 hearing on September 11, 1970. Then he began rereading the transcripts and official reports. Jeffrey MacDonald remained under house arrest.

Six weeks later, Captain Hammond Beale, Colonel Rock's legal adviser, paid MacDonald a visit. Beale had just come from a meeting between Colonel Rock, Major General Edward Flanagan, and Flanagan's legal officer, Major Pedar C. Wold. Beale told MacDonald that Rock's findings on all key points explored during the hearing soon would be released in a report. Beale assured MacDonald this would include the staged-scene theory and the sloppy crime-scene preservation.

Most important, Rock's report recommended that all charges be dismissed against MacDonald because they are "not true." And in a second recommendation, resulting from disclosures made by witness statements, Rock asked "that appropriate civilian authorities be requested to investigate the alibi of HELENA STOKELY [sic] . . . reference her activities and whereabouts during the early morning hours of 17 February 1970, based on evidence presented during the hearing."[18]

Captain Beale told MacDonald that General Flanagan had been surprised at Rock's findings because the general had been assured by the CID that MacDonald was guilty. But Colonel Rock told him about the crime-scene evidence and declared there was no case against MacDonald. "It isn't there," Rock told the general.

"What standards of proof did you use?"

"No matter what standards of proof you use, it just isn't there."

Flanagan's legal adviser, Major Wold, then asked Colonel Rock an ominous question: "Is there anything else the government can do now to solidify the case?"

"No," Colonel Rock said. "You shot your wad."

Beale told MacDonald that Rock at first thought Ivory was just a dumb cop, but as the hearing progressed he thought Ivory might be "dirty with something in town." Also, according to Beale, Rock had considered pressing charges against some of the CID and the prosecution team, but he feared that the army would interpret such an act as inappropriate advocacy of MacDonald. They might then throw out the Rock report, and bring another Article 32 proceeding against him. Rock didn't want that. He hoped that the civilian authorities who had jurisdiction over Helena Stoeckley[19] would look into the matter and set the case straight.[20]

When the Rock report was made public in late October 1970, the colonel was widely criticized among the troops and leadership at Fort

Bragg as being deficient in mental capacity because of his ruling. Some said that MacDonald's charisma must have mesmerized him. The CID agent who admitted that he and Ivory had picked up and interviewed Stoeckley two days after the murders[21] said, incredibly, that he had heard in CID circles the rumor that the army had discovered that the American Medical Association had "leaned on Colonel Rock" because it didn't want "one of their own accused of murder." Others would say that the AMA paid for MacDonald's high-powered Philadelphia lawyer. Some CID agents felt that Kenneth Mica, who said he had seen the suspicious young woman on the nearby street corner at 3:55 A.M., should have been polygraphed, because the MP was "probably lying."

Fred Bost and I learned that Major Wold, as General Flanagan's legal adviser, had been faced with the duty of advising the general about how to officially dispose of the unpopular Rock report. Fred located Wold in 1992, finding him now to be a colonel serving at Schofield Barracks near Honolulu. I phoned Wold and learned that he hadn't actually attended the Article 32 hearing himself, but the CID agents had convinced him that MacDonald was guilty. After the army hearing Wold went back to Fort Bragg CID headquarters, and the agents again reassured him that MacDonald was guilty no matter what Rock had said. Their assurances convinced him, even though he had not seen any of the defense case.

During our telephone conversation, Wold told me he "synopsized" Colonel Rock's ninety-page report, then gave this shortened interpretation to the general. And, since Wold "knew" MacDonald was guilty,[22] he advised Flanagan to distance himself, as much as possible, from Rock's potentially embarrassing ruling about MacDonald's innocence.[23]

General Flanagan chose the middle ground, officially dropping charges against MacDonald, not because they were "not true," as Rock had stated, but because of "insufficient evidence," a far more ominous pronouncement which left the CID free to continue their claim that MacDonald was guilty—and it left them free to renew their pursuit of him.

Neither Segal nor his client was aware of what was happening in the background. Assistant U.S. Attorney James C. Proctor began pressing the Justice Department for a chance to prosecute MacDonald in federal court. J. Edgar Hoover and the FBI, however, just as adamantly refused to be drawn into the investigation. Hoover said he would fight any attempts by the army to drag the FBI into the case because, he told his men, "the Army handled this case poorly from its inception."[24] Even after Hoover's death, it was with reluctance that the Justice Department later allowed itself to be pulled into the case by a federal judge who, like the army brass before him, had been impressed by the CID's claims.

Following the exoneration of MacDonald by Colonel Rock, Bernard Segal suggested that MacDonald should apply for a hardship discharge because, he advised, a satisfactory career as an army doctor now would be impossible. The discharge would be listed as "honorable." MacDonald agreed. He was sick of the army, to be sure, but he had another reason. His mother had sold her house to pay Segal's fees, and the young doctor needed to find a job to repay her.

"So, start a new life," Segal told him the day the lawyer left Fort Bragg. "They can't bother you any more."

Segal really believed it was over.

PART
TWO

The Trial

5

■

Reversals

After his discharge from the army, Dr. Jeffrey MacDonald worked for a few months as an emergency physician on the construction site of the World Trade Center in Manhattan. In July 1971, about seventeen months after the deaths of his wife and daughters, he accepted an offer from Dr. Jerry Hughes[1] at the emergency department of St. Mary Medical Center in Long Beach, California.

He helped Dr. Hughes transform St. Mary's emergency department, using the modern emergency techniques first tested in the field by the American army in Vietnam. He ultimately became director of the department, one of the finest in the state. His professional reputation was further enhanced by the authorship of articles in prestigious medical journals, and his co-authorship of a book on the management of emergency medicine departments.

Still active in sports, MacDonald helped organize intramural softball at the medical center. He also taught emergency medicine at UCLA Harbor General Medical Center, and he became a public speaker in the effort against child abuse, and in CPR. For saving the lives of policemen in difficult cases, MacDonald was made an honorary lifetime member of the Long Beach Police Department.

He was well known, well liked, and extremely successful professionally. But, more to the purpose of the army CID, who were still in pursuit of him even though he was a civilian, he also dated a number of beautiful women, and bought a boat and an oceanside condo. When later asked about this flurry of activity during those years after the murders, MacDonald told close friends that he had to keep his mind on something besides the loss of his family. But his detractors would claim that he was trying to quiet a guilty conscience, or that he was simply "living it up." And the CID were very busy clearing Helena Stoeckley.

In the Government Files

After finding that the 1970 charges against MacDonald were "not true," Colonel Rock had asked civilian authorities to investigate Helena Stoeckley. That never happened. The only civilian authority who might have looked into the whereabouts of Stoeckley and her friends in relation to a crime on a military post was the FBI, but when J. Edgar Hoover learned on October 27, 1970, that the army had dropped all charges against MacDonald, he refused to be drawn back into the investigation.

Documents finally revealed via FOIA, years after the trial, show that Warren Coolidge, the United States Attorney for the Eastern Division of North Carolina, didn't see things in the same light as Hoover. Coolidge had been convinced by the local CID that MacDonald was guilty, and he immediately moved to prosecute the army doctor who was "getting away with murder." On October 31, 1970, with Jeffrey MacDonald still a serviceman, Coolidge telephoned chief FBI agent Robert Murphy in Charlotte to say he intended to bring MacDonald before a grand jury within ten days. Coolidge threatened to "subpoena anyone who has knowledge of this case, including FBI agents."[2]

But when Coolidge and Proctor sought support from their bosses at the Justice Department, they were told an FBI investigation would never be requested without a substantial new lead in the case.[3] The government decision to excuse the FBI from action left the CID in a predicament. Once MacDonald was discharged, only the FBI could legally pursue him. With no office actively investigating, the army could easily be left as a scapegoat for an unsolved triple murder.

That would have pleased Segal. His attempts to drum up publicity for the case led MacDonald to accept an invitation to appear on Dick Cavett's television talk show in December of 1970, where MacDonald sharply criticized the army's handling of the case. Those who thought

MacDonald was guilty saw this personal appearance as a blatant display of arrogance. But the army might have seen it in a different light, especially when Cavett, whose show reached millions of viewers across the country, criticized the CID, and remarked about "an incredible bungling on the army's part."

Sometime during those trying days in the fall of 1970 a decision was made by unidentified army brass to allow the CID to pursue Jeffrey MacDonald into civilian life despite the Posse Comitatus Act, which makes it illegal for military authorities to investigate a civilian.[4,5]

MacDonald, at that time still busy with efforts to gain his discharge, remained unaware that he was still targeted for prosecution. He was telling others that he had to find ways to repay the $30,000 legal debt he had accrued, to get the obviously stalled investigation of Helena Stoeckley moving, and to force a probe of the CID's conduct.

To help him with the latter cause, his friend and former legal counsel, Lieutenant Mike Malley, offered to bring charges through army channels against Kriwanek, Somers, Thompson, Shaw, Ivory, and Grebner. Freddie Kassab also prepared to make similar charges through Congress.

When news reached Malley (by then in Vietnam) and Kassab (at home in New York) that MacDonald had been successfully discharged on December 4, 1970, the two men submitted their respective complaints. As a result of Kassab's allegations, Senators Sam J. Ervin, Mendel Rivers, and Peter W. Rodino, Jr., as well as Representatives Allard K. Lowenstein and Emanuel Celler, sought explanations from the Pentagon.[6]

Within a week of MacDonald's discharge, and the beginnings of this pressure from Capitol Hill, the army general counsel ordered the U.S. Army CID agency in Washington to conduct an internal investigation of the way the case had been handled.[7] The complaints made by Malley and Kassab resulted in a formal investigation of Grebner, Ivory, and Shaw, with a view toward possible charges of perjury, dereliction of duty, suppression of evidence, and conduct unbecoming officers.

In most instances when police probe the conduct of a fellow officer, they follow a set pattern. The assigned investigator first familiarizes himself with the case documentation. Then he interviews complainants and others who might have knowledge of the alleged infractions. Next he interrogates the accused officer, forcing him to explain specifically any deviant material, accepting no excuses or generalizations.

In this instance the assigned chief investigator was agent Peter E. Kearns, from the CID headquarters in Washington, D.C.[8] His graying temples were matched by an ashen cowlick above his right forehead, suggesting aged experience. However, experience wasn't evident in the order in which he questioned witnesses. For example, the Article 32 hearing officer, Colonel Rock, was in a good position to address the allegations, and, Rock told Kearns, he felt there was a possibility that Grebner had perjured himself. The colonel also gave his opinion that the Fort Bragg CID agents had failed to inventory the crime scene properly and had failed to interview MacDonald adequately in those first crucial days following the crime.[9]

But Kearns was already absolving the suspects at the time he approached Rock. In fact, on January 5, 1971, the same day that Rock was signing his transcribed statement, a CID headquarters memorandum declared Grebner, Shaw, and Ivory innocent of all charges.[10] Colonel Henry H. Tufts, the CID commander, enclosed to each congressman and senator a twenty-nine-page packet which answered each allegation previously made by Malley and Kassab. Most of the answers, though, failed to fit the facts as established by investigation.[11]

Kearns's group of Washington CID agents, when first charged with investigating Grebner, Ivory, and Shaw, leased a downtown Fayetteville office for a full year. While the internal probe was yet unresolved, they already looked beyond the issue of the three CID suspects toward the case itself. Upon learning that Helena Stoeckley was on a holiday visit to Fayetteville, one of the visiting agents phoned and asked her for an interview. Reluctantly, she consented, but only if the meeting was kept secret.

Agents Robert Bidwell and Richard Mahon sat down with her at a large table in the staff conference room at Womack Army Hospital on December 29, 1970, to learn what they could about her and her friends. They quickly discovered not only that the girl couldn't account for her whereabouts at the time of the murders eleven months earlier, but that she herself was worried about it.[12]

The agents attempted to talk her into being photographed, taking a polygraph test, and surrendering hair samples and fingerprints. They told her that if she wasn't involved, they would prove it through negative physical evidence. But Stoeckley said she wanted time to think about the requests. She agreed to meet the agents the following day at the Cumberland County Courthouse in Fayetteville.

When Bidwell and Mahon greeted her at the somber gray courthouse the next day, they found the girl adamantly hostile. She told them she would be a fool to take a polygraph test, to give fingerprints, or to pose for a photograph. "I'm not certain whether or not I was there," she said, according to Bidwell's description of the conversation in the case log. "I could only hurt myself by cooperating with you."[13]

On the morning of January 6, 1971, CID agent Peter Kearns drove to the airport to greet Lieutenant Colonel Jack G. Pruett, the director of the CID's internal affairs unit in Washington.[14] Pruett, while awaiting reassignment to Vietnam, was to be the figurehead leader in Fayetteville for a proposed case reinvestigation once the Kassab-Malley allegations were disposed of.

At Fort Bragg that afternoon, Pruett assured key officials that the charges made against the army by Malley and Kassab had been refuted. He told his listeners that the document which cleared the accused CID agents had already been accepted by the Pentagon.[15] Now, the CID team from Washington planned on successfully completing a reinvestigation of the MacDonald murder case, and MacDonald, before the end of 1971.

With the new investigation now officially under way, CID questioners moved into geographically widespread areas to investigate persons who were possible suspects. These persons were interrogated, their alibis checked, and their fingerprints and hair samples compared with unidentified hairs and fingerprints from the crime scene. Despite discrepancies in most of their stories, each would-be suspect was rapidly cleared—except for Helena Stoeckley.

The task of investigating Miss Stoeckley fell to Richard Mahon, one of the two agents who had spoken with her in December of 1970. Mahon learned that Fayetteville detective Prince Beasley had been close to the girl, so he arranged for Beasley to accompany him on a trip to Nashville, Tennessee, where Helena Stoeckley was taking a course in criminology at Aquinas College.

On the morning of February 25, 1971, Beasley and Mahon were aboard a commercial flight out of Raleigh when Beasley suggested that the girl might balk at discussing the MacDonald affair. Beasley claims that Mahon assured him, "She'll say something to me. All I want to do is eliminate her as a suspect."[16]

But Mahon was wrong. Following three days of frustrating effort, he was unable to get a photograph, hair or fingerprint samples, or a signed statement. The girl had refused to cooperate in any fashion unless she was first granted immunity.[17] Beasley signed a statement for the CID which included his observation that Helena wouldn't surrender her hair and fingerprints because "she had strong convictions that she was a witness to the MacDonald murders."[18]

Shortly after that trip Mahon received unsettling news from Nashville. Helena Stoeckley, now an informant for the Nashville Police Department, had told an officer she witnessed the MacDonald murders and knew who committed the crimes.[19]

Mahon rushed back to Nashville on April 21, 1971. At the police station he learned that Helena was now the key informant in an important drug probe aimed at ferreting out some crooked cops in the force.[20] Her handlers were two young patrolmen, James T. Gaddis and John J. Rohtert, who had gained Helena's confidence and had been using her information. Rohtert confirmed for Mahon that Helena told him she had been involved in the murders.

The next day Mahon approached Nashville police lieutenant Milburn E. "Jack" Bowlin, the commanding officer of the Internal Affairs Section, seeking help in getting a polygraph exam plus hair and fingerprints from Helena Stoeckley.[21] Bowlin shook his head no. "She's doing a good job and we need her for a few more days," he said. He suggested that Mahon leave her alone until the job was finished, and in return the Nashville police would help in gaining her cooperation in the MacDonald case.

Despite Bowlin's plan, early the next morning Helena was arrested by the Nashville Police Department vice squad, caught with marijuana and mescaline.[22] Initially, following police pressure, she agreed to submit to a CID polygraph test in return for the drug charges being dropped. Mahon put through a call to the Virginia home of Robert A. Brisentine, Jr., the CID's leading polygraph expert, awakening him at 4:15 A.M. to summon him to Tennessee.

At the police station that evening, Mahon remained hidden while Brisentine and patrolman Gaddis took turns speaking to the girl. She told them separately that she had firsthand knowledge of the murders and would tell what she knew if she was granted immunity. The interviews continued from 6:15 P.M. until 10:45 P.M. with the girl continuing to refuse the polygraph exam. Stoeckley looked beat, so the detectives let her go home when she promised to return to the station by ten the next morning.

Brisentine had made notes of Helena Stoeckley's statements. She claimed that she didn't take part in the homicides but may have been physically present; that she suffered nightmares since the deaths; and that she had worn boots, a floppy hat, and a blond wig that night, all of which she discarded after the homicides. She said that on the day of the memorial services for the MacDonald family she had worn black and meditated; that she knew who killed the MacDonalds; and that if she were given immunity she would name the killers and explain the circumstances surrounding the murders.[23]

But when immunity was still denied her, Stoeckley changed her story at the next day's meeting. She said she had no knowledge of the murders and that she had "talked too much." Brisentine and Gaddis spent the morning trying to convince her to accept the polygraph exam. At 2 P.M. she was still refusing, so Mahon, who had been watching through a one-way mirror, decided to speak to her alone.

After forty minutes he managed to attain what the others had failed to accomplish; at 3 P.M. she began a grueling two hours and forty-five minutes of polygraph-monitored questioning. She continued to insist that she was not involved in the crimes.

Brisentine analyzed the results and informed Mahon that the examination showed "deception" when Stoeckley denied being in the MacDonald home and denied knowing who killed the MacDonalds. The polygrapher's official report submitted to CID headquarters concluded "that Miss Stoeckley is convinced in her mind" that she knows who committed the murders, and is convinced "that she was physically present when the three members of the MacDonald family were killed."[24]

Now that Stoeckley's polygraph exam indicated she was lying about not being in the murder apartment, the CID had a problem. Brisentine eased the predicament by saying in his polygraph report that because of Stoeckley's "admitted confused state of mind and her excessive drug use during and immediately following the homicides in question, a conclusion cannot be reached as to whether she, in fact, knows who perpetrated the homicides or whether she, in fact, was present at the scene of the murders."

Still, the polygraph hadn't cleared her. To the contrary, as Brisentine himself would later reveal, it had implicated her even more deeply.

The CID turned, finally, to Stoeckley's friends. If they could establish that she had been somewhere else at the time of the murders, the contrary polygraph exam, especially since it was not admissible evidence, would have little meaning.

But the CID ran into problems here, too. FOIA documents in the form of investigators' reports prove that the stories of her drug-using friends didn't mesh. On May 5, 1971, CID agents Richard Mahon and William Ivory visited a girl Stoeckley had roomed with at 1108 Clark Street.

Kathy Smith told the agents that upon learning they were coming to see her, she telephoned Diane Cazares (née Hedden), the other former Stoeckley roommate, to discuss the situation. Cazares at that time reminded her that Stoeckley had been with Greg Mitchell on the night of the murders. To the CID, Cazares said she herself was out with friends, driven around by Bruce Fowler on the murder night.[25] Ivory didn't press Cazares on the issue, yet Ivory himself had testified at the Article 32 hearing that Stoeckley told him it was *she* who had used Bruce's car and she was alone. These exchanges represented troubling discrepancies between the memories of Cazares and Stoeckley.

Each remaining interview of the group members also brought discrepancies. Both Kathy Smith and Diane Cazares had placed Stoeckley with Greg Mitchell on the night of the murders. But Greg Mitchell, interviewed by the CID three weeks after the Smith and Cazares interviews, told the agents still a third version. He said he believed Helena was with Kathy Smith on the murder night. This represented a marked discrepancy between the claims of Mitchell, Stoeckley, Smith, and Cazares.

Mitchell now said that he believed that he himself had spent the night with a friend named Don Harris. But Kathy Smith and Diane Cazares, during their interviews, said that Harris had helped Smith paint the apartment that night. Smith contradicted Cazares by saying that Don Harris stopped painting and departed before Cazares returned to the apartment. Cazares said Harris was still there when she got back from being out with Bruce Fowler in Fowler's blue Mustang. Yet, when Fowler was interrogated on May 11, 1971, he failed to support either claim. He didn't remember being with Cazares that night, and he didn't recall lending his car to anyone.

Each story was contradicted by another. Yet, even with these inconsistencies, the stories were never challenged, nor, apparently, were they checked by the CID, nor did the CID make these contradictions available to Segal for the 1979 trial.

During this time, the CID agents were trying to get Stoeckley's fingerprints to check against the prints collected at the crime scene. Strangely, however, her fingerprint file had disappeared from the Fayetteville police records; and throughout the Nashville encounter she had resisted attempts to gain her fingerprints, and had actually physically fought off officers trying to print her. Mahon was ordered by Pruett via telephone to remain in Nashville until the fingerprints were obtained.

The Nashville police, however, refused to force fingerprints from the girl for fear of alienating her and losing her cooperation as an informant. By April 30, 1971, Mahon admitted defeat. That night in his log, before leaving Nashville, he addressed the frustrating alliance of Bowlin and Stoeckley: "I know that he isn't going to break up a good thing as long as she is playing the role of the good informant," Mahon wrote. Then he added: "I don't blame him."

Not long afterward, the Nashville police, having finished with Helena Stoeckley, forwarded legible fingerprints from the girl. After comparisons, the CID investigators by the end of May 1971 stated that Helena Stoeckley's fingerprints had not been found in the murder apartment. On the basis of this, the CID agency soon decided to write Stoeckley and her friends out of the case,[26] even though dozens of fingerprints from the apartment had been lost or destroyed, and even though Stoeckley's and her friends' stories contradicted each other, and even though the CID possessed still-secret knowledge that long blond wig hairs had been found in an unidentified hairbrush only a few feet from where MacDonald said he saw the blond female intruder.

After this cursory, problem-plagued "investigation" of the Stoeckley group, Stoeckley was cleared, and MacDonald still remained the CID's chief suspect.

Grand Jury

During this time, in the early 1970s, the army's collection of evidence from the crime scene was examined in the FBI laboratories, and a new forensic theory was presented to a Raleigh, North Carolina, grand jury in late 1974 and early 1975. Of course, in a grand jury hearing the defendant has no defense attorney present in the hearing room, and the evidence presented by the government against the defendant is not challenged by experts and is usually accepted by grand jurors as factual.

Bernard Segal managed to get the grand jury prosecutor in the Mac-Donald case to promise to call to the stand Dr. Robert Sadoff, the defense psychiatrist who had found MacDonald to be normal, sane, and not of the personality type to have murdered his family. The prosecutor from whom Segal had received this assurance was Victor Woerheide, a Justice Department special prosecutor, who was especially adept at securing indictments. Woerheide was a large, gruff man known by his contemporaries for his tenacity in tough cases, and he did nothing in the MacDonald case to diminish his reputation for success.

During MacDonald's initial appearance at the opening of the grand jury hearing in August 1974, Victor Woerheide had made it known to Segal that he wanted MacDonald's psychiatric records, privileged defense team documents which he knew he could obtain only through the cooperation of the defense attorney. The unsuspecting Segal agreed to surrender the documents, and immediately kept his part of the bargain, on a promise from Woerheide to allow defense psychiatrist Dr. Sadoff to testify in front of the grand jury.

MacDonald was recalled to the grand jury hearing on January 21, 1975, and at that time Segal chastised Woerheide for not yet calling Sadoff to the stand according to their agreement. Woerheide stalled Segal on the issue, for the truth is he had no intention of calling the psychiatrist as a witness; five days prior to this discussion he had informed fellow attorneys at the Justice Department that immediately following MacDonald's testimony he intended to seek a quick indictment. He told them that he would request the indictment to be furnished "sealed" in order "to afford time for press releases to be issued out of Washington." He added that he expected to have the indictment in the middle of the workweek of January 20–24.[27]

But things began to go awry for Woerheide.[28] With MacDonald on the stand, a juror begged him to undergo a sodium amytal examination to prove his truthfulness. MacDonald tried to explain the psychological perils of such an experience, but when the juror remained adamant, MacDonald requested a recess to talk it over with Segal and Malley, who were in a nearby anteroom.

He returned to say that he would submit to such an interview if Dr. Sadoff approved, and that the psychiatrist, who was at home in bed with the flu, was being called at that moment. The phone call caught Sadoff by surprise. He voiced his reluctance to allow such a test because of the trauma which usually results, so he told the attorneys he would have to discuss it with MacDonald himself, and personally hear MacDonald agree to the examination. But, by that time, MacDonald was back on the witness stand, where at 3 P.M. on January 21 he agreed to take the exam if Dr. Sadoff would attend him.

That's the way it stood at the end of the day when Woerheide dismissed MacDonald from further questions. MacDonald traveled with Malley to

Malley's home outside Washington, D.C., with the expectation that Sadoff was to be called to the stand when he was well, and that a sodium amytal examination would be arranged in the interim to satisfy the jurors. MacDonald and Segal had great hopes that this exam, to which they were now fully committed, would end the entire affair. But documents suggest that Woerheide had no intention of allowing the test. On the following day he requisitioned a court reporter and flew to Sadoff's home in Philadelphia, accompanied by his fellow prosecutor, James "Jay" Stroud, an Assistant U.S. Attorney for the Eastern District of North Carolina. Unaware that the prosecutor was on the way to Sadoff's home, MacDonald phoned the psychiatrist and convinced him to make hospital arrangements for a sodium amytal interview at the earliest date.

Sadoff received the surprise visit by Woerheide with cordiality, despite his flu miseries. With the conversation being recorded by the court reporter, he patiently answered questions by the attorneys concerning MacDonald's psychological makeup and about the use of sodium amytal. In discussing the forthcoming interview, he agreed to a promise solicited by Woerheide that he would ask MacDonald certain questions about specific crime-scene evidence when he administered the sodium amytal. When the entourage departed Sadoff's house, the psychiatrist was left with the impression that everyone, including Woerheide, was in agreement concerning his administering the test. Accordingly, on the following day he reserved a Philadelphia hospital room for February 1, the earliest reservation possible. MacDonald, informed by Segal that he would not be needed for another week, boarded a plane for California on January 23.

When Segal was told, also on January 23, that Woerheide had flown to Sadoff's home with a court reporter in tow he suspected that Woerheide might not be playing fairly. Segal sent a Mailgram that very day to the grand jury foreman beginning with the words: "The government's attorneys are trying to block the personal appearance of Dr. Robert Sadoff as a witness before the Grand Jury after they had assured me he would be called in person." In the telegram Segal explained to the grand jury that Sadoff was arranging the sodium amytal interview as they had requested and that the psychiatrist's personal appearance before the jury would allow them to ask questions specifically about the test results. Segal ended his Mailgram with the words: "It would be unforgivable of the government's attorneys to block this direct and personal testimony on a subject which the members of the Grand Jury have stated firmly they want to hear about."

Unforgivable or not, Woerheide was intent upon ignoring his agreement with Segal. On the same day that Segal sent the Mailgram, Woerheide made arrangements with the FBI for MacDonald's arrest, overlooking the fact that MacDonald had not yet been indicted. At 9:02 that evening the FBI sent a telegram to outlying units saying that an indictment was forthcoming and that a bench warrant was to be issued without recommendation for bond. The FBI was unaware that MacDonald had departed for California, so Virginia agents were ordered to keep Malley's home under observation to assure an early arrest.

The next day Woerheide told the grand jury he had interviewed Dr. Sadoff and that Sadoff's responses made it clear that the inquiry would receive no benefit from a sodium amytal examination. Sadoff had expressed no such opinion, yet Woerheide called for an immediate vote for indictment. With these assurances from the prosecutor that the sodium amytal issue was dead, the grand jury at 4:45 P.M. on January 24, 1975, indicted Jeffrey MacDonald for three counts of murder, and the presiding judge, Franklin T. Dupree, released the already prepared bench warrant. Woerheide's tactics, fair or not, had garnered another "win." MacDonald was immediately arrested in California, and held against a bail of $500,000.

Bernard Segal fought the indictment with an appeal based on speedy-trial issues, the sodium amytal "deception," and prosecutorial misconduct. He won that effort in 1976, then lost in 1978 when the government appealed, in turn, to the Supreme Court. He also filed a writ for relief on grounds of double jeopardy, claiming constitutional protection against being tried a second time for the same crime. But the courts found that the army hearing back in 1970 didn't actually constitute a judicial proceeding, so the double jeopardy ruling didn't apply. Finally, after much legal jockeying, a trial date was set for the summer of 1979, more than nine years after the murders. Meanwhile, MacDonald had been released from jail after he and friends put up bail money which had been reduced to $100,000. He arranged for other doctors to take over his work at St. Mary's emergency department. Then he departed for trial in North Carolina.

Bernard Segal's Grievance

The official version of that trial, and the story reported by the overwhelming majority of the media, was that a team of superior FBI laboratory analysts had finally coaxed the truth from the circumstantial evidence and unmasked MacDonald as a murderer. The physical evidence itself, they insisted, cries out MacDonald's guilt. This official version has long been a matter of public record. But before Fred Bost and I completed our study of the trial evidence, we continued the practice of reading the official public records, then hearing the defense complaints, then going to the newly released FOIA records to weigh the disparate claims of both prosecution and defense. To that end, we wanted to know what MacDonald's lead defense counsel, Bernard Segal, had to say about it. Segal had served MacDonald well for more than twelve years, and he made no secret of his feelings that his client had been cheated.

I had encountered Segal only as a bold and belligerent signature slashed across countless legal papers. In 1988, nine years after the MacDonald conviction, I visited the attorney in his stylish San Francisco office overlooking the bay. I waited a few minutes until he came out of a meeting. He was a small man with striking, azure eyes, a quick smile, and a wild shock of white hair.

"It's a simple equation," Segal said when I told him Fred and I wanted to know what happened at trial. "I had an innocent client, and we lost to a malicious prosecution."

"Malicious. You're convinced of that."

"Yes, I am. In 1970 I didn't know, for certain, that Jeff hadn't killed his family, no matter what he or the psychiatrists said, until I heard the army's evidentiary case at the army's Article 32 hearing."

I reminded Segal that Colonel Rock said he recommended MacDonald's release because the evidence cleared him, but, I added, "when you got to trial, from what I've heard and read, that same evidence proved he was guilty."

"Well, sir, what you have heard and read is a lie," Segal barked, his eyes flashing blue fire. Then, with an effort, he half smiled, and in a softer voice said, "Technically speaking, it was the evidence *as presented*." He stabbed the table with his finger. "And that's an important phrase, *as presented*. And the evidence that was *not allowed*," he added, "and the evidence that was completely *suppressed*. There is absolutely no evidence that Jeff did this thing and there's a surfeit of evidence that shows he *didn't* do it. That is what anyone will learn if they look at the government records, all of them, the records that were suppressed throughout the trial and for years beyond, at Brian Murtagh's insistence, I might add." Murtagh had become Segal's nemesis when as an army captain during the grand jury investigation he suddenly appeared in the role of Woerheide's assistant, only later to take charge of the case as a Justice Department attorney. Obviously their personalities had clashed.

"That's pretty strong," I said.

"You aren't supposed to have to prove your innocence," Segal said. "That's supposed to be presumed. It wasn't presumed in this case, but with what we now know, if MacDonald's new lawyers could get him back into court, we could, without doubt, prove he did not commit these crimes."

"But they won't let you back into court."

"They can't afford to. We couldn't lose if we went back before a jury and showed them everything. This is the quintessential case of suppressed evidence, and it's a very, very visible case."

Like Gunderson, the eloquent, animated Segal sounded like a publicity agent spouting puffs for the defense team's media releases. But also, like Gunderson, he knew that Bost and I now possessed the FOIA papers and that we would check out everything he was saying. I asked him our key question. "How could the physical evidence, as presented by the prosecutors at trial, be so unlike the evidence presented by the army nine years earlier? After all, it came from the same crime scene."

Segal steepled the fingertips of one hand, one by one, to the fingertips of the other, his eyelids narrowing in concentration. "We weren't afraid of the physical evidence at first," he said, "and for good reason. The evidence the army had in 1970 proved, as you say, exactly the opposite of Ivory's claims. So, when the prosecution made noises at the grand jury in 1975 as if they were going to present a purely physical evidence case at trial, we said, 'Hey, we'd better get our hands on this stuff and see what it is.'"

For this purpose, Segal said, he retained forensic expert Dr. John Thornton, of the University of California, Berkeley, immediately following the indictment in 1975. "With Thornton on board, I pressed the government for four long years before the trial to let Thornton analyze the crime-scene evidence they claimed against MacDonald," Segal said. "But, the government's case was being run by a former army lawyer, Brian Murtagh, and this guy insisted we couldn't test the evidence. What!?" Segal said, throwing his hands up in disbelief. "Incredible. It was, after all, only circumstantial evidence, evidence which, *by their interpretations alone*, without substantiation by source documents, I might add, made

MacDonald *seem* guilty. Now, this sounded like the tactics I had faced in the South when I defended a civil rights leader against trumped-up local charges. Thornton and I were shocked by the government's refusal to let us look at evidence that might send our guy away for the rest of his life. 'We are the *government*,'" Segal mocked. "'Would we lie?'"

After many such requests to lab-test the evidence, followed by as many refusals, Segal said he received a letter from Dr. Thornton warning him that the prosecution's stalling tactics suggested that the government was hiding something. Thornton later told Segal that there could only be one reason that the government didn't want him looking at the source documents. "Of course, they were hiding things," Segal said. "We know that for certain now, but we knew, or *thought* we knew then. Otherwise, why didn't they let us analyze the stuff? Why not let us see the lab notes?"

Segal said he sent Thornton's letter to Judge Dupree in his next request. "Then, at the last minute, Murtagh finally agreed to allow lab testing, but then Dupree immediately proceeded to hamstring us with prohibitions which made it impossible, in the end only days before trial, to lab-test anything except a few swatches of material which was too old to test successfully for blood type, anyway. And they knew it. Big deal. They still weren't giving us the handwritten laboratory notes. Then, only a few days before trial Murtagh finally let us *eyeball* the evidence. They stacked it all up in a holding cell, not a laboratory, mind you, and they said, 'Okay, now come see the evidence, but, hey, remember, guys—you can look at it, but you can't test anything.'"

"You just looked at it, then?"

"Not really. Not even that. It was a farce. After fighting four years, Dr. Thornton actually was only allowed a tour through the cell to look at stuff in stacks upon stacks of boxes. There wasn't even any way to catalog it. Finding what we might need, without the lab notes to determine what it was we needed, was like looking for the needle in the haystack," Segal said. "Only they knew where and what the needle was. We didn't. And they weren't going to help us."

I wondered whether Segal's ire had risen out of the ashes of his own defeat, or from an actual violation of the law by the prosecutors.

"Okay," I said, "so you didn't get to lab-test the evidence. What happened when it was finally presented at trial?"

"*Now*," Segal said, "we get to the physical evidence, so called." The defense attorney placed his small hands palms down on the polished table, and leaned over toward me. His voice lowered in pitch and trembled with barely contained anger. "It had all changed."

"Changed?"

"Changed incredibly. Something had happened throughout that nine years that the government and the army had the evidence in their labs. It simply wasn't the same stuff and it *definitely* wasn't the same case."

Segal began telling me about some of the items MacDonald's investigators had found in the FOIA, discoveries that seemed, on the surface at least, to support his claims. "But," he said, waving his hand in the air, "I won't try to convince you. You guys are going through the same documents. See for yourselves."

In the Government Files

Official documents show that the chief architect of the government's new case against MacDonald was a foe with considerably more talent than William Ivory, or Joe Grebner, or any of the prosecution team which MacDonald's lawyers had faced back in 1970. Brian Murtagh, a bright and ambitious young lawyer who joined the army in 1971, was one of the circle of military personnel who were convinced that Colonel Rock had erred at the Article 32 hearing the year before. And, like Major Wold, the attorney who synopsized Rock's report for General Flanagan, Murtagh decided to do something about it. Having become heavily involved in the case, when it passed from army hands he resigned his commission in 1975 and joined the Justice Department. There his chief duty was to pursue Jeffrey MacDonald.[29]

Murtagh, a small, bespectacled man with thin, brown hair, had loaded the CID evidence into his station wagon in 1974 and delivered it, in his capacity as army attorney assisting the Justice Department, to the FBI labs where lab techs examined the items according to Murtagh's new theory about how the murders occurred.

Grand jury prosecutor Victor Woerheide, with young Murtagh's eager assistance, used the new theory, and some surprising, newly found evidence, to get an indictment for three counts of homicide. When Woerheide died after the grand jury hearing, Murtagh stepped in to square off against Segal at the 1979 trial on precisely those matters in which Segal had soundly trounced the army in front of Colonel Rock.

Segal had told me, years after trial, that Brian Murtagh and Judge Franklin Dupree had erected various hindrances which effectively prohibited Dr. Thornton's efforts to properly lab-test the evidentiary materials before trial. When Bost and I examined the case records on this point, we discovered that Segal indeed had made his first requests for lab testing soon after the 1975 grand jury indictment, but the prosecutors claimed his requests were too broad. They were denied. Segal then made other, more specific, lengthy, written requests, but Murtagh again resisted, and Judge Dupree refused to rule that Murtagh turn over the evidence for laboratory analysis.[30] He also refused to force Murtagh to produce hand-written lab notes of evidence examinations, notes which Segal wanted desperately to compare to the published laboratory reports furnished him. Such sparring continued for nearly four years. Finally, a few weeks before trial, Murtagh suddenly agreed to allow lab testing—but with severe conditions soon imposed by Judge Dupree.

In the first of Dupree's restrictions, he ruled that he would allow Thornton a one-time-only, supervised visit to the jail cell where the evidence was being safeguarded. Thornton would list the items he wanted to examine, not in his own labs in California, as he had been requesting, but only in the laboratory of the North Carolina State Bureau of Investigations. Murtagh would still have the right to refuse Dr. Thornton lab testing on any specific item. Murtagh would submit such objections to Dupree, who would make the final decision on each contested item.

The procedure never even began. Dupree's rules for the operation were theoretically feasible, even if they were time consuming, and that was the sticking point. The one thing that Segal wasn't offered was time. Dupree's ruling, incredibly, demanded that all laboratory examinations and tests, including the arguments over which tests could and couldn't be made, including Judge Dupree's ruling on each argument, including writing and filing of all subsequent reports—Dupree demanded that all this be accomplished, without exception, not later than July 12, 1979. This date was only three weeks away from his ruling allowing the tests, tests yet to be individually ruled upon, tests which still might be completely disallowed, and tests which Segal had been seeking, and the government denying, for four years.[31]

This behavior, which seemed to Dr. Thornton patently unfair, caused him to repeat his earlier cautions to Segal. "There is something there they don't want us to find." With the trial date upon him, and now encumbered with witness preparations, Segal indignantly repudiated the judge's belated lab-testing solution as ridiculous. The army laboratory had required more than six months to complete their own initial examinations on the same evidence, examinations that had continued for years, and the FBI had been working with the evidence for many years since. In the end, Segal and Thornton decided it would be impossible to attempt it in the few days they had left.

On July 6, 1979, now only ten days before opening day of the trial, the prosecution ended the bickering with a sudden unexplained switch. There would still be no real lab testing, but Murtagh himself now asked the court to allow the defense to "microscopically examine fibers that are connected with the physical evidence in this case. . . ."

"This was terribly frustrating," Segal told me in one of our interviews years later. "Since the government had eaten up four years in denying us access," Segal said, "there was no reason to believe they really were going to let us have the evidence and the time it would take to examine it on the very eve of trial. And without the lab notes for comparisons, how would we know that room even contained everything they'd found in the apartment?"

"No," Segal added, "the reason for the prosecutor's belated offering, even with Dupree's hindrances intact, was so he could later claim that we were not *really* denied the evidence. They had no intentions of actually letting us fully examine anything."

Indeed, documents prove that, as Segal had expected, Judge Dupree then took five agonizing days to consider Murtagh's new offer. His belated ruling, only days before the trial commenced, allowed Dr. Thornton and Segal only to enter the evidence cell and, visually only, examine "the contents of any sealed vial, pill box, or other container having within it certain fibers which the government proposes to introduce as evidence." But Thornton could only look. He could use a microscope, but, of course, only if he could find what he needed among hundreds of exhibits, and many hundreds more fibers, splinters, hairs, blood samples, and fabric samples. Thornton could perform no tests, and he couldn't see the handwritten lab notes Murtagh was still holding back. Effectively defeated, Thornton and Segal finally went to the evidence cell at the courthouse and haplessly viewed the hundreds of boxes. There were no lab facilities there, and no time. They found nothing to help them. The trite but perhaps appropriate phrase "needle in a haystack" became a lament the bitter defense attorneys would use for years afterward.

"In almost any state court," Segal later pointed out, "the examination of evidence in a murder trial would be a given right of the defense experts. But not with the feds. It's up to the judge's discretion. They're afraid we're going to somehow change something—that's sort of the unofficial official version. The truth is that, if they want, they can keep problems for their own case all safely tucked away." Whether Segal's assessment of the government's motives is correct, it is a fact that he was required to face Murtagh's experts at trial unarmed with information which the government had. Segal saw it as one man trying to sell another man a house, without allowing the buyer ever to inspect it. After losing a four-year fight, Segal entered trial without knowing whether there even *was* a foundation to the structure.

6

■

The Evidence
at Trial

A crowd of observers pushed into the Raleigh courtroom on the morning of July 19, 1979. As reporters jockeyed for seats, a writer recognized author Joe McGinniss, who revealed that he was indeed planning a book on the case. Jeffrey MacDonald arrived fit and handsome in a dark, well-tailored business suit. Looking more like a successful trial attorney than a doctor, he carried his briefcase down the crowded aisle and seated himself next to Bernard Segal. MacDonald's mother, Dorothy, nervously watched her son. Colette's stepfather, Freddie Kassab, stout and dark of visage, sat quietly watching MacDonald, thinking his own thoughts. Colette's mother, Mildred Kassab, sat next to her husband. Her thin face revealed the bitter pain of losing her daughter and her grandchildren. She had made it no secret that, in her view, MacDonald had evaded justice for nine long years. Now, the prosecutors had assured her, he would suffer his due.

The bailiff cried out for everyone to rise in honor of Judge Franklin T. Dupree, Jr. The crowd quieted as a white-haired, black-robed man, tall and gaunt, entered and took his place at the bench. At exactly 9:46 A.M., Assistant U.S. Attorney James Blackburn, the lead prosecutor, rose to thank the jurors for their service. He introduced the other members of the prosecution team: Brian Murtagh from the Justice Department; Jack Crawley,

134

Assistant U.S. Attorney; and George Anderson, United States Attorney for the Eastern District of North Carolina.

Assisting Bernard Segal for the defense were Michael Malley, the former army lawyer and longtime MacDonald friend who had served with Segal in the army hearing, and Wade Smith, a former North Carolina football hero and prominent defense attorney of great repute.

In his opening statement, James Blackburn, a trim and handsome dark-haired man, concentrated on the basis of the government's claims against MacDonald—a crime scene that had been well controlled, Blackburn insisted, yielding evidence that had been impeccably preserved.

Blackburn assured the jurors that everything in the murder apartment had been photographed, implying that he possessed a reliable record of the crime scene as first found. Some of the weapons came from inside MacDonald's house, Blackburn insisted, and perhaps all the weapons were MacDonald's. In a pleasant southern accent, Blackburn quietly described the gruesome overkill inflicted upon Colette and the children by those weapons. Then he gave the jury a much truncated version of MacDonald's wounds, saying MacDonald only suffered a "bump on the head . . . a cut on the left arm . . . a paper cut on his finger . . . several abrasions on his chest . . . and an incision in his chest." The prosecutor then paused and pointed an accusing finger at MacDonald. Blackburn reminded the jurors soberly that the defendant, unlike his wife and daughters, was "very much alive."

The army sealed the murder apartment after the crimes, Blackburn told the jury, implying, as in his earlier reference to photographic proof, that the government would present evidence from a crime scene that had been unquestionably well guarded.

Blackburn said there was a lot of blood in the house, but what was important, he added, was where the blood was *not* found, for in the living room where MacDonald's struggle with the intruders was supposed to have occurred, Blackburn said there was no blood except on the *Esquire* magazine.

The prosecutor stated that MacDonald had said that his pajama top was torn and pulled over his head in the fight, yet there was not a single pajama thread in the living room. And Blackburn promised to prove that Colette's Type A blood was on the pajama top *before* it was torn and therefore could not have gotten onto the fabric when MacDonald placed the garment on his wife, as MacDonald had claimed.

Blackburn also said he would show proof that MacDonald had stabbed

Colette in the chest twenty-one times with an ice pick. "Basically," Blackburn concluded, "we believe that the physical evidence points to the fact, unfortunately, that one person—not two, three, four, or more—killed Colette, Kimberly, and Kristen and that person is the defendant.

"We are concentrating, ladies and gentlemen, on the physical evidence. . . . This is not a complicated case—it is straightforward. We are going to make it easy for you to understand that the circumstantial physical evidence in this case points swiftly and unerringly to the fact that one person killed his family." That charge echoed another which Blackburn used throughout the case when speaking about the physical evidence. "Things do not lie," he said, "but people can and often do."

At Trial

William Ivory Takes the Stand

CID agent William F. Ivory, the lead army investigator in the case, took the stand early in the trial. Responding to Blackburn's questions, the investigator described his actions and those of his men in the crime scene as meticulous and competent. Ivory assured the jurors that he had seen no one in the neighborhood as he drove toward the home that morning. And when he arrived at the MacDonald apartment he saw only "about four" military policemen outside and none in the bedrooms.

Ivory had arrived about fifteen minutes after the first MPs on the scene, but he said Lieutenant Paulk had assured him that nothing in the house had been moved by anyone who had been in the house during that time. Ivory was a government witness, of course, and he didn't volunteer the crime-scene disturbances he and his team had admitted to back at the army hearing nine years earlier.

Ivory said the dishes in the dining area china cabinet hadn't been disturbed, and Valentine cards standing on edge atop the cabinet hadn't been moved, suggesting to him that no violent struggle had taken place between MacDonald and intruders in the adjoining living room.

Ivory's claims about a staged scene were similar to those he'd made at the 1970 army hearing. Colonel Rock hadn't believed those claims, but at the 1979 trial James Blackburn introduced selected crime-scene photos to illustrate and corroborate Ivory's testimony. This was clearly meant to revive the staged-scene theory that had suffered an ignoble death before Colonel Rock in the army hearing. Not surprisingly, Segal objected heartily to this early use of the crime-scene photographs. He approached the bench for a conference. Out of the jury's hearing, Segal told Judge Dupree that the prosecutors obviously intended to use these photographs to establish that nothing had been moved in the crime scene. For such proof, logically, of course, the government would need photos taken immediately upon the MPs' arrival. But such photographs weren't made. Segal charged that if the army's photos were introduced, the government should at the same time introduce all the MPs and army personnel who said things were moved, that they personally saw things moved, including all three bodies, before the photos were taken. "Everything Ivory has *seen* has been moved." Segal added, "It is not only false—"

But Judge Dupree interrupted him. "You seem to be anticipating that the testimony of this witness will be at variance with some witness . . . and, if it is, so be it."

Segal, his blue eyes intent, angrily retorted, "It is not right to introduce a photograph when it does not represent the crime scene as it was found. They simply want to skip how they found it."

Segal attempted to object further, but the judge ignored him, looked at Blackburn, and said tersely, "Ask your questions."

In this manner Judge Dupree allowed the prosecution to introduce the photos, which Blackburn and Ivory continued to use to represent the crime scene as it was found, and to support Ivory's claim that this was exactly the crime scene the MPs had entered fifteen minutes before his arrival, with absolutely nothing changed during that first quarter hour and for the next several hours before the photographers arrived. Using these hotly contested photographs and the prosecution's scale model of the apartment, Ivory then explained how he directed all the other agents to various tasks in the yard or in the bedrooms collecting what Ivory many times called "fragile evidence," a term which intimated Ivory's respect for the forensic data, and an expression Blackburn soon began using as well.

Like the case itself, William Ivory had undergone a drastic change since 1970. Back then, he had worn ill-fitting suits, and his well-oiled hair had been combed with a curl falling across the middle of his forehead. Before Colonel Rock, the youthful Ivory had been an inexperienced investigator with an attitude. Now, before Dupree, the swagger was gone. The suit was filled out, his manner reflected years of experience, and he had discarded his rock star hairdo. Segal and Malley realized immediately that this new William Ivory was a more formidable foe than the brash youth he had been when they faced him on the stand in 1970.

THE ROCK REPORT DISALLOWED

Bernard Segal had anticipated Ivory's testimony. And he had expected this initial skirmish over the crime scene. As he had prepared for trial, he had petitioned Judge Dupree to allow the defense to show the trial jurors Colonel Rock's official report of the Article 32 hearing. Segal believed that this report, based, in part, upon Colonel Rock's analysis of the activity in the crime scene, would create doubt in the jurors' minds regarding the government claims of a murder apartment untrammeled by the boots and hands of military personnel and others. In the absence of lab testing, and without the lab notes, Segal sorely needed Rock's report on the army hearing.

That crucial report, which had exonerated MacDonald in 1970, had already come into play long before trial. After the grand jury indictment in 1975, Segal had attempted to thwart the government's attempt to try MacDonald by claiming that he had already been tried once, at the army hearing, and he had been found innocent. But the government lawyers claimed, and the courts ruled, that the Article 32 hearing wasn't a *judiciary* affair, it was an *investigative* effort, and, as such, did not qualify as a legitimate defense claim of double jeopardy.

Now, however, at the trial the government lawyers switched their stand, claiming that the army hearing was actually a *judicial* proceeding; therefore, they argued, the Rock report should not be allowed as evidence. Judge Dupree agreed. He ruled he wouldn't let Segal introduce the report to the jurors. Segal cried "foul," complaining that the government had used the report both ways, as an investigation and not a judicial proceeding when that posture benefited their double jeopardy arguments, and then as judicial and not investigatory when that new claim suited their purposes to block evidence at trial. But Dupree would not relent.

Having failed to get the critical, fact-laden Rock report before the jury, Segal again asked Brian Murtagh to turn over to the defense certain army investigative reports. These long-sought, long-denied items included certain witness statements, grand jury testimonies, and all the handwritten laboratory notes created by the lab techs as they worked on the evidence. This, Segal hoped, would better equip him to fight government claims that nothing untoward had occurred in the crime scene or in the analysis labs. But again Murtagh refused to give Segal the desired documents.

SEGAL'S FINAL PLEA FOR DISCLOSURE

As the trial proceeded, Segal asked Dupree, one more time, to make Murtagh turn over the still withheld handwritten lab notes and other documents. The importance of such items to Segal's case or to the case of any defense team cannot be overstated, for it is upon just such reports and notes that the government's charges are made. But, again, to Segal's anger, the judge quickly ruled in Murtagh's favor, saying, "I will not so rule." Dupree promised the disconsolate Segal that if any of these withheld notes were later found to contain exculpatory information, which is to say, information supporting MacDonald's claims, the government's case would "get reversal."

Years later Segal said that this promise seemed hollow and especially cruel, because the time to see whether the lab notes and other items contained material helpful to MacDonald was pre-trial, or, failing that, at trial—not after MacDonald might be convicted on erroneous claims by the prosecutor. Segal knew, even then, that it would require years of legal jockeying to get his hands on notes Murtagh was then refusing, and which Dupree saw no reason to share with Segal.

Segal and his team were not only dejected by Dupree's final refusal to force Murtagh to give Segal the documents, they also feared that the judge's own language and behavior revealed that the magistrate himself, long before the end of trial, already seemed to have accepted that Jeffrey MacDonald would be convicted. What occurred here, one defense team member later remarked, is tantamount to hanging an alleged rustler on the word of a powerful ranch owner without even looking at the brand of the cow in question.

IVORY'S TESTIMONY CONTINUES

Needless to say, Segal hadn't gotten off to a good start at trial. He knew that the photographs, taken long after the first MPs and even after William Ivory arrived, did not depict the crime scene as found by the responding MPs. Colonel Rock, after hearing many witnesses, had determined that things had indeed shifted positions. Strangers had been in the apartment that morning, touching things, moving things, sitting on the furniture. The wallet had been stolen. The rings had been taken. Clothing had been moved, windows were opened and closed, drawers shut. The flowerpot had changed position, as had the baby's bottle. The position of MacDonald's glasses had shifted slightly. There was evidence that the bodies of the victims had been moved. The phones had been wiped free of prints, and the knife wiped, and the baby's bottle wiped—all this *after* the MPs arrived. But the photos Dupree had allowed included no such information.

If Segal hadn't earlier realized that Brian Murtagh and James Blackburn were more talented adversaries than those attorneys he'd faced in the army hearing, he now knew it, with Ivory still on the stand, only a few hours into trial.

Ivory on Cross

Segal began his cross-examination of prosecution witness William Ivory knowing he would have to work hard to dispel the idea that the crime scene was well controlled. This task had been easy at the army hearing in front of Colonel Rock, who had asked his own questions, and who had apparently rankled at the unmilitary investigative sloppiness he encountered in the CID efforts. It wouldn't be that simple in front of Judge Dupree.

The defense lawyer remarked to Ivory that, in his direct testimony, the agent had stated at least twelve times that the scene had been well protected. Yet Ivory's responses to Segal's questions about the flowerpot were vague, as if the investigator had never learned that a stranger had touched it. Ivory continued to talk about the careful and competent collection of "fragile evidence." Incredibly, the CID agent even claimed that he hadn't known that MP Kenneth Mica had seen a woman with a floppy hat in the neighborhood that morning.

Segal then broached the subject of MacDonald's story about the woman carrying a flickering light. "Mr. Ivory, did you ever learn during the period of time that you were collecting physical evidence that Dr. MacDonald described the woman he saw in his home as carrying a candle which gave off a flickering light?"

"Yes, sir, I did."

"And that he said he saw that woman in the living room of his house?"

"That is correct."

"By any chance, as you were gathering up the physical evidence, did you find any wax in the living room?"

"Yes, sir, there was some wax in the living room."

"You sound like it didn't seem very important. Did you think that was a significant clue—to find wax?"

"Yes, I believe it was significant."

"When and where did you find this wax?"

"There was wax on one of the slats of the upturned coffee table as I recall."

"The coffee table?"

"Yes, sir."

"In the living room?"

"Yes, sir."

"The very place that Dr. MacDonald says he was engaged in a struggle and in which he saw the woman with a candle; is that right?"

"As I recall, that wax that was found there was old wax on the table, and it was found to be similar to some candle wax of candles from within the house."

Of course, Segal knew Ivory's statement contradicted the CID wax report which had been reluctantly surrendered to Colonel Rock in 1970. The report confirmed that the wax did not match any of the candles in the MacDonald home, and Segal would later establish when he cross-examined a CID lab tech that the wax had been deposited about the time of the murders. It was not old wax.[1] Ivory was wrong, but the jurors, for now, had heard the errors from the mouth of the lead investigator.

But Segal wasn't finished. He asked, pointedly, "Mr. Ivory, is it your testimony, sworn testimony, that you are not aware that there was wax that was located in the MacDonald living room that to this very day has not been identified as coming from the MacDonald house; is that your testimony?"

"As I recall right now, I cannot think of any that wasn't."

So Segal asked Ivory when he had last read the lab reports and when he had collected the wax samples. Ivory couldn't remember. Segal called his attention to a CID consolidated lab report on wax samples.

"I have seen that consolidated lab report, yes, sir."

"You have, sir?"

Blackburn called out, "Your Honor, we object to this line of questioning. It is going outside the scope."

Blackburn correctly recognized that Ivory was in trouble, but the question certainly wasn't out of the scope of Ivory's earlier statements. Dupree realized that as well, but he offered the prosecution relief in another way. He sustained the objection, "not necessarily on that ground," the judge added, "but as being an improper way to get in evidence of some report."

Segal tried again. "If I were to suggest to you, Mr. Ivory, that the CID consolidated lab report Number 58 states that the samples of wax taken from the living room in the MacDonald house—"

"Objection."

"Sustained."

"Your Honor," Segal offered, "he has already testified that he thought that these samples of the mysterious wax he found had been accounted for. I intend to show—"

But Judge Dupree quickly cut him off, explaining that this was an improper way to get the report before the jury since Ivory did not prepare the report himself. Segal thought it trivial that Ivory hadn't been the one who prepared the report. Ivory was, after all, the government's lead investigator, and he had just made a statement contrary to a report he had said he'd read, about an important piece of evidence that had helped scuttle the army's case in front of Colonel Rock.

Without the inadmissible Rock report and other documents held back by Murtagh, including the laboratory notes, Segal found himself hard put to cope with Ivory's apparent ignorance of inadequate crime-scene protection and the discoveries of evidence favorable to the defense in the apartment. Segal was an experienced trial lawyer, and was well aware that whether feigned or real, Ivory's ignorance of these defense claims could cause the jurors to suspect that Segal might simply be insinuating things which didn't exist. Thus, Ivory softened Segal's cross-examination thunder on central issues by saying, "I don't know," or "I don't remember." The jury had to decide whom to believe, a government agent seemingly trying hard to recall hazy details, or a voluble defense attorney cleverly advocating for his client. And, without the still undisclosed source documents, neither Segal nor the jurors knew anything about the bloody syringe, or the blond wig fibers, and other things Ivory's men had found, and they didn't know the truth about the still secret piece of skin Ivory himself had examined in the CID lab.

Many things were left undisclosed as Ivory remained in the witness chair as a kind of official sponsor for the physical evidence the prosecutors now began placing on a table in the courtroom. One by one came boxes and vials, and bloody bedsheets, photographs, flipcharts of body outlines, pieces of rugs, sections of wall, boards sawn out of the floor, surgical gloves, magazines, a bed slat, a pocket torn off MacDonald's pajama top.

Higher and higher the evidence pile grew. The prosecutors sang out the name and description of each item in a manner which exhibited complete confidence that the FBI and CID laboratories had established that this piece of evidence proved MacDonald was lying about his version of events that morning.

This damning litany continued into the next day with more vials; a plastic sheet from Kristen's bed; part of the north bedroom (Kristen's room) west wall with bloodstains; hair ribbons from the master bedroom; items from the kitchen and the north bedroom. In all, 175 objects were introduced in a manner suggesting that these items formed a comprehensive and seamless web of verification that caught MacDonald in lie after lie. "Things do not lie," Blackburn told the jurors, "but people can and do." He would repeat this slogan like a battle cry throughout the trial.

Following Ivory's appearance and the dramatic presentation of these "proofs," Murtagh and Blackburn now revealed to the jurors a new interpretation of the evidence which had failed to convince Colonel Rock back in 1970.

According to the revised government explanation, prosecutors contended that Jeffrey MacDonald had fought his wife in Kristen's room after he beat her in the master bedroom. Blood evidence confirmed she had bled in both rooms. The prosecutors contended that after this second beating, Colette was moved to make it seem she had never left her own room. They claimed that MacDonald stripped the blue bedsheet from the master bed, wrapped her beaten and unconscious form in it to mask blood flow, and carried her back to the master bedroom. He then stabbed her to death with the Old Hickory knife and the ice pick which he obtained from his kitchen. This became the government story which unfolded at the trial.

BLOODSTAINS ON THE BLUE BEDSHEET

That McDonald, and no one else, did these things was intimated by the apparent lack of evidence that any intruders had been in the home. To prove this, the prosecution called Paul Stombaugh, a former head of the FBI chemistry laboratory. The white-haired, quiet-natured Stombaugh was the epitome of what a government trial witness should be. In a kindly, unhurried manner, the old gentleman showed the jurors some bloodstains on the sheet, which had been found on the floor of the master bedroom. He said these stains were the murderer's handprints and shoulder print. This appeared to support the prosecutors' theory that

MacDonald had moved Colette in the sheet. In the absence of evidence of intruders, the jurors would have no reason to suspect that anyone but MacDonald had done these things, if, indeed, they were done.

During cross-examination Segal pressed hard to discredit Stombaugh's testimony, and soon the lab man admitted, in a characteristically calm voice, that he hadn't attempted to duplicate such stains by applying a marking liquid such as ink to a model's shoulder and hand, then pressing the inked shoulder and hand to the sheet. He also admitted, upon Segal's questioning, that he had failed to use a microscope to search for hair follicle patterns within the stains, a normal procedure when determining the source of stains.

Stombaugh finally acquiesced to Segal's charge that his findings regarding the stains were subjective, and that no scientific comparison of the patterns to knowns was even attempted.

To further combat Stombaugh's claims, Segal called two defense witnesses. Dr. John Thornton, the lead forensic expert for the defense, and Charles Morton, an experienced fabric impression expert, both testified that they believed Stombaugh was wrong about the source of the "hand" and "shoulder" stains on the sheet.

Thornton pointed out how the bloodstains comprising the "handprints" on the sheet were uniformly thick. He explained to the jury that if these were genuine handprints the stain would show varying thicknesses; each finger stain would be thinnest in the middle where pressure was greatest, and would be thicker on the edges where blood had been pushed outward. But this explanation seemed feeble when matched against the other government claims regarding the bedsheet. More damning to MacDonald were the unmistakable patterns of stains on the sheet which appeared to be from his pajama top and from Colette's pajamas. This seemed to link Colette and Jeffrey and that blue bedsheet.

STOMBAUGH'S CREDENTIALS

Without complete lab notes, and having been denied Stombaugh's personnel records by Judge Dupree, Segal could only attempt through questions to show that the retired laboratory technician had received very little formal instruction in the fields for which he claimed expertise. Stombaugh claimed hundreds of court appearances as a laboratory expert; strangely, though, he could not name a single trial in which he had ever been recognized as an expert in fabric impressions. At a bench conference, Segal requested that Stombaugh be rejected as an expert in that field.

Against the attorney's protestations, Judge Dupree, despite the lack of documentation, let it stand that Stombaugh was an expert on the subject.

But Segal wasn't through with Stombaugh's credentials. In touting those credentials during a bench conference the week before, Murtagh assured everyone, "I know he has a bachelor's degree in chemistry from, I believe, the University of North Carolina."[2] Segal had sought proof of this claim and had come up empty. During preliminary questioning at the trial, however, Stombaugh said he received his bachelor of science degree in 1949 from Furman University in Greenville, South Carolina, with a major in biology and a minor in chemistry. As Stombaugh was being led through direct examination by Blackburn, a defense researcher contacted Furman University seeking facts. Thus, when Segal began his cross-examination, he was armed with new information and attempted to show through questioning that Stombaugh had received only one year of instruction in chemistry, that his chemistry grade had been minimal, and his grade in physics had been even worse. But Judge Dupree, visibly angry at such attempts to discredit the former head of the FBI lab's chemistry section, quickly cut the effort short.

BLOODSTAINS ON THE PAJAMA TOP

Therefore, despite Segal's discoveries, Stombaugh was allowed to remain on the stand as a fabric impressions expert, and his appearance as a distinguished, soft-spoken scientist continued to buttress his believability. In his direct testimony he said that certain bloodstains on the pajama top proved that it had been torn after it had been stained with Colette's blood, proof, the government said, that MacDonald got her blood on it while fighting her. Then, Stombaugh calmly said, as this alleged fight continued, MacDonald's pajama top was torn *across these bloodstains.*

It infuriated Bernard Segal that this new theory suddenly had appeared after nine years, without the defense being allowed to examine the source documents from which it had been produced. This was especially true because visual examination of the pajama top itself certainly did not show the stains running across the rip. In fact, Segal asked Stombaugh himself to produce one of the photographs which showed the stain proceeding across the tear. Stombaugh chose one, but the lab man himself admitted he could not see the bloodstain continuing across the rip into the fabric on the other half of the garment. Segal then asked Stombaugh to select any one of the five different stains on the pajama top which best demonstrated the theory that the top had been bloodied before being torn.[3] Stombaugh did select a stain, looked at it closely, but again admitted that the stain was not visible across the tear in the fabric.

Segal asked the man to produce any other laboratory photograph supporting his claim. Stombaugh could not. The lab didn't have one, he said. He then amended his earlier assertion, saying now that "photo facilities just did not bring it up"[4]

Nevertheless, the mild-mannered FBI retiree insisted he still could prove his point. He asked that a lightbox be brought to the courtroom so he could demonstrate how the stains on either side of the rips matched up. Stombaugh then placed the garment over the opaque lighted window of the box and examined it, but *still* he could not see that the stain continued across the rip. Stombaugh finally explained to Segal in a now almost apologetic tone that "in 1971 these stains were much more visible than they are now."[5] He seemed genuinely surprised that the years had done so much damage to this evidence which he claimed once clearly pointed to MacDonald's guilt.

Since Segal didn't possess the CID bench notes about the pajama top stains, he couldn't prove that Stombaugh was wrong. And, again, Segal realized the jurors had to decide whether this decent and gentle-appearing old lab tech, with apparently impeccable credentials, was misleading them about such an important issue or Segal, the little long-haired, Jewish lawyer from up north, was just badgering a competent witness.

But what would the jurors have heard about those bloodstains if Segal had been given the documents he had been denied?

In the Government Files

Bernard Segal and Jeffrey MacDonald would forever lament Judge Dupree's refusal to make Murtagh turn over the contested lab notes and other documents Segal had requested. When senators and congressmen finally forced the release of these papers years later, the defense team found a rich vein of evidence Segal could have mined for material to challenge each government charge.

THE DISCOVERIES OF SHEDLICK AND DANNELLY

The most important evidentiary discoveries in the FOIA papers were found in the late 1980s by private detective Raymond Shedlick, Jr., and his daughter, Ellen Dannelly. Shedlick, a retired New York City homicide detective whose colorful career involved undercover work in mob cases, was hired as a private investigator for a security firm handling the Mac-Donald case. Shedlick later opened his own office to work solely for MacDonald. Interviews by Shedlick and Dannelly produced scores of witnesses who had been missed or simply passed over by the army CID. This irked Shedlick, who said that "the CID agents never did the basic neighborhood investigation, knock on every door, ask everyone what they saw and heard, and they didn't consider the crime-scene forensic evidence as a whole. *Any* pair of NYPD detectives would have wrapped this thing up in short order."

Shedlick also had begun studying the FOIA forensic notes before learning he suffered from terminal lung cancer. When he was told at the hospital that his death was imminent, he insisted upon returning to his home where in his final days he continued his search through the army CID and the FBI lab notes. When Shedlick became too weak to work in late 1988, Ellen continued the analysis in the next room, from time to time reporting to her father what she was finding.

Shedlick died in January of 1989, but Ellen Dannelly, herself now a licensed private investigator, continued her dad's search through the eleven file boxes of FOIA papers. She gathered more than 250 of the handwritten laboratory notes that Murtagh had denied Segal. She found that these notes addressed sixty-four exhibits of trial evidence; and, as Segal had suspected, thirty-seven of these exhibits, more than one-half, contained findings which the defense experts could have used at trial to challenge prosecution claims there. Yet of these thirty-seven findings, only three were ever transcribed into typed reports to be turned over to the defense.

Dannelly also found that Dr. Thornton had been correct when he guessed the government was hiding something in the lab notes. For one thing, there were major discrepancies between separate findings by the CID and FBI labs in the same exhibits. She noted that the FBI laboratory experts had disagreed with the CID lab (and sometimes with their own fellow lab technicians) over the identification of hair findings in twenty-two exhibits, and over the actual type, number, or physical characteristics of fibers in nineteen exhibits.[6] All of this was unknown to the defense at trial. If Segal had possessed this information, he could have impeached the government's claims of forensic solidarity. The prosecutors' stance that the lab findings were competently arrived at and inarguably definitive would have been empty words.

But the discrepancies between the CID and the FBI lab tests of the evidence were secondary to an even more important question. Do the laboratory notes and other heretofore withheld government files actually *contradict* the prosecutors' central claims at trial?

For instance, if Segal had possessed the lab notes, what might he have learned about Paul Stombaugh's trial claim that the bloodstains on the pajama top had continued across the rip? During Shedlick's and Dannelly's forays in the FOIA documents they discovered that the government failed to reveal at trial that CID lab tech Janice Glisson, years earlier, had explored the same bloodstain theory and had come to a different conclusion. She had determined that the stain edges on either side of the rips did not intersect, that the pajama top was, therefore, stained *after* it was ripped, not before.

Yet the jurors would hear many other, even more damning, government claims whose true histories, as detailed in the FOIA documents, Segal well could have used at trial to discredit these claims.

At Trial

THE PAJAMA TOP FOLDING EXPERIMENT

During his lengthy appearance on the stand during trial Paul Stombaugh presented astounding new evidence which the government said was proof MacDonald had stabbed Colette with the ice pick through his own pajama top as the garment lay over her chest. This experiment was the key government exhibit, and would become famous due to Joe McGinniss's representation of it in *Fatal Vision*.

Stombaugh explained to the jurors that he and assistant Shirley Green had folded MacDonald's pajama top so that the forty-eight tiny round holes found in the fabric exactly matched the twenty-one stab wounds in Colette's chest. He presented a large photograph of his folding experiment, which featured metal skewers piercing the folded garment on a dummy form meant to represent Colette's chest. The skewers in the form protruded outward like arrows piercing a body, or like the blade of an ice pick being thrust repeatedly into Colette MacDonald.

Stombaugh explained that he had used actual crime-scene photos of the pajama top draped over Colette's chest as a basis for his work. He said he had refolded the garment "exactly" the way the MPs had seen it covering her. He also assured the jury that the one-eighth-inch width of some of the holes in the garment indicated places where the tapered ice pick blade had been driven into Colette's chest "up to the hilt."

The photograph of the experiment showed the skewers extending at various angles in silent testimony that a brutal Jeffrey MacDonald knelt over his wife's already dead body, and repeatedly pounded the cruel blade into her. Coming from no less than the former chief of a section of the FBI laboratory, the jurors could hardly fail to understand that the pajama top experiment was meant to be taken seriously.

Without the benefit of lab notes to trace the evolution of Stombaugh's experiment, Segal had little direct information to prove his hunch that Stombaugh had performed the folding experiment at the expense of scientific method. But Segal's own forensic expert, Dr. John Thornton from the University of California, Berkeley, had offered Segal some ideas about how to approach the problem during Stombaugh's cross-examination.

Segal, under Thornton's direction, asked Stombaugh whether he had really folded the pajama top as it had been found. Stombaugh again confidently insisted he had done so. Segal then produced the crime-scene photograph of the pajama top draped over Colette, the same crime-scene photo Stombaugh had reported he had worked from. Then he handed Stombaugh the FBI photograph of his own laboratory experiment showing the garment draped over the form meant to represent Colette's chest. He asked Stombaugh to examine the two photographs closely and tell him if they were the same.

The old lab tech did so, and now told Segal, quietly, that he and Mrs. Green had indeed made "some" changes from the photographed position of the folded pajama top.[7]

In Dr. Thornton's later testimony on the issue, he further pointed out that a loose garment would not have remained steadfastly in position while being repeatedly and violently stabbed twenty-one times. In his opinion, subsequent powerful thrusts of the blade would move previous holes out of alignment with the stab wound beneath it so that a single folding configuration could not account for fabric holes which had moved away from an earlier wound as the body moved under the violent blows. To duplicate the alleged event, one would have to devise at least twenty-one such folding configurations, each one representing a shift of the fabric after each blow of the ice pick. Thornton thus rendered the government pajama top experiment as arbitrary and unscientific. The experiment only showed, Thornton believed, that one could use up all the fabric holes by folding the garment in various ways. It proved nothing.

Segal wasn't finished with Stombaugh or the pajama top experiment. The attorney also pointed out that Stombaugh's experiment suffered problems other than his failure to adhere to the photographic evidence he claimed to have used. The blade of the ice pick is tapered, Segal reminded him, and Stombaugh should have measured the width of each hole to ensure that the sizes of the holes were compatible in those instances where the blade was supposed to have passed through several layers of cloth. Stombaugh admitted he had made no such measurements, which would mean that a smaller hole in the cloth might be situated above a larger hole in a lower layer of the folded cloth, and this would be an impossibility if the thrusts of a tapered blade went one way through layers of cloth.

Relying again on Dr. Thornton's observations, Segal insisted that the direction of the blade's passage through those multiple layers of cloth, as signified by the bent angles of tiny broken fibers, would also have to be compatible.[8] In other words, the ice pick would have gone through various layers of cloth in the same direction, and so logic demands that all the broken fibers in various layers over a single wound would have to be bent in the same direction. When confronted with this reasoning, Stombaugh said he hadn't taken the broken fibers into account.

Continuing to attack Stombaugh's laboratory methods, Segal pointed out that Stombaugh, inexplicably, had also failed to consider the thirty puncture holes and eighteen cuts that appeared in Colette's own pajama top which had lain between the blue pajama top and the wounds in Colette's chest. Stombaugh acknowledged that this defense claim, also, was true.

Stombaugh also admitted he ignored the knife cuts in Colette's body. "Someone says to you," Segal said, "'See if you can take forty-eight puncture holes in Dr. MacDonald's pajama top, and match them to the holes in Mrs. MacDonald's body, but ignore the cuts in her body'?"

"They didn't say ignore the cuts," Stombaugh said. "They did not ask that we do that."

"Didn't you say, 'I'm a scientist here in a forensic laboratory; I don't understand why you ask me to just match up puncture holes and not match up the cuts in the same part of the body'? Did you not ask them that kind of question as a scientist?"

"No, sir, I did not ask that kind of question."

"You just accepted their request and did what they asked?"

"That is right."

"The persons who made this interesting request of you were whom?"

"Mr. Woerheide and Mr. Murtagh," Stombaugh said.

Then the beleaguered Stombaugh abandoned his own earlier claims about the pajama top exhibit. "We are not saying this is what happened," Stombaugh now admitted. "We are only saying this *could* have happened."

This was far removed from Stombaugh's earlier assertions, and from the prosecutors' inference that the pajama top folding experiment proved MacDonald murdered Colette.

Pleased with Stombaugh's admission, Segal attacked still another point. Because the ice pick blade was tapered, the width of a garment hole over a given wound would have to be compatible with the actual depth of that wound as indicated by the width of the blade at that depth. In other words, if the ice pick were thrust halfway into the chest, and therefore halfway into the fabric, the width of the fabric hole should be exactly the diameter of the blade at its halfway point. Stombaugh conceded that he also had ignored these measurements.

Related to this issue, Stombaugh had earlier told the jurors, confidently, that the width of some of the holes in the pajama top proved that the ice pick blade had punctured the fabric "up to the hilt." Since the blade was four and a half inches long, this would have resulted in deep wounds in Colette's body. But no deep ice pick wounds existed. The autopsy report, one of the documents that were released to Segal, said that sixteen of these puncture wounds were superficial—in other words, they did not penetrate muscle. The deepest wounds were no more than four centimeters, or about an inch and a half in depth. This was hardly "up to the hilt."[9] Knowing this, Segal asked, "Mr. Stombaugh, could you tell us which of the various holes here were the ones that went up to the hilt of the ice pick?"

Stombaugh replied that he could not remember which fabric holes were wide enough to have suggested that, and, again, he had failed to make any notes about it.

Still related to the problem of the depth of the wounds was Stombaugh's statement to the jury that the autopsy report said that some of the ice pick wounds in Colette's chest were "deep and penetrating." Segal knew that the autopsy report did not support this claim.

Referring to that autopsy report, Segal asked Stombaugh if he had ever read that the ice pick–like wounds in Mrs. MacDonald's body were superficial.

"No, sir."

"Did you ever read that any pathologist had ever measured the depth of any ice pick wounds in Mrs. MacDonald's body?"

"I don't recall it, sir."

"If I were to suggest to you that there is no evidence that any pathologist found any bruising—"

"Objection," Blackburn shouted.

"Sustained," Judge Dupree said.

As Segal had expected, the pajama top arguments so far had been complicated and confusing. Segal's next question was designed to simplify the concepts for the jury. He asked Stombaugh, "How many other combinations are there possible of fitting forty-eight holes into twenty-one?" Segal knew that if the garment could be arbitrarily folded in such a way that all forty-eight fabric holes were used up over twenty-one ice pick wounds, then the ability to fold the pajama top one way or another was no proof that Colette was stabbed through the garment, especially if directionality, depth of wounds, width of fabric holes, and photographic evidence were either ignored or violated by the scientist performing the demonstration.

"Sir," Stombaugh said, "I have no idea. All I'm saying is that we used up all forty-eight holes with twenty-one thrusts, and we're just saying that it can be done. We are not saying this actually took place. It could have taken place, and that's all this demonstration represents."

"You mean this is one way it could be done?"

"That is correct."

"And you agree that there are numerous other ways that it could be done?"

"I have no idea how many other combinations."

"Do you agree that there are other ways it can be done?"

"Yes sir."

"And you have never experimented or attempted to compute in any way the number of other possible combinations in which the same thing could be done?"

"No, sir."

That was what Segal had wanted. For a moment he believed he had won. And proving that the government's lead expert had, in effect, finessed the government's key exhibit would impeach the credibility of everything else the prosecution team would present. For even though the principle of broken-fiber directionality, a tapered blade, and the depth of wounds was complicated, Segal had just reduced the experiment to a principle the jurors could not fail to have understood—merely folding the garment one way among many, and admittedly not even the way the photographs had showed it, was not proof that MacDonald had stabbed his wife through the garment.

But the old FBI agent got some unexpected help. Before Stombaugh vacated the witness chair, a single question by Judge Dupree breathed new life into the momentarily discredited pajama top experiment. "Now, my question is simply this," the judge said, leaning toward Stombaugh. "Is there any way that you can turn it and put the holes in a different place and they will still line up or is there only one way if they are randomly spaced? That is a simple question."

It was not a simple question. Dupree didn't explain what he meant by "randomly spaced." Was he referring to an arrangement of fiber holes as already lined up by Stombaugh, or was he referring to making new "holes in a different place" on the garment? But Stombaugh, badly in need of help at the moment, apparently had no trouble with the concept. Only minutes earlier, while under fire, he had admitted there were indeed other ways the pajama top could be folded over the wounds, yet he now revived the prosecutors' earlier claims regarding the garment. "Oh, I see, sir," the beleaguered Stombaugh answered, ignoring his earlier admissions. "There would be only one way."

This exchange left the jury believing precisely what Segal's questions had just disproved, that the forty-eight holes in the top could only be lined up one way, Stombaugh's way, which was the unspoken, and unsupportable, purpose of the experiment from its beginning.

Segal, sick over the exchange, had told Judge Dupree, even before the experiment was presented to the jurors, that it was false science, and that he and Thornton feared that if it were allowed to be presented by a former director of a branch of the FBI lab, the jurors, unable to follow the complex issues involved, would think it must be good science. But Dupree had ruled he would let Murtagh and Stombaugh present it anyway, saying that the jurors could make up their own minds about it. Strangely, then, during a bench conference two weeks after Stombaugh's pajama top testimony, Judge Dupree rendered his own private opinion on the subject. He said that Stombaugh's offering "was a question of demonstrating that square pegs could indeed be made to fit into round holes which you could demonstrate here for everybody if," the judge added, "they are willing to believe it."[10]

But the jurors, of course, never heard that incredible bench conference statement. And they never saw the CID bench notes that would have challenged Stombaugh's experiment more strongly than could Segal and Thornton in the absence of documentation. What would the jury have seen had Segal been given a peek at the lab notes about the pajama top experiment?

In the Government Files

THE PAJAMA TOP FOLDING EXPERIMENT

FOIA documents finally tell the full story about that folding experiment. They prove that, in the summer of 1971, at the specific request of the CID, Stombaugh of the FBI lab had examined the pajama top to determine the directions in which the tiny, broken fibers were bent by the force of the ice pick as it was thrust through each of the fabric holes. Although the pajama top had been handled a great deal, Stombaugh and his assistant, Shirley Green, were still able at that time to discern the directionality of the ice pick thrusts through eleven of the holes.[11] Stombaugh dutifully reported these findings to the CID laboratory. Then, three months after receiving Stombaugh's data, Janice Glisson of the CID laboratory attempted to fold the garment so all its ice pick holes would align over the stab wounds in Colette's chest. After days of effort the attempt was abandoned; Glisson was unable to adjust the folds so that the thrust holes remained compatible with Stombaugh's findings of directionality of the tiny broken fibers.[12]

The failure of the pajama top folding experiment became a dormant issue until 1974 when Stombaugh and Green secretly tried it themselves at the FBI laboratory. They might have met with the frustrations the CID had experienced, but Stombaugh and Green simply ignored their own 1971 findings on broken-fiber directionality in the various layers of fabric holes, findings which earlier had foiled the CID's efforts.[13] Without these pesky lab standards to hinder them, Stombaugh and Green succeeded in folding the garment so that all forty-eight fabric holes lined up over the twenty-one ice pick wounds, as the prosecutors had requested.

Even though Stombaugh had studied broker-fiber directionality in this very garment, at trial he said he hadn't taken the issue into account in the folding experiment. But his own documents prove he *had* taken it into account. He had discovered the discrepancies in the directions of the broken fibers, wrote them in his notes, and then ignored them. It is interesting that in most government explanations of how MacDonald was convicted, this flawed experiment is cited as the leading indicator of MacDonald's guilt.

At Trial

THE ISSUE OF FIBER DIRECTIONALITY

Bernard Segal, of course, was unaware at trial of CID technician Glisson's earlier failed attempts at this pajama top folding experiment. During his cross-examination of FBI technician Shirley Green, he asked whether she had made use of the 1971 FBI findings concerning the fiber directionality of exit and entry holes.

"Yes, I believe I did," Green replied.

"And which ones are they?"

"I don't recall."

Segal asked, "Where are your notes in that regard?"

"I did not make any notes," Green said. "I just had the information at that time when I first did it, and they seemed consistent."[14]

"Seemed" apparently wasn't close enough according to the laboratory notes, for the tiny broken fibers in various layers of fabric over a given wound should all have been bent in the same direction. They were not. Dr. Thornton compared notes of the finished FBI experiment with notes of the directionality studies Stombaugh and Green had made in 1971. He discovered that in Green's folding experiment in 1974 she had actually reversed the directions of the broken fibers in six of the eleven holes in which she established directionality in 1971. This is a 55 percent error ratio and should have caused the experimenters to abandon that approach. It had stopped Glisson, yet Stombaugh and Murtagh presented the experiment to the jury as valid science.

THE MOCK FIGHT

If Segal had made any progress with the jurors, it was threatened by still another prosecution demonstration regarding the pajama top. MacDonald had said the puncture holes were made in the fabric when he used the pajama top, bound around his wrists, as a shield to keep from being stabbed by his assailants. To disprove this, prosecutors Brian Murtagh and Jim Blackburn performed their own lively and entertaining fight scene in the courtroom. Murtagh placed a similar pullover-type pajama top on his arms, binding his wrists with the garment the way MacDonald had claimed that his wrists were bound during the tussle with the intruders. Blackburn then played the part of an assailant wielding an ice pick. The lawyer raised the weapon overhead and began flailing downward into the fabric, repeatedly puncturing it as Murtagh moved the garment from side to side. This caused excitement and laughter in the courtroom, and the action inflicted a bleeding scratch on Murtagh's wrist.

But the mock fight wasn't for entertainment. After their demonstration, Murtagh and Blackburn showed the jurors that the holes in the fabric were ripped, not round and even as were the holes in MacDonald's pajama top. The prosecutors then asked the jurors a question. If MacDonald had used the fabric to fight off assailants' blades, as he claimed, why weren't the holes in his pajama top also ripped? The prosecutors suggested there were no rips there because the pajama top had been stationary when the ice pick penetrated the fabric. And it was stationary because it lay upon Colette's lifeless chest.

On this issue, MacDonald complained to Segal that the prosecutors' graphic courtroom demonstration was grossly unlike the fight he had lost to assailants in his living room. MacDonald insisted that Segal put on his own courtroom demonstration to show the jury that the prosecutors had presented a false picture of the fight, one that MacDonald had never described. He reminded Segal that he had told the investigators that he first thought the men were only punching him, not stabbing him, and now the government was ignoring this. Segal took his point well, for punching is not done overhand. It seemed to Segal and Thornton that the prosecutor's technique of striking downward in an overhanded manner was less intended to cause harm to a combat-trained Green Beret than to cause the fabric to rip.

Segal and Thornton agreed that this, like the pajama top folding experiment, was false science, but Segal left it up to MacDonald to explain the problem during his own testimony later in the trial. MacDonald tried, complaining while on the witness stand that the mock fight the prosecutors had performed for the jury was misleading. He told the jurors he had described the attackers striking at him with straight-in thrusts, which, interestingly, is the way all American military knife fighters are taught to fight, not overhanded in the manner in which Blackburn had flailed away with the weapon for the laughing jurors.

MacDonald also told the jury he had pushed the pajama top toward his attackers, a defensive move he said he had to use given his position on the sofa. This, he claimed, was entirely unlike Murtagh's side-to-side motion which caused the puncture holes to be ripped. In the end, however, it seems evident that the jurors believed the prosecutors on this issue, not the defendant.

THE STAB WOUND INTO MACDONALD'S CHEST

Still another government charge worried the defense team. The prosecution claimed that MacDonald's worst injury, the knife wound into his right lung, had not been inflicted by knife-wielding intruders. A doctor who had examined MacDonald in the hospital on the morning of the murders had told Colonel Rock that he didn't believe MacDonald could have stabbed himself in the lung in that particular location with any guarantee of survival. Now, however, that same man, Dr. Severt Jacobson, stated that MacDonald might have stabbed himself there with a good chance of success.

Dr. Jacobson had explained in 1970 that MacDonald could not have expected to control the depth of the wound due to the uncertain plasticity of the skin. When the skin finally gave way, Dr. Jacobson had said, it would be difficult to control the depth of the knife point, dangerous in an area so near the tip of the liver.

Again, a key element in the case had changed. When Fred Bost and I interviewed Dr. Jacobson in 1989, he told us that during the grand jury hearing prosecutor Victor Woerheide showed him their evidence and explained that the FBI laboratory analyses, including radiocarbon testing on some of the evidence, fully condemned MacDonald. Jacobson said he then believed he was testifying about a guilty man.[15]

With his opinion now in line with the prosecution's charges, Jacobson's medical opinion also seemed to have changed. He told the trial jurors that he thought MacDonald might have been able to control the depth of the knife thrust into his own chest. This statement was vastly different than his opinion given nine years earlier at the army hearing.

A PAJAMA FIBER AND A BLOODY HEAD HAIR

When Segal believed things could get no worse at trial, he learned that something else had changed. In a vial of debris collected from the bedspread in the master bedroom, Paul Stombaugh said he had found a bloody head hair of Colette MacDonald twisted around a fiber from MacDonald's pajamas. Like the pajama top folding experiment, this was silent testimony that a life-and-death struggle had taken place in the

MacDonald apartment, not with drug-crazed intruders, but between Colette MacDonald and her husband. On cross-exam, Segal could only attack the government's method and intention. He asked Stombaugh who had brought him this new evidence that the CID strangely hadn't found on the bedspread over nine years earlier. Stombaugh said that Murtagh had brought the vial to him, and that Stombaugh then had found the hair wrapped around the pajama fiber.

Segal's question had been tacit accusation that Murtagh may have tampered with the evidence, but the defense lawyer could not afford to press the matter. In the absence of laboratory notes to detail the various previous examinations of this evidence exhibit by the army, Segal had no way to fight this claim. He had heard of no report about a bloody hair entwined with a fiber prior to trial, but there was nothing he could do to combat it now.

In the Government Files

Comparative lab examinations by the CID and the FBI create serious problems for the government in the matter of Colette's bloody hair entwined around a pajama thread. Documents released long after trial show that, years before Paul Stombaugh told the trial jury about making this critical find amid the debris collected from the bedspread, the CID laboratory had examined this same debris, not once but three times, and had found nothing entwined.[16] Various CID laboratory notes and charts unavailable to Segal in 1979 now detail the history of that exhibit.

DEBRIS FROM THE BEDSPREAD

The debris from the bedspread was placed in a vial at the crime scene before it was delivered to the CID laboratory. Dillard Browning had inventoried the vial's contents on March 5, 1970. By March 10, Browning had separated the hairs in the debris and microscopically compared them to hairs of the dead victims. He determined that among the hairs found in the bedspread, a hair from *Kimberly*, not Colette, was bloodstained, and that it was the only bloodstained hair in the vial. And he had found no hair, neither Kim's nor Colette's, entwined around a pajama thread.

Later, during those first months after the murders, the CID laboratory technicians compiled two lists, one citing all the exhibits in which hairs from the victims were found, the other citing those exhibits which contained fibers matching those in Dr. MacDonald's pajama top. The first list specifically stated that none of Colette MacDonald's hairs found on the bedspread was bloodstained. Neither list mentioned a hair being found entwined with a fiber, a discovery that undoubtedly would have been used by the army prosecutors at the Article 32 hearing had they known about it.

Given the later discovery by Stombaugh of the entwined hair and fiber, one might conclude that Browning had simply erred in his examination and had missed this key evidence. But the records show that Browning had examined the exhibit yet another time six months later, again placing each item under the microscope. His findings remained constant. He found no bloody hair from Colette, and certainly no head hair entwined around a pajama fiber.

The lab notes force the question: How could this same vial with its oft-examined contents suddenly be found to hold such graphically damning evidence? Government documents divulge no answer either for such a change in contents, or about reasons why the change in findings was kept secret. Apparently no one but government representatives handled the exhibit.

In fact, rather than shipping it by registered mail, which was the normal method of transporting such things, Brian Murtagh himself had hand-carried this critically important vial from the CID evidence depository to the FBI laboratory on September 24, 1974. Nevertheless, like the brown hair in Colette's left hand, this evidence somehow had changed sometime between Browning's last look at it and Stombaugh's first.

One defense team researcher remarked that it was almost "too cute" in a grotesque way. For what more could the prosecutors desire than to find a victim's bloody head hair entwined forever with a fiber from her murderer's garment during a death struggle. It made for vivid testimony at trial, but as in other government claims, the jurors never learned the truth—that no such intertwined fiber was found when the evidence was first examined in 1970.

At Trial

The Ice Pick
The government prosecutors continued to present crime-scene evidence loaded with blame against MacDonald. He had continually claimed he

never owned an ice pick and didn't keep one in the house; therefore, he swore that the ice pick found in the backyard had to have been brought in by the intruders. But the prosecutors presented a former MacDonald neighbor and babysitter, Pam Kalin, and MacDonald's mother-in-law, Mildred Kassab, to say that they remembered seeing an ice pick in the home. Therefore, the prosecution claimed, MacDonald had lied.

But what do the FOIA releases offer in regard to the testimony about the suddenly revived memories of these two witnesses?

In the Government Files

THE ICE PICK

The government had introduced Pam Kalin and Mildred Kassab to establish the existence of the ice pick in the MacDonald household. But in the documented history of the case, neither government witness has been consistent on this issue, nor, when the facts are known, can either be regarded as an unimpeachable witness.

Mildred Kassab told the jury in 1979 that during her 1969 Christmas visit to the MacDonald home she had taken an ice pick from a kitchen drawer. Yet when Mrs. Kassab was first questioned on the subject by CID agents Ivory and Shaw during an interview on Long Island on March 19, 1970, Mildred told them she had never seen an ice pick in Colette's home. A careful reading of the CID's final report of March 1972 shows that, even though by this time Mrs. Kassab had turned against her son-in-law, she still had not recalled seeing an ice pick in the home. It wasn't until she was summoned as a witness before the grand jury, four years after the murders, that the memory seemed to occur.

The other witness to an ice pick in the home had experienced similar memory problems. At the time of the murders, Pamela Kalin was a sixteen-year-old girl who had lived next door to the MacDonalds and babysat for them on occasion. Shortly after the murders CID agents reported that this girl recognized the bent Geneva Forge knife, the knife found in the master bedroom, as being from the MacDonald kitchen.[17] But by the time the army Article 32 hearing began less than five months later,[18] the girl denied she had said that. CID agents had made her mother so angry by pressing the girl on the issue that the mother refused to allow her family to cooperate further with the investigators. As part of the army CID reinvestigation, on February 2, 1971, Pamela was reinterviewed in Heidelberg, Germany, by CID agent John Reynolds, and she insisted again that she did not recognize any of the weapons as being from the MacDonald home, not the club, not the ice pick, and not the knives.

But by the time the grand jury was convened, Pamela Kalin seemed ready to name a weapon she had seen in the home. She was brought to the witness stand on the morning of August 27, 1974, not to identify the Geneva Forge knife as MacDonald property, which was the original claim of the CID, and not to name the ice pick, but instead to name as MacDonald's property the Old Hickory knife which had been found in the backyard.[19]

Assistant prosecutor James "Jay" Stroud, assisting Victor Woerheide at the grand jury hearing, asked Pamela some questions about the club while she was under oath at the hearing. She said it wasn't familiar to her. He showed her the bent Geneva Forge knife in a plastic bag and asked her if she recognized it. She didn't. Neither did she recognize the ice pick, although she said the MacDonalds may have had one, but she didn't know where they kept it. Stroud then produced the final weapon, the Old Hickory knife. He asked the girl: "Can you recognize that knife?"

"I think," she replied.

"You think?"

All Stroud got from her was a nod. When the girl continued to deny a positive recognition of the knife, he became vexed. "When you and I were talking yesterday," he reminded her, "I believe—at least you gave me the impression—that you *did* recognize it, and that you felt like you recognized it from the MacDonald household. Is that not your recollection, or is it?"

"I'm not sure," Pamela Kalin replied. She indicated there were some ten different homes where she babysat, where she may have seen such a knife, but it was unclear where.

She was excused. However, when jury members reconvened that afternoon, they were surprised to find Pamela Kalin called to the witness stand for a second time.[20] Prosecutor Stroud put her at ease by reminding her that she had just reviewed some photographs with Brian Murtagh, then after a few minor questions, he said, "Now it is my understanding at this point that you have some further recollection which came to you today with regard to the ice pick which I earlier asked you about. Is that right?"

"Right," she said.

"Would you go ahead and state for the Grand Jury what that recollection is, please?"

After years of saying she could not remember anything about the weapons she'd been asked about, now, after a meeting with Brian Murtagh, Pamela Kalin had suddenly regained her memory. She said, "I remember using the ice pick that was on top of the refrigerator to get popsicles and ice cream out of the freezer, which was always very full, and I needed to break the ice away in order to get the popsicles out, or whatever." She said she had used the ice pick in the MacDonald home "twice that I remember," and that she had always found it on the top of the refrigerator. Her reborn memory after years of stating she knew nothing about the weapons helped indict MacDonald, and later was effectively used to help convict him.[21]

A Question about the Bedsheet

As Fred Bost and I reviewed the findings of Ellen Dannelly and the defense team, we learned that every key government presentation was challenged by facts discovered in the lab notes and other investigative reports.

For instance, prosecutor Murtagh had proposed to the jury that bloodstain patterns on Colette's pajamas got on the blue bedsheet when MacDonald supposedly used the sheet as a buffer to shield him from blood as he carried Colette's battered, unconscious body into the master bedroom. Indeed, the evidence made such an event seem possible, if not probable. But Shedlick found a witness who had seen something in the murder apartment only moments after the MPs arrived. It was a witness who, incredibly, lived in the same building as the MacDonalds, yet, contrary to all expectations, the man had never been questioned by the CID agents.

MacDonald's neighbor, Chaplain Kenneth Edwards, told defense investigator Ray Shedlick that he saw a bedsheet spread over Colette's bloody body when he entered the apartment early on the murder morning.[22] Shedlick's excitement over this find would continue till his dying day. He reasoned that the bloodstain patterns which had appeared so damning to the prosecutor might therefore have been placed on the sheet not while MacDonald allegedly carried Colette's body, *but when an unwitting MP stripped the sheet off the bed to cover Colette's partially nude chest.*

In support of their new theory, Ray Shedlick and Ellen Dannelly also learned that the lab notes indicate that *no blood of MacDonald's type was found on that blue sheet.* This fact held immense interest for them, for if MacDonald had carried his wife from Kristen's room to the master bedroom, as the government alleged, he would have been forced to move through Kristen's two-and-a-half-foot doorway and down the three-foot-wide hallway. Colette was pregnant and weighed 135 pounds. Shedlick believed it would have been impossible for MacDonald to carry her weight without holding her close to his own bloody body, thereby putting himself in contact with the sheet which covered her. By this time, in theory, according to the government's own account, Colette would have already wounded her husband in the stomach and at the left bicep. Yet when the bedsheet was carefully examined in the laboratory, not a speck of Type B blood, MacDonald's type, was found on it.[23] Shedlick asked: How could he have carried his wife in the sheet without, in some small measure, staining it with his own blood?

Although Chaplain Edwards had shared the same building as the MacDonald family, the government during twenty years and two separate investigations had never questioned him about what he'd seen. If Lieutenant Paulk is accurate about seeing the sheet and bedspread pushed to the bottom of the bed, and if Chaplain Edwards saw Colette covered by a sheet, then someone that morning, possibly one of the military policemen, took the "pushed down" bedding off the bed and used the sheet momentarily to cover the body.[24]

THE BEDSPREAD AND TWO FOOTPRINTS

Other things also challenge the government theory. Prosecutors claimed that MacDonald took the sheet and bedspread into Kristen's room for the purpose of transporting his wife's body. He supposedly used the bedspread to keep her blood off the floor. The government claimed he then inadvertently stepped on the blood-soaked bedspread and left two bloody footprints just inside Kristen's room as he was leaving. The blood type of the footprints was the same as that on the bedspread found crumpled in the master bedroom, Type A, Colette's blood type. This was the only physical evidence supporting the prosecution hypothesis.

From the long-withheld government files, it is now known that in November 1974 the FBI lab techs passed an intense light through the bedspread looking for impressions of MacDonald's feet. They realized that if MacDonald stepped on the bedspread while carrying his wife, their combined weight—about 310 pounds—would have exerted tremendous force. Fabric impression experts know this would have left an indelible signature—a thinner layer of blood where the pressure existed directly under the foot, a heavier crusting of blood surrounding the foot, where blood had been displaced outward. But, even with the strong light, the technicians could find not a single footprint in the bedspread.[25]

This failure by the FBI laboratory to validate the government theory was never made known to either the defense lawyers or the trial jury. It was among the secrets contained in the withheld documents, and the prosecutors continued to claim that MacDonald had so used the sheet and bedspread.

As Bost and I worked through the thousands of pages of previously withheld documents, we were struck by yet another problem with the government's footprint theory. Among the more graphic images which the trial prosecutors presented to the jurors was the idea that Jeffrey MacDonald supposedly left the two bloody footprints in Kristen's room as he carried away his bleeding and unconscious wife.[26] Segal and his experts thought it curious, however, that this allegation had MacDonald leaving only two footprints, one from each foot, and no more. Why wasn't there a following trail of bloody footprints through the hallway? The curiosity of MacDonald's attorneys was finally satisfied when they read FOIA reports on the issue years after trial. Those reports show that the CID had pursued the same question. According to a December 1971 CID report, William Ivory stated: "In addition to making visual searches for evidence, the entire house was searched with an ultra-violet light in an attempt to determine, if possible, whether or not the walls, floors, or ceilings had been recently wiped or washed to obliterate any evidence."[27] The investigators knew that ultraviolet light, commonly called "black light," will cause otherwise unseen blood particles to glow faintly.[28] Ivory ended his report with the words: "The test was negative."

This satisfied Bernard Segal's question whether a footprint trail had been made—it hadn't, but it didn't solve the mystery of how the two bloody footprints, clearly visible, came into existence. The defense attorneys knew from the various witness statements that those first minutes on the scene in the master bedroom while the MPs waited for an ambulance had been hectic ones. MacDonald had moved around quite a bit and had to be restrained. MacDonald's attorneys, however, didn't know until 1983 when they viewed an FOIA document that MacDonald at one point actually had gotten to his feet while struggling off the gurney.

Donald Kalin, MacDonald's neighbor, had told an FBI agent that he had entered MacDonald's residence with the first MPs through the front door, and had seen MacDonald standing in the master bedroom before he collapsed into the arms of two MPs. The FBI interview report thus established a possibility that MacDonald stepped in fresh blood of Colette's type in the bedroom just prior to his removal from the home.[29]

Then, while being wheeled out on the gurney, MacDonald again began to struggle. Mica and Tevere helped ambulance attendants get him onto the stretcher before rolling him feet first into the narrow hall. Multiple witnesses agree that as the stretcher moved through the hall, MacDonald grabbed the door jamb on the left, at Kimberly's room, and momentarily fought his way off the stretcher, shouting, "God damn MPs. Let me see my kids!"

After wrestling MacDonald back onto the gurney, the medics moved him along. However, this action in the cramped hallway became the focal point for a defense theory about the bloody footprints. Ray Shedlick recognized that the narrow width of the hall precluded MacDonald's getting off the gurney between it and a wall, so the detective reasoned that the distraught MacDonald must have slipped off the gurney, as witnesses observed, into one of the doorways. When he grabbed Kimberly's door jamb, he would have pulled himself around to face that door. If his feet and legs had swung off the gurney to the opposite side at that moment, his feet would have hit the floor in Kristen's room about at the point where the footprints actually were found, pointed toward the hall, just inside the door. Only five feet separate Kimberly's door jamb from the location of the footprints on the other side of the narrow hall. Since MacDonald is almost six feet tall, and since he would have been stretched at arm's length across the gurney, Shedlick believed that the mathematics as well as the geography supported his theory. Using an army quarters built to the exact specifications as the MacDonald apartment, Fred Bost demonstrated Ray Shedlick's theory to producer Allan Maraynes of the ABC television show 20/20.[30] He repeated the demonstration for attorney Donna Bruce Koch at the same locale.[31]

Shedlick's theory is further supported by laboratory evidence which became available under FOIA. A CID lab note made by Dillard Browning states that two fibers were recovered from one of the two bloody footprints in Kristen's room. The fibers did not match the bedspread upon which the government claimed MacDonald had stepped just prior to making the footprint; instead, the fibers matched a throw rug in the master bedroom, a rug where Donald Kalin had seen MacDonald standing only minutes before he was carried from the premises, a rug near the freshly shed blood of Colette MacDonald.[32]

And, finally, there was yet another reason to believe that the footprints had been freshly made just prior to the arrival of the CID investigators. Detective Robert Shaw is on record under oath as saying that when he arrived at 4:55 A.M. he noticed that the blood of the thin imprints was "glistening," still coagulating.[33] Thus, multiple events at the crime scene offered a possible explanation for two bloody footprints at the entrance to the baby's room, but like many other things that occurred during those first, crucial fifteen minutes, they were ignored in favor of the government's idea that MacDonald must have made those footprints while carrying his wife's body in the sheet.

James Blackburn

For more than two years, Fred Bost and I weighed the Shedlick-Dannelly findings and, going directly to the source material, we delved into the torturously detailed laboratory notes themselves. In our view, these badly copied pages of lab tech scrawl clearly supported each defense claim that evidence had been undisclosed. After our studies we believed that no government claim, which previously seemed to point to MacDonald's guilt, was left uncontradicted in the government's own long-secret records.

Fred and I wanted to talk with the prosecutors in late 1988 about the contents of the lab notes they had denied Segal at trial, but by this time Brian Murtagh was under siege by the media due to accusations brought against him by MacDonald's new lawyers, Harvey A. Silverglate and Alan Dershowitz, of Boston, and Murtagh was resisting comment to the media. By 1989 Silverglate was publicly saying that the "so-called evidence against MacDonald is a myth." Dershowitz told a nationwide television interviewer, "I believe that the government of the United States deliberately covered up evidence to convict Jeffrey MacDonald."

Murtagh was saying almost nothing, but considering the possibility of future litigation, we couldn't blame him for reserving comment, and, after all, it wasn't as if Murtagh had never spoken. We did have nearly twenty years of case documentation to represent the government's official point of view.

But I still wanted to talk with Murtagh's co-counsel, James Blackburn, who had since become a civil attorney in Raleigh.[34] First, I called Fred Bost at his home in North Carolina and asked him what he knew about Blackburn as a person. "You live there, Fred," I said. "What have you heard. Is this guy likely to open up if he learns that Murtagh held back information that affects the very claims Blackburn himself prosecuted MacDonald on?"

"From what I hear," Fred said, "he's highly respected, a family man, and, I think, a very religious man. I couldn't even guess what he would do when he learns, if he doesn't know already."

"But," I said, "if Murtagh kept anything back and it was now showing up in the lab notes, it should bother the hell out of Blackburn."

"I would think so, if he's a good guy."

From California, in February of 1989, I phoned Blackburn at his home in the Raleigh area. He wasn't in. I talked to one of his children whose manner seemed very warm and especially competent. So, he was a family man, and the Blackburns had cared enough about their children to teach them how to conduct themselves with a stranger on the telephone. I left word I'd call back. I did, and got Mrs. Blackburn. I told her I'd like to speak with her husband about the MacDonald case. She was as friendly as her child, as she told me, laughingly, that Jim was always eager to talk about the case.

I finally reached him, told him who I was, and that Fred Bost and I were writing a book. I asked him for an interview.

"First, answer one thing for me," Blackburn said. "Are you guys writing the book from the point of view of MacDonald being innocent or guilty?"

I told him we had found things which made us feel that MacDonald hadn't been given his fair day in court, and that we were leaning toward believing in his innocence. "At any rate," I assured him, "we're going to report what we've found, seen, and heard, and leave it at that."

"Not that it makes that much difference to me which way you go," he said. "So, sure, I'll talk with you." His manner had been warm, open, and friendly.

A couple of days later I flew across the country, and got a room near the Raleigh-Durham Airport. That night I phoned Prebble, my wife, and she told me Blackburn's secretary had called. She said, "Mr. Blackburn is canceling his appointment." Disappointed, I asked Prebble what the woman gave as a reason for the change. She had offered no reason.

I met Fred for breakfast, and told him what had happened. We decided to phone Blackburn and let him know we were already here. Maybe he would still see us.

He apologized for getting the message to my wife only after I'd gotten on the plane, but he said he was sorry, he just couldn't talk with us. He apologized again for our trouble, but said he'd "best not make any comments pending possible litigation."

I assured him that our research showed Brian Murtagh's name, not his, connected with documents involving items we had recently seen in the long-withheld lab notes, and that Fred and I thought that Blackburn probably hadn't even known about problems with some of the evidence.

He said he couldn't say anything about that.

I asked him if he had been aware, back during the 1979 trial, of the evidence the defense team had discovered only post-trial in the handwritten notes, evidence that hadn't been turned over to the defense.

He said, still in a kindly manner, that he couldn't comment.

I asked him whether he would have turned the evidence over to the defense if he *had* been aware of it. In a voice now noticeably cautious, Blackburn said he had "turned over everything the defense team was entitled to."

"Then you didn't know about the information now in question?" I asked.

"I'm not saying anything," he said, "and I didn't say I didn't know. I didn't say that. I didn't say anything. You're making a jump there."

He was correct. I had indeed made a jump to see if he'd jump with me, and he hadn't taken the bait. But I thought I had hit a nerve, so I tried once more, suggesting that he let us visit him and at least show him the lab notes and other newly discovered information that Murtagh had denied Segal at trial. Then Blackburn would know whether Murtagh had held any of this information back from him, too. I wanted to watch Blackburn's face as he read the laboratory notes that were in variance to items which he and Murtagh presented at trial.

But, again, the man who had been so eager to condemn MacDonald as a liar was hesitant to discuss the truthfulness of the prosecution. He signed off cordially and hung up.

I left the conversation thinking that Blackburn was probably a good man who had been kept unaware of the explosive laboratory information. I felt sure he would look into the situation and demand to see the lab notes themselves. Either way, as I mentioned to Fred, this former prosecutor would eventually have to take a side. Fred agreed, adding that Black-burn's position was hardly envious, a case of being damned if you do and damned if you don't.

"Things do not lie."

Throughout the trial James Blackburn repeatedly told the jurors, "Things do not lie." Yet, in the MacDonald case, the "things" didn't speak for themselves.

Stombaugh had performed the pajama top folding experiment only after discarding the inhibiting scientific studies he himself had made.

The government offered the idea that MacDonald had carried Colette wrapped in the blue bedsheet, in spite of the lack of MacDonald's blood on the sheet, and without the evidence presented by Chaplain Edwards, who had seen Colette covered by the sheet.

The government had pressed the theory that the pajama top had been torn after Colette's blood had gotten on it, saying that it proved MacDonald had lied, but they had done this without revealing that the CID lab had found otherwise, and without considering that Stombaugh himself couldn't even see the bloodstains supposedly continuing across the fabric on either side of the rip.

The government claimed that the footprints in Kristen's doorway prove MacDonald carried Colette's bleeding and unconscious body to the master bedroom, but they didn't reveal their own unsuccessful search for the necessary trail of such footprints, and they ignored eyewitness accounts that MacDonald had gotten off the gurney with bare, bloody feet at the baby's room where those footprints had been found. The government's theory depended upon MacDonald stepping on the blood-soaked bedspread, but the government's experts didn't reveal that they had searched for, and failed to find, footprint impressions in the bedspread. In fact, they failed to find any evidence that the bedspread had ever been in the baby's room.

The government claimed that pajama fibers in the children's bedrooms proved MacDonald lied about when he took off his ripped pajama top, but they ignored that the bottoms were ripped, too, and they omitted their knowledge that a pile of blue fibers had disappeared from the hallway where MacDonald said he had fallen unconscious, with the ripped pajama top still bound around his wrists.

The government brought forth a doctor who said MacDonald could have stabbed himself in the chest with good chance of survival, without revealing that that same doctor had said otherwise in the Article 32 hearing, and without revealing that they had, secretly, convinced that doctor of MacDonald's guilt pre-trial by sharing with him their view of the forensic material.

And, to preface all these claims of MacDonald's culpability, they posited a well-protected crime scene that ostensibly contained no proof of intruders, yet they held back knowledge of a lost piece of skin[35-38] on Colette's fingernail, a bloody syringe, blond wig hairs, and many other items. They didn't account for the phones and baby bottle having been wiped *after* the MPs arrived. The documents that should have spoken about these things remained hidden, and therefore mute, while the government prosecutors thundered about a case which Bernard Segal, and even the army CID lab people, had never seen before. As the trial went on, other items would continue to damn MacDonald, and each claim would send Bost and me, years later, to compare the government's statements with their own secret documents.

■

Bernard Segal faced the grim prospect of failure at trial. He feared that if the jurors had actually entertained a presumption of MacDonald's innocence pre-trial, it was now being gnawed away by the government claims. Segal knew that the jurors faced a dilemma. Who was lying, the government or MacDonald? The United States government and the revered FBI laboratory insisted the liar was MacDonald, but all Segal theoretically needed to do, of course, was to introduce an element of doubt in the jurors' minds. To that end he sought to introduce Helena Stoeckley and witnesses who had heard her confessions.

7

Helena Stoeckley
at Trial

Eight years after her CID polygraph indicated deception regarding the night of the murders, Helena Stoeckley was located by the FBI during the trial proceedings, at Segal's request and upon Judge Dupree's order. The agents brought her from South Carolina to Raleigh and billeted her in jail as a material witness. Gathered around a table in a meeting room of the courthouse during a recess in the trial, Segal and his team asked her questions, and showed her photographs of the interior of the MacDonald apartment and the neighborhood surrounding it. But contrary to what she had told others, she now refused to admit any knowledge of the murders.

Helena had just turned twenty-seven. She was a slightly plump and plain, brown-haired woman with expressive, even coquettish eyes. And, in Segal's view, she was maddeningly stubborn. The best he could get out of her was a half-hearted admission that she "might" remember something from the photos of the neighborhood and the interior of the murder apartment.

That wasn't enough, but Segal had planned for her reticence. Prior to the trial he had located six witnesses who, upon her refusal to talk, were ready to tell the jurors that she had admitted to them her actual presence in the MacDonald apartment on the murder morning. William Posey, Stoeckley's neighbor in Fayetteville, had elicited self-incriminating admissions from her.

Twice-decorated narcotics detective Prince Everett Beasley, for whom Stoeckley had worked as an informant on fellow drug users in Fayetteville, was prepared to tell what he had learned from Stoeckley the night after the murders. Detective James Gaddis, of Nashville, had worked in undercover sting operations against dirty cops for internal affairs. Stoeckley, working as his informant in some of his operations, had admitted to him that she had been in the MacDonald home during the murders. Still another law enforcement officer was Robert Brisentine, Jr., the CID agent who had polygraphed and interviewed Stoeckley in 1971. Agent Brisentine believed Stoeckley may have been in the murder apartment that night. He also confirmed to Segal that her polygraph had indicated deception when she said she wasn't there. Brisentine was now prepared to tell a jury what he knew.

Segal's investigators also had found two of Helena's former Nashville neighbors, Charles "Red" Underhill and Jane Zillioux, in whose separate presence Stoeckley had wept uncontrollably and talked about the murder of babies, and about having blood on her hands.

Strangely, except for her former neighbor, William Posey, all of these witnesses were at the time of trial, or had been in the past, law enforcement officers or had worked in some capacity of law enforcement. And these six witnesses had come to Raleigh to tell the judge and jury what they knew about Stoeckley's admissions of guilt in the MacDonald case.

During breaks in her pre-appearance interview with Segal and his lawyers, Stoeckley talked with her friends. And, again, outside of Segal's hearing, she told them about that murder morning. Red Underhill, Prince Beasley, and Jane Zillioux all said that she again admitted to them that she remembered being in the murder apartment. Segal's pictures of the MacDonald living room, she said, brought back memories of her standing over a body while holding a candle. She said that when she ran out of the MacDonald house during the mayhem she stood outside and stared at her bloody hands. She said she was the one the MP saw standing on the corner of Honeycutt and Lucas shortly after the murders. And she told her friends again that she knew who had committed the murders.

But Red Underhill cautioned Segal, informing him that Stoeckley had no intention of testifying in MacDonald's favor. According to Underhill, who was a retired police officer, Helena told him that she would simply step into the courtroom, act "spacey," say she didn't remember anything, and walk out a free woman, "laughing all the way home."[1]

Segal still intended to put her on the stand, but if he had known Helena

Stoeckley more intimately, and if he had known the world she came from, he might have understood Red Underhill's cautions better.

In the Government Files

Long-withheld records now show that on October 31, 1978, two days after North Carolina newspapers reported that the Supreme Court had cleared the way for the MacDonald trial, Helena Stoeckley telephoned an FBI agent in Raleigh and told him she had been involved with the MacDonald killings. She said she wanted to clear the record. The agent sent a report to his boss in Charlotte on November 3, 1978, saying, "She stated she is now under treatment for drug abuse and wants to get everything off her chest and desires to talk with an agent. She appeared to be under the influence of either drugs or alcohol during this telephone call and she provided no additional information."[2]

Hospital records, however, challenge the agent's guess that Helena Stoeckley was under the influence of drugs on the date of the phone call to the FBI. She turned herself in for psychiatric treatment at Dorothea Dix Hospital in Raleigh two days after that call. Her admission record has her telling her doctors, "I have been trying to kill myself." Yet, she wasn't on drugs. The record states, "On admission the patient was alert, neatly dressed and cooperative. Her mood was depressed and her affect was blunted. [Her] thoughts showed no loose associations or delusions. She showed no blocking. She admitted to suicidal ideations without a definite plan. . . . Immediate, remote and recent memory were intact." The report also said, "She was placed on suicidal precautions." The discharge summary, signed a month later, on December 1, 1978, stated, "The patient showed no signs of drug withdrawal on admission."[3]

On previous occasions Stoeckley had said she would name the real killers provided she herself was given immunity to any charges. With this pre-trial telephone confession to the FBI, she finally had reached an agency that could arrange such immunity for a civilian, but it is not known whether such immunity ever was discussed at the Bureau. The knowledge of this phone call was never revealed to the court or to the defense by the prosecution. In fact, the record of the phoned confession to the FBI did not surface until May 1990, more than eleven years after it happened, and only after MacDonald's attorneys applied pressure via the Freedom of Information Act. Although the last paragraph of the November 3,

1978, FBI report said that a special agent in Fayetteville would interview Stoeckley as a result of her telephone call, no written record of that interview has yet surfaced. Specific requests through the Freedom of Information Act for the results of that promised FBI interview have gone for naught.

At Trial

After the defense team failed to elicit anything helpful from Helena Stoeckley's pre-testimony interview during the trial in Raleigh, detective Prince Beasley spoke to her in the courthouse hallway. Beasley approached her because he believed Segal had handled Stoeckley "all wrong. You could never push her," Beasley said. "Not a bit. You had to talk nicely to her and get her to come along; but Segal pushed her and she got her back up." Beasley talked with her a little bit about old times, then he asked her to tell what she knew.

According to Beasley, she now shrugged off his pleas and asked, "Why should I stick my neck out for MacDonald?"

"Because he's innocent," Beasley said, "and you know it." He reminded her that, due to a change in the death penalty laws, the federal statute of limitations had expired for her. "They couldn't prosecute you, anyway."

"I know they can't," she said, "but my friends can." Beasley believed she was referring to, and was genuinely afraid of, someone from her former drug crowd.

Before he placed Stoeckley on the stand, Segal had set the stage by bringing on James Milne. This MacDonald neighbor told the trial jurors that he had heard voices behind his house on the night of the killings, at about midnight. Concerned because his car had been broken into recently, he left the model airplane he was working on and went to the back door. About thirty-five feet away he saw three figures, two men and a woman, dressed in white sheets. They each carried lighted candles which they shielded with their hands, and they chanted in weird, singsong voices. The woman had light brown or blond hair. They walked away in the direction of the MacDonald house across the street.[4]

Having elicited Milne's vivid preparatory testimony, Segal called Stoeckley to the witness stand on August 17. Now, however, Segal says she wasn't the same Stoeckley he had talked to just the day before. She entered the courtroom slowly, with a blank expression on her face. She raised her hand as if in a dream, or as if on drugs, and repeated the oath to tell the truth. Helena spoke softly, almost inaudibly. In response to Segal's opening questions, she said she had graduated high school two years early, at age fifteen.[5] She said she attended Aquinas Junior College in 1971 and 1972, taking a course in police science. After seven months she dropped out with "drug problems." In 1974 she took a course for surgical operating room technicians, but after six months she left that, too. She said that in 1975 she completed a one-year nursing course, but never took her nursing boards.

When Segal showed her a picture of the MacDonald neighborhood, she said she did recognize Castle Drive on Fort Bragg. She soon admitted she used the word "pig" often and the word "acid" pretty often. And, yes, she was aware of who Charles Manson was.

Segal then asked her about witchcraft. She said she was "interested in it," and owned a two-volume set of books on the subject.[6] She said, "A lot of the rituals involved killing the animals and using their blood."

"What animal," Segal asked her, "was most commonly used?"

"A cat," she said, very softly.

"Beg your pardon?"

"A cat."

"Cat? Was there some special relationship that you believed between cats and witchcraft?"

"A cat is generally the familiar in witchcraft," she said. "Its blood could be sprinkled on a person or a thing, anything."

Segal had no doubt that the testimony of James Milne, about three robed figures carrying candles, was still on the jurors' minds. So Segal asked her about candles. Candles, she told him, were used in rituals usually to signify death or growing old. "It's a belief that the Devil is afraid of any kind of artificial light."

Stoeckley told him that on the way to a ritual a high priestess might carry a lit candle.

Having established that Stoeckley had been involved in ritualistic animal sacrifice, and that she had a special affinity for candles, Segal now asked her what she was doing late on February 16, in the hours before the murders. She said that the last thing she remembered was standing in her driveway talking with her friend, Greg, who had given her mescaline. She said her friends were painting her apartment when she returned at about 4:30 or 5 A.M. She was a passenger in a car that dropped her off. She could not recollect where she was between midnight and being dropped off the next morning.

"Who was in the car, Ms. Stoeckley?"

"I can't remember their names. Just some soldiers from Fort Bragg. Two or three—I don't know."

"Do you know their race?"

"Not for sure, no."

She admitted she talked with her neighbor, Bill Posey, about the MacDonald murders about a week or a week and a half after the murders. She said Posey seemed to be trying to put her on the spot so she told him to tell his wife to keep her door locked.

"May I ask," Segal said, "do you recall talking about the MacDonald murders before this remark was made?"

"Objection," Blackburn said.

"Sustained," said Dupree.

Segal tried again. "Did any of those conversations involve the subject of the MacDonald murders?"

"Objection," Blackburn said. This time Dupree allowed the question.

"Did they?"

"Yes, sir."

But Stoeckley couldn't remember what she told Posey except that she didn't know where she was that night. She remembered talking with Jane Zillioux, but didn't remember what she had told her. She remembered talking with Red Underhill, but could not recall what she said to him. She remembered talking with Jim Gaddis, the Nashville police detective for whom she had been an important internal affairs informant, but could not remember "specifically" what was said. She remembered talking with CID agent Robert Brisentine, but couldn't remember what was said. She remembered talking with Beasley and considered him "a very good friend," but couldn't recall what she had said to him regarding the Mac-Donald murders.

When Segal pressed her further, she admitted that she had owned a floppy hat in 1970, and had worn a blond wig, shoulder length. She had two pair of boots in 1970, one white and one brown pair, and she was about 115 pounds at the time of the murders. When shown the picture taken of her on August 10, during the Article 32 investigation, the one that showed her as much heavier (the same one MacDonald had been shown at the army hearing), she said that at that time she had been on "the usual heroin and barbiturates."

She said she had burned the wig because "it connected me with the murder." She also said she had broken the heel on the boots and threw them away. Segal showed her the same picture of the MacDonald living room he had shown her during his pre-testimony interview of her. On the day of that interview, the day before her appearance at trial, she had told some of her friends, who were in Raleigh to testify about her earlier confessions, that she remembered standing over a man's body in the room depicted in that photograph. Those friends told Segal that she had just admitted again that she was in the murder apartment. But now, from the witness stand, Stoeckley said that she had no reason to believe that she had ever been there.

Segal approached the bench and petitioned Judge Dupree to allow him to further examine Helena as a hostile witness, which would give him the right to vigorously cross-examine her. The lawyer told Dupree that Helena had told her friends she remembered trying to ride the rocking horse in the child's bedroom. Segal informed Judge Dupree that she had remembered standing outside the MacDonald house, looking at her hands, saying, "My God, the blood. Oh my God, the blood!"

Dupree allowed Segal to question her as a hostile witness, but when Segal resumed his questioning, she again denied remembering anything. Segal reminded her that her friend Jane Zillioux had been present during her confession just the day before. Then Helena admitted she might have said something about the rocking horse being broken, but she stated that she never said that she "used or touched" the horse. Contrary to what she had told her friends the day before, she now denied that she remembered holding a candle over a body in the house. Again, when pressed, she relented only slightly, and said, "It was only like in a dream or something like that."

She did remember standing the funeral wreaths along her fence the day of the MacDonald family funerals at Fort Bragg, and she remembered that she had worn black that day.

Segal asked her about violence in her group, but Blackburn objected, saying, "There is no connection between Helena and the crime except that she doesn't know where she was."

Under Blackburn's friendly cross-examination, Helena said that she sometimes went back to Castle Drive, "Just to see if anything looked familiar."

"Did it?"

"No."

She told Blackburn there was no connection between the funeral wreaths and the MacDonald funerals. Blackburn asked her if, because of all the police interviews, she'd begun "to worry yourself about your involvement in this killing?"

"Yes sir," she said.

Blackburn asked if it was uncommon for her to be out all night. She replied that it happened all the time.

"Isn't it true that you might have been at Dunkin' Donuts that morning?"

Stoeckley had said numerous times from the stand that she didn't remember where she was, yet now, offered an alibi by the prosecutor, she said, "That is where I was coming from at that time."

Helena stepped down from the stand that Friday morning having admitted no direct involvement in the MacDonald murders. She was freed from her jail cell, and Segal got her a motel room in town. There was still hope that she would break, Segal believed, perhaps when her friends testified about her confessions. Back at trial early that afternoon, Segal told Judge Dupree he wanted to offer the testimony of those friends. His plan was simple. The judge and the jurors had heard Stoeckley talk about candles and cats and the devil and rituals. "Now," Segal told MacDonald, "we'll let the friends reveal what Stoeckley had said to them about being in the murder apartment."

Segal planned to introduce the six witnesses, all of whom were prepared to inform the jury that, according to Stoeckley's own words, she had been in the MacDonald home on the murder morning. Each of these witnesses thought Stoeckley seemed tormented by the murders. Segal's reasoning was evident; the prosecutors had no motive for MacDonald to have murdered his family. And Segal believed he had raised enough questions about Stombaugh's forensic methods, however complicated, to force the jury now to consider any evidence that someone else, not MacDonald, had committed the murders. If, that is, he could only get those witnesses to say that Stoeckley had confessed to being in the home during the murders.

But when Segal called the first of those witnesses, Brian Murtagh rose up to register a resounding, and historic, objection. Once again, Segal found himself in a war with Murtagh. As with the Rock report and the physical evidence, Segal wanted full disclosure of this potentially explosive issue. Murtagh did not.

The Stoeckley witnesses would only relate "hearsay evidence," Murtagh complained, and Judge Dupree should disallow them all. Segal argued that under certain conditions the federal rule does, in fact, allow hearsay testimony about someone who has been heard to say he has committed crimes which could cause him to be prosecuted.[7]

Segal's hearsay argument invoked the classic tenets of hearsay law: Since people generally do not make self-incriminating statements without good reason, the law allows that such statements may be examined in open court if they cast suspicion toward the person who made the statement, and away from the defendant on trial. Another requirement of this rule is that the maker of the original statement be unavailable, and, as Segal pointed out, a legal definition of "unavailable" is lack of memory about the event or time of the event in question.

Helena Stoeckley's statements about witnessing the murders were clearly self-incriminating, and most certainly did cast suspicion upon her and her friends. And, Segal argued, since Stoeckley had claimed to possess no memory of the specific few hours in question, this made her legally "unavailable." He said that, by law, the hearsay witnesses were admissible.

Segal thought he was on firm ground, especially in a triple homicide with nothing but circumstantial evidence against his client. But Judge Dupree wanted to hear for himself what these witnesses would say, before he decided to let the jurors hear them. Dupree excused the jury and the witnesses were brought in, one by one, to be heard out of the presence of the jury. Such a preliminary procedure to determine competency is called "voir dire" testimony.

Prince Beasley told the judge that he had waited for Stoeckley and her friends at her apartment early the morning after the crimes. When they arrived, he said, Helena had revealed to Beasley that she might have been there. She told Beasley, "In my mind I saw this thing happen."

William Posey told Judge Dupree that Stoeckley indicated to him that "although she did not kill anyone herself, she held a light" while the crime was in progress. She said she saw "a hobby horse thing" which was broken, in the MacDonald home. Posey also said that Stoeckley told him that she thought she had been seen by a policeman while she was standing on Honeycutt Road on the morning of the crimes.

Jane Zillioux told the judge that Stoeckley had said that she couldn't return to Fayetteville because she was involved in the killing of a woman and two children. Helena talked to Zillioux of "So much blood. I couldn't see or think of anything except blood. . . ."

Charles "Red" Underhill said that while emotionally distressed, agitated, and crying deeply, Helena once told him that "(t)hey killed her and the two children. . . . They killed the children and her."

Nashville police officer James Gaddis informed Dupree that Stoeckley was his chief informant in an important internal affairs case that occurred after the MacDonald murders. Helena had told Gaddis she had been present during the murders, and that she knew who was involved. She said that one of the individuals drove a blue Ford Mustang. Judge Dupree asked Gaddis, "On the basis of what this girl told you, had these murders happened in Nashville, would you have issued or signed a warrant for her?"

"I'm not sure, sir. I have a feeling I would have tried to have her indicted." Gaddis paused, then said, "I would have investigated further, and I would have indicted her; yes, sir." This, from a law enforcement officer who had known her and had worked with her, was precisely the kind of testimony that Segal wanted the jurors to hear.

Next he called army CID polygrapher Robert Brisentine, who said that she confessed to him that she had been present during the murders, but said that she was not guilty of participating herself. Brisentine said that she talked about the amount of blood on the bed; and she further stated that the hippie element was angry with MacDonald because he wouldn't treat them with methadone. He said that "since the deaths of Mrs. MacDonald and her children, Stoeckley has suffered nightmares. Due to frightening dreams she is afraid to sleep."

Brisentine also told Judge Dupree that Helena claimed to know "the identity of the persons who killed Mrs. MacDonald and her children. That if the army would give her immunity from prosecution, she would furnish the identity of those offenders who committed the murder and explain the circumstances surrounding the homicides."

He said that she "further explained that it had been drizzling rain during the night, but that it did not start to rain hard until after the homicides." Brisentine, who had been intrigued by this admission from one who had claimed to have no memory of the time in question, said he asked her how she could possibly know the heavy rain didn't start till later unless she had been there. "Then Stoeckley said, 'I've already said too much.'"

Judge Dupree, with the jury still out of the room, asked Brisentine if Helena honestly believed these things were true. Brisentine, who had polygraphed Stoeckley in conjunction with his interview, obviously based his personal opinion on both the prior conversations and the machine results. Although at the time of the polygraph interview she was telling him she had *not* been in the MacDonald home, Brisentine thought the test results indicated that she truly believed the opposite.

Judge Dupree recessed court that Friday afternoon without revealing whether he would allow the Stoeckley witnesses to tell the jurors what they knew. This pending decision created one of the most tension-filled periods the defense team had yet experienced. And during that electric weekend, bizarre incidents continued to highlight Helena Stoeckley.

According to witnesses at the hotel where Segal had placed Stoeckley, her fiancé, Ernest Davis, had argued with her about her admissions to her friends, people who were now Segal's witnesses. When Davis and Stoeckley were in the hotel swimming pool, the argument became so heated he held her head underwater, causing such a disturbance that the hotel manager asked her to leave.

Segal moved her to the Hilton Hotel and assigned Wendy Rouder, one of Segal's assistants, to stay with her for the rest of that night. Helena also requested that her friend Red Underhill take a room next door to hers because Davis's violence scared her, Underhill said. She wasn't afraid only of Ernie Davis. She told him that after she testified, if she implicated anyone in the murders, her life wouldn't be "worth a nickel on the streets."

Segal offered to pay for Davis's trip to go back home and Davis accepted, but before leaving Raleigh he visited Helena one more time. Red Underhill said he was buying a soft drink from a machine in the hotel hallway when Ernie Davis ran out of Helena's room angrily complaining that she was insisting on "doing something." Underhill hurried into her room to find Helena bleeding from her nose. She told him she had run into the bathroom door. Segal would always wonder whether the "something" Helena had planned to do was finally to come clean about the murders of the MacDonald family.

Underhill took her to a local hospital for treatment for a broken nose. Even at the hospital, Helena, who had just denied under oath that she was involved in the murders, made a self-incriminating statement to still another person that placed her in the murder apartment. Lynne Markstein, who had just been in a traffic accident, was sitting in the X-ray waiting room when a girl began talking to her. The girl told Markstein her name was Helena Stoeckley and she was in town to testify at the MacDonald murder trial. According to Markstein, Helena told her that she was at the MacDonald house during the murders and she remembered looking down and seeing the bloody child in the "crib." She said there was a lot of blood and that it was horrible. Markstein says that Stoeckley then told her, "Can you imagine someone like me doing that to those babies?" Markstein especially remembered that Helena's hands were quite animated while she talked about the baby. Helena reportedly told her that she had been on drugs at the time of the murders and at first had difficulty remembering, but now she did remember it.[8]

Segal wondered whether Stoeckley, fearful of going on the stand and confessing directly, was actually trying to get others to do her confessing for her? Nevertheless, the attorney believed this last incident was something Judge Dupree should know. Then surely, Judge Dupree would believe that Stoeckley was serious about having seen something on the murder night and he would allow the jurors to weigh the confessions for themselves. Segal hoped that MacDonald's sighting, Mica's sighting, Milne's sighting, and Stoeckley's floppy hat, blond wig, boots, and the racial mix of her group of drug-dealing friends might cause the jurors to doubt the government claims against Segal's client.

When court reconvened the next Monday morning, an encouraged Segal informed Judge Dupree of the curious incidents involving Stoeckley over the weekend. And the judge, again out of the hearing of the jury, listened to defense team attorney Wendy Rouder, who had spent the night with Helena in her hotel after her altercation with Ernest Davis. Rouder told Judge Dupree that Helena had continued to talk about the murders outside the courtroom. She had "a memory" of "standing at the couch holding a candle. . . ." Rouder explained that she asked Helena if she ever felt guilt. Helena had replied that this is why she takes "all those damn drugs." Asked why she wouldn't state her recollections in court, Helena answered, "I can't with those damn prosecutors sitting there."

Segal believed that the conditions of the Stoeckley issue completely satisfied the legal obligations for hearsay testimony. Even after Stoeckley, on the stand, had claimed no memory of the murder morning, she had within two days confessed to two more people. Segal thought Judge Dupree would now have to let the jurors hear this testimony about her confessions. Segal believed he had put together the key to winning his case.

But, again, Brian Murtagh had other ideas. Murtagh, still outside of the jurors' hearing, stood up to argue that Stoeckley's statements to these people were nothing but the product of a drug-stimulated imagination. He insisted that "the statements should not be admitted unless there are corroborative circumstances which clearly indicate the trustworthiness of the statement."[9] And he and Blackburn had earlier insisted that no such forensic corroboration of intruders had been presented. Indeed, based upon the crime-scene evidence that the army and the prosecutors had allowed to surface, Judge Dupree had little reason to believe that the investigators had found anything in the apartment to corroborate either MacDonald's story or Stoeckley's self-damning confessions to her friends. There were, of course, many such things.

In the Government Files

There were the three wax drippings at key locations in the murder house, and James Milne's testimony that he had seen three figures carrying candles and moving toward the MacDonald home, and there was Stoeckley's own testimony that she and her friends used the blood of sacrificed cats, and that they used candles in ceremonies on the way to initiations, and that she had gotten rid of the floppy hat because it tied her to the murders. And there was Mica's testimony that just after MacDonald's telephone call for help he saw a woman in a floppy hat not far from the murder site; and there was Beasley's testimony that Helena Stoeckley traveled with a black man wearing a field jacket, another parallel in the Stoeckley group to MacDonald's description of one of the intruders.

With the passage of time it was learned that Murtagh also failed to reveal other things, physical items that MacDonald's attorneys now say logically point toward Helena Stoeckley and corroborate her many confessions.

Back in 1971, on March 9, CID agent Peter Kearns had made a request to the CID laboratory to reexamine certain items of evidence. These included hairs collected from an unidentified clear-handled hairbrush found on a stool within a few feet of the place where MacDonald said he saw the blond woman in his living room. In this brush, Janice Glisson found synthetic blond hairs up to twenty-two inches in length.

The subsequent CID laboratory report, which was published on April 20, 1971, strangely failed to mention the blond wig hairs found in the brush, even though it already had been established at the 1970 army hearing by William Ivory himself that Helena Stoeckley owned and had worn a blond wig. When the wig fibers were discovered in withheld lab notes many years after the trial, MacDonald attorney Harvey Silverglate substantiated the pre-trial fears which had been repeatedly and vehemently voiced to the judge by Segal. The lab notes did hold things that had been kept off the typed notes, and the defense lawyers believed that these things went directly to the heart of the case.

Instead of revealing pertinent information that possible wig hairs had been found in the home, the 1971 CID laboratory report, in contrast to the lab notes, stated only that hairs found in the brush were "similar" to the blond hairs found in Colette's right hand, hairs that had been matched to her own natural hairs.[10] Defense lawyers who studied the official typed laboratory reports before and during trial were led to believe, by the report's wording, that nothing significant was found in the brush, and that all of the hairs found there belonged to Colette MacDonald. Absent from the official reports, but not from the withheld lab notes, was the mention of *synthetic blond hairs,* hairs that could reasonably be from a blond wig. And twenty-two-inch blond hairs matched MacDonald's description of the intruder he said he saw.

Could Glisson have been mistaken about her initial analysis of the synthetic hair? The documents themselves answer that question. On May 6, 1971, Kearns forwarded samples of Helena Stoeckley's real hair to the CID laboratory for comparison. Janice Glisson reinventoried all the hairs found in the murder apartment, and she *again* identified synthetic blond hair taken from that brush. The official laboratory report issued on May 25, 1971, revealed an attempt to compare the various unknown hairs in the case with natural hairs taken from Helena Stoeckley, but again, in this latest report, Glisson and the CID failed to disclose the now fully confirmed existence of the blond synthetic hairs. Like the foreign hair in Colette's hand, this knowledge, too, could have been used by Segal at trial to claim the presence of intruders.

In years to follow, the prosecution would belittle the defense's discovery of these artificial blond hairs in the brush, claiming that such an intruder would not use a hairbrush. But at the 1979 trial, long before the defense knew of the artificial hairs, defense witness Jane Zillioux told of remarks made to her by Helena Stoeckley concerning the night of the murders, including Helena's stated fear that her wig would be ruined by the rain.[11]

THE MYSTERY HAIR IN COLETTE'S HAND

Something else was held back at trial, something which, by itself, might have cleared Jeffrey MacDonald from the very first, and something which, if known, might have convinced Dupree to allow the Stoeckley witnesses to tell about her confessions. At trial Stombaugh told the jurors that the unidentified hair found clutched in Colette's left hand was simply too small to test. This was the hair that had caused such a ruckus during the army hearing. But was it true that the hair was unfit for comparison purposes, as Stombaugh maintained?

Army documents show that during the early CID investigation Janice Glisson compared this mystery hair to at least nine persons without finding a source. It remained a foreign hair. The official report of the test of that hair against the hair samples taken from all points of MacDonald's head and body had been kept from Colonel Rock back in 1970 while efforts were made to change the wording during the army hearing. Years later, on September 24, 1974, this unmatched hair was delivered on a glass slide to Paul Stombaugh at the FBI laboratory. It was hand-carried by army captain Brian Murtagh.

Stombaugh had looked at the slide and deemed its contents useless. His written report stated, "This hair fragment does not exhibit enough individual microscopic characteristics to be of value for comparison and identification purposes." This, even though the hair had already secretly been compared with samples from many people, including Jeffrey Mac-Donald.

Had Segal known about the previous comparisons, CID lab technician Janice Glisson might have testified at trial that she first suspected a foreign hair in Colette's hand to be from an arm of the murderer. She could have shown a drawing she made of the hair's characteristics, and she could have testified that she compared that hair's characteristics to dozens of samples taken from many people, including Jeffrey MacDonald. She could have testified that, although its features were distinctive enough for comparison purposes, the hair remained unmatched. But Janice Glisson at trial was not allowed to talk about hair. She was used by Murtagh to introduce blood evidence. Because of this, the defense and the jury never knew about her hair evaluations. The disagreement between her findings and those of Stombaugh regarding this vital exhibit was never exposed, and *the jurors never knew that a mystery hair found in Colette's hand wasn't Jeffrey MacDonald's.*

To Ellen Dannelly and other members of MacDonald's defense team, the discrepancy was more than a disagreement between the results of two lab experts. There can be no question that the hair was actually of sufficient quantity to test, for the army did test it against MacDonald and others. If Stombaugh, as he claimed, found the hair either of insufficient quantity or of too few points of comparison to attempt a match with other hair, then something ugly had happened. Either the hair had been altered, or another hair had been substituted in its place.

Bernard Segal later said that knowledge of a foreign hair in Colette's hand would have been one of the most explosive facts he could have delivered at trial. When reminded that he knew about that hair back at the army Article 32 hearing, and asked why he had not jumped on this at trial, Segal pointed out that he had been misled. He had been led to believe that MacDonald's hair, taken from him during the army hearing, had been tested against *another* hair in Colette's hand, a longer blond one later determined to be her own.

"That unmatched and therefore foreign hair," Segal insisted, "since it definitely was not Jeff's, could have destroyed the government's circumstantial case. For the question would have to have been asked: If it wasn't Jeff's hair, then whose hair was found in Colette's dead hand?"

That was an important item. There were many others which would have been of lesser value to Segal, yet even an accumulation of smaller things might have helped sway a jury. One of these items was the ice pick, which Mildred Kassab said MacDonald never owned, and which babysitter Pam Kalin had never seen, until both of them later changed their stories four years into the case. Also, for instance, the full truth about the wooden murder club, too, escaped the jurors. The prosecutors said that the murder club was a piece of household wood which they claimed was kept indoors where MacDonald could easily have picked it up to use on his daughter and his wife. Although tests showed that it had been cut from the same wood as a bed slat in Kimberly's room, the statements of three government investigators suggest it had lain outdoors for a lengthy time. In fact, it was so weathered, its surface wouldn't accept fingerprints.[12] These offerings tend to refute the prosecution theory that the makeshift club was an indoor object readily available in an unplanned bedroom confrontation. More reasonably, since photographs show excess weathered wood of this type lying outside under the edge of the apartment, this very piece might have been a weapon of opportunity picked up in the backyard by an intended housebreaker.

At Trial

Segal pressed hard to have his witnesses tell their stories to the jury that Monday morning, but Dupree was favoring Murtagh's motion to prevent them from learning of Stoeckley's confessions. The judge remained skeptical despite a reminder that Stoeckley had admitted to Brisentine that the rain hadn't started in earnest until after the murders. Without the still-suppressed lab notes containing references to the yet-undisclosed items, Segal had nothing left on this crucial issue except to continue arguing points of the hearsay rule. And Dupree appeared to agree with him on some points. Yes, the Stoeckley witness issue had met the first two requirements of the hearsay rule. Stoeckley's statements did actually implicate her in a serious crime, and her lack of memory made her "unavailable" under legal interpretations of the rule. But from there, Dupree sided with Murtagh's arguments. Applying his right of judicial discretion in such matters, the judge ruled the statements Stoeckley made to the witnesses to be "clearly untrustworthy." He said they were, in fact, the most untrustworthy statements he had "ever seen or heard."[13] He would allow the witnesses to testify in the presence of the jury, but he warned them and Segal that he would tolerate no questions or answers which touched on Stoeckley's confessions. In other words, Dupree allowed the Stoeckley witnesses to testify, but wouldn't let them say anything about Stoeckley's admissions about the very case the jurors were hearing. This was a devastating blow to the defense.

Years later, Judge Dupree's decision not to allow the Stoeckley witnesses' testimony about her confessions would become a major issue on appeal. The appeals judges would find that the wide discretion afforded to trial judges on such issues left Dupree fully within his rights to have denied the jurors those Stoeckley confessions. However, one appeals judge, Francis Murnaghan, Jr., stated that had he been the trial judge, he would have allowed "the testimony to come in." Murnaghan clarified his statement by adding: "My preference derives from my belief that, if the jury may be trusted with ultimate resolution of the factual issues, it should not be denied the opportunity of obtaining a rounded picture, necessary for resolution of the large questions, by the withholding of collateral testimony consistent with and basic to the defendant's principal exculpatory contention."

It also seems that even Justice Murnaghan found himself believing in the possibility that Stoeckley was telling the truth about being in the MacDonald home that night. He said that prior to the Manson tragedy, Stoeckley's story "would have been dismissed as so incredible as to merit no serious attention." But after Manson, "the possibility of such an occurrence, while still macabre, was considerably enhanced." The appeals judge went even further: "The evidence, in my humble judgment, tended to show an environment where MacDonald was stationed in which persons might indeed emulate Manson or independently behave in such a fashion. Helena Stoeckley was shown to be a person of no fixed regularity of life, roaming the streets nocturnally at or about the time of the crimes, dressing in bizarre fashion, and capable of so short-circuiting her mental processes through an indiscriminate taking of drugs that she could well accept her presence and, to some extent, her involvement in the MacDonald murders and she could become so separated from reality that, on the fatal evening, she was ripe for persuasion to participate."[14]

In this statement Murnaghan sounds like a MacDonald defense attorney, but his appeals duties were strictly limited to finding whether Dupree had abused his legal discretion in not allowing the Stoeckley witness testimony. Under the letter of the law, if not under Murnaghan's own interpretation of fairness, Murnaghan could not find that Dupree had overstepped. Incredibly, however, Murnaghan did point out that if Dupree had allowed the jurors to hear about the Stoeckley confessions, the damage to the government's case would have been "incalculably great." Bernard Segal, reading this later, could not help but translate Murnaghan's extreme and surprising language to understand that this appeals court justice, at least, thought that if the Stoeckley confessions had been allowed, they might have saved the day for the defense.

Because of Dupree's decision to disallow the Stoeckley confessions at trial, Brian Murtagh and James Blackburn had won on still another issue to keep key defense evidence out of the courtroom. But Murtagh and Blackburn still weren't pleased, for Dupree was allowing these witnesses to tell the jurors about other things, and one of these witnesses, in particular, worried them. Consequently, during a bench conference, Murtagh said he didn't want Jane Zillioux to testify before the jury in any manner whatsoever. Blackburn complained to Dupree that the woman might just "blurt out" objectionable material. It would be all right, Blackburn said, "if Zillioux wants to testify that Helena lived in a little house and worked at Bonnie's and that she had hepatitis." But the prosecutors specifically did not want Zillioux to tell the jurors that Helena Stoeckley "looked down at her hands that night and saw blood."

Even while these arguments proceeded, a strange event came to Segal's attention. Wat Hopkins, a Fayetteville reporter, called Segal and told him about a man named James E. "Jimmy" Friar, who had been a soldier in 1970 at the time of the murders. Friar had told Hopkins that one night while he had been hospitalized at Fort Bragg he left his bed and went to town. Drinking and disoriented early in the morning, Friar asked the operator for the telephone number of Dr. MacDonald. He was trying to locate his psychiatrist, Dr. Richard M. MacDonald, in another state, to come help him. Friar said that when he called the local number the operator had given him, a giggling woman answered the phone at the other end, and a man's voice in the background told her, "Hang up the damn phone!"[15]

Segal understood the possible value of this event. One might conjecture that apparently Jimmy Friar called the MacDonald home by mistake at precisely the time the murders were taking place.

Segal immediately considered bringing Friar onto the stand as a witness to corroborate MacDonald's story that someone had been in the house. Friar's testimony might also be used to persuade Judge Dupree that there was corroboration to Stoeckley's story as well. But there were serious problems, not the least of which was Friar's record. He had been hospitalized with emotional problems back in 1970, and nine years later Friar had contacted the reporter from jail.

Segal faced still another problem with Friar. If he introduced the man, and the prosecutors then succeeded in impeaching his admittedly bizarre claims, the defense could stand to lose, and lose big, in the eyes of the jurors, for they might think Segal had simply gotten a witness to say something, anything, to attempt to create doubt regarding MacDonald's guilt.

Segal decided Friar's unsupported story would not be worth the ordeal in red tape to have him delivered from prison as a witness. Unknown to Segal, however, this wouldn't be the end of the Friar claim.

■

Segal had been defeated on the issue of lab-testing the evidence, and on the issue of reading the laboratory notes which he felt might contain evidence to corroborate MacDonald's story. He had been beaten on the issue of presenting the Rock report. And now, defeated on the Stoeckley issue, Segal watched the trial continue without the jurors learning anything about Helena Stoeckley's frequent admissions of involvement in the crimes or her requests for immunity.

Many years later the defense team would learn that Murtagh and the FBI had withheld more information about Stoeckley than Bernard Segal could have imagined, information that undoubtedly would have changed the outcome of the trial.

In the Government Files

When Harvey A. Silverglate became lead defense counsel in 1989, he and his staff studied the entire MacDonald case history. He knew about various Stoeckley confessions, her requests for immunity, her three polygraph exams all indicating that she was in the MacDonald home. He knew that MacDonald's previous attorneys had learned that Stoeckley had confessed to the FBI only months before the trial, and that this confession was suppressed until the release of FOIA material four years after trial. But it wasn't until late 1990 that Harvey Silverglate's team discovered Stoeckley had confessed before the trial *directly to the prosecuting attorney*.

The discovery came by accident during the research of something else. Brian Murtagh was quoted in Joe McGinniss's book, *Fatal Vision*, as saying, on day 21 of the trial,[16] that the government had "no physical evidence whatsoever to tie her [Stoeckley] to the crime scene." But the defense team, after their work with the FOIA-released lab notes, knew a great deal of evidence was never turned over to MacDonald, and they wanted to know more about the background of this intriguing quote by Murtagh.[17] They looked for the quote in the typed court transcript. But the transcript of the day McGinniss had specifically referred to revealed no such words.

Intrigued, the defense team searched further and finally found the quote as part of a bench conference that had been held much earlier, on the ninth day of trial. That McGinniss had put the quote in Murtagh's mouth to support an argument that occurred seventeen days later was of little consequence to Silverglate. What suddenly became important was the discovery of a statement *preceding* the words that had been used by McGinniss, for in those words Murtagh told Judge Dupree that he himself had once interviewed Stoeckley and she had tried to confess to him. This disclosure was made while Helena Stoeckley was being sought for testimony, so it had occurred sometime before Stoeckley was brought to Raleigh for the trial.

Even though Murtagh has never turned over to the defense any record of this heretofore secret meeting between Stoeckley and himself, Murtagh told Dupree of the specific exchange he had with the woman: "'Well, why do you think you were there.' And she says, 'Because I think I was there.' You know, you go round in circles on that one." Then Murtagh made the statement which McGinniss quoted in *Fatal Vision:* "We have no physical evidence whatsoever to tie her to the crime scene."[18]

It infuriated Silverglate that Helena Stoeckley had confessed directly to MacDonald's prosecutor, and yet no details of this exchange had surfaced. A report should have been made and filed, and it should have been released under laws governing the Freedom of Information Act, not to mention the requirements of the *Brady* rule regarding the surrender of exculpatory material to the defense prior to trial. A defendant's right to know about and use such evidence is one of the fairness factors built into the justice system. Sometimes called the process of discovery, this doctrine is more often referred to simply as the *"Brady* rule," named for a court case which confirmed that a prosecutor breaks the law when he withholds evidence useful to the defense.[19]

It might be argued that Murtagh did indeed share the knowledge of his interview with Stoeckley, and that he did so in front of the judge and the defense lawyers during that aforementioned bench conference. But the defense team still might claim a right to the further details of a meeting with a confessor who matched the descriptions of MacDonald's female intruder and the floppy-hatted woman Mica saw in the neighborhood, a confessor who had no alibi, a confessor who had violent friends, a confessor whose polygraph exam had indicated deception. As Bost and I encountered the well-shrouded events involving Stoeckley's confession to Murtagh and her confession to the FBI, we were reminded of her secretive relationship in Fayetteville to William Ivory, the CID, and the Inter-Agency Narcotics Bureau. All these events seem of a kind. For Helena Stoeckley, while being denied official immunity, nevertheless enjoyed a peculiar brand of protection. Was it because her admissions, if made public, would destroy the prosecutors' case, as they had destroyed the army case before Colonel Rock in the 1970 hearing?

Fourteen years after the trial and Murtagh's almost flippant aside to

Judge Dupree, Bost and I received still another packet of information previously withheld from MacDonald. This packet was direct from the FBI files. It included a report written by the FBI agents who transported Stoeckley to the trial in Raleigh. Three days before she went on the stand to testify she told FBI agents that she "honestly does not know what she did that night and therefore, could not categorically state that she was not involved in the murder."[20]

Whether one believes Murtagh should have shared the content and conditions of his own heretofore secret interview with her, it is inescapable that this FBI interview and her admissions should have been provided to Segal. Her statements to the FBI contradicted her denials to Segal during his meeting with her and, it could be argued, her statements to the FBI may indicate she was designing her testimony when she appeared on the witness stand. One thing is certain: Her statement to the FBI contradicted both her denials and her many outright confessions, and Segal could have used it to show that, given a chance to officially deny involvement, she refused, contrary to government claims.

What's more, this interview with Stoeckley, held in the government files for fourteen years, also contained information about her involvement in witchcraft, her use and sale of hard narcotics, her informant status, and information about the intriguing polygraph examination which showed deception when she said she wasn't in the murder apartment. The defense charge that this critical information was withheld is compounded by still another discovery. This FBI report wasn't put into final form until trial testimony ended, a full thirteen days after Stoeckley was interviewed. Was the delay and the subsequent failure to deliver the report to the defense merely bureaucratic bungling? Or, as Silverglate suspects, were these faults deliberate as a result of prosecutorial suppression? If so, the government showed absolutely no conscience in withholding this information at a time when the court was wrestling with the admissability of Stoeckley's other confessions.

■

Whether the FBI report was buried as a result of bungling or deliberate intent, the damage was the same. Its use to the defense was denied, as was the case with other things. Brian Murtagh had succeeded in blocking the defense use of the Rock report and the laboratory notes. He had stalled, and therefore blocked, the defense team on the issue of laboratory testing of the evidence. He had successfully held back details of Stoeckley's confession directly to him. He had failed to turn over the FBI interviews of Stoeckley. And he had argued successfully against the testimony of the Stoeckley witnesses regarding her confessions to them. But still another leg of the defense case threatened the prosecution. Bernard Segal wanted to bring psychiatrists into court to tell the jurors that MacDonald was normal and sane, and was not of the personality type to have committed the murders.

Brian Murtagh and James Blackburn had an agenda of their own on that issue as well.

8

■

The Psychiatric
Issue at Trial

The question of MacDonald's mental state had begun on the day of the murders. During the very first week of investigation, CID agents were confounded by MacDonald's sterling reputation as a decent and caring human being. They learned that he had been an exemplary youth, an above-average student, and a spirited high school athlete. In nothing less than storybook fashion he married his childhood sweetheart, attended Princeton, and worked his way through medical school. As if that were not enough, he became a paratrooper who actually looked forward to dropping out of airplanes. That was unusual for a doctor. He joined the Green Berets, became group surgeon to his unit, and was preparing to seek field duty with his former unit commander in Vietnam. He was a volunteer, a romantic, a man's man; and people liked him.

In the days preceding the murders MacDonald was seen by everyone as a loving father. On the Christmas before the murders he bought the girls a Shetland pony as a surprise gift, and later added a bunny rabbit. Richard Love, the man who owned the land MacDonald rented for the animals, said that MacDonald built a little barn himself, and often dropped by in the evenings or at night to see to their welfare. "I told the investigators that boy didn't kill his family," Love said. "He'd bring the girls out here and walk around the lot holding the baby on the horse's back. He just loved them too much."

The Kassabs, Colette's mother and stepfather, insisted early on that their son-in-law was near perfect, that he'd loved his wife and daughters far more than the average father. MacDonald's fellow soldiers swore he was well balanced and very devoted to his family. Doctors who worked with him lauded his talents and his innately caring nature.

These things interested Bernard Segal back in 1970 when he realized that the sheer brutality of the murderer or murderers of the MacDonald family indicated that whoever did it was "sick, really mentally ill." MacDonald, however, seemed normal, albeit currently mired in grief and apparently suffering from loss and from having failed to protect his wife and daughters. Segal decided he must seek a professional opinion. He arranged to have his new young client evaluated by Dr. Robert Sadoff.

Besides having practiced psychiatry in the Army Medical Corps, Sadoff had served a residency at the UCLA Neuropsychiatric Institute. He had been director of the Forensic Psychiatry Clinic at Temple University in Philadelphia, and had worked as the first clinical director of the State Maximum Security Forensic Diagnostic Hospital at Holmesburg County Prison in Philadelphia. In 1970, at the time of army hearings in the MacDonald murders, Sadoff enjoyed an active private practice, and served as a consultant to the Norristown State Hospital in forensic psychiatric matters and as training supervisor in forensic psychiatry at Temple University.

After Dr. Sadoff performed an exhaustive examination of Captain MacDonald, Sadoff's clinical psychologist, Dr. James L. Mack, put MacDonald through an extensive battery of psychological tests. Based upon Mack's reports and his own examination, Sadoff concluded that MacDonald was normal, sane, and not of the personality type to have committed the murders.

"You really cannot slaughter your own flesh and blood," Sadoff told Segal. "You really can't destroy them the way these people were destroyed without being extremely disturbed in a number of ways. This act was so horrific it would leave a trail a mile wide. That trail just isn't there," Sadoff said. "MacDonald isn't crazy. Your client didn't kill his family."[1]

As part of his defense, Segal called Dr. Sadoff as an expert witness at the army hearing. "At the time I examined Dr. MacDonald," Sadoff told Colonel Rock, "his sadness, more than sadness, but actual depression was accompanied by difficulty sleeping, some problem in eating, some irritability, and he was prone to tears in discussing the events of the night of February 17th. He was reacting to the deaths by what I would consider a normal depression."

Sadoff had added that he found no signs of mental illness in MacDonald. He found no character or behavior disorders, and no evidence of sociopathic personality disorder, or psychopathy. "Based on my examination of him and all the data that I have, Captain MacDonald does not possess the type of personality emotional configuration that would be capable of killing his wife and children and react the way he did during my examination of him."

Having allowed the defense an opportunity to explore MacDonald's psychiatric makeup, Colonel Rock ordered MacDonald to travel to Washington, D.C., for a psychiatric examination by doctors at Walter Reed Army Hospital. During a hearing recess over the next two weeks, MacDonald was interviewed at length by the army's top psychiatrists: Lieutenant Colonel Bruce Bailey, chief psychiatrist; Lieutenant Colonel Donald W. Morgan, director of research psychiatry; and Major Henry E. Edwards, chief of psychiatric consultation.

The evaluation consisted of multiple psychological tests, extensive psychiatric interviews by all three examiners, and an electroencephalogram (EEG). In addition, the Walter Reed team called in their own consultants; and they were briefed by both prosecution and defense attorneys.

Following this evaluation, Dr. Bailey of Walter Reed testified in behalf of his fellow army psychiatrists who had examined MacDonald. As Sadoff had done before him, Bailey said that MacDonald was not of the personality type that was likely to kill. Like Dr. Sadoff, Bailey found "no derangement" in Dr. MacDonald. He described him as "an engaging, personable young man, who establishes rather quickly a sense of warmth." And Dr. Bailey—when specifically asked during the army hearing— said he didn't believe MacDonald was contriving his version of the events of February 17. The only significant difference between the testimony of the defense psychiatrist, Dr. Sadoff, and the government psychiatrist, Dr. Bailey, was that Sadoff claimed MacDonald was incapable of killing his family, while, on that subject, Bailey said that psychiatric evaluation alone doesn't allow one to make such a far-reaching conclusion.

In preparation for the trial nine years later, Segal had requested still another psychiatric evaluation of MacDonald, this time at the hands of University of North Carolina's Dr. Seymour Halleck, a forensic psychiatrist and an author of considerable repute in the field. Halleck agreed with

Sadoff and Bailey and the other Walter Reed specialists. MacDonald showed no signs of pathology, and he was not of the personality type to have murdered his family.

Not surprisingly, then, since Segal possessed nothing but positive psychiatric information to present at trial, the prosecutors pressed Judge Dupree not to allow any of the psychiatrists to testify. But how could Murtagh and Blackburn offset the defense's psychiatric testimony, knowing full well that army psychiatrists already had agreed, in effect, with the defense psychiatrists' claims? Each defense psychiatrist had legitimate qualifications and each had examined MacDonald personally. Yet Murtagh had a plan; and Segal, even while castigating Murtagh's methods and motives, would later admit that Murtagh's idea was brilliant.

Immediately following the opening remarks at trial the prosecutors called for a bench conference out of the hearing of the jury, where Murtagh pressed the judge to forbid psychiatric testimony absolutely. Murtagh didn't want Segal to be allowed to mention anything about MacDonald's state of mind. Murtagh said he feared the subject would "permeate the trial."

Blackburn, in turn, argued that if the prosecutors could prove that MacDonald did the crime, they wouldn't have to prove that he's the type of person who *could* do the crime. Psychiatry, he claimed, should have no part in the trial.

Judge Dupree postponed a decision about the issue, and Murtagh pursued it at other bench conferences, saying at one such conference, "We think this whole psychiatric thing is a can of worms, Your Honor. It is going to prolong the trial." And at a later bench conference he said that the testimony of Dr. Robert Sadoff was "not competent, and will only confuse the jury."

Even though Robert Sadoff was a founder of the American Board of Forensic Psychiatry, and a recognized expert in the subject of the criminal mind, and even though his expertise had been relied upon many times by the court system, Judge Dupree agreed with Murtagh, and mused, out of earshot of the jury, whether psychiatric testimony should *ever* be admissible. Dupree said that Congress had erred in allowing psychiatric evidence in trials.

On Thursday, August 9, 1979, as the prosecution was running out of witnesses in its presentation, Murtagh put his psychiatric plan into action. At a bench conference he told Judge Dupree that he had secured a forensic psychiatrist who "tells us that the Rorschach Test that Dr. MacDonald took in 1970, for the defense—which was furnished to the Army—is inadequate. I don't know the specifics," Murtagh said, "but apparently he didn't react to the ink blots or whatever. In that regard, Your Honor," Murtagh continued, "if psychiatric testimony is going to be offered by the defense, we would move the court to order the defendant to submit after court, perhaps on Monday, to any and all psychiatric or psychological tests. I don't think it would be lengthy, they are what the experts would require."

This was not exactly true. A Rorschach test *is* a subject's reaction to the inkblots, and MacDonald did take the test. The defense had no knowledge at this time that for years the CID had been attempting to get their hands on MacDonald's original Rorschach test. In accordance with his plan, Murtagh on the following Monday informed Dupree at a bench conference that he had his psychiatric team waiting and suggested that the judge either forbid psychiatric testimony outright or else allow the new team to examine MacDonald. Segal objected to the proposed ban on psychiatric testimony and began to argue the issue, but Murtagh pressed hard, calling for fairness through an impartial evaluation of MacDonald by a neutral psychiatrist. "If there is going to be psychiatric testimony, we have got to have him examined at the earliest possible time," he said.

"Then make a motion in writing for God's sake," Segal barked, angrily. "These are serious questions."

But Judge Dupree didn't wait for a motion in writing. "I think you should have him examined at the first available time," Dupree said. He further clarified his ruling, saying, "Yes, I would require that, if I let the [psychiatric] evidence in."

Thus it was that Judge Dupree, who himself had stated he didn't believe in psychiatric testimony, but who indicated he was now about to allow it, ordered MacDonald to be interviewed and tested that very afternoon by yet a sixth psychiatrist in the case.

Segal had been whipsawed on the issue. If he wanted to bring on Sadoff and Halleck and their psychologists, he would have to abide by Murtagh's wishes in the matter. The defense lawyer returned to his table and explained the situation to a balking MacDonald. He told his client that it was essential that the defense psychiatric testimony be presented to the jury, and there was only one way to see that happen. "Dupree won't let any of the psychiatric evidence in," Segal explained, "unless you submit to this one additional examination. They have us over a barrel, Jeff. You have to do it."

Defense attorneys Wade Smith and Mike Malley adamantly opposed the examination because they feared a setup. "It's obvious what's happening here," Malley told MacDonald. Malley had been his friend since their days at Princeton, and MacDonald trusted him. His new friend, author Joe McGinniss, who had become a legal member of the defense team, also openly opposed it. McGinniss told MacDonald's mother at the courthouse that he "wouldn't watch them screw Jeff." She said that McGinniss was so disgusted he said he would rather "go get drunk."[2] But MacDonald had little choice. At about 5:15 P.M. that Monday MacDonald and the defense team[3] left the courthouse and headed for Wade Smith's law offices where the examination was to take place.

The new government psychiatrist, Dr. James A. Brussel, and his psychologist, Dr. Hirsch Lazar Silverman, met MacDonald and the defense team at Smith's offices. Segal said Dr. Silverman seemed to be intelligent and rational, but Brussel, in his seventies, appeared stroke ravaged. He drooled from the side of his mouth and seemed disoriented. MacDonald, who knew nothing of Brussel's background, feared the setup Malley only moments earlier had warned him about. He stepped over to Segal and told him quietly that he would not submit to an examination by this apparently senile old man.

Segal again reminded MacDonald that he had no choice, that Murtagh and Judge Dupree had them in a bind. When MacDonald remained unconvinced, Segal decided to draft a quick statement outlining the terms within which the examination would occur. Segal wrote that the product of the Brussel-Silverman interview was to be kept in strict confidence, and was to be shared with no one without Dr. MacDonald's written consent, unless Judge Dupree allowed the psychiatric evidence to be heard by the jury.[4] Brussel and Silverman both agreed in the presence of several witnesses, and MacDonald then decided to go ahead with the examination.

At approximately 6:30 P.M. Brussel, Silverman, and MacDonald closeted themselves in Smith's personal office. Segal's team had worried about a setup connected with this new psychiatric evaluation, which had been so suddenly imposed upon them, and, in time, they would have need to determine who, exactly, was Dr. James A. Brussel, for Brussel was no "new man," as the government allowed Segal and Judge Dupree to believe.

In the Government Files

Much of what the public has heard regarding Jeffrey MacDonald's character has come from the father-in-law who turned against him. Alfred Kassab's opinions were persuasively delivered by Joe McGinniss in *Fatal Vision*. This view of MacDonald has served the prosecutors well, but defense team members complain that such a treatment elevates uncorroborated rumor to a higher position than it deserves. And rumor, not fact, the defense team argues, has driven the case from the beginning, thereby giving the government license to proceed without fact.

What part, then, did rumor play as MacDonald's public face changed from that of "golden boy" to "monster"?

RUMORS

Upon completion of the army hearing, and the exoneration by Colonel Rock back in 1970, the CID agents insisted that MacDonald was a murderer hiding behind the pleasant visage of a charismatic healer. Rumor pursued him as relentlessly as did the CID during their secret surveillance during the new investigation.

Some of the rumors were vicious. During the defense team preparations, Michael Malley, the young army attorney who assisted Segal at the army hearing, visited MacDonald's hometown in Patchogue, New York, where MacDonald's friends told him that the CID agents who preceded Malley's visit had intimated to witnesses that Jeff and Colette were using drugs.

It was rumored at Fort Bragg that Colette had threatened to kill Jeffrey. The source of this claim by the CID agents might have been a passing statement attributed to Colette by a neighbor when MacDonald bought a stereo system. Colette allegedly said, "I could kill him for buying that."

Rumor had it that MacDonald had refused his children's toys[5] when offered them after the hearing because he didn't care about them. And CID agents still thought MacDonald had a woman somewhere, a woman he would kill for.

Some made the preposterous allegation that the American Medical Association pressured Colonel Rock into releasing MacDonald because it didn't want one of its own accused of murder. Word was that the AMA had even paid for Bernard Segal, MacDonald's "high-powered Philadelphia lawyer."[6]

Another rumor had it that William Posey's Article 32 testimony about Helena Stoeckley had been "bought." Following a meeting of CID investigators on December 31, 1970, agent Robert Bidwell wrote in the case log: "Everyone seems to agree that the theory Posey was paid is a credible one." Yet, at this point in time, Posey had not yet been interviewed by the CID.

Another tale had MacDonald's sister, Judy Alvey, saying that she believed MacDonald was capable of murdering his family.[7] CID investigator Robert L. Colombo, who had interviewed Alvey, had actually reported, "When asked whether she thought her brother Jeffrey was capable of killing anyone, she hesitated and after some thought responded that although she does not believe he did kill his family she felt he was capable of killing if he were provoked." During Franz Grebner's Article 32 testimony he construed this to mean that Alvey had said that her brother was capable of killing his family.

But Mrs. Alvey said that her statement had been misconstrued. When the agent had asked whether her brother could kill anyone, her words were, "I think anyone, under certain circumstances, could kill someone else, but Jeff could not have killed his wife and children." Mrs. Alvey said that she related the substance of the CID interview to her brother soon after the interview. She added that she at no time ever believed, or ever stated, that her brother could have killed his family and that her words had been misused "over and over" both in the courts and by the media.[8]

Rumor, or something quite like it, had affected General Flanagan's decision to release MacDonald from custody and drop all charges, not because he wasn't guilty, as Colonel Rock had found, but because of "insufficient evidence." Rock had told the general there was no evidence—"It just isn't there." But Flanagan's legal officer, Major Wold, said that the CID had convinced him that MacDonald was guilty, nevertheless. Wold, who had not attended the hearing, synopsized Rock's report and gave that to the general. In other words, the defense team now complains, he filtered Rock's findings and gave Flanagan reasons not to completely clear MacDonald.

The CID, without revealing everything they knew about Helena Stoeckley, had also convinced some FBI men that MacDonald was guilty, and the CID agents had convinced people in the local U. S. Attorney's office. With little knowledge of Stoeckley and her group, these men began clamoring for MacDonald to be tried, and would have continued had not the Justice Department insisted there wasn't enough evidence. Rumor is not supposed to substitute for hard evidence.

But did rumor play a part in the official psychiatric issues of the case and in the turning of Alfred and Mildred Kassab? The CID, under serious fire for the way they handled the case, were still secretly in pursuit of Jeffrey MacDonald after Colonel Rock exonerated him. They recognized in those waning days of 1970 that, among other obstacles, they faced two formidable hurdles. One was the psychiatric evaluations which seemed to show that MacDonald couldn't have committed the crimes. If the CID were to succeed, these evaluations would eventually have to be neutralized. The second hurdle? MacDonald's father-in-law was making life hell for the army on Capitol Hill. With good reason, the CID agents regarded Alfred Kassab as MacDonald's most dangerous ally.

Unknown to the CID, not everyone on the defense team during the army hearing saw Kassab as an ally. During Article 32 preparations Bernard Segal had called MacDonald aside and advised him to keep his father-in-law out of the case. "The guy is dangerous," Segal told MacDonald. "He's uninformed. And he's a zealot." Segal's complaint was that Kassab had called press conferences on his own and had badly misstated some things. MacDonald defended his father-in-law, reminding Segal that Kassab had put up a $5,000 reward for the killers.

Michael Malley, the young legal officer who had assisted Segal at the Article 32 hearing, also feared Kassab's zeal. Malley recalled that the first day he had met the Kassabs, Freddie had immediately "launched into a tirade," first about the army, then about the provost marshal, and then about Jeff's commanding officer. Malley wrote, "He showed me the press release he had prepared for when Jeff was released—he was single-mindedly obsessed with not only vindicating Jeff, but with catching the killers and embarrassing the army."

Malley recorded his realization that Mrs. Kassab was equally fixated. He wrote, "Mildred, while not as voluble, shared his views more intensely than even he did, I think. I was surprised at how their sorrow had turned into hatred, so that only the hatred showed, though I knew and respected its genesis. It was a militant grief, and it scared me."[9]

Helen Fell, a friend of both families, attended a New York press conference in the summer of 1970 during which Kassab attacked the army and announced his reward offer. She often visited both families, the MacDonalds and the Kassabs. What she observed between Alfred and Mildred worried her, too.[10]

Helen said she watched as Mildred's sarcastic words constantly imposed an imaginary rivalry between her husband and her son-in-law. "Mildred swore that Jeff would find the murderers and avenge the family. Freddie, on the other hand—as his wife constantly reminded him—was accomplishing nothing."

According to Helen, Mildred would belittle him for not tracking down the killers, telling him he was "a poor excuse for someone [who had been] in [military] intelligence. . . ."[11] Helen Fell said that in an effort to placate Mildred and regain stature in her eyes, Freddie became more and more obsessed with finding the killers, to a point where the obsession for revenge "eventually seemed to take on a life of its own."

Based on records, Freddie Kassab in those days saw the killers as evil strangers, and he saw his son-in-law as the likable "kid" who would one day help gain revenge. MacDonald says that this constant "vigilante attitude" led him in November 1970 to tell Kassab a very dangerous lie. During a telephone conversation while still at Fort Bragg awaiting discharge, he fabricated a story for Freddie Kassab. MacDonald told Kassab he had found and had killed one of the murderers.

MacDonald later admitted at both the grand jury investigation and the 1979 trial that he had fabricated the story. He said he did it because after he had been released from "arrest in quarters" the Kassabs kept hounding him about finding the murderers. On a few occasions, MacDonald said, he submitted to his own hopes of finding the murderers, and gave in to the Kassabs' urges, and made investigative trips into Fayetteville, but each time he was recognized by someone who had known him on post or who had seen his picture in the media. Fellow soldiers would then gather around, buy him a drink, and tell him they'd "blow the killers away" if MacDonald would point them out. After several such incidents MacDonald said he lost heart in the effort, realizing, finally, that one doesn't stumble across the guilty ones as in a television show. Yet, he said Mildred and Freddie kept insisting that if he really cared about his family he would get the killers.

MacDonald later explained that with his lie he hoped he could make Freddie Kassab believe one of the murderers was dead, that it might sober the man's ambitions and cause him to draw back. "It seemed that only good could come from it," he said. "No one would really be dead, and the Kassabs would see that it didn't bring my family back."[12]

After telling the bizarre lie, MacDonald claims he quickly came to his senses. "It was a totally inappropriate and wrong thing to do," he confessed to the trial jury. He says it failed to accomplish what he intended, for after his discharge Kassab began visiting him for lunch at his new job in New York, spending the time trying to pressure him into a joint search for the killers.[13]

Kassab, by his own later admission, had learned within weeks of the telling that the story had been untrue. North Carolina newspapers failed to report any murder with the necessary characteristics. And Kassab has made claims that it was at this time that he first began to suspect his son-in-law as the murderer; the suspicions deepened, he said, as he spent the 1970 Christmas holidays reading the transcript of the army hearing; and, according to him, he became certain of the fact upon making a visit to the murder apartment in March 1971. Kassab often says that he told the CID of his feelings at that time and swore to them then that he would see MacDonald prosecuted. He has repeated this story during television and radio interviews, and the television docudrama *Fatal Vision* included this dramatic scene.

But statements and documents fail to corroborate Kassab's recollections of events. For one thing, he made his most pro-MacDonald plea to Congress *after* being told the lie, and he continued to hound authorities pressing MacDonald's innocence and the CID's shenanigans after the Christmas holidays. One letter to the Department of Justice defending MacDonald's story was apparently so virulent that someone in attorney Jim Robinson's office considered taking Kassab to court for making a "threat." Instead a decision was made and recorded on a memo routing slip, dated January 20, 1971, to write "poor daddy" and feed him "another dose of gobbledy-gook."[14] Apparently, Kassab never knew how he was viewed by the law enforcement officers.

When Kassab on February 9, 1971, forced the CID to terminate an interview of his stepson, Bob Stevenson, and Bob's wife, Pep, Lieutenant Colonel Jack G. Pruett recognized the man had to be neutralized. Pruett, the director of the CID's internal affairs, was on transfer orders to Vietnam, and was temporarily in charge of the reinvestigation. Kassab had requested, without success, to be allowed to inspect the crime scene. Pruett, in an attempt to placate the man, finally acceded to the request. On March

28, 1971, he and Peter Kearns played host and allowed Kassab to roam the apartment at will. Afterward they treated him to dinner at the post Officers' Club.[15] The defense attorney, Bernard Segal, was never allowed such access to the crime scene. The CID's apparent friendliness to their most strident nemesis was an unusual situation.

Despite the stories now told by Kassab, and despite the drama of the scene depicted in the TV movie *Fatal Vision*, apparently the CID agents hadn't succeeded in softening Kassab's defense of MacDonald, for in a telephone conversation between Pruett and Kearns five days *after* the crime-scene visit the two agents discussed the need to pressure Kassab further.[16] Then on the following morning in a telephone conversation between Pruett and Major David B. Reed, the two CID officers agreed that Kassab would have to be visited prior to Pruett's departure for Vietnam "to avoid additional congressional pressure" from the man.[17]

Pruett and Kearns made that visit on April 27, 1971, to find the Kassabs still favoring their son-in-law. Kassab told them that Jeff had visited nine days before on Kimberly's birthday after taking flowers to the child's grave. Kassab said MacDonald had lost weight and appeared to be suffering an emotional strain, perhaps partly due to the two jobs he was working to try to pay off his legal fees. Kearns, writing in the CID casebook following the visit, summed up the Kassabs' feelings: "Both Kassabs still exhibit a strong feeling that Dr. MacDonald did not participate in the murders."[18]

Thus, government records reveal that Freddie Kassab was still supporting his son-in-law five months after the "big lie," four months after reading the Article 32 transcript, and a month after his visit to the murder apartment. The FOIA documents offer a different scenario of Kassab's involvement in the case than that perceived by the public through the book *Fatal Vision*, and through Kassab's interviews on television and radio.

As the summer of 1971 approached, MacDonald made a decision to leave the East Coast to accept a job in California. MacDonald explained to Helen Fell that he wanted to "put it all behind him, live a new life."[19] Fell says that Mildred's enthusiasm for MacDonald had begun to wane when her son-in-law became too busy to visit them. Suddenly, Fell said, MacDonald was no longer Mildred's hero. Helen Fell, as a friend of both families, attended the "parting dinner" hosted by the Kassabs for MacDonald just days before he left for his new job in California in July 1971. It was a small group—MacDonald, his mother, Helen Fell, and

Mildred and Freddie. Mildred, suffering from cancer, didn't want to accept Jeff's leaving. Fell says Mildred tried to persuade him to remain in New York and take care of her. But Jeffrey told his mother-in-law that he would keep in constant telephone touch with her doctors on her behalf. Helen recalls that Mildred then said, "Stay and mourn with me." And when MacDonald said he couldn't remain on the East Coast, Mildred became furious and told him, "If you leave, you will live to regret it."[20]

After that farewell dinner argument, Alfred Kassab and Peter Kearns quickly moved to a first-name basis. Having taken up the reins upon Pruett's departure for Vietnam, Kearns was handling his job well in wooing Kassab. MacDonald, far away and working as an emergency physician at St. Mary's Medical Center in Long Beach, California, had virtually removed himself from the lives of the Kassabs, and the relationship began falling apart. Within six months Kassab began petitioning for MacDonald's prosecution as actively as he had earlier defended him.

Most of Kassab's letters were aimed at the Justice Department, demanding now that they prosecute his son-in-law. Eventually the Justice Department tired of the harangue and on January 10, 1974, a letter was forwarded to Kassab informing him that no indictment would be sought against MacDonald.

Infuriated, Kassab wrote CID commander Colonel Henry H. Tufts and presented an ultimatum. In a three-page letter dated March 4, 1974, delivered by certified mail, Kassab told Tufts that he was proceeding on his own to file a criminal complaint, and that he wanted CID support. "Your command can take one of two positions open to it," Kassab wrote. "Either you agree with me, OR the Dept. of Justice. You cannot take a neutral ground. Either you prepared a bona fide case or you did not."

Kassab demanded a letter from Tufts to be presented to the court, containing an opinion that Jeffrey MacDonald committed the murders, and that the CID believed enough evidence existed for indictment and prosecution. He added, "Your command stands accused by the U.S. Dept. of Justice of bungling this whole matter. Now it is up to you to take a stand."[21]

After about a week of discussion, the CID commander conceded to give Kassab the letter he desired.[22] Once again the CID was stepping outside its legal mandate. It had now imposed itself into civilian litigation. When these documents became available to the defense team years later it was learned that the CID officers had claimed their letter was a gesture of "good faith"[23] in response to a "Freedom of Information Act" request,[24] which, of course, was untrue.

The Kassabs, their attorney Richard Cahn, and Peter Kearns then made a dramatic end run. They visited Judge Algernon L. Butler in Clinton, North Carolina, on April 30, 1974, where they presented the CID letter supported by an affidavit from Kearns, who by now was retired from the army.

Judge Butler, in turn, pressured the Justice Department,[25] which appointed Special Prosecutor Victor Woerheide in mid-May of 1974 to head up a grand jury probe, which finally indicted Jeffrey MacDonald in January 1975.

The resultant negative publicity, unlike that of late 1970, caused MacDonald's "golden boy" image to lose a good bit of its shine.

While the CID agents were turning Alfred Kassab in their favor, they had also attempted to neutralize the problem of the clean bill of health given MacDonald by psychiatrists. Back in early 1971 someone on the CID team came up with the idea to recruit another psychiatrist. They chose Dr. James A. Brussel, then an assistant commissioner of mental hygiene for the state of New York.

Brussel, who also conducted a private practice, was a gun-toting[26] celebrity psychiatrist who at one time had been an army colonel/psychiatrist.[27] While in the service he had written a medical treatise on "The Military Malingerer."[28] He also claimed to have been an agent for the Central Intelligence Agency, spending the years immediately following World War II engaged in counterespionage activities in Mexico. One of his books, Casebook of a Crime Psychiatrist,[29] lists him as a consultant to various police agencies, including the FBI and the army CID in counterespionage activity. But Brussel's dominant reputation was that of an almost psychic criminalist with the power to describe a suspect without interviewing him, without seeing the crime scene, and without questioning witnesses. It was said he often needed only to talk with police on the telephone to make his diagnosis. His fame was tied primarily to the cases of the "Boston Strangler" and New York's "Mad Bomber," both involving psychotic killers. In these cases Brussel gave a physical description of the assailants which was close to the actual description of the chief suspects when later arrested.

Brussel was also an innovative researcher into novel methods for controlling inmates in psychiatric institutions. Lamenting the frustrations of managing unruly patients and the cost of housing them in the late 1940s, Brussel and an associate instituted electric shock experiments on the brains of female inmates. Brussel had come up with the idea after learning of its success in controlling unruly, shell-shocked soldiers being transported home on troop ships. Due to the intensity and frequency of the treatments, he called his technique the "Blitz Electric Shock Therapy." Brussel's initial experiments were performed on fifty severely disturbed female patients whose brains were shocked morning and afternoon with 600 milliamperes for a half second per application over two successive days, some receiving "40 to 50" such shock sessions in their initial courses. Today such a procedure is considered as indiscriminate overuse.[30] Brussel wrote that the women exhibited marked improvement in "noisiness, assaultiveness, destructiveness, resistiveness, idleness, carelessness in appearance, and uncooperativeness." One woman who had refused to speak anything except Italian had been allegedly shocked into speaking English. Another finally revealed her age. Brussel claimed that another woman even cleaned her room.[31]

Such therapy, in much reduced frequencies, is now called electroconvulsive therapy, and is legitimately applied today to pathologically depressed patients who have been prescreened, adequately informed and counseled, and heavily sedated, as a means of relief. Brussel, however, did not write about relief of psychic pain, or freedom from suicidal impulses, which was, from its inception, the treatment's purpose—Brussel wrote only on issues of patient control. "So uniformly gratifying have been the results that it has been found most difficult to restrain enthusiasm. No better judge of therapeutic results can be had than the exhausted and pessimistic employees who have labored for years with these people." All patients improved, Brussel claimed. Only one patient failed to enjoy a six-day remission. That patient was given a second series of shock treatments which resulted in a longer remission of her earlier, unsatisfactory behavior. This led Brussel to set up a schedule of repetitions of the initial therapy, applying shock on a regular basis, "enabling patients to enjoy unbroken remissions and maintain improvement as long as B.E.S.T., at intervals, is not omitted."

Brussel also performed an experiment in which he injected methamphetamine hydrochloride (the drug dubbed "speed") into depressed patients. The drug caused them to be unable to lie still in one position, causing "an almost uncontrollable thrashing about the bed." One woman suffered convulsions and exhibited psychotic-like behavior, seeing hallucinations. A man, a stammerer, fell into a deep sleep, awoke to go to the bathroom, and fell, lacerating his forehead. During the methedrine interview his stammering "failed to disappear, but the stuttering element did." One woman, a "paranoid, suspicious, and resistive schizophrenic patient," began to cry. Brussel hadn't expected this and surmised it was because she couldn't control the force of words the methedrine was "forcing her to release" against her will as Brussel fired questions at her "in rapid succession." After the methedrine interview, however, the woman was very cooperative and "ladylike," according to Brussel.

In his article, entitled "The Use of Methedrine in Psychiatric Practice," Brussel recommended that other doctors employ this treatment, if for no other reason than to elicit confessions, explaining that if they would add amytal to the methedrine and inject it into a psychopath, "sooner or later he 'tips his hand.'"[32]

"It is remarkable," Brussel wrote, "to watch one of these individuals . . . turn his head from side to side, his eyes darting furtively from person to person, consternation written all over his face as he realizes consciously that he cannot check his flow of speech at least long enough to weigh his words." What the patient then says, Brussel claims, will be the truth, in contradiction of what he has previously told "investigating authorities."

As in his shock experiments, Brussel's published work about amphetamine injections was entirely concerned with issues of control. This, no doubt, helped form his reputation for an uncanny ability to elicit confessions from patients.[33]

Once the CID agents had selected this gaunt, pipe-smoking man as a possible recruit in their reinvestigation, Peter Kearns and William Ivory visited him in his Manhattan home on the weekend of February 7, 1971, nearly one year after the murders. The sixty-four-year-old psychiatrist scanned the crime-scene photographs and autopsy reports, and the two agents briefed him about the crime and statements allegedly made by MacDonald. Brussel offered an immediate opinion. He told the agents that he didn't believe intruders had entered the MacDonald apartment. He told them that he believed the carnage began with a struggle between Jeffrey MacDonald and his wife.[34]

Ivory's report, released in the 1980s, years after trial, has Dr. Brussel claiming in 1971, upon Ivory's first visit to Brussel, that the words of MacDonald's alleged female intruder themselves proved MacDonald a liar. If a girl really had been there, Brussel told the agents, and if that girl had mentioned "acid," she would certainly have been under the influence of LSD herself. This also meant, he reasoned, that her companions, too, would have been under its influence because the drug "is a group doing."

Brussel also had a pronouncement regarding the weapons. Hippies, the psychiatrist insisted, wouldn't have used paring knives and ice picks. They would have "been involved in ritualistic killings and would use daggers or similar ceremonial type weapons." Furthermore, hippies wouldn't have "entered the house by walking only on the side walk. They would 'stroll' and not care where they walked."

Brussel reminded the agents that whoever had committed the murders had been very active, and this ruled out LSD, he believed, because "acid" users are "always lethargic." Since MacDonald had said the female intruder mentioned acid, this was implied as another reason not to trust his story.

Whether Brussel had, in fact, made such statements, or whether Ivory had so interpreted them, they were not in character with what was known, even then, about LSD. Dr. Albert Hoffman, the Swiss chemist who discovered LSD, wrote about his first LSD "trip," during which he thought a "demon invaded me, had taken possession of my body, mind, and soul. I jumped up and screamed trying to free myself from him."

Comparisons between the powerfully disruptive LSD experiences of Hoffman and the pleasurable trips of English writer Aldous Huxley revealed early on that the effect of LSD on different individuals is varied, both in the intensity and in the reactions of its subjects. Universally, however, it has been shown first to induce euphoria, then depression. The overall evaluation of individual experiences as either enjoyable or torturous seems dependent upon dosages, environmental condition, and personality. And contrary to Brussel's reported view, violence has been associated with the use of the drug from the beginning. Few people in 1970 hadn't heard stories of subjects jumping to their deaths while under the influence of LSD.[35] *The Encyclopedia of Human Behavior*, published the year before Dr. Brussel allegedly told Ivory that LSD always causes lethargy, reports that LSD is "particularly dangerous in the hands of thrill seekers and cultists, since it can produce terrifying reactions and outright psychosis in unstable persons." In fact, the New York State Council on Drug Addiction, the state where Brussel practiced, reported that 12 percent of the cases treated at Bellevue Hospital during an eighteen-month period exhibited "uncontrolled violence. Nearly 9 percent had attempted either homicide or suicide."[36]

Nevertheless, Kearns and Ivory credited Dr. Brussel's opinions regarding LSD and lethargy as true and found they had no difficulty in persuading Brussel to work with the CID toward solving the case. One thing they specifically promised before they left him that day was that they would furnish him with Jeffrey MacDonald's Rorschach tests completed by the psychiatrists at the time of the army hearing. He insisted that these "inkblot" tests were necessary if he were to disclose effectively MacDonald's true character. So on this day in 1971 Brussel became the CID's secret psychiatric expert, and they used his words and theories to legitimatize their own claims in the continuing illegal investigation.[37]

Kearns and Pruett tried unsuccessfully to get Bernard Segal to supply MacDonald's Rorschach tests during two 1971 interviews of MacDonald in Philadelphia, but backed off without divulging the fact that Dr. Brussel was working with them. They did learn at the second interview, however, that the Rorschach tests were still in the file at Walter Reed Army Hospital. The CID then tried to pressure the doctors at Walter Reed into relinquishing the tests, only to be rebuffed by Colonel Bailey on ethical grounds. Bailey told them that the tests were the property of MacDonald's civilian psychiatrist, Dr. Sadoff, and, as such, could not be released without his permission.

Sadoff had recommended to Segal not to release the tests unless they were going to a qualified psychiatrist, and the CID, of course, did not want to give up Dr. Brussel's name. Their continuing efforts to force Bailey to surrender the tests failed, and the day came when they recognized they were at a stalemate. It was on that day, May 17, 1971, that the CID agents reluctantly wrote a letter to Segal stating they wanted the tests for a Dr. Brussel. However, the letter crossed the path of a letter from Segal stating he would give no further cooperation to the CID because he had discovered that the "new" investigation was specifically aimed at his client, and was not aimed at what Segal termed the real assailants.[38]

Although Dr. Brussel continued to work with the CID while that agency remained in the case, he never did get a look at the Rorschach tests during that time period. Segal later turned these records over to prosecutor Victor Woerheide during the 1974–1975 grand jury hearing, but the CID wasn't controlling that hearing, so Brussel was not involved. Brian Murtagh acquired the records following Woerheide's death; and, in 1979, as preparation for the trial, he sent them to Brussel whom he had recontacted for the prosecution.

Of course, Murtagh wanted no psychiatric testimony allowed in the trial, but in the event that such testimony would be allowed, he wanted to prepare Dr. Brussel to participate.

And Brussel was ready. On Friday, July 6, 1979, ten days before the trial was to open, the psychiatrist sent a letter to the prosecutors reporting that he had concerned himself not only with psychiatric issues but also with case evidence. He wrote, "I have carefully read the testimonies of the MacDonald case sent to me my [sic] your office and have copious notes thereon."

It was this Dr. Brussel to whom Segal unknowingly delivered MacDonald during the trial in 1979. Brussel was not, of course, a new man, as the prosecutors had intimated. Brussel had been working for them for eight years. Nor was he interviewing MacDonald to determine whether he was insane and capable of murder. He had already decided that question in his own mind in 1971 after listening only to William Ivory and without ever meeting Jeffrey MacDonald or fully reviewing the crime-scene evidence. In fact, the CID had specifically used Brussel's opinions to justify their own continued and illegal pursuit of MacDonald into civilian life.

At Trial

Not surprisingly, two and a half hours after MacDonald entered the room with Brussel and Silverman, the subject stepped out of the room pale and shaken. In a tape-recorded statement that night,[39] a troubled Mac-Donald said that for the first two hours he was put through a bank of seven psychological tests including a new Rorschach. After the tests, Brussel asked him questions from a typed document which the aged psychiatrist said had been given him by "the little guy," referring to prosecutor Brian Murtagh, who had driven Brussel to the meeting. Mac-Donald told Segal that the larger share of Brussel's questions had not been psychiatric, but forensic, including questions about the crime scene, and Brussel had asked them in the manner of a police investigator, not as by a psychiatrist.

"He did ask me a number of questions about homosexuality, my sex drive, virility and masculinity, and whether I lied to investigators," MacDonald told Segal. "But at no time did Dr. Brussel discuss my childhood, my marriage with Colette, my feelings about my children, my capacity for violence, my aggressiveness."

MacDonald said Brussel read to him portions of Victor Woerheide's interview of Dr. Robert Sadoff that had taken place in Sadoff's home during the final days of the grand jury investigation. MacDonald said that Woerheide's questions were read by Brussel as if they were Sadoff's answers, asking MacDonald to respond to them. When MacDonald pointed out that Brussel had confused the two men, Brussel pushed the paperwork aside and commented, "Well, it's not important anyway. This is just a bunch of crap."

Brussel asked more questions such as "Why was there no evidence of intruders?" and "Did these murders involve homosexual activity?" Finally, at the close of the interview the psychiatrist informed MacDonald that he shaped up to be "a homicidal maniac with pathological tendencies," as well as "a chronic liar." MacDonald challenged Brussel's basis for the remark, pointing out that the psychological tests he had just taken were not even graded yet.

According to MacDonald, Brussel replied, "They will be graded soon."

"As we were getting ready to leave the room," Dr. MacDonald said, "Dr. Brussel's disorientation became more apparent. He asked me if I had taken his hat. I replied I arrived in the room after he did and that I did not see him with a hat. He then asked me if I had his coat. I replied I didn't know anything about a coat. He asked me what motel he was staying at. I asked Dr. Silverman what motel he was staying at and he replied the Royal Villa, so I told this to Dr. Brussel. I then asked Dr. Brussel if he knew where he was. He said somewhere in the South. I asked Dr. Brussel again, 'What motel are you staying in?' He was still unable to tell me at this point what motel he was staying in. He then went to Wade Smith's waiting room and began trying on a hat from the hat rack and he asked me if it was his hat. I told him I didn't know but it didn't appear to fit his head. He then asked how was he to get back to the airport and Dr. Silverman said he wasn't going to the airport—he was going to the motel."

MacDonald's allegations that Dr. Brussel was somehow mentally incapacitated and was being used by Murtagh are seemingly corroborated by the manner in which the diagnostic findings were produced three days later, on August 16, 1979. Normal procedure is for a psychiatrist to prepare and sign the main report, with reports of attending psychologists appended. But in this case the whole of the paperwork produced over the weekend was prepared and introduced not by the psychiatrist, Brussel, but by the psychologist, Dr. Silverman, who submitted the report under his own signature to Brian Murtagh. Segal and MacDonald, incredibly, did not receive a copy of it until after the trial.

Upon hearing MacDonald's story of the questions asked by Brussel, Segal became furious. The lawyer assured MacDonald that Brussel's testimony wouldn't hurt them because he intended to "demolish the old psychiatrist on the stand."

But Segal never got his chance. In violation of the agreement made by Brussel and Silverman, someone[40] immediately and secretly furnished their report to Judge Dupree. This report gave legal and professional credence to ugly rumors which had followed MacDonald for nine years. Finally, after five government and private psychiatrists had found him sane, well balanced, and not likely to have been homicidal, Brussel and Silverman destroyed the last remaining leg of the MacDonald defense, the integrity of his character and his mental stability.

"Psychologically," the Silverman-Brussel report stated, "Dr. MacDonald musters a strangely foundational repression, even an unconscious denial, of the murders of his wife and children." It said, "He lacks a sense of guilt; he seems bereft of a strong conscience." And it stated, "The animal content in the Rorschach further indicates homicidal tendencies. . . . The inanimate movement responses in his Rorschach indicate latent homosexuality approaching homosexual panic; and the depreciated female contents in his projections suggest more than a possibility of homosexuality, latent or otherwise. . . ."

The summation paragraph practically named Jeffrey MacDonald as the killer of his family. Silverman had written, ". . . Dr. MacDonald may well be viewed as a psychopath subject to violence under pressure. . . . Dr. MacDonald in personal and social adjustment is in need of continuous, consistent psychotherapeutic intervention, coupled with psychiatric attention."[41]

With the Silverman-Brussel report in the judge's hands, Murtagh was now able to point to variances between the experts, even though the balance was five doctors to one. Murtagh now argued that the judge shouldn't allow any psychiatric testimony at all because psychiatric testimony seemed to be just another form of character testimony. "The whole thing is a can of worms, Judge," Murtagh complained again.

Segal's angry protests were useless. Upon receipt of the psychiatric report which the judge himself had ordered at Murtagh's insistence, Dupree immediately agreed with Murtagh, saying that psychiatric evidence would only confuse the jurors, ruling it "not cognizable to the ordinary human mind not versed in psychiatry." Segal recalled bitterly that Dupree had earlier removed a potential juror precisely because he possessed a knowledge of psychology. Segal angrily told the judge that the psychiatric testimony was important specifically because the jurors were *not* versed in psychiatry.

But Dupree held his ground. He cautioned both sides not to tell the press anything about the ongoing conversation about psychiatrists. He told Segal that the psychiatric testimony that Segal was trying to offer was just another form of character testimony, and MacDonald already had enough character witnesses. On the twenty-fourth day of trial, August 22, 1979, the "can of worms" was closed. Dupree ruled that psychiatric testimony "will not be admissible." The defense had been fooled into the Brussel examination, and through Brussel's efforts Segal had lost still another leg of MacDonald's defense.

Dupree's ruling against psychiatric testimony in court also kept the jurors from viewing videotapes taken of Dr. MacDonald, under hypnosis, describing the murders. MacDonald was "taken under" by Dr. William S. Kroger, then Richard Doucet took over. Doucet, a former FBI agent and expert hypnotist, regressed MacDonald, who "relived" the attack on him in his living room. MacDonald wept for his wife and children, cursed his assailants, and described them for police artist F. G. Ponce. At one point, MacDonald remembered a cross around the neck of one of the assailants.

MacDonald detractors decried the hypnosis as an act, a consummate MacDonald performance, but many defense team members found themselves unable to view the tapes without weeping, one remarking that "if it's an act, MacDonald should get an Academy Award." Other observers have pointed out that one reason they believed the hypnosis was "real" was that throughout the four-hour hypnosis interview, even though MacDonald appeared to be suffering the agony of the damned, one of his hands remained suspended and unmoving. This suspension was the result of an instruction given by the hypnotist, a form of control to assure that hypnosis remained unfaked, for it is a fact that a person under hypnosis can ignore muscle fatigue far longer than would normally be endurable.[42]

After ruling the jurors could not view the videotapes, or hear the testimonies of the psychiatrists, Judge Dupree proceeded to allow the prosecutors themselves to psychoanalyze Dr. MacDonald at will, presenting him to the jurors as a man in a psychotic rage rampaging through the small apartment stabbing and clubbing and slashing his wife and daughters to death.

Through the Brussel affair the public psychology of Jeffrey MacDonald was completely transformed. The only psychiatric report that was allowed in the official trial record, which allowed no cross-examination, presented him as a homicidal maniac. The positive findings of Dr. Sadoff, Dr. Halleck, and the government's own high-powered three-man team at Walter Reed Hospital were buried by Dupree's ruling. When, years later, Segal read the FOIA releases about the Brussel-CID relationship the defense lawyer charged that the change to MacDonald's official and, consequently, public psychology had been engineered according to a government agenda completely hidden from public view, and outside any fair protections of due process, or normal courtroom procedures, or cross-examination.

Years after the MacDonald trial, Dr. Emanuel Tanay, clinical professor of psychiatry at Wayne State University, and a recognized expert and author on homicide, became interested in the case after reading *Fatal Vision*. In a review of the book for the *Journal of Forensic Sciences* he denigrated the actions of the judge and the prosecutor in the Brussel affair and in the way they handled psychiatric evidence.

> The prosecution's case against Dr. MacDonald was in large measure built upon character assassination. Every possible indiscretion that Dr. MacDonald had committed over his lifetime had been paraded before the jury time and time again. However, psychiatric testimony offered by the defense was kept out because it was ruled to be "character testimony." This was clearly unfair.
> . . . . The judge ruled against "the shrink" testimony but permitted the prosecutor to give "psychiatric" reconstruction in closing argument. The judge allowed state of mind testimony by Mr. Stombaugh, a chemist, but excluded testimony about state of mind by a psychiatrist.

Eventually in 1983 a document released under the Freedom of Information Act revealed Brussel's early role in the CID investigation. By then Bernard Segal had been replaced as the lead defense counsel by attorney Brian O'Neill of Los Angeles. O'Neill, upon seeing the release, complained that Dr. Brussel had certainly not been a "new man" as intimated by Murtagh during the 1979 trial. The old doctor had been aboard the prosecution team, waiting in the wings, for years.[43] With this as a clue, O'Neill compared the government questions asked of MacDonald in court to the questions asked of MacDonald by Brussel during the psychiatric interview. The comparison revealed a pattern.

O'Neill pointed out that when MacDonald was on the witness stand at trial the prosecutors had pressed hard on questions for which MacDonald had few or no answers during his interview with Brussel. But the prosecutors tended to ignore at trial those questions which MacDonald had answered fully and readily for the psychiatrist. Brussel had told MacDonald that his list of questions about the physical evidence was given to him by "the little guy." O'Neill suspected foul play, for MacDonald understood "the little guy" to mean Brian Murtagh. O'Neill's key question in this matter was: How could it be fair for a prosecutor to type up a list of forensic questions to be asked of a defendant by a supposedly neutral psychiatrist?

But Judge Dupree ruled against that 1984–1985 appeal, saying that the prosecutor's action in the Brussel affair was "beyond reproach."

Thus, the prosecution had managed to replace MacDonald's "golden boy" image with that of a twisted monster, and Judge Dupree's edict actually invested the dubious transformation with the sanctity of law.

Dupree's refusal to allow "shrink" testimony at the trial meant that the government had effectively blocked most of the issues upon which Segal had won at the 1970 army hearing. At the army hearing Colonel Rock had insisted upon full disclosure, but at trial that troublesome principle had been beaten back. The defense had not lab-tested the evidence, and they hadn't even been allowed to compare the handwritten lab notes to the official, typed reports. The jurors hadn't been allowed to hear psychiatric testimony, the Rock report, or the Stoeckley confessions. As Bernard Segal had angrily pointed out in my interview with him years later, a lack of disclosure allowed the government's case to undergo a drastic metamorphosis. Now, with each leg of MacDonald's defense cut out from under him, and with the presentation of a crime scene "devoid" of evidence of foreign intruders, MacDonald must have appeared more and more guilty to the jurors.

One more key issue whose character had changed radically was the question of MacDonald's wounds. Had he been badly hurt? Was he faking? Did he stab himself to throw the investigators off the track? And to what extent would allegations about his injuries affect the jurors' verdict?

9

The Verdict

Soon after the crime, the CID agents began claiming that Jeffrey MacDonald wasn't badly hurt. They said they believed that his chest wound was self-inflicted, and that he had faked unconsciousness when the MPs arrived. Words like "barely hurt, only scratches," and "a few cuts and bruises" were often used to describe his condition. By the time of trial, nine years after the murders, that smooth rumor had become so "matter-of-fact" that prosecutor James Blackburn apparently felt quite comfortable to tell the jurors that MacDonald only suffered a "bump on the head . . . a cut on the left arm . . . a paper cut on his finger . . . several abrasions on his chest . . . and an incision in his chest."

The prosecutors also officially claimed that Jeffrey MacDonald "sustained no wounds on his arms, hands, or body consistent with wounds inflicted by an ice pick."[1] Therefore, the prosecutors claimed, MacDonald had lied about an attack on him.

At trial, even some of the doctors who had treated MacDonald downplayed, from their earlier statements, the number and severity of his wounds when they testified. Dr. Frank E. Gemma, chief of surgery at Womack Army Hospital at the time MacDonald was treated, was asked at trial how many ice pick wounds he had seen on MacDonald's body. He replied that he "did not count or actually pay much attention to any of the ice pick wounds. There were none of the ice pick wounds that were so severe on any part of the body that seemed to cause any complications with his treatment."[2] Dr. Severt Jacobson, who had treated MacDonald in the emergency room the day of the murders, told the jurors at trial that MacDonald might have stabbed himself, as the prosecutors claimed. He might have done so, even in the right chest near the liver, with a good chance of survival. Perhaps Dr. Jacobson had reconsidered his earlier position, but this was not what he'd told Colonel Rock nine years earlier. Back at the army hearing Jacobson had insisted that, due to the uncertain elasticity of the skin, it would be difficult to control the depth of the knife point, perhaps causing serious damage to nearby internal organs.

By the time *Fatal Vision* was published, four years after trial and thirteen years after the murders, the canon on the wounds was so well established in the official story that author Joe McGinniss apparently didn't even see the need to detail MacDonald's injuries according to medical records and the documented observations of the physicians treating him on the morning of the murders. Even Judge Dupree would later discount MacDonald's wounds, claiming he had suffered only "scratches." These statements, not the record itself, finally became the public "truth" of the matter, which is that MacDonald suffered only cuts and bruises in a fight with Colette preceding her murder.

But what do the official records actually show?

In the Government Files

When MP Kenneth Mica at the crime scene saw other MPs standing around MacDonald, doing nothing to help him, Mica immediately applied mouth-to-mouth resuscitation, "at least three times," until MacDonald began pushing him away. After hearing MacDonald's initial explanation about what had happened, MPs and medics forced MacDonald onto a gurney only to struggle with him again as he fought the medics and got off the gurney while trying to get into the baby's room just down the hallway.

At Womack Army Hospital, Michael Newman, the noncom in charge of the emergency room night staff, noted that Dr. MacDonald's mouth area was bloody, a fact which supports MacDonald's statement that he had used the mouth-to-mouth revival method on his family members.

The wounds in his chest and abdomen bled only slightly. The only garment he was wearing upon his arrival at Womack Army Hospital was the pajama trousers, and they had been ripped along the inseam from knee to knee. Newman noted that his patient did not seem to be in heavy shock, although MacDonald's emotions were extremely ragged. His body shook visibly, and he cried about his family. The wound in his right chest bubbled bloody froth with each quick breath, creating a mound of pink foam over the wound, an unmistakable sign that the lung had been punctured.

Another jagged knife wound in his upper left abdomen was larger than the chest wound and looked worse, but didn't seem as serious as the stab wound into his lung. During his treatment, the records say MacDonald suddenly bucked upright and fought the attendants. He tried to get off the table, telling his caregivers that he had to get to his kids. "You've got to stay put," an attendant said, trying to hold him down.

In spite of MacDonald's periodic resistance, Newman checked his blood pressure and pulse. "Vital signs stable," the medic reported to Dr. William Straub, the treating physician who had begun the examination. This was a good sign of no serious internal bleeding.

"I checked their pulses. They had no pulses," MacDonald cried. "When is the ambulance coming with them?"

After X-rays, Dr. Severt Jacobson, the surgeon on call, arrived to examine MacDonald, and discovered "four or five" additional wounds in the left upper chest, as opposed to the stab wound in the right chest which had collapsed his lung. These left chest wounds were like ice pick wounds, small round punctures made by an instrument with a pointed shaft.

Dr. Merrill Bronstein, another surgeon, showed up to take charge at 5 A.M. in the intensive care ward. He found MacDonald still semi-hysterical and, despite the presence of blunt-trauma head wounds, Bronstein decided to sedate his patient. MacDonald told Bronstein, "Don't leave me." Then he asked him, "Why aren't you helping my family?"

The collapse of MacDonald's right lung seen on X-ray worsened, and he was moved to an operating room where an incision was made to allow the insertion of a tube between the chest wall and the lung to prevent more blood and air from filling the chest cavity.

When Lieutenant Paulk, accompanied by his driver, Dickerson, arrived at the hospital shortly after 7 A.M. to question MacDonald regarding his descriptions of the attackers, MacDonald had already been given four intravenous sedation injections. MacDonald's doctors insisted that he couldn't talk now, but Paulk had been ordered by Colonel Kriwanek to interview him, so the young lieutenant persisted and was allowed a few minutes with MacDonald.

Despite the influence of the four intravenous pain medications and sedatives in his bloodstream, MacDonald was able to give the junior officer a somewhat lucid account, explaining that he had awakened to Colette's scream, "Jeff, why are they doing this to me?" And Kimberly's cries, "Daddy, Daddy, Daddy, Daddy." He explained that he was confronted immediately, while still on the couch, by the black man and two white men. Behind them was a woman wearing a floppy hat and carrying what he thought might be a candle, since the light on her face was flickering.

MacDonald also told Paulk, in response to Paulk's questions, that he had been threatened by a heroin addict, a corporal named Badger, in his office the day before.

About two hours later CID agent Paul Connolly showed up to ask the patient more questions. Again, MacDonald tried to go through the sequence of events. When he described the black man swinging the baseball bat, Connolly stopped him. "You're sure it was a baseball bat?" There was no baseball bat among the weapons found at the crime scene. Yes, MacDonald explained, saying he had grabbed the club at one point, and that it was smooth like a bat. He said he then lost his grip on it and the man hit him with it.

To other questions about weapons, MacDonald, apparently groggy from the effects of the drugs, replied, "There was a knife in my wife's chest. I pulled it out and threw it. I'm not sure where it went."

Even as CID agents began constructing a view of the crimes without interviewing the first-arriving MPs or others who soon entered the crime scene, MacDonald's four attending physicians also arrived at conclusions regarding his wounds without consulting one another's notes. A cumulative list of MacDonald's wounds can only be determined by examining documents and statements by the many physicians who saw him throughout the day.

Wounds to Dr. MacDonald's head included one discolored, swollen, and scraped blunt-trauma bruise to the left forehead at the hairline. Most doctors saw and reported this bruise, although some reported it lower than the hairline. Others, intent upon caring for the worsening stab wound into the lung, overlooked or completely disregarded it. A smaller bruise on his right forehead, at the hairline, was observed by several people, including medics and Captain Jim Williams, who was a Medical Service Corps officer and former administrator of "MASH"-type units in Vietnam. Doctors who examined him a few days later saw additional contusions on the left posterior portion of Dr. MacDonald's head, hidden by his hair. In all, at least three head injuries were reported.

MacDonald's left shoulder and upper left arm suffered a large bruise attributed to blunt trauma (blow from a club), a "through-and-through" knife wound into the biceps muscle (the knife blade entered in one place and exited in another), and several puncture wounds. The left forearm was also bruised, a wound usually considered defensive.

A cut on a finger of MacDonald's left hand and a cut in the web of the index finger and left thumb were also noted but apparently disregarded by prosecutors, who stated during the trial that there were none.

"Four or five" ice pick wounds were found in the left chest, above the heart area (reports differ on the number). The right chest suffered a stab wound listed as one-half to three-quarters of an inch wide into the anterior chest between the ribs at the seventh intercostal space. This is the wound which collapsed the lung.

In addition, a three-inch-long laceration down to the rectus muscle in the left upper quadrant of MacDonald's abdomen crossed another knife laceration that extended outward and down. These two different knife wounds formed an upside down "V" with the outside laceration of the "V" being slightly shorter than the inside, deeper, laceration.

Across the center of MacDonald's abdomen were several ice pick wounds that were never charted, although one doctor did list them. Two other surgeons later testified to having seen these wounds, describing them as "a bunch" of wounds.

During that first morning it became apparent to his physicians that the first chest tube inserted into MacDonald's collapsed lung was not functioning, so a second surgical operation was required. Another incision was made in his right side and a second chest tube was inserted. Following this, the now heavily drugged MacDonald submitted to a third interview that day. CID agent John Hodges and FBI agents Robert Caverly and Robert Williams of the Fayetteville office required that MacDonald again tell his story.

FBI agent Caverly noted that by this time, as Captain MacDonald attempted to relate the occurrences of that morning, he could not easily follow a logical sequence of events. Caverly ascribed this to the shock and to the drugs, but the CID investigators insisted later that this was not due to the sedatives and anesthesia, but because he was lying. His "noncooperation" was added to the CID reasons for believing MacDonald was the murderer.[3] It is interesting that even though the CID had already decided MacDonald was guilty, none of the investigators who interviewed him informed him of his suspect status, and none of them read him his rights guaranteed under the *Miranda* case.

Even though his accusers have stated that MacDonald never showed any emotion about the deaths of his family, witnesses claim that all that day, and periodically in the days that followed, MacDonald erupted into uncontrollable weeping. Newsmen observing his behavior at the funeral the following Saturday also reported that at times he cried hard.

The record, if not the myth, is clear. MacDonald spent ten days in the hospital, underwent two surgical operations to reinflate his right lung, and, contrary to rumor, he seemed to express shock and grief over the deaths of his family, even after heavy sedation. Contrary to prosecutors' claims, he suffered three blows to the head, and five or six defensive wounds on his hands and arm. He experienced from twelve to seventeen ice pick wounds and at least four stab wounds from a knife. Yet, as time progressed, and as rumors gained official status, memories changed for those who were willing to ignore the original observations in the record.

Alfred Kassab documented his own knowledge of the stab wounds, which he numbered at nineteen, plus multiple head contusions, in a letter of complaint to Congress. Yet, later, after Kassab had changed his opinion regarding MacDonald's guilt, he sometimes told interviewers that when he visited MacDonald at the hospital on the day of the murders he didn't see any wounds on MacDonald's bare torso except for the one in his chest. This "observation" by MacDonald's own father-in-law undoubtedly helped further the myth that MacDonald was "barely hurt," since it was reported in many interviews during television talk shows.

Likewise, Dr. Gemma's failure at trial to remember ice pick wounds on MacDonald's body is contrary to the record he himself filed after treating MacDonald back in 1970. At that earlier time Gemma had indeed paid attention to ice pick wounds and actually recorded them. A narrative summary of MacDonald's clinical record, signed by Gemma on March 12, 1970, included the following statement about wounds to MacDonald's abdomen: "also several small puncture wounds that may have been from an instrument, such as an ice pick."[4]

Interestingly, during the early years of the case, even Brian Murtagh had corroborated the official reports of ice pick wounds. Captain Murtagh, working as a young army lawyer for the CID during its forced reinvestigation of the case, decided in 1972 that MacDonald had attempted suicide immediately after murdering his family. The attorney concluded that MacDonald had wielded a knife and an ice pick against himself. In a report forwarded to the Department of Justice, Murtagh actually mentioned the "ice pick prick marks on his [MacDonald's] chest," and described these marks as "hesitation" wounds.[5]

Dr. Severt Jacobson was yet another doctor who had noted ice pick wounds in MacDonald in 1970. When testifying before the grand jury on November 13, 1974, he said of MacDonald's wounds, "Also, on his skin he had multiple, multiple punctures, ..."[6,7] In each of his sworn testimonies, and in an interview with Fred Bost and me, Jacobson never hesitated to call these punctures ice pick injuries.

It was only after the piece of skin from Colette's fingernail had been lost at the CID laboratory in 1970 that the prosecution tried to present these "punctate wounds" as fingernail scratches. Dr. Jacobson, the initial responding surgeon, has since specifically stated that these wounds definitely were not fingernail scratches.[8] Prosecutors at the trial also implied that MacDonald had lied about the knife attack on him by intruders. They told the jurors that MacDonald could not have been attacked because he had "no defensive-type wounds on his hands and arms." But even as they made these claims to the jury, Brian Murtagh's own files contained documents that challenged them. During testimony before the grand jury in 1974, Dr. Severt Jacobson said he had examined a knife wound on MacDonald's forearm in addition to a cut in the web of one of his fingers.[9] And the official medical records recorded a knife wound all the way through his left bicep, another cut on a finger, and a bruise on his left forearm and shoulder.

At trial in 1979 the prosecution continued to ignore or downplay the severity of MacDonald's 1970 injuries. They waved aside the wound to his left abdomen because it hadn't required stitches, and insisted that the "self-inflicted" lung puncture wasn't a dangerous wound. Yet in transcripts of grand jury testimony the defense team later found contradictions to both these presentations as well. Dr. Merrill Bronstein called the stomach laceration "kind of gaping. It was open. And you could see down to the bottom of it. You could see—every muscle in the body has a covering called a fascia—you could see the fascia of the muscle there."[10] Bronstein said it really should have been sutured, but in the concern over the more serious chest wound and collapsed lung it was overlooked, and simply was taped closed.

As to the severity of MacDonald's collapsed lung (a condition called "pneumothorax"), when Dr. Jacobson reviewed the X-ray in 1974 for the grand jury he said, "I think one could call this up to forty percent pneumothorax. . . . At the time we called it twenty percent."[11] This judgment was confirmed by Dr. Gemma.[12] And Gemma also explained why visitors saw MacDonald "sitting up" in his hospital bed on the day of the murders. It wasn't because MacDonald was unhurt and relaxing, as claimed by Alfred Kassab, or "showing off his bare chest," as claimed by CID agent Paul Connolly, but because his chest wound was serious and "air will rise when you are upright, and the fluid will be down." Thus, his position in bed was part of the treatment for a collapsed lung from a stab wound.

At the army hearing in 1970 each of the doctors who attended MacDonald was asked if he would risk stabbing himself in the seventh intercostal space, the place between the right ribs where MacDonald suffered his apparently most threatening wound. At that time, each one of the doctors considered it too dangerous, due to the proximity of the liver. As Dr. Gemma explained, the liver changes position with every inhalation and exhalation of breath. He told the grand jury that if the knife was angled just a bit downward "it might only have to go in two or three inches to damage the liver."

Gemma explained the seriousness of such an attempt. If a person held a knife at two and a half inches from its point, to allow one inch for elasticity and the rest for penetration, the person might get the safe depth of penetration he wanted, but on the other hand, "he might get more than two full inches penetration when the skin 'gave.'" Gemma insisted that a two-inch depth at this location, so near the liver, might be critical.

But at the trial Gemma didn't offer these earlier observations in Mac-Donald's favor. The possibility that Jeffrey MacDonald had stabbed himself in the lung was now enforced with the solitary medical testimony of Dr. Jacobson, who seemed to have changed his earlier opinion. Jacobson now testified that he thought it *was* possible to control the depth of such a wound if it were self-inflicted.[13] Asked, during a 1989 interview,[14] why his feelings about MacDonald's guilt had changed, Dr. Jacobson said that during the grand jury hearing, the prosecutor's offerings convinced him that he was now testifying about a man who definitely had murdered his family. "The prosecutor showed me evidence that looked pretty sophisticated," Jacobson said. "They even had radiocarbon dating on some of the evidence. It seemed clear, from what they showed me, that they had the proof that he had done it."

On cross-examination at the trial, Dr. Jacobson, nevertheless, had made it just as clear to Bernard Segal that he was not suggesting that Jeffrey MacDonald had wounded himself. He also reconfirmed his earlier testimony that if he were inflicting a wound upon himself he would choose some other location because "there are some vital structures in this area that could make the condition much more serious."

But based upon Jacobson's trial statements, and upon blood of MacDonald's type found at a sink where MacDonald said he had examined his wounds in the mirror, Jim Blackburn told the jury in closing arguments, "I think you can infer from the evidence, ladies and gentlemen, that this defendant with his medical knowledge, with his medical ability, knowing that MPs would soon be on the way, very likely inflicted one—not all, but one—injury in the bathroom. . . ." In light of the indications now available via the government records, however, blood on the bathroom sink may as easily be called evidence for MacDonald's own story, that he had examined his wounds at that sink after he had attempted to revive his family members by applying mouth-to-mouth resuscitation.

Ironically, the army and the government were actually rewarded at trial by the CID's failure to have MacDonald's wounds photographed, and thereby documented, on the very day of the crimes. The lack of a photographic record has allowed a great deal of disinformation to survive, despite the existence of MacDonald's actual hospital records and the various testimonies of the doctors who had treated him.

There is no doubt that MacDonald received more wounds than James Blackburn told the jurors, but still another difficult question plagued the MacDonald defense over the years. Why was Jeffrey MacDonald left alive in the wake of the overkill suffered by his family members?

Helena Stoeckley's words on the subject may cast some light. When Stoeckley returned to her apartment after the crimes that early morning, a girlfriend asked her why they had done it. Stoeckley said she responded, "He deserved to die," as if she thought he had been killed. And she later told Gunderson that they thought MacDonald had been dead when they left the house. She told Fred Bost that when the group learned he was still alive they worried that he might have recognized some of them.

This was still another indication that the group thought they had killed Dr. MacDonald along with the other members of his family.

Joe Grebner alluded to this subject when he asked MacDonald at the April 6, 1970, CID accusation interview why the intruders hadn't just hit him in the head with that club on their way out of the house. MacDonald did not express to Grebner what he, in private, expressed to his own attorneys, that he was ashamed of having remained alive when Colette, Kimberly, and Kristen had died. But he suggested to his own lawyers that, apparently, the intruders *did* hit him in the head while he lay in the hallway. He says he believed he suffered only one or two blows to the head during the actual struggle, but at the hospital later that day his mother and others found three contusions on his head and ice pick wounds which he didn't remember receiving during the struggle. Perhaps a third blow *had* been made while he lay unconscious.

Indeed, during an active struggle, it would be virtually impossible for an assailant to inflict four repetitious ice pick wounds in such a narrow straight line patterned like the "tines of a fork," as recorded by Dr. Jacobson. But such wounds easily could be driven into an unconscious man. And if at the same time the ice pick passed through MacDonald's pajama top stretched taut and ropelike across his chest, the holes in the layered cloth would be multiple, perfectly round, and would be produced without tearing, the way the holes, in fact, did appear in the garment.

Investigator Raymond Shedlick also pointed out a possibility which might have been overlooked by prosecutors intent upon proving him guilty. If MacDonald fought people in the living room after having heard his wife and child screaming in the back of the house, then Colette was fighting someone else. Was that someone more vicious and powerful, and perhaps more combat skilled? Also, MacDonald was much stronger than his family members. He had boxed. He had played football and other sports. He was a paratrooper accustomed to strenuous physical endeavor. And, of course, he had recently received army hand-to-hand combat training. Ironically, if he is telling the truth, his hands getting bound in the pajama top perhaps kept him from fighting back as effectively as he might have, but because he used the garment as a shield, it might have kept many of his chest wounds from being far deeper and therefore lethal.

Defense investigator Raymond Shedlick suggested that one other thing might have saved MacDonald's life. When Shedlick learned about the phone call of Jimmy Friar to the wrong Dr. MacDonald, the detective considered that the intruders may have been frightened away by the possibility of exposure by this early morning caller.

At Trial

When Bernard Segal called Jeffrey MacDonald to the witness stand, the doctor told his story again, standing by his earlier claims that he had awakened to the screams of his wife and older daughter. He again told about three males wielding weapons, and again he described a woman in a floppy hat. She had blond hair, was carrying a flickering light, and wore boots. Then Segal turned MacDonald over to James Blackburn.

During his cross-examination, Blackburn demanded, time after time, that MacDonald explain various "findings" at the crime scene. The pajama fibers found under Colette and in the children's bedrooms were again and again presented as proof that MacDonald was wearing the garment in those bedrooms, and that he had lied about discarding it upon finding his wife. How else, the prosecutor intimated, could fibers have gotten into those other bedrooms? When MacDonald suggested to Blackburn that the ripped pajama bottoms might have deposited the fibers, the prosecutor kept pressing as if he had not heard that MacDonald still wore the ripped pajama bottoms, and this led MacDonald to speculate further. Perhaps, he surmised, the fibers had adhered to his bloody hands, perhaps to the hairs on his arms, and when he bent over the children to try to revive them by mouth-to-mouth breathing, the fibers were deposited there. The prosecutor gave no consideration to the defense's longtime claims that many MPs and CID people had compromised the crime scene, moving things, long before the evidence was collected. No thought was given to Shaw's statement about seeing a pile of blue fibers in the hallway, a pile that had disappeared by the time the CID got around to processing that hallway floor days later, only after the area was traversed by scores of boots and shoes.

Blackburn asked MacDonald if Colette had bled on the pajama top before it was torn. He answered "no," but the prosecutor failed to allow for the secret CID lab report that indicated, in MacDonald's favor on this point, that the bloodstain got onto the garment *after* it was torn. Blackburn pressed this point made by Paul Stombaugh, despite the fact that Stombaugh's photographs and light box had failed to show a bloodstain continuing across a tear.

Blackburn kept firing questions MacDonald could not answer, or, as Blackburn intimated to the jury, MacDonald *would* not answer. The prosecutor referred to "the struggle" between Jeffrey and Colette, to which MacDonald curtly replied, "I'll repeat, Colette and I did not have a struggle."

Blackburn asked how the bloody impression of a cuff of MacDonald's pajama top got onto the blue bedsheet. MacDonald couldn't answer that damaging question. He wouldn't learn for nearly ten years that his neighbor, Chaplain Edwards, saw Colette's body—with the pajama top presumably on her chest—covered by that same sheet. The prosecutor's question implied, however, that MacDonald had used the sheet to carry her unconscious body back to the master bedroom where he finally murdered her, as the government had earlier claimed.

Often during these exchanges, a furious Bernard Segal objected on the ground that the so-called facts being questioned "haven't been proven in this case." Even though, in one instance, the defense experts agreed that the bloody cuff impression did appear on the blue bedsheet, Judge Dupree suggested during a bench conference that Blackburn change the form of his question to: "If the jury should find from other evidence certain facts, do you have any explanation. . . ?"

This form of the question, while legally acceptable, still left MacDonald apparently unable, or in the government's view unwilling, to explain facts that weren't proven. The judge told Blackburn to simply "put it in the hypothetical." The judge looked at Segal and said, "Even Mr. Segal won't have any objection to that, will you?"

Segal, defeated again, didn't even answer. The bench conference was terminated; Blackburn had been instructed how to ask questions of MacDonald about "facts" which had never been established.

During the following exchanges he used Dupree's suggested technique often and well. Each exchange that began with "If the jury were to find . . . do you have an explanation . . ." carried with it an implication that MacDonald had a requirement to prove his innocence. Finally Segal, with his objections being overruled, asked Dupree to ensure that the jury understood the law, that the burden of proof is never on the defense, but only on the government.

Judge Dupree complied, telling the jurors, "That is the rule of law under which all cases are tried in this court. . . . and it is in full force and effect from the inception of the trial right on through to the final verdict." Segal could only hope that the judge's instruction would act as a sobering filter for the unusual type of questioning going on.

Blackburn continued with his hypothetical questions using varying findings or assumptions—such things as the distribution of pajama fibers, the bloody footprints in Kristen's room, the "stepping upon" the bloody bedspread, the lack of blood on the Geneva Forge knife, the wiping of a knife and ice pick on the bathmat, and the lack of fingerprints on the telephones.

Although cross-examination of a prior government witness had touched lightly on a blood spot found in the hallway where MacDonald said he had lain unconscious, that blood spot had never been introduced by the government as part of the collected evidence. Neither had it been included on any of the charts prepared by Murtagh.[15] Blackburn, ignoring knowledge of this bloodstain, now asked MacDonald, "Suppose, sir, that the jury should find that no Type B blood—your type blood—is found in the living room area where the struggle with the intruders allegedly occurred, and you were allegedly stabbed—do you have an explanation for that?"

MacDonald answered, "Nothing other than the obvious. The wounds weren't bleeding very much."

So the jury was left with the impression that MacDonald had once again failed to prove a point in his story.

When testimony at the trial finally ended, the jurors were faced with a sobering duty. They had to decide who was telling the truth. Was it MacDonald? Or was it the combined forces of the army and the Federal Bureau of Investigation and the United States government? To help the jurors' thought processes, both sides were allowed closing arguments.

There is no doubt that by standards of proficiency the prosecution team had done its job well. Most things which challenged the government's views and which Segal had wanted to present had been denied to the jurors through the prosecution's efforts. Now in the closing arguments Jim Blackburn added to that proficiency by reminding the jurors that MacDonald couldn't answer a great many questions about conditions at the crime scene. Blackburn asked the jurors, "Don't you think if he could have, he would have?"

Then Blackburn introduced his final point in dramatic fashion, meant to be the determining blow. Back in 1970 the CID laboratory had discovered two tiny dark threads adhering to the splintery wooden club that had been used against Kimberly and Colette. The lab determined that these fibers were purple cotton sewing threads from the seams of MacDonald's pajamas. Although the army attorneys at the Article 32 hearing lent little importance to this finding, Blackburn considered it the ultimate proof of MacDonald's guilt.

He used these two fibers well. Blackburn reminded the jurors of the mass of evidence he and Murtagh had presented, then he told them they "could throw the whole shooting match away except for two pieces of evidence." He held up the torn, bloodstained, blue pajama top which MacDonald had worn on the night his wife and daughters were slaughtered. Blackburn then lifted high the crude wooden club that had felled Colette and had crushed Kimberly's skull. He asked the jury, "Why are they so important?"

After due pause, he answered his own question by reminding them that two threads from the pajama top were found caught on the club. "This sounds sort of minor, really," he said, "until you think about something. How did they get there?"

Blackburn said it was because the murder club "was not outside the back door until after—not before—that pajama top dropped threads and yarns and blood on the floor, and as it fell on the floor it picked up the threads and picked up the yarns with the blood and it was thrown out the door." Blackburn's point, of course, is that MacDonald was lying about this club. The implication was that MacDonald, not intruders, used it, dropped it on the floor strewn with fibers, then picked it up and threw it out the door to make it appear that an assailant had thrown it down on his way out.

Prosecutor James Blackburn wasn't the only person in that courtroom who thought those dark fibers on the club were important and damning. MacDonald later claimed that when the prosecution told the jurors that agents had found pajama top fibers on the murder weapon, the defense team sagged noticeably and never mustered the strength to recover. Segal also later said that he had absolutely no defense for the fibers, no convincing explanation at all except to guess that the CID agents had lain it down in the house and picked up pajama fibers on it that morning. But since he had no proof of this, those reported pajama top fibers on the rough wooden club that had struck down Colette and Kimberly now threatened—because it bore two fibers—to strike the death blow to MacDonald's chances in court.

What do the government documents reveal about Blackburn's pivotal evidence? Did the government really find two dark little pajama top fibers on that murder weapon, or is even this "most important" proof of MacDonald's guilt challenged by Murtagh's own records?

Let us leave prosecutor Blackburn holding that murder weapon up over the jurors' heads. Leave him there for a moment, suspended in time, and move back a few feet to the valises of Brian Murtagh's case records, the records Segal had fought in vain to see. And, via the time travel provided by the FOIA records, we back up just a few months to visit Murtagh pre-trial, when he ordered further secret laboratory examinations on some key items which included the debris found on the club. What do those documents say that the FBI laboratory technician really found on that club?

In the Government Files

When the studies of the FOIA documents were nearly completed in the late 1980s, these two fibers were considered the only evidence for which the defense researchers still had not found government documentation which opposed key government claims. Consequently, for years, the effort to understand how the fibers might have arrived on the club underlay nearly everything else in the MacDonald defense effort. Defense team members, most still working gratis for MacDonald on evenings and weekends, searched through more than 10,000 pages of documentation for proof that perhaps the CID had mishandled the club and somehow brought it into contact with pajama fibers strewn throughout the house.

The suspicion that the CID discoverers could have brought the club from the backyard into the house and contaminated it with fibers, either from the rug or the pajamas, was still uppermost in the minds of defense researchers. And they had encountered tantalizing hints that they were right. For one thing, discrepancies exist in statements as to when the weapons were found and how well they were protected. Robert Shaw swore under oath that he discovered the weapons after daylight, sometime after 6:30 A.M. and that he took extreme care to have them photographed in place and to protect them. But statements by four other people, including his boss, Joe Grebner, maintain that the weapons were found about an hour and a half before that, and that their positions had actually changed in the yard. If so, then perhaps the club had been handled during that ninety minutes by someone who had somehow caused pajama fibers to adhere to it, then put it back out in the yard in the wrong place.[16]

Equally intriguing to the defense team was a story that surfaced a decade after the trial, told by a soldier who claimed to have known Ivory in Germany after 1979. The soldier said that Ivory had told him the weapons had been brought into the house; then, when the agents realized the weapons had never been photographed in place, they were taken back out into the yard for photos. If so, then perhaps the club, still wet from rain and blood, picked up pajama top fibers in the house. There was no way to corroborate this claim, however,[17] and nothing else was found to buttress the defense team's efforts to discredit Blackburn's claim that pajama fibers were found on the murder club.

The months of research on this issue continued, with the poorly photocopied handwritten lab notes being examined and reexamined. On one of these eye-wearying excursions Ellen Dannelly spied the words "black wool." They appeared in FBI laboratory exhibit Q89. And after the words "black wool" appeared the word "Source?"

She'd read these notes before, but she had always been looking for references to known exhibits. "Black wool" had never before registered with her. Dannelly immediately sent copies of that note out to defense team lawyers, detectives, and volunteer defense team researchers. Dannelly also sent copies of the note to Fred Bost and me. My wife, Prebble, who was at the time compiling a computer database of names and subjects of all the FOIA and other case-related documents, cross-checked the FBI exhibit identification number in the lab note against Bost's previously compiled list of FBI exhibit numbers.

"Guess what?" Prebble said to me. She was smiling broadly.

"What?"

"Q89 is some fiber debris," she said.

"That's a good guess," I said, smiling back at her. "Black wool would have to be fiber. So?"

"This isn't just any fiber. Remember the two dark fibers Blackburn called pajama top fibers?"

"Okay." *Now* she had my attention. "Go on."

"Exhibit number Q89 is fiber debris from the murder club," she said.

"You're kidding."

"Nope. They found two black wool fibers on the murder club and they didn't report it. Blackburn's little closing drama, holding up that murder club saying they'd found pajama fibers on it, was misleading at best, maybe even a complete farce."

Excited, we phoned Fred Bost and he and Ellen Dannelly, working separately, began meticulous studies of all CID and FBI examinations of the club, the debris on the club, and anything else having to do with black wool. By reviewing the government lab work, we learned that black wool also had been found on Colette's mouth where she had been struck with that club, and on her pajama top. Neither the CID nor the FBI reports list any black wool as having been found in the murder apartment. Like the hair in Colette's hand and the blond synthetic fibers in the hairbrush, and like the fresh wax drippings in the house, there was no match among the known fiber products at the crime scene. The black wool appeared to be foreign to the MacDonald household.

This discovery sent shock waves through the defense ranks. In the view of the defense lawyers, at least, the last piece of previously unassailed government evidence, after eighteen years, seemed to have fallen. For, according to the government's own documents and court testimony, those fibers on the murder club were supposed to be purple cotton, not black wool.

Still reading the FOIA documents, Fred Bost sought out the history of the lab analyses that produced the discovery of the black wool. He wanted to know who had ordered the examination and what else was found. The records show that as Brian Murtagh prepared for trial, even while Segal was requesting and being denied laboratory access to the critical documents and fibers, Murtagh had asked that certain evidence be reexamined by the FBI laboratory. The debris from the club happened to be among that evidence. The lab notes Murtagh had fought so hard to keep in his possession now proved that Murtagh's FBI laboratory examiner had indeed found two dark fibers on the club, as had the CID examiners years earlier, but the 1979 lab notes revealed dark black wool fibers, and listed no dark cotton fibers from MacDonald's pajama top among the fibers on the club.

Bost's further analysis of all previous lab documents proved that the first examinations on the debris from the club had taken place at the army CID laboratory back on February 28, 1970, just eleven days after the murders. The lab note from that exam stated that the fibers consisted of "two purple multi-strand cotton fibers identical to the purple thread used to sew the seams of the pajama top." The note also indicated the presence of multicolored nylon fibers, most of them bloodstained, all of them identical to the multicolored rug in the bedroom.[18]

The CID's description of this debris never changed. In all future notes cataloging the debris there were always two dark fibers and *only* two dark fibers, among numerous light-colored fibers. When CID lab tech Dillard Browning testified for the government at the 1979 trial he told the jurors that upon receipt of this debris directly from the crime scene, he found the two purple fibers had already been separated from the rest, placed in their own vial by field agents, signifying the agents' belief that these were pajama fibers—a belief that might have influenced Browning's own interpretation when he, too, called them pajama fibers.[19] Janice Glisson had made a similar mistaken identification, later rectified, when she at first said that the blond fibers from the clear-handled hairbrush matched Colette's hair—an error which, it seems, can only be made by a lab tech failing to use a microscope.[20]

At the trial, long before the defense team even knew about the black wool, Segal cross-examined CID lab tech Browning about the fibers on the club which he claimed were from MacDonald's pajamas. "I assume you counted the number of fibers?"

"Yes, I did," Browning said. "The number of fibers present in the vial were two."

"There were two in the vial?"

"Yes, that's two purple cotton fibers."[21]

So, in the mix of the *colors* of the various fibers, Browning's testimony was perfectly consistent with the CID lab reports. He said he had seen two, *and only two*, dark fibers. His 1970 report on the entire collection of debris from the club showed the same color mix found by the FBI just before the trial, two dark fibers among other lighter fibers.[22] Only in the FBI's 1979 tests, the two dark fibers reported weren't purple cotton at all, they were black wool.

With the additional discovery that black wool fibers had been collected from Colette's mouth and from her pajamas,[23] the defense team had finally found what they considered to be proof that Blackburn's most dramatic claim at trial, the evidence that Blackburn touted most highly, was in error. For even if the government persisted in the claim that the earlier CID reports prove two purple cotton pajama top fibers were on the club, the defense team could now point to the devastating find of foreign black wool fibers on the *murder* weapon, *and* on Colette's bruised mouth, *and* on her bloody pajamas. Since the government had failed to match any of these fibers to source garments in the apartment, despite attempts to do so, it was logical to infer that the black wool fibers came from an assailant who fled the scene. And, finally, even if one ignores the obvious possibility of intruders having somehow gotten the purple pajama top fibers on the club as they assaulted MacDonald or poked at his unconscious form while he lay in the hallway, the defense certainly should have been notified by the government of the existence of the black wool fibers found in such crucial locations.[24]

When, in his tenth year in prison, MacDonald's new defense attorney Harvey Silverglate filed the 1990 habeas petition which relied heavily upon the black wool, the government once more had the fibers from the club examined, this time by FBI technician Michael P. Malone. When Malone's carefully worded affidavit was submitted to the courts, it, too, failed to address the presence of, or the examination of, any "pajama" fibers as being in the debris found on the club. Malone did, however, find and examine two dark fibers among that debris. They weren't dark cotton pajama top fibers at all. Again, they were black wool. Malone's 1990 exam thus confirmed the long-secret 1979 FBI testing.

At Trial

Now, we return to James Blackburn holding that club high above the jury box. Co-prosecutor Brian Murtagh, sitting behind Blackburn, has just now reached a point of no return. He has fought very hard to get this case to trial. He has successfully argued to keep out all psychiatric testimony and all testimony about the Stoeckley confessions and the troublesome Rock report; and he has successfully hindered Segal's chances to lab-test the evidence. He hasn't even allowed Segal to know that the FBI lab retested the fibers on the club as a result of Murtagh's own request, so Segal wasn't aware that the FBI test results did not agree with the results of the earlier CID lab tests. As chief prosecutor James Blackburn completed his claim to the jurors that these "pajama top fibers" prove that MacDonald used this club to destroy Colette and Kimberly, Murtagh sat behind him in silence, leaving the ill-informed and unsuspecting jurors to imagine an enraged Jeffrey MacDonald wielding that splintery piece of wood, smashing it down upon Kimberly and Colette, crushing their skulls, removing them in a horrible way from his otherwise charmed life.

The prosecution's failure to reveal the existence of the black wool[25] allowed the jurors to accept Blackburn's imagery as if it were proven unequivocally by both the CID lab and FBI analysts. But, as in all other key government exhibits, the FOIA documents reveal that the jurors saw only part of the evidence. What might have happened if Murtagh had brought to the witness stand James C. Frier, the FBI laboratory examiner who had found the black wool fibers? What if Segal had asked Frier, under oath, if he'd examined the two cotton fibers Blackburn was claiming? What if Frier let slip that he examined two *black wool* fibers? Blackburn's key proof would have been in jeopardy, but that never happened. Why it didn't happen is interesting and, no doubt, crucial.

James Frier was on Murtagh's list of government witnesses to be called during trial. He was apparently in Raleigh waiting to be called. But before he could be asked to appear, Murtagh filed a stipulation, avowedly in the interests of time and expense, that there was really no need for lab tech Frier to take the stand because all he'd be saying was that he'd matched a green bloodstained yarn found on the floor of Kristen's room to a number of colored yarns found on Colette's nightstand. Murtagh added that Frier was also prepared to testify that he had compared some fibers from the murder club to fibers from the throw rug in the master bedroom, and "in his [Frier's] opinion, they could have a common source." In short, Murtagh led Dupree and Segal to believe that Frier really had nothing of importance to tell.

Segal believed Murtagh's claims, and he agreed to excuse Frier. But since Segal didn't have Frier's handwritten lab notes, his agreement to the stipulation effectively excused from the stand the one man, besides perhaps Murtagh, who could have told him that Frier found something on that murder weapon besides some fibers which matched the rug.

In light of what was learned about the Frier examination more than ten years after the trial, the salient facts regarding the fibers on the murder club seem to be that the CID lab said they found two dark pajama fibers, but when the FBI lab reported on the same debris taken from the club, they listed *no pajama top fibers*. They listed, instead, black wool fibers, black wool which matched no other wool in the house. If Frier had testified as scheduled, Segal might have shown the jurors the murder club with foreign fibers on it, fibers for which no match was found in the house, fibers which Segal therefore could have suggested came from the clothing of outside intruders. But Murtagh, whether or not knowingly, protected Frier's discovery of black wool fibers on the murder weapon, and Blackburn was free to show the jurors the murder club and claim, without opposition from the still-hidden documents or the FBI lab tech, that only two dark fibers, MacDonald's pajama top fibers, were found on it.

BLOOD ON THE HALLWAY FLOOR

Blackburn's dramatic presentation of the fibers on the club would not be the final blow to MacDonald's attempt to prove himself innocent at trial. Another, perhaps equally critical, if not as dramatic, incident would come within hours. After closing arguments were finished, Judge Dupree gave the jury their instructions then sent them to their solemn task. But the twelve jurors could not immediately agree to a unanimous vote either way, and their arguments somehow brought them around to MacDonald's wounds and to his claims that he had fallen, injured and unconscious, onto the hallway floor. They wondered whether MacDonald had indeed lied about his wounds as Murtagh and Blackburn claimed. This was a critical juncture. Nine years of investigation and six weeks of trial had arrived at a single question: Had Jeffrey MacDonald been untruthful about lying unconscious on that hallway floor?

The jurors tried to remember whether any evidence had been found to support MacDonald's claim of falling to the floor. They had no way of knowing, for instance, that a pile of blue fibers had disappeared from that end of the hallway floor, and that a pubic hair had been found there, then had been lost at the lab. But they reasoned that MacDonald certainly should have been bleeding if he had been stabbed in the chest and abdomen and arm.

Blackburn had set the stage for just such a question when he told the jurors on the very first day of trial that there was a great deal of blood in that house, but what was important, he also had told them, was where the blood was *not*. When Blackburn cross-examined MacDonald after the accused had told his story about facing intruders and being stabbed, the prosecutor challenged MacDonald with the "fact" that no blood was found in the hallway.

On August 28, 1979, Blackburn skillfully pressed this false point home during his summation before the jurors. "You know," Blackburn told the jury, "he [MacDonald] said he lay unconscious—for how long he did not know—right there." Blackburn pointed and every head in the hushed courtroom turned to the blood chart, every eye became fixed upon the hallway portion of that blood chart.

"How much blood of Type B was found on his pajama top which he said was under his wrists?" Blackburn cried. "Very little." Then Blackburn delivered the killing blow. "How much Type B blood, if any, was found here?"

Of course, according to the chart, there was none.

When Judge Dupree sent them to the jury room to deliberate, he told the jurors that if they thought MacDonald had lied about events in the house that morning, they could find him guilty. Not surprisingly, then, the deliberating jurors called out for the official FBI blood chart to be brought into them—a chart which, over the objections of Segal, had been deemed bona-fide evidence by Judge Dupree. The jurors examined the chart carefully, and, as Blackburn had earlier shown, they found blood noted in many places in the house—the bathroom, the bedrooms, the kitchen. But the government's official chart showed no blood in the one place where blood would have supported MacDonald's story, in the hallway where he said he had lain unconscious. The jury simply could not reconcile such evidence with MacDonald's story. MacDonald, not the government, had to be lying.

By withholding critical evidence Murtagh and Blackburn finally had destroyed the jurors' perception of MacDonald's innocence. Yet Fred Bost, while studying government documents years later, discovered that the consolidated CID laboratory report issued in 1972 listed Exhibit D-144, a blood spot recovered from the west end of the MacDonald hallway, shown as being Type B or Type O blood. Bost searched out the original handwritten lab notes on this item, notes that had been recently released through the Freedom of Information Act. The analysis note indicated that the blood was most likely Type B (MacDonald's type). But the note went on to say that the contamination of floor wax made this Type B finding inconclusive, and thus the blood more remotely could be of Type O. Bost wondered whether this last note, about Type O blood, was a convenient "out" for the CID in case the Type B blood was ever discovered. Bost also wondered what the lab would have found if the blood on the hallway floor had been collected when it was fresh instead of three days later, after scores of shoes and boots had tread on it. And Bost and I both lamented often that Segal's team had not found the obscure mention of Type B or O blood in perhaps the most critical location within the murder apartment.

Bost found not only that blood evidence had been withheld from the jury by the government, but that fiber evidence from the same area of the hallway had also been excluded from the government's offerings. CID agent Robert Shaw had seen a "pile" of blue fibers on the floor at the entrance to the hallway. That pile wasn't mentioned in the evidence reports even though MacDonald had told the agents that he had fallen there during a fight after his pajama top had been pulled over his head by one of the intruders. In addition to this deletion, the consolidated CID laboratory report showed that Exhibit E-32 was debris from the hallway near the living room steps, and that it included several fibers which matched Jeffrey MacDonald's pajama top. In examining the lab notes on this, Bost found that Dillard Browning of the CID lab had discovered two pajama fibers in the debris, and that Stombaugh of the FBI, when reexamining the debris four years later, found only one such fiber. So the fiber evidence had diminished, from a "pile" of fibers, to two fibers, to one fiber, and then, like the vanishing Type "B" blood, the fiber count in that hallway fell to zero on the official FBI charts, charts whose construction was overseen by Brian Murtagh.

The jurors' deliberations took less than six hours. On August 29, 1979, the jury found Jeffrey MacDonald guilty of second-degree murder in the deaths of his wife, Colette, and older child, Kimberly, and of first-degree murder in the death of little Kristen. MacDonald's mother and other family members broke into sobbing. People in the gallery cried aloud, as did members of the defense team. Even Joe McGinniss wept. A stern-faced Judge Dupree immediately asked Jeffrey MacDonald if he had anything to say. MacDonald, stunned, stood up shakily, and replied, "I'm not guilty. I don't think the court has heard all the evidence."

But Jeffrey MacDonald had no idea how much secret evidence still lay in government files. As Bost and I worked in the files we made lists of the items the CID had found which never appeared before the jurors. Besides the vanishing blood and fibers in the hallway, there was the piece of skin from Colette's fingernail. That piece of skin had been lost or destroyed even before it had been lab-tested—but *after* the chief CID investigator had gone to the lab, picked it up, put it under a microscope, and looked at it long enough to establish for himself and for the lab manager that it was, indeed, skin. Then, mysteriously, it was gone. A similar fate awaited the mystery hair from Colette's left hand, a hair which was, at first, of sufficient quantity to test secretly against MacDonald's hair samples, and against hair from investigators and family members. Yet by trial time the hair somehow had been altered so that Paul Stombaugh now told the jurors that this hair was simply too small to test—without telling them the whole truth which lay in the government files, that this mystery hair *had* been tested against MacDonald's hair and it wasn't his.

The list goes on. Multiple pairs of bloody gloves, the unmatched black wool fibers on the murder weapon and on Colette, the unmatched blond wig hair, an unmatched blue acrylic fiber in Colette's hand, an unmatched pubic hair beneath Colette's body—the jury knew about none of it, yet the prosecutors would continue to tell the world for years to come that "the evidence" proved MacDonald guilty.

MacDonald's "fair trial" was over. MacDonald awaited his fate. A poker-faced Dupree quickly sentenced him to three consecutive terms of life imprisonment.

Jeffrey and Colette MacDonald on their wedding day. (*Dorothy MacDonald*)

Colette and the MacDonalds' children, Kristen and Kimberly. (*Dorothy MacDonald*)

WEATHER
Cloudy, foggy tonight. Clearing, warmer Wednesday. Low, mid-30s; high, 55-63. Warmer Thursday. Details on 1B.

The Fayetteville Observer

STOCKS
Today's complete New York, American Exchange prices, other financial news. Pages, 12-13A.

Established 1817

VOL. CLIII—NO. 170   TWENTY-SIX PAGES   FAYETTEVILLE, N. C., TUESDAY, FEBRUARY 17, 1970   FINAL EDITION   PRICE TEN CENTS DAILY, TWENTY-FIVE CENTS SUNDAY

Dial 484-6121

Victims Of Hippie Cult?

Officer's Wife, Children Found Slain At Ft. Bragg

14 Caught In Huge Drug Raid

Local Youth Is Included

DURHAM (AP)—Hearings will begin Wednesday for some of the 14 young persons arrested in what state law enforcement officials call a crackdown on major suppliers of illegal drugs in a three-county area of North Carolina.

The 14, including the 18-year-old son of University of North Carolina Chancellor J. Carlyle Sitterson, were arrested Monday.

Ages of the youths ranged from 17 to 22. Four are college students and one is a high school pupil.

The director of the State Bureau of Investigation, Charles Dunn, said the youths are believed to have been major suppliers of narcotics to high school and college students in Orange, Durham and Moore counties.

"We feel a major illegal drug operation has been broken up," Dunn said. He said the arrests came as a result of four months of investigation by his agency and the police in Chapel Hill, Durham, Southern Pines, Pinehurst and Moore County.

Dunn said several cars were confiscated in the arrests, along with quantities of marijuana, LSD, DTP and Heroin.

He said the investigation is continuing and he expects more arrests.

Sitterson's son, Carlyle Howard Sitterson, was charged with four counts of possession of narcotics for the purpose of sale. His bail was set at $20,000.

Sitterson, reached at his home in Chapel Hill, said he would have no comment on his son's arrest. Young Sitterson is a freshman at UNC.

(See RAID, Page 2A)

By PAT REESE
Observer Staff Writer

An Army doctor's wife and their two young children were stabbed to death in their Ft. Bragg home early today, apparently murder victims of a "ritualistic" hippie cult.

The doctor, Capt. Jeffrey MacDonald, 26, 6th Special Forces, was reported in satisfactory condition late this morning at Womack Army Hospital where he is being treated for multiple stab wounds.

The victims were identified as MacDonald's wife Colette, 26, and the couple's two daughters, Kimberly, 6, and Kristen Jean, age 2.

Military authorities said MacDonald told them four people—three men and a woman—burst through the rear door of the home at approximately 4 a.m. chanting "LSD is great. LSD is great" while the family slept.

One of the suspects, a blonde woman wearing a floppy hat and muddy white boots, was carrying a candle, according to a report from the investigating officers.

Officers said another suspect was a Negro man wearing a jacket with sergeant stripes on the sleeves. The two other suspects were reportedly white men, they said.

Military police said when they arrived at the couple's Corregidor Courts home, a six-room, one-story brick structure, they found the front door locked. They went to the rear door, which was open, and entered the home.

They reported finding the two small girls in a bedroom where they had died from stab wounds. One military policeman said furniture in the living room had been overturned.

(See OFFICER'S WIFE, 2A)

This Is The Home Of Capt. MacDonald At Ft. Bragg   (Observer photo by Bivens)

New Probe Opens On Viet Policy

WASHINGTON (AP) — A U.S.-aided program under which South Vietnam seeks to capture, convert or kill leaders of the Viet Cong faced a critical Senate inquiry today in the opening round of new war policy hearings.

The operation is called the Phoenix program, and Sen. J. W. Fulbright, D-Ark., already has characterized it as a system of assassination.

The Senate Foreign Relations Committee, which Fulbright heads, will consider Phoenix as part of a wider inquiry into U.S. aid and advisory operations in Vietnam.

Fulbright said the committee will hold hearings in March on the activities of U.S. military advisers, and American economic aid to (See NEW PROBE, Page 2A)

Senate Reaches Time Of Decision On School Integration Measure

WASHINGTON (AP) — The Senate reached the time of decision today on proposals designed to check the drive toward school integration now in full swing in the South.

The initial vote was set on an amendment by Sen. John Stennis, D-Miss., to a $33 billion education bill seeking a uniform policy for school desegregation throughout the nation.

Stennis' amendment provided the government must move its vigorously against Northern de facto segregation—that caused primarily by neighborhood patterns—as it does against de jure, or legal segregation in the South.

Scott Flies To Washington

RALEIGH (AP) — Gov. Bob Scott planned to fly to Washington today to confer with the North Carolina congressional delegation on school desegregation problems.

He was to be accompanied by two aides — David Murray, an administrative aide, and Fred Morrison, staff legal aide.

The North Carolina governor did not plan to meet with the governors of three other Southern states who were to gather in Washington today to discuss their school integration problems.

Scott's office said he was not invited to the meeting and the timing of the trip was just coincidental.

The meeting will bring together the governors of Alabama, Mississippi and Louisiana.

Scott was to arrive in just Washington income tax time.

(See SCOTT, Page 2A)

Today's Chuckle

Ruling Asked On Racial Balance

WASHINGTON (AP) — The Supreme Court, which has been slowly spelling out its school desegregation policy for 16 years, has been urged to say finally whether racial balance in every school is the only way to achieve integration.

WASHINGTON (AP) — Nathan P. Volosen, a longtime friend of House Speaker John W. McCormack, and four other men were indicted by federal grand jury today on charges of defrauding a corporation in connection with a $775,000 Navy contract proposal.

Jury Indicts Friend Of McCormack

Blue To Seek Nomination

By JIM CARR
Observer Staff Writer

ABERDEEN — Newspaper publisher H. Clifton Blue of Aberdeen made weeks of speculation Monday as he announced that he will seek the Democratic nomination for Congress in the 8th District.

Blue's entry into the race sets up what is expected to be a hotly contested battle for the nomination between two of Moore County's leading political figures. Former State Sen. Voit Gilmore of Southern Pines paid his filing fee last week.

ROTC Offices Leveled

EUGENE, Ore. (UPI) — A four-alarm fire broke out in the Physical Education Building at the University of Oregon Monday night and destroyed the ROTC offices and other facilities, including irreplaceable records.

(See ROTC OFFICES, Page 2A)

Where It Is Today

Amusements 10-11A
Bridge 11A
Classified 7-11B
Comics 11A
Crossword Puzzle 11A
Deaths 4A
Editorials 4A
Financial 12-13A
Horoscope 11A
Sports 5-6B
Social 1-4B
Television 10-11A

• Planners Seek Pollution Solution, 1B
• Soldier Held In Cross Creek Slaying, 1B
• Dream Gathers Dozor Nominations, 10A
• Housing Order May Slow Construction, 14A

(Fayetteville Publishing Company)

544 Castle Drive, Fort Bragg. The MacDonalds' ground-floor apartment is at right in top picture and left in bottom picture. (*Exhibits in* U.S. v. MacDonald)

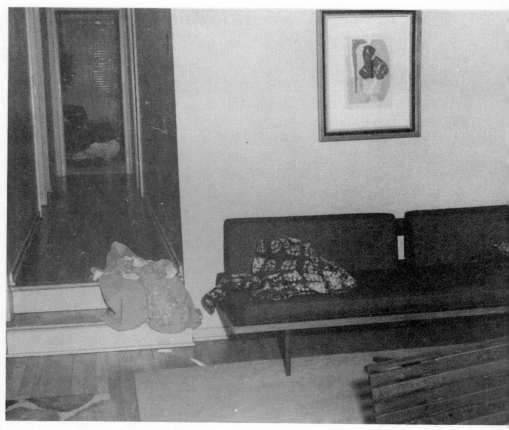

At the end of the corridor, Colette MacDonald's body. *(Exhibit in U.S. v. MacDonald)*

The overturned coffee table, and the white plastic flowerpot standing upright rather than on its side as observed by the first MPs on the scene. *(Exhibit in U.S. v. MacDonald)*

Two photographs of the MacDonalds' kitchen show how items were moved by MPs and CID investigators before they could be logged as evidence and examined: the coffeepot, at first on the counter and then on the washing machine, was used by CID investigators for coffee breaks; the telephone handset, reported dangling from its cord by the first MPs on the scene, was put back on its hook. (*Exhibits in* U.S. v. MacDonald)

#13 one hair - bloody

—————————————————

#13 <u>E-5</u> apprex 1 inch : curved - worn end -

worn end   narrow diam at
                            the same width
                            fine pigment gr
                            interrupted medul
                            darker color along
                            broken end   sides

E 305 = too black
E 306 = ~~grey~~ ~~brown~~ diam varies = bulges
E 307 = ~~grey~~ ~~brown~~
E 308 = "   "   tapered
E 309 = "   "   "
E 310 = "   "   diam varies - tapered - worn end but not
E 311   "   "   "   "   like #13
E 312 black brown - diam varies ;
E 313 medulla too heavy ; diam varies ; tapered
E-5 #13 ~~tapered~~ Compared to ~~304~~ 306
       mounted E-5 between the two hairs of 306. the
       two hairs of 306 ~~were~~ had more pts of similarity
       to each other than E-5 #13 had to them. Some areas

1141

Lab note written by CID technician Janice Glisson records comparison tests of the bloody hair found in Colette MacDonald's left hand against hairs taken from Jeffrey MacDonald (none of which matched). At trial, the prosecution said the hair was too small to be tested. *(FOIA document)*

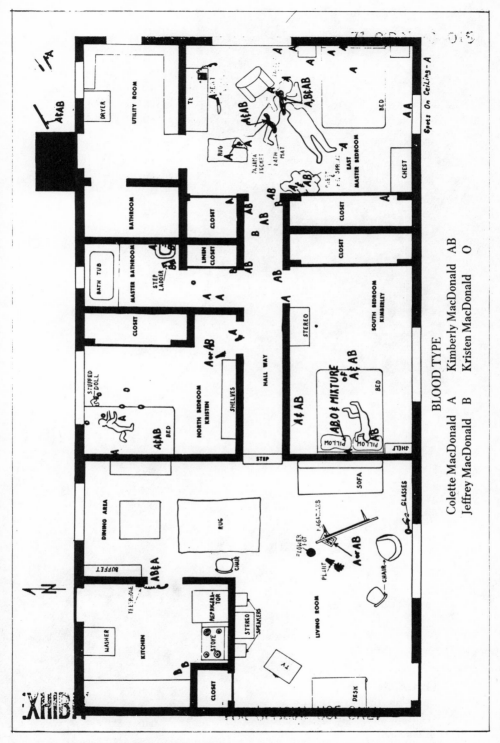

FBI floor plan of the MacDonald residence as presented to the jury, omitting bloodstains of MacDonald's type found in the hallway entrance where he said he had lain injured and unconscious. (*Exhibit in* U.S. v. MacDonald)

James Blackburn, co-prosecutor in the trial. *(Fayetteville Publishing Company)*

Brian Murtagh, co-prosecutor in the trial. *(Fayetteville Publishing Company)*

Bernard Segal, lead defense lawyer in the trial. *(MacDonald defense file)*

Harvey Silverglate, MacDonald's lead appeals lawyer. *(Ann Fuller)*

Joe McGinniss, author of *Fatal Vision*, at a gathering of the defense team during the trial. *(Dorothy MacDonald)*

Jeffrey MacDonald in prison, a quarter-century after the murders. *(Donna Bruce-Koch)*

REQUEST TO THE PUBLIC FOR INFORMATION CONCERNING TRIPLE MURDER SUSPECTS

| ...TE FEMALE | BLACK MALE | WHITE MALE | WHITE MALE |

DESCRIPTIONS:

NOTE: The ages, heights and weights are approximations as of 1970.

16-22	Age in 1970: 20 - 25	Age in 1970: 20 - 25	Age in 1970: 20 - 25
5'2" - 5'4"	Height: 5'10"	Height: 5'7"	Height: 5'10"
110 - 130	Weight: 160 - 180	Weight: 140 - 150	Weight: 170 - 180
Long, blonde (or wig).	Hair: Dark, Kinky, Well-kept.	Hair: Dark	Hair: Brown
Medium	Build: Medium	Build: Slight to medium.	Build: Medium
Floppy hat, boots.	Clothing: Army fatigue jacket, E-6 stripes.	Clothing: Grey hooded sweatshirt	Clothing: Tan jacket
	Other: Clean shaven, chubby face.	Other: Thin mustache, deep-set eyes, pock marks on cheeks & chin.	Other: Clean shaven, wore cross on chain around neck

On Tuesday, February 17th, 1970 The home of Dr. Jeffrey R. MacDonald at 544 Castle Drive, Ft. Bragg, N.C. was entered and Dr. MacDonald was stabbed & beaten and his family murdered. The drawings above were prepared by a police artist from descriptions given by Dr. MacDonald.

Anyone having information concerning this case is requested to contact John D. Myers, A licensed private investigator by calling collect at the following number: (919) 828-4376 in Raleigh, N. C.

MacDonald's defense team ran this newspaper ad during his trial in 1979.
(Exhibit for MacDonald defense, 1984 appeal)

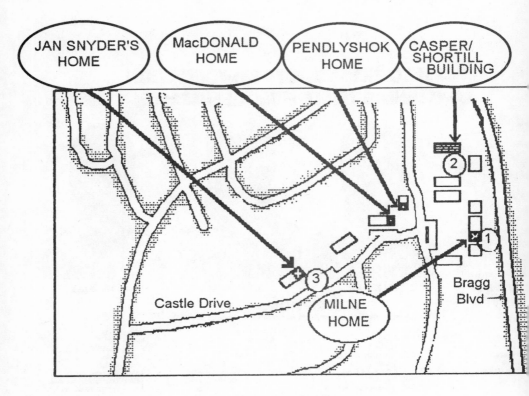

LEGEND

①   Robed trio carrying candles at about midnight

②   Group heard passing at about 2 a.m.

③   Group seen entering vehicles

A map of the neighborhood showing where neighbors observed strangers around the time of the murders. *(Fred Bost)*

Greg Mitchell, who confessed to taking part in the MacDonald murders shortly before his death from liver disease on June 3, 1982. *(Exhibit for MacDonald defense, 1984 appeal)*

Helena Stoeckley at the time of the murders and in 1981, when she repeated earlier confessions to having taken part in the murders. *(Bottom left: exhibit for MacDonald defense, 1984 appeal; bottom right: Fred Bost)*

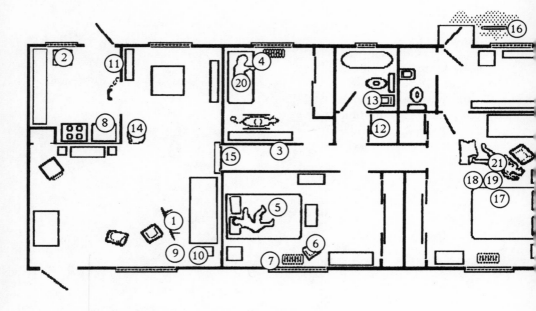

Did intruders commit the murders? *(Fred Bost)*

Physical evidence indicating the presence of intruders at the crime scene. In legend below, "unidentified" and "unmatched" mean that the items could not be traced to any source; numbers correspond to map above.

   1. Unidentified candle wax was found on the living-room coffee table (*CID Exhibit G-201*). MacDonald reported that he saw flickering candlelight when he woke and struggled with intruders.

   2. Unidentified wax was found on the west side of the washing machine in the kitchen (*CID Exhibit D-27K and lab notes, March 3, 1970*), but not disclosed to the defense and jury. Bloodstains were found on both sides of the washing machine (*CID Exhibits D-19K and D-27K*). Fingerprints on the washing machine were noted but not collected (*CID technician Hilyard Medlin's sworn deposition, June 29, 1970*).

   3. Unidentified yellow wax with an unidentified hair embedded in it was found on the hall wall (*CID Exhibit F-60; CID technician Craig Chamberlain's lab note 60, February 18, 1970; undated lab note "wax = 60, 131"*), but not disclosed to the defense and jury.

   4. A burned match was found near the radiator in two-year-old Kristen's room (*CID Exhibit 39NB, collected February 19, 1970, by CID technician Walter Rowe*), but not disclosed to the defense and jury.

   5. Unidentified candle wax was found on Kimberly's bedding near her corpse (*CID Exhibit D-123*); an unidentified hair was found on the bed (*CID lab note, September 1, 1970*); an unmatched flat black thread was found on her bottom sheet near a bloody splinter (*CID Exhibit E-119 and lab note, March 3, 1970*); unmatched pink and blue fibers were also found on bottom sheet, and unmatched purple and black nylon fibers were found on her bed quilt (*CID lab notes*). The fact that the hair and fibers were unmatched was not disclosed to the defense and jury; the lab notes which would have revealed this were withheld.

6. Unidentified candle wax was found on an arm of a chair in Kimberly's bedroom (*CID Exhibit G-131*).

7. Unidentified red and blue wax was found on Kimberly's window curtain (*CID Exhibit 160 and note made by FBI agent H. Warren Tool, Jr., during CID briefing on February 21, 1970*), but not disclosed to the defense and jury.

8. Unidentified pink wax was found on the kitchen floor near the refrigerator (*CID Exhibit D-9K; undated CID laboratory spreadsheet; CID lab notes of March 3 and 4, 1970*), but not disclosed to the defense and jury. A bloodstain was found on the refrigerator door (*CID Exhibit D-5K*).

9. An unidentified red-pink wool fiber was found on MacDonald's reading glasses, along with a speck of Type O blood (*CID lab reports R34 and R35 and lab notes; Janice Glisson's search, August 2, 1973*). Human blood of undetermined type was found on the living-room floor near the reading glasses (*CID Exhibit D-161*). The fiber on the glasses was not disclosed to the defense and jury.

10. A stemmed drinking glass bearing an unidentified adult fingerprint, apparently female, was found on the living-room end table; the glass held dregs of chocolate milk purchased by Colette MacDonald on the night of the murders (*CID technician Hilyard Medlin's deposition, June 29, 1970; Medlin internal CID memorandum, April 1, 1971*).

11. Three bloodstained gloves were found in the kitchen (*CID Exhibits D-33K and D-34K*).

12. A bloody syringe containing an unknown liquid was found in the hall closet (*Note made by FBI agent H. Warren Tool, Jr., during CID briefing on February 21, 1970*), but not disclosed to the defense and jury.

13. An unidentified hair covered with a tarlike substance was found in the bathroom sink (*Sworn grand jury testimony of CID technician Dillard Browning, October 24, 1974*). Two unidentified blue cotton fibers were also found in the sink, crumpled in a pink facial tissue (*Browning lab note*), but not disclosed to the defense and jury.

14. Blond wig hairs, up to 22 inches long, were found in a hairbrush on a chair next to the kitchen phone (*CID lab notes, April 20 and May 7, 1971*), but not disclosed to the defense and jury.

15. An unidentified fiber was found where MacDonald claimed to have lain unconscious (*Based upon the FBI's 1974 reevaluation of CID Exhibit E-32, redesignated FBI Exhibit Q12*). An unidentified hair was also found there (*CID Exhibit E-32 and lab notes of March 10 and September 1, 1970*), but not disclosed to the defense and jury.

16. Two unmatched black wool fibers were found on the murder club (*FBI lab notes and post-trial 1992 court arguments*), but not disclosed to the defense and jury. The CID recorded three unidentified "human pubic or body hairs," which apparently shook loose from the club in the evidence bag (*CID Exhibit E-206 and lab notes of Feburary 28 and March 10, 1970*); the hairs were called "animal hairs" in a 1974 FBI reevaluation *(FBI Exhibit Q92)*.

17. Two unidentified hairs *(CID lab note, September 1, 1970)* and an unmatched flat pink fiber *(CID lab note)* were found on the master bed, but not disclosed to the defense and jury.

18. Two hairs were found on the bloody bedspread in the master bedroom *(CID Exhibit E-229 and lab note of September 1, 1970)*. The fact that these were unidentified was not disclosed to the defense and jury.

19. An unidentified hair was found on a fragment of rubber glove in a crumpled blue sheet in the master bedroom *(CID technician Craig Chamberlain's lab note 21 made at the scene, February 17, 1970)*, but not disclosed to the defense and jury. A piece of skin tissue was found in the same sheet *(CID Exhibit E-211 and lab note of March 4, 1970)*, but not disclosed to the defense and jury; the skin tissue disappeared after it was catalogued. Near the sheet on the bedroom floor the CID found an unmatched clear nylon fiber adhering to a splinter from the murder club *(CID lab note)*.

20. Two unidentified hairs were found on Kristen's bed near her body *(CID Exhibit E-52NB and lab note of September 1, 1970)*. An unmatched pale blue nylon fiber and several unmatched clear nylon fibers were found on her pink blanket; a clump of unmatched purple nylon fibers, some unmatched cotton fibers, and an unmatched pale yellow fiber "with deposit of blood" were found on her bedspread *(CID lab notes)*. The fact that these hairs and fibers were unmatched was not disclosed to the defense and jury.

21. Items on or near the body of Colette MacDonald: An unidentified piece of skin tissue was found on one of her fingernails *(Autopsy and CID reports)*, but was subsequently lost by the government; the loss was not disclosed to the defense and jury. An unmatched blue acrylic fiber was found in her right hand *(CID Exhibit E-4; CID lab note, February 28, 1970; internal FBI report, November 5, 1974)*. An unidentified hair was found clutched in her left hand *(CID Exhibit E-5)*. A black wool fiber, a purple fiber, and a pink fiber, all unidentified as to source, were found around her mouth *(CID lab note, March 6, 1970; FBI lab notes and post-trial 1992 court arguments)*, but not disclosed to the defense and jury. An unmatched black wool fiber was found on her right bicep *(FBI lab notes and post-trial 1992 court arguments)*, but not disclosed to the defense and jury. Two unidentified body hairs were found near her left arm, close to three bloody splinters, and another unidentified hair was found under her body *(CID Exhibit E-301, CID lab note of March 20, 1970)*; the fact that these hairs were unidentified was not disclosed to the defense and jury. Also found under her body was an unmatched greenish brown cotton fiber and an unmatched, "heavily blood-stained" nylon gold fiber *(CID lab notes)*. A clump of fibers was found adhering to a bloodstained hair of Colette's: a blue fiber in the clump was matched to the throw rug in the master bedroom but the others could not be traced to any source *(Lab notes of CID technician Dillard Browning and FBI agent James Frier)*.

PART
THREE

Reverberations

10

Post-Trial Admissions
and Confessions

Years after the trial, interviews with the jurors who condemned MacDonald reveal that when they left the courtroom to begin their deliberations that last day of trial many of them were unhappy with the government's case. But the glaring absence of physical evidence of intruders in the murder apartment, and the absence of blood on the floor where MacDonald should have bled, caused them finally to accept the prosecutors' claim that MacDonald was lying and therefore had to be guilty.

Yet before their last vote, two holdouts in the jury room still had resisted pressure to condemn MacDonald. After a barrage of questions, one jurist escorted the couple, who had become upset, to a small vestibule. While calming them, the man finally convinced the pair to surrender their opposition, and they finally agreed to vote against MacDonald. In the courtroom, after the sentence was announced, MacDonald had no difficulty recognizing which two people had been holding out for his acquittal. In a letter to author Joe McGinniss the day after his conviction, MacDonald wrote about "the look of 'please forgive me' on the faces of the black juror and the lady who cried so much."

Holdouts on a jury are nothing new. What proved interesting in this case were thoughts entertained by another juror while the two holdouts were out in the vestibule. During a 1988 interview, juror Fred Thornhill confided that if the holdouts had continued to resist, he, not totally convinced himself, might have swung the other way, to vote for MacDonald's acquittal.[1] So uncertain was he that he called the evidence against MacDonald "interesting," and blamed the conviction not on a strong prosecution but on a "lack of defense." In short, that MacDonald was unable to prove his innocence, which, of course, the defendant is not supposed to have to do.

Arnold Clary, another of the jurors interviewed in 1988, said that throughout the trial he wanted to acquit MacDonald. "I wanted Perry Mason to come in and tell us just exactly how it happened," Clary said. "I wanted that to happen so bad I didn't know what to do."

Mrs. Gloria Hayes was one of those two persons who had held out for Jeffrey MacDonald's innocence until the final vote. According to Hayes, of all the evidence presented, the strongest thing against MacDonald was the small size of the murder apartment.[2] She had visited 544 Castle Drive with the rest of the jurors during the trial, and she had trouble visualizing it holding the number of assailants Jeffrey MacDonald had projected. It is interesting that she held this view while simultaneously ignoring the defense efforts which revealed that the apartment had been even more crowded following the arrival of the military police and CID agents.

Richard Embrey was the man who cinched the final guilty vote by taking Gloria Hayes and the other holdout juror aside for their quiet talk.[3] Embrey said the majority group had put a number of specific items before the two holdouts, including the government claim that no blood had been found in the hallway where MacDonald had supposedly lain unconscious. Embrey said it was impossible for MacDonald to have suffered the wounds he alleged, "yet not leave even one speck of blood in that hallway. And there was no carpet in there. It was a wooden floor." Embrey assumed, erroneously, and fatally, that the government had reported truthfully about what they found on that wooden floor.

If this blood spot had been represented on the official government chart, it is possible, based on post-trial remarks,[4] that even the jury foreman, David Hardison, and others also might have voted for MacDonald's acquittal. As it turned out, though, it was Hardison who was credited with nudging the jury to its unanimous conclusion.

Eddie Parker, the only black juror, complained that after the last witness testified and the trial was brought to a halt, he wasn't at all satisfied with what he had seen.[5] He said he told the other jurors that there were a lot of things that should have been heard. One thing, in particular, bothered him. He said, "We should have been told more about that woman."

Parker recalled, "A few of us didn't believe he was guilty. The arguments went on for a good while. It would always come out the same. David Hardison, he did the heaviest arguing.

"It was Dave—he was a truck driver—who sent for the pajama top to spread it out there on the table to show where the punctures was in it. Dave was trying to show that there was really no other person that would have did a thing like that. He was determined that Dr. MacDonald was going to be guilty. Dave said that Dr. MacDonald knew how to' cut himself or stab himself without inflicting death."

As Bernard Segal had feared, Parker's statement suggests that the jurors had failed to grasp the complicated arguments about the depth of the ice pick wounds in Colette (they weren't deep, as Stombaugh had claimed). Apparently they had failed to understand the directionality of the bent and broken fibers in the garment's puncture holes (the FBI had performed the experiment with a number of the fiber directions going the wrong way), and they hadn't understood that the garment had not been folded the way the photographs showed it over Colette's chest, as Stombaugh had earlier claimed, and later admitted was incorrect.

Parker said the thing that got under his skin the most was the way Hardison kept saying, "Show us what proof you've got that he's not guilty. . . ."

The elderly man said he had no defense against Hardison's pressure. To him, there had been no real proof in either direction. He wasn't happy about the final decision, he said, and his frustration plagued him. Many years later his eyes filled with tears as he recalled his last view of Jeffrey MacDonald standing in shock in the crowded courtroom. "When I walked out of that jury box that day I walked to the door and I turned around and I looked at him. That thing hurt me. It hurt me," he said.

Eddie Parker summed up his view of the ritual he had helped perform that fateful day. "I still don't think Doctor MacDonald's guilty," the old man said. "I try to put it out of my mind. I don't feel like he's guilty, and I'll tell anybody I don't feel like he's guilty."

Others, who claimed to have been in the MacDonald home on the night of the murders, seem to share the tortured sentiments of juror Eddie Parker.

Confessions — Helena Stoeckley

MacDonald spent the year after his conviction incarcerated at Terminal Island Federal Correctional Institute at San Pedro, California. During that year, on April Fool's Day, 1980, Helena Stoeckley married Ernie Davis, the man who had allegedly broken her nose and held her head underwater at her hotel during the MacDonald trial. As she and Davis began planning a family, the MacDonald murders still hung over them. Meanwhile, private investigator Ted Gunderson had entered the case the previous November, and he was tenacious. Within six months of their marriage, her new husband had signed a statement for Gunderson saying that, from the things he had seen and heard, Helena was remorseful about what had happened. Ernie Davis observed other things that caused him to think that Helena was telling him the truth about the murders. He said she had a kind of spotty memory of the murder morning, as she might have if she had been on drugs as she claimed. Davis said his wife could remember approaching the MacDonald apartment, then the next time period would be a dark blank. She could remember seeing MacDonald on the couch, then again experienced a blank space in her memory, then she'd see Colette in the bedroom fighting with Mitchell, then the children, and all the blood. Davis told Gunderson that Helena refused to allow him to have an ice pick in their home. And once, when Helena and Ernie were walking together, she saw a child's hobby horse and suddenly began to cry uncontrollably. All these things, Davis said, made him believe Helena had been present at the murders, but he insisted that she hadn't killed anyone herself.

Davis's bold statement seemed to motivate Helena's own next move. Beasley and Gunderson told her they would try to arrange immunity for her, and she signed a confession for them on October 25, and another on December 6, 1980. She really was present in the MacDonald apartment while the murders were being committed, she said; and, contrary to what she had said in court, she did remember the night in question. Inside the house, she remembered a child's hobby horse that was broken (its condition could not be discerned from newspaper photos). She remembered seeing Colette's tiered jewelry box, open on the dresser, the same jewelry box where the two missing rings had been (the jewelry box was never shown in newspaper photos). And she said she knew the people who had killed Colette, Kimberly, and Kristen.

In conjunction with these confessions, polygrapher Scott Mero admin-istered three "lie detector" examinations, and felt that in two of them Stoeckley did not show deception when she claimed she had been in the home and knew the names of the killers. This supported Brisentine's earlier CID polygraph. (In a third test, Mero's data were inconclusive. Stoeckley was shaken up because Gunderson had gotten tough with her and told her she could still go to jail.) Beasley complained that Gunderson possessed no better skill at working with Helena than had Segal. In Beasley's view, neither of them really understood how to deal with drug informants, especially Helena Stoeckley.

Helena had told Beasley earlier that she was upset about Judge Dupree's public characterization of her as a burnt-out hippie who had lost command of her faculties. Beasley expressed this to Gunderson, who consulted Segal. They took this opportunity to suggest that she see a specialist who would determine whether she was still in control of her faculties and thus set the record straight. She readily agreed, and Gunderson arranged for her to see Dr. Rex Beaber, a prominent psychologist at UCLA, on December 7, 1980.

Beaber interviewed her at length about the murder night and related events. At one point she graphically described her group stringing up a cat and killing it during a cult ritual. She liked cats, she said, and didn't like killing them, but she explained, "The cat died immediately after its throat was slit. After that there was nothing to it. I was tripping. It could turn into something nice, doing heroin, opium, smoke. . . ."

Following this taped interview, Dr. Beaber told Gunderson that Helena Stoeckley was intelligent and in control of her faculties. He said he felt certain her memories were genuine, and added, "She is sure she was there the night of the murders."

Stoeckley accompanied Gunderson and Beasley back to Fort Bragg where she showed them the routes the group took to and from the MacDonald home. She also walked down the sidewalk to point out the place the group's vehicles had parked. That location coincided with the story about vehicles told by MacDonald's neighbor, Jan Snyder.

Her confession to Gunderson and Beasley had given the defense team further reason to believe Jimmy Friar's strange tale about phoning the MacDonald home on the murder morning. Stoeckley told the detective that during the murders the phone rang in the MacDonald apartment. She said she picked up the receiver to hear a man ask, "Is Dr. MacDonald there?" She said she laughed at the caller, then when someone else in the house yelled at her to "Hang up the God damn phone," she put the phone back on the hook. Her words were an eerie echo of Jimmy Friar's recollection of his phone call to the MacDonald home that night.

In time, after much cajoling, Gunderson managed to put a reluctant Stoeckley on the public airways with her confession. On August 18, 1982, Stoeckley was interviewed by the television staff of columnist Jack Anderson in Washington, D.C., where she confirmed her earlier confessions, including her story about answering the phone during the murders and being told to hang up the phone.

Stoeckley had given the defense team much to please them, but she also presented distortions as well as untruths that did not become apparent until further investigation. Her claim of having seen no weapons was an apparent distortion, for in another part of her confession she described an attack in the master bedroom against Colette MacDonald by Greg Mitchell, her boyfriend at the time. In addition, she denied seeing the children attacked, but only recalled seeing them "sleeping." Given the extreme guilt the affair must have generated in her, Bernard Segal could understand this kind of lie, especially in the continued absence of official immunity.

There was another lie. When she gave the names of five companions she alleged were involved in the crime, she definitely lied about at least one of them, a drug dealer named Allen Mazerolle who, it turned out, was being held in the Cumberland County Jail at the time of the slayings. It is likely that Stoeckley knew where Mazerolle was because she was the one who had turned him in on an LSD charge. In fact, she was with Mazerolle the night he was arrested, a night in which she had actually signaled Prince Beasley to move in for that arrest.

According to her husband, there was a reason for that lie. Ernie Davis said that Helena later told him that she had thrown in Mazerolle's name for her own safety. If the immunity she required were denied, then her "mistake" about Mazerolle would "prove" she didn't really know who was in the home that night. Davis said that she promised him that the moment she was granted immunity by the government, she would correct the discrepancies and reveal the full truth.

In December 1980, Fred Bost, retired from the Green Berets and working as a reporter, was the first newsman to reveal that Helena Stoeckley had confessed to being involved in the murders.[6] Then, at Bost's request, Prince Beasley arranged an interview with her the following month in Seneca, South Carolina. On a cloudy but warm winter day the two men waited in Bost's car for her arrival. They were parked in a post office lot near the outskirts of the small city, where trees outnumbered buildings. At the appointed time Bost saw a woman come into sight at the bend of the rural road, walking toward them.

"Is that Helena?"

"That's her," Beasley said.

"I was expecting a hippie," Bost said.

"That was a long time ago."

As she approached, Bost saw she was a heavyset woman in her late twenties. She walked proudly, with her shoulders straight and her chin high. She wore a gray sweater and slacks, and as she neared the car, she smiled at Beasley. He got out, got in back, and let her sit in the front next to Bost.

They made small talk while Bost drove the Pinto station wagon to an inner city parking lot where they wouldn't attract attention. The reporter noted her neat attire, soft voice, and educated vocabulary as she mentioned nursing manuals and medical books she was studying.[7] Bost expressed his surprise that she didn't fit Judge Dupree's description of her. Helena smiled grimly and told him that she had long been upset over what Dupree said. She insisted that she had not exhibited behavior that justified Dupree's judgment that she was a burnt-out case. Indeed, one of the reasons for submitting to an interview was to dispel that error.

After a few preliminary questions, Bost asked her about reasons for the attack on the MacDonald family.

"MacDonald was just one of several people giving the drug users a hard time," she said. "And I don't really know who started the idea."

"How did they get the others to get into this thing?" Bost asked. "Did they use any particular methods, force you, or kid you? Ridiculing you if you don't go along?"

"No. It's kind of like if you tell somebody that they're going to be cut off [from drugs] or something if they don't do something about it. They said, 'Look, you know it's happening to us now. It could be you next.' That's the way it was."

"How long before the murders was the decision made?"

"Well, I had heard talk about it up in the Village Shoppe for two or three months already, and then it started getting more intense and started narrowing down to the people that did hang around the apartment on Clark Street to about maybe two weeks beforehand. I told Gunderson and everybody else that no one ever specifically mentioned murder."

"The raid on the house was going to be—what?"

"Well, from what I understood, there was simply going to be a little pushing around, you know, and trying to get a point across, and that was it."

"What about the business of the cult? Did that come into it?"

"Things started blending in more and more to kind of form a pattern, you know, how they could work things out under the guise of something else. During that time, I was into my own thing. But as far as the cult went I didn't approve of a lot of the things they did, but I figured if I was going to become a member, there were certain things I was just going to have to learn to do."

"What was their theme? Was it actually devil worship or was it supposed to be some kind of powerful occult practices?"

"Yeah. It was more the practice of witchcraft, mind over matter and things like that. It wasn't so much devil worshipping. I mean, they didn't go overboard as far as devil worshipping. There were anti-Christ symbols everywhere, but that's about it."

"I heard of a picture that was at 908 Hay Street up on the wall, of Christ being fellated—do you recall that picture?"

"Yeah. There was that painting on a lot of walls, but the head shops at that time, too, were selling the anti-Christ symbols and I don't think a lot of people knew what they were buying. But if they had paid attention, it was the cross upside down, crow's foot, witch's foot."

"Did they take turns leading? Was there a particular leader?"

"Sheila was really the one that instigated this—you say 'cult,' I just say 'group.'"

"Who was Sheila?"

"She was just a friend of mine who was interested in witchcraft, well, I was interested in witchcraft. She was pretty much an authority on it."

"You know what she looks like—blond, brunette, redhead?"

"She had sort of bamboo-colored hair, more towards the blond side."

"Did you ever see her again afterwards?"

"No. Because after the murders, I planned on leaving, and I stayed pretty much off the streets. And then after that, shortly after that, I think I went to Chapel Hill to get off heroin and when I came back there was a lot of people gone. There was a lot of people gone a few hours after the murders."

A few minutes later Bost started asking questions about the murder night. "What's the first thing you remember about MacDonald's house?"

"I think the weather is probably one of the things that really strikes me because it was rainy that night—more misty than rainy."

"And they let you off at Honeycutt to walk into the house, is that right?"

"Somewhere in the vicinity because about the first thing I remember is going into one door."

"Why did they let you off? Why didn't they just drive up to where they were parked?"

"I don't know why anyone did anything else. I don't even know why it happened."

Bost later remarked that Stoeckley seemed to be what he as a reporter called a "thinking talker." If she had the answer ready, she gave it. If not, she seemed to think a moment before speaking.

"Did you have any trouble finding the place?"

"I wasn't there at first anyway because I had been going up with Bruce. He had to park the car, and I remember the weather, and when we got there, people were having a hard time with the door. Somebody said something about the dog was going to bark if they weren't more quiet."

"Did you see the dog at that time?"

"That's when I paid attention to the dog, but he didn't bark."

"Was the dog behind a fence?"

"No."

"Was it tied up?"

"It had to be tied up some kind of way or it would have been over where we were because try as we may, we weren't really that quiet."

Fred Bost knew that the Pendlyshoks, behind the MacDonald apartment, owned a light-colored German shepherd. Helena had alluded to the type and color of the dog in other interviews. He asked her again about the white German shepherd and she repeated that she had thought the dog was white but it could have been tan.[8]

Then Bost asked whether they were quiet going in.

"Around that time, yes."

"What was the first thing you heard?"

"Someone must have gone into the back because I think that's what woke him up to begin with before anyone even said anything to him. I think Colette yelled out to him."

"What about the child? Did the child yell before Colette did?"

"No. She yelled first because I didn't know anything about how many children were in there or anything. It was after I heard a small child's voice call for 'Daddy' that I knew there was children in the house, and that's when I went towards the back."

"Did the child call 'Daddy' right after Colette called?"

"Not right afterwards because by that time, he [MacDonald] was already awake and knew pretty well what was going on."

"How much time did he have to get a look at things before he was hit the first time?"

"As dark as the room was, he didn't have much time at all. I mean, I'd say that he maybe woke up, if he ever did really wake up, you know, before being knocked back down, and with the TV set off and everything, I don't think he had time at all to see much of anything."

"Do you remember anything you saw in the room at the time?"

"Everything I remember is the TV set, I found the glasses on the floor, and the book upside down on his chest that led you to believe he was probably reading while watching TV or something like that, fell asleep either reading the book or watching TV. There was something—there was a Valentine's Day card and something that looked like a child's— just how kids, you know, put construction paper, things together. I don't know if they were cards or what. Those were on the table."

"What about this flowerpot that they were arguing about being knocked over?"

"I don't remember it being knocked down. I don't know anything about that. It wasn't until later. Now, if you want to say, you know, I read the papers and found out about such and such, that's when I found out about a flowerpot."

"You went into the other room and you saw Colette being attacked?"

"Well, I saw her more or less fighting off, being attacked."

"Who was she fighting off at the time? Do you remember?"

"At that time, I think it was Mitchell."

"Just Mitchell alone?"

"Yeah."

"Was she screaming much, much noise?"

"Yes, and that's when I noticed the child lying next to her. I think that may have been why she was fighting."

"Was the child moving?"

"I thought she was sleeping."

Helena told Bost she left the master bedroom and "somewhere along there the phone rang." She said she answered it, laughing, "peaking out on mescaline." It wasn't until sometime after she hung up the phone that she went back to see what was happening with the woman in the bedroom. "She wasn't on the bed anymore, she was on the floor. That's when blood started appearing all over the place, and that's when I started freaking out." She told Bost she had been in another room with a child. "It was dimly lit in there. You couldn't see anything. I sort of backed into something behind me, and I guess that was the [hobby] horse because one of the springs was loose, and I went out of there. I didn't know who was fighting with who but by then there was blood, and I realized that things were out of control, and I didn't have anything to do with it. That's when I screamed and went out the other door."

"You went out alone?"

"As far as I know. I went out. I don't know."

"And the others were still in the house?"

"No one was with me, yes."

"Is that when the dog started barking at you?"

"No, that was when everybody left."

"Were you outside when the others came out, or did you go back in the house again?"

"I don't remember. I don't know if I was standing in the hallway or not because every time that I would reenter a room, somebody was struggling with somebody, and I just wanted to get out. That's all."

"Supposedly you had gone to Dunkin' Donuts again [after the murders]. Do you remember that?"

"As far as going there, no. But I know that we were getting back from Dunkin' Donuts. We had a box from there and it was nothing for us to go there at that hour, anyway."

"Now when you went home to your apartment, what did you do? What were your feelings? What happened to you then? What thoughts went through your mind?"

"It's just a complete blank as far as feeling anything or thinking about anything. Then the first thing that occurred to me was that Kathy [Smith] was in there with Diane [Hedden] painting on the wall and she turned to me and said, 'Why'd you do it?' And I remember saying, 'He deserved to die.'"

"You thought MacDonald was dead when you left?"

"No one had been listening to the radio, so that seemed kind of funny, and then they took off somewhere."

"Kathy?"

"Kathy Smith and Diane Hedden."

"They weren't with you [at the MacDonald house]?"

"No. They were painting the wall."

"When you said, 'He deserved to die,' you thought he was dead, that MacDonald was dead then, apparently from that statement?"

"I don't know. And for days after that I couldn't understand why I said that."

"Did you still have these memories [about the MacDonald apartment] at this time or had everything left you and then come back to you later?"

"No. I knew we had been somewhere and something had been done, and people would give you these knowing glances. And I would go back to the Village Shoppe and I used to think it was just a dream and stuff. And then the newscast came on that they had been murdered and then it was like denial—like, 'No, I wasn't there.' So I went to [one of our group members who was at the house that night] to tell him I'm leaving town, and he said, 'Well, if you're going, I'm going, too, because they'll be looking for me.'"

"Were you and [he] very good friends?"

"Yes, we talked a lot because he was a very sensitive person. He was fresh back from Nam, and that left a really deep thing on him. He was temporarily separated from his wife, and that shook him up, besides being strung out. With him, he was like a typical—you could understand why he was using heroin because he would escape, and I used to like to go and talk to him a lot."

"When did you get together with your friends again, with those that took part in the raid?"

"Off and on, for several weeks afterwards, no one would meet at the Village Shoppe. You might run into someone and they would have somewhere to go or you would go in the other direction. No one wanted to be seen with anyone else."

"When your group got together, what did they say to you? How were they acting about this? Were they giving you any kind of threats to keep you quiet, or were they just cautioning you to keep quiet?"

"Everyone was more or less trying to pretend nothing had happened because at that time MacDonald was still alive, and he was in—from what we understood, he was in pretty bad condition. But he was still alive, so we weren't going out that much, and the Village Shoppe did thin out quite a bit during those days."

"Did any of them give any indications that they felt MacDonald may have recognized them?"

"Well, there was a paranoia, if that's what you mean."

"Who was this?"

"Well, Greg [Mitchell] was always paranoid, so you never knew about him."

"But were they worried that they might have been recognized?"

"Yes."

Stoeckley acknowledged to Bost that one of the men was concerned about the cross around his neck, and another quit wearing his field jacket.

As his interview with Stoeckley continued, Bost remembered that she had moved to Nashville where she became an informant working for the police in internal affairs. CID agents Mahon and Brisentine had interviewed her back in 1971 after a Nashville police officer, John Rohtert, told a local CID agent that she had implicated herself in the MacDonald murders. Bost asked her, "How many times did the CID interrogate you? I'll tell you the reason I'm asking that. CID agent Kearns says they have interrogated you half a dozen or more times."

"That's not true."

"You know, when he was talking about that you had confessed so many times. Do you remember how many times they actually talked to you?"

"I think a grand total of about four times, and that wasn't interrogation."

"What kind of questions did they ask? Did they ever ask if you were in on the MacDonald thing? Did they ever ask you any direct questions like that?"

"Not directly, no."

"What kind of questions did they ask?"

Bost knew that Helena had been arrested and jailed on September 2, 1970, for trespassing at the Village Shoppe. While in jail she was questioned by William Ivory and the assistant prosecutor at the army hearing, William Thompson. Helena alluded either to that night or to one of Ivory's other interviews with her. "Ivory just asked me where I was that night, and I said, 'I don't know,' and that was that."[9]

"They never pursued it any further?"

"No."

"And they didn't ask you, 'Do you think you may have been involved?'"

"No, not really. I just said I didn't know where I was, but he said that was to be expected as messed up as I was that night. So he accepted that, and that was that."

"Were you aware that the colonel who had held that Article 32 hearing, were you aware that he said that they should look into Helena Stoeckley?"

"I was really scared because out of that whole thing was only two recommendations, [that the charges against MacDonald are not true] and I was the second one. I think I called—maybe I called Truitt, detective Truitt,[10] and I asked him did I have anything to worry about, and he said, 'No, they know he's guilty.'"

"And he thought MacDonald was guilty?"

"Sure. Everybody I talked to said, 'MacDonald is guilty.' [CID agent] Mahon, when I saw him in Nashville, he told me to just keep my mouth shut and let sleeping dogs lie. He said, 'Everybody knows MacDonald did it. You've got nothing to worry about.'"

"How did you feel about this, knowing that you had these feelings that you were there, knowing that you remembered seeing these things? What were your feelings about the police saying, 'Don't worry about it?' Was it relief?"

"Well, it was kind of frustrating because I knew—I knew I didn't sit around and make these things up in my head, and these people who knew nothing about what was going on, my own family included, just for the sake of keeping my name out of it, said, 'Forget about it.' It used to really tick me off, too, when they would say this thing about, 'You just want publicity.' I really didn't want it, you know, a murder or something. They all just said, 'He's guilty. Leave it alone.' So I shut up, and then something would always come back up. By the time I talked to Beasley, I had just had it. This is one of the reasons I never got married before or tried to get into an active career or anything, you know, because it was always cropping up, and it's playing havoc on it right now, too."

Helena told Bost that this was one of the main reasons she wanted it cleared up. She said she thought that if the CID had come out to her house the night Beasley radioed for them, she would have told them everything, and that even some of the others might have talked. She told Bost that she felt guilty about the murders themselves, then felt guilty about not saying anything to the CID at the time of the murders. Then, much later, Gunderson and Beasley had approached her and convinced her they would do everything in their power to see that she would get immunity, and wouldn't be indicted. "I'm tired of living in a private hell. Nobody else can know what this is, not my husband, not my family, not people reading the newspaper. I do."

Helena Stoeckley Davis gave birth to a baby boy on June 2, 1982. Seven months later, in January 1983, she phoned Prince Beasley. She was scared, she said. Always in the past she had refused to agree to testify without immunity. This time she didn't say anything about immunity, she said she finally wanted to tell Beasley the whole story about the MacDonald murders. She would "blow the lid" off Fort Bragg, she told him. She said she had recently been interviewed by the FBI, and she now was being watched by two men in suits who sat in a car in front of her apartment in Seneca, South Carolina.

Before Beasley could arrange for another trip south, the news media announced on January 14 that Helena Stoeckley Davis had been found dead in her Seneca apartment. She lay on her sofa, nude from the waist down. An ice tray sat in the kitchen sink with water from the open tap still running into it. She was believed to have been dead about four days. Her baby was alive, but was suffering from dehydration.

Fearing foul play, the MacDonald defense team asked Dr. Ronald Wright, chief medical examiner of Broward County, Florida, to fly to South Carolina and observe the autopsy. Wright could find no sign of foul play. The autopsy on the body, which had deteriorated for four days, revealed nothing that would contradict that Stoeckley apparently had died of pneumonia and sclerosis of the liver. She was thirty years old.[11]

MacDonald's defenders, who had relied heavily on the Stoeckley post-trial confessions to reopen the case, felt crushed. But they did have videotapes of Stoeckley's confessions made by the news media. They would soon acquire audiotapes of Bost's interviews with her, and they knew more about the CID's apparent efforts to clear her as a suspect. The defense team also were beginning to receive the FOIA material, and soon other confessions from the Stoeckley group would come to light.

In the Government Files

There was a point in time when the government claimed that Helena Stoeckley Davis had fully retracted her confessions. This supposedly occurred after Ted Gunderson attempted in the spring of 1981 to force a new FBI investigation. Knowing that Segal had furnished Stoeckley's confessions to the U.S. Solicitor General on February 4, and seeing no action forthcoming, Gunderson decided to push. In early May he arranged for Fred Barbash of the Washington Post to publish Helena's confession nationwide.[12] Barbash's story circulated throughout the country on May 17 and, not surprisingly, cost Stoeckley her job as a babysitter. As a result, when the FBI finally got around to questioning her in September 1981, she was feeling unkindly toward Gunderson.

Murtagh and the FBI took this opportunity to claim that Helena had fully recanted the confessions made to the former FBI man, Ted Gunderson. They put this supposed recantation to full use against MacDonald's appeal efforts, even though FOIA documents finally proved the recantation story wasn't true. These FOIA papers, not released until June 4, 1993, nearly twelve years after they were filed by the FBI, show that Helena had indeed attempted to waffle a bit when the FBI confronted her with her own signed confession of complicity in the MacDonald murders. But contrary to Murtagh's claims, the documents also prove that she stopped far short of recanting. The fact, based upon the government's own documents, is that Stoeckley never recanted her confessions.

The proof lies in a paper signed by her in Seneca, South Carolina, on September 9, 1981, witnessed by an FBI agent.[13] Helena wrote: "I have previously furnished signed statements regarding the MacDonald murders to Mr. Ted Gunderson, a private investigator in Los Angeles, California. I have read the statements I furnished to Mr. Gunderson, dated October 25, 1980, and December 4, 1980. I have also read some of the statements I furnished on December 6, 1980. These statements are basically accurate: however, the statements and the facts of the statements are what I think happened or dreamed and are not a positive recollection of events on February 16–17, 1970. The fact remains and the truth of the matter is that I do not know if I was present or participated in the MacDonald murders."

Even faced with the possibility of prosecution, and without an offer of immunity, Stoeckley still did not go so far as to claim she definitely wasn't in the murder apartment. There was no recantation. Despite several follow-up sessions imposed by the FBI, the woman adamantly held her position. Denied immunity, she continued to claim confusion. *The government has never released to the defense team any document in which Stoeckley recanted her confessions.* The fact remains that Stoeckley did sign confessions, and when she was offered the opportunity to recant them, she either refused outright or claimed confusion, leaving the door open, perhaps, to clear the air officially if immunity were ever offered.

Eventually Helena grew tired of the FBI pressure, and finally told an agent that she would never again speak with anyone from the FBI or sign anything because she felt the FBI "had lied to her in the past."[14]

During this period of jousting with federal agents, Helena expressed herself more openly in a letter of July 25, 1981, to Gunderson, with whom she was clearly angry:

> Never have I seen a bigger mockery made of justice or such a shambles made of an investigation. . . . Granted, I have a past history of drug abuse and cult involvement, but, in my opinion, I do possess clear and sound mental faculties and judgments, and a moderate level of intelligence. . . . When I finally agreed to cooperate with you, I felt I was doing what was morally right. I would also be freeing myself from a private hell, so I gave you as conclusive a review of the night in question as I could.

Stoeckley had, indeed, signed full confessions for Gunderson which reflected crime-scene events she had talked about with other people. She had submitted to polygraph exams for Gunderson, and had even undergone Dr. Beaber's psychological evaluation. But Gunderson had promised to seek immunity for her, and before that immunity was granted, he had arranged the story by Fred Barbash of the *Washington Post*, which got her fired from her job and opened up old wounds in a manner that, given the lack of immunity in return for her testimony, couldn't be easily healed. And the remainder of her letter to Gunderson proves she was still angry with him.

> You, in turn, misconstrued and distorted all statements I made to you, to be used against me at your convenience. . . . Any and all fears and anxieties that I now have, I will deal with myself. Contrary to statements made by Judge Dupree, and countless other people, my life is no longer one big drug-crazed stupor that I cannot face.[15]

Within a few months Helena's anger toward Gunderson had melted. The following spring, while still staving off overtures from the FBI, she allowed Gunderson to arrange two separate television interviews in which she repeated her confessions in front of the cameras of *60 Minutes* and on Jack Anderson's interview show.[16]

Confessions—Greg Mitchell

At the time of the murders Greg Mitchell and Helena Stoeckley were apparently quite close. Mitchell was or recently had been her boyfriend.

He was a lean, brown-haired, nineteen-year-old soldier, a vehicle mechanic recently back from Vietnam, and like Helena, he was heavily
hooked on drugs.[17] Following the murders Mitchell requested immediate
discharge and reenlistment in order to return to Vietnam (a rare request
from a recently returned soldier). While awaiting the request to be processed and movement orders to be forwarded, he volunteered to be the
first patient in the new live-in Operation Awareness drug rehabilitation
program on the army post, virtually placing himself in seclusion and in
the presence of a ready supply of methadone beginning on June 7, 1970,
which was just prior to the opening of the army's Article 32 hearing
against MacDonald.

Just before that, sometime in May or June, neighbors of Greg Mitchell's
mother saw a tussle between her and her son. The neighbors, Betty Jean
and John Bishop, looked across at Mitchell's residence and saw the mother
and son struggling in front of a window. The Bishops called the police,
but an officer told them that nothing could be done unless a complaint
was made from the household in question. The next morning, Mitchell's
mother told Mrs. Bishop she was worried about her son's drug use and
didn't know what to do about it. She told Mrs. Bishop that when they
had fought in the house, Greg had screamed at her, "We have to go and
kill them. We have to kill all the ten-year-olds we can find."[18]

Four days after Colonel Rock closed the Article 32 hearing, and while
the colonel was evaluating what he had learned, Greg Mitchell graduated
from the Operation Awareness drug program as "cured."[19] With his
orders to Vietnam in hand, he furloughed to Florida where he soon
overdosed on heroin and was hospitalized. Upon his release from the
hospital, he proceeded to Vietnam[20] to assume vehicle mechanic duties.
Again he fell into trouble with drugs, underwent a psychiatric evaluation,
and was diagnosed as suffering from chronic drug dependency. In February 1971, he accepted a general discharge rather than face a military
board.[21]

After this, Mitchell didn't stray far from his troubles. At a halfway
house in Fayetteville the following month, a troubled young man who
called himself "Jim" asked for help. He moved into the place, known as
the Manor, and worked in mission projects. Anne Sutton Canady, one
of the caregivers, had helped found the institution with President Carter's
sister, Ruth Carter Stapleton. Canady recalls the young man once saying
that he had been a member of a cult. Shortly afterward, during a Saturday
night prayer meeting, "Jim" began trembling and crying uncontrollably,

and he confessed that he had murdered people. On his knees, weeping and shaking, he begged God to forgive him. Others prayed with him. The next morning he was gone.

That Sunday afternoon several members of the establishment drove out to an old farmhouse that Jim and others had been helping to renovate for mission use. As their vehicle approached, they saw the young man they knew only as Jim run from the building into some nearby woods. Inside, freshly painted on a wall, were the words:

I KILLED MACDONALD'S WIFE AND CHILDREN

After Mrs. Canady made her information known to the MacDonald defense team, private detective Ray Shedlick showed her a large array of photographs on March 30, 1983. She picked out a photograph of Greg Mitchell as the young man she had known as Jim.[22] It should be noted, though, that at the time the CID interviewed Mitchell in May 1971 they say that he passed a polygraph examination while claiming no knowledge of the MacDonald murders. Bost and I remembered that the name "Jim" also had been used by Greg Mitchell during the time following the murders. On the day Stoeckley admitted to her neighbor, William Posey, that she might have held the light during the murders, Posey had spoken to Helena's boyfriend, a violent, angry man calling himself Jim. And, that day, this "Jim" drove a car whose description loosely fit that of Mitchell's light yellow Plymouth.

Sometime after the halfway house incident, Mitchell married a former high school girlfriend and the pair settled in the area of Charlotte, North Carolina. A decade later he fell sick and died in a Lynchburgh, Virginia, hospital on June 3, 1982, just two days before his thirty-second birthday. Apparently, he had fallen victim to the same affliction that would take the life of Helena Stoeckley Davis some seven months later—a diseased liver.

During those years in the Charlotte area, the Mitchells had become friendly with another couple, Norma and Bryant Lane. Just before his business trip to Virginia where he fell ill and died, Greg Mitchell began exhibiting nervous behavior. He confided in Mrs. Lane that he had recently been interviewed by the FBI and that he needed to borrow some money to get out of the country because they were after him. She told him that if he wasn't guilty, he didn't have anything to worry about.

He replied, "That's just it. I am guilty."[23]

The following year Norma Lane was reading the newly published *Fatal*

Vision, by Joe McGinniss, when she suddenly realized that one of the characters in the book was their friend, the late Greg Mitchell.[24] She recalled how unsettled he had been just before his death, and she remembered his desire to borrow money to get out of the country. She remembered him telling her that he had once done something wrong and "was guilty of a serious crime that had happened a long time ago at Fort Bragg, North Carolina."[25]

Norma Lane's statement had been offered by MacDonald in his bid for a new trial in 1984. It served no use, however, because Brian Murtagh argued to the judge that Mitchell must have been referring to something terrible that had happened not at Fort Bragg, but in Vietnam. Murtagh assured Judge Dupree, "Mitchell, we do know that in his second tour in Vietnam, was severely wounded and apparently was never the same subsequent to that."[26] However, contrary to this absolute assurance given to Dupree by Brian Murtagh, Mitchell's service records confirm that he saw no combat during that quickly interrupted second tour in Vietnam, and he was never wounded during either tour. Murtagh's misinformation, introduced as substantiated fact, and accepted unchecked by Dupree, helped convince the judge that Mitchell's confession had nothing to do with the MacDonald murders.

Unknown to Norma Lane, Greg Mitchell had specifically cited the MacDonald murders to her husband. But Bryant Lane had kept silent, first, because he wasn't sure he believed his friend. Also, Mitchell had asked him to keep his secret so that he could get his life together. Lane had promised to do so. Later, however, Lane became troubled about holding back his knowledge. He says that during a period in which his friend was emotionally troubled, Mitchell told him, "I personally know MacDonald is innocent, because I was the one that killed the MacDonald family."[27] Lane also said that during the much-publicized MacDonald trial, Mitchell told him that there was "a bitch out there which if she didn't keep her mouth shut she could get a lot of us in trouble."

It was during that period of time that Greg Mitchell attended a party at Lane's home. He was drinking heavily and crying when he confronted another man who was at the party. Sam Lee, a builder, says that this stranger asked him if he had seen the girl at the murder trial on television, adding something "about her not testifying or they wouldn't let her testify because of drug problems." Lee asked the crying man what he was saying and the stranger replied, "We did it, man. We did it." At that moment, Bryant Lane came back into the room. Soon Lee told his host what the stranger had said. Lane told him he already knew about it, that Mitchell had told him about it earlier. Lee, who had formerly been a policeman, said they later phoned the FBI together, but no agents ever showed up. Lee eventually told two other policemen about it. One didn't seem interested. Lee said the other man took a statement but nothing ever came of it.[28]

Confessions — Cathy Perry

Nine months after the murders, in November 1970, a Green Beret named Jackie Don Wolverton noticed Cathy Perry, a former companion of Helena Stoeckley.[29] Perry was a young, slim brunette who lived in a hippie pad near Fort Bragg called Cottonade Farms. She was disoriented, acting strange, getting in the way of the other people, so he took her to his own pad after they agreed that he would care for her if she did the cleaning and cooking.

When Wolverton gave the girl a puppy as a companion, she took it into the backyard and killed it, stabbing it continuously with a knife. A police report said she stabbed it till it was "flat."

Not long afterward, on December 23, Wolverton was sleeping when she attacked him, stabbing him with a kitchen knife in the back of his shoulder. She tried to stab him again, but he managed to wrestle the knife away from her. A friend drove him to Womack Army Hospital for treatment where he said a stranger had attacked him in his unit parking lot. The authorities didn't believe him and placed him on restriction. He broke restriction, claiming he feared Cathy Perry would take her own life, which he said she had threatened to do. Wolverton's actions resulted in an investigation to determine whether his security clearance for the Green Berets should be withdrawn. While being interrogated under oath, on March 17, 1971, he talked about Cathy Perry's stabbing him.[30] Years later Wolverton told private detective Ted Gunderson that Perry told him "forces from the supernatural" made her attack him.[31]

Mrs. Betty Garcia, the woman who drove Wolverton to the hospital on the day he was wounded, told others that Cathy Perry was so despondent after stabbing Wolverton that she thought of killing herself that night. On March 23, 1980, Mrs. Garcia telephoned Gunderson on the West Coast to tell him she knew something that might help Dr. MacDonald. She told Beasley in person (and Gunderson by telephone) that on the night of the Wolverton stabbing her son had found the girl behind a grocery store attempting to kill herself with a knife. The son brought her home and Mrs. Garcia cared for her and called authorities. Not long afterward Cathy Perry also tried to stab a second person, Mrs. Garcia's son.

Cathy Perry told Mrs. Garcia that she and her boyfriend had run away from home in Florida and that after arriving in Fayetteville they joined a witchcraft cult in the Haymount area, which is where Stoeckley lived.[32] Perry kept denying she was a witch, Mrs. Garcia told Gunderson, even though no one was accusing her of being one. "She would tell us that she 'just lived with witches,'" the woman said. "She complained that the Black Cult kept making her do things she didn't want to do." At one time, according to Mrs. Garcia, Cathy Perry said, "I have killed several persons." She would refer to a "white car of death," and would cringe when she saw a light-colored automobile on the street. "I kept all the knives and potential weapons locked up or hidden," Mrs. Garcia told Beasley. "Her state of mind was bad."

Mrs. Garcia said that eventually she coaxed the girl into telling where her family lived in Florida. Arrangements were made for an uncle nearby in North Carolina to take charge of her. After she had departed, Mrs. Garcia noticed what appeared to be bloodstains on some clothing Perry had left behind with some other items. Garcia said she called the girl's home in Florida, and Perry's mother instructed her to burn everything.

But Mrs. Garcia feared the items might be important to the MacDonald case, given the statements made to her by Cathy Perry. The CID case progress file discloses how Garcia arranged to surrender the clothing to authorities through the cooperation of two civilian lawyers, former district attorney Charles Kirkman and his law partner, James Nance, Jr. Nance, who had worked as a local representative for Bernard Segal during the Article 32 hearing, delivered the items to MacDonald's former military defense attorney, Jim Douthat, at Fort Bragg on January 5, 1971. Douthat arranged to surrender them to Kearns and Ivory of the CID.[33]

Records show that nothing ever came of the surrendered items except for a CID agent's indifferent interview of Cathy Perry fully nine months later on October 5, 1971. The interviewer, Darrell Bennett, didn't even bother having Perry sign a statement; in fact, he thought so little of the effort that he himself didn't put the results into written form until April 5, 1972, a year and three months after the clothing had been turned in. Bennett's report, totaling nineteen lines, stated that Cathy Perry admitted she was in Fayetteville at the time of the murders, that she used drugs, that she had once stabbed her pet dog to death, that she had stabbed another person, that she denied being involved in the murders, and that she could furnish no leads as to others who might have been involved.[34]

But by 1984 Cathy Perry, like her friends Stoeckley and Mitchell before her, felt she had something to say. In that year, while notices of the upcoming NBC-TV docudrama *Fatal Vision*[35] were being aired on television, Cathy Perry Williams, now married and living in Florida, called the FBI and told an agent that she wanted to confess to the MacDonald murders. The FBI did not respond. She called a second time the following day and said that she no longer wanted to confess. It was only then, after she had changed her mind, that the FBI dispatched Special Agent Edward M. McGrath to her home on Saturday, November 17, 1984, one day before the first airing of the TV movie *Fatal Vision*.

Now having to justify her earlier promise to confess, she gave McGrath a disjointed story of being induced into entering a car on the night of February 16, 1970 (the night before the early morning of the MacDonald murders), by two white females and five or six white males. She told how they broke into the front door of a house where a white male was lying on a couch. One of the group allegedly injected the man with a narcotic and he collapsed. They claimed he was a doctor who turned in drug users. She said "everyone went upstairs" where she saw them pounding on a baby under a blanket. She said she took the baby in her arms to prevent him from being further beaten. She told how they "forced her to hit the baby." She told of hiding another child in a closet, and later called the child "the other little boy."

She told a bizarre tale of trying to get the woman in the house to jump out of the window with her. She claimed she was ordered to "tie the woman up and kill her." She said she stabbed the woman in the leg and abdomen, murdering her. According to her statement, the group was in the house from approximately 11 P.M. until 4 or 5 A.M., and that the weather was warm and clear and there was no rain.

According to McGrath's November 17 report, Cathy Perry Williams told him that "shortly after this incident she had a nervous breakdown and was placed under psychiatric care. She further advised that she has been seeing a psychiatrist on a regular basis for the last 6 years, and is taking Thorazine on a daily basis."

As noted, some of the details offered by Cathy Perry Williams fail to fit the MacDonald crime scene. The children weren't boys. There is no evidence that MacDonald was injected. True, the children were very young, and might have been seen as boys. And records reveal that a CID lab tech had told an FBI man that his team had found a bloody syringe. This syringe never showed up, but the man said it contained a clear liquid. Might that syringe have held a narcotic, which Perry thought was going to be used at the crime scene? If the FBI had been interested in pinning Perry with the murders instead of MacDonald, what better evidence to support her story than to point to that mention of a bloody syringe? But the FBI, who recorded the information about the syringe in the first place, didn't bring it up.

The discrepancies in Perry's account of multiple murders at the home of a doctor who turned in drug users force questions: Was this a confession of real occurrences recorded by a sick person perhaps also on drugs that night? Was the confession made deliberately unbelievable during a moment's bid for self-preservation after the FBI waited to visit her until she had changed her mind about confessing? Or was the confession nothing more than the wild imaginings of an innocent, uninvolved, drug-tortured woman?

Whatever the truth, several of her statements caused serious conjecture about certain crime-scene findings. Back in 1971, Dr. Russell S. Fisher, then serving as the CID's paid consultant, had focused attention on a bruise on Colette MacDonald's right arm which he thought resembled a rope burn. Fisher's observation was brought to mind in 1984 with Cathy Perry's words, "Tie the woman up." Little Kristen's hair was found in Kimberly's bedroom closet, mirroring Perry's story of "hiding another child in a closet." Blood spots of Colette's type were found near both windows in the master bedroom, bringing to mind Perry's words of "trying to get the woman of the house to jump out the window with her."[36]

The confession of Cathy Perry Williams was presented to the court as part of Jeffrey MacDonald's bid for a new trial in 1984–1985, but Judge Dupree gave it scant attention, calling it "bizarre." Despite the findings of ligature marks on Colette's arm, despite a reference to tying up the woman, and despite the baby's hair being found in Kimberly's closet, and blood spots at the window, and the statements by the CID's own consultant, Dr. Fisher, prosecutor Brian Murtagh argued there was no physical evidence that corroborated anything the woman had said.

But defense lawyer Brian O'Neill pointed out that there had been physical evidence, in the form of bloodstained clothing among the items left by Cathy Perry at Mrs. Garcia's home. Cathy Perry Williams had confirmed this fact during an interview with private detective Ray Shedlick. Yet, Murtagh steadfastly denied the existence of the clothing. To prove his point, he showed the judge a CID handwritten receipt made when the Perry items were accepted, and the receipt listed no such clothing.[37]

That receipt recalls the presence of a man who had handled other evidence which had disappeared, for the man who had accepted the items and prepared the receipt was William Ivory. His signature appeared on it. And it had been countersigned by Jim Douthat. But the "receipt" argument satisfied the judge, who later ruled, "The court therefore finds that he [Douthat] . . . did not deliver any articles of clothing to the agents."[38] Yet information that afterward came to light not only indicates that the clothing existed—as so many other persons said it did—but also makes it obvious that the receipt had to be in error and the clothing *had* been accepted by Ivory and then had disappeared, as had the piece of skin he had handled earlier. The clothing was specifically mentioned in the CID's own case log. On April 2, 1971, agent Mahon referenced certain items left behind by Cathy Perry, namely, "A pair of white boots, an article of clothing which appeared to have blood on it, and some photographs of Perry and her associates."

The CID apparently made photographs of the items in question, but the article of clothing, whatever it was, had vanished. This was learned by television producer Ted Landreth some four years after Judge Dupree accepted the "receipt" argument. Landreth was best known for his 1982 documentary about the death of Marilyn Monroe and for the 1988 award winning story on Americans missing in action in Southeast Asia, *We Can Keep You Forever: The Story of the MIA*. In 1988, in conjunction with the British Broadcasting Corporation, Landreth arranged to produce a television documentary entitled *False Witness*, focusing on questions which challenged the verdict of MacDonald's conviction.[39]

In October 1988, Landreth asked MacDonald's former military attorney, Jim Douthat, to provide some background materials about the Article 32 hearing. Among his documents Douthat came across pictures of the items, but the clothes weren't in the photos. To be precise, what Douthat found were pictures he had made of pictures. To explain, back when the CID was still handling the case, two CID agents, armed with pictures of several items including white go-go boots, called upon Douthat at his home. They showed him the pictures and wanted to know if any clothing had been inadvertently turned over to him. Clearly, they were looking for clothing that had once existed, apparently clothing listed by Mahon in the CID case log, clothing that was now lost. Douthat later explained to Landreth that he grabbed his camera and took photographs of the CID's pictures.

But there are no indications that clothing ever reached a laboratory. Documents suggest that William Ivory was the only CID agent to control the Perry possessions accepted from Mrs. Garcia. No laboratory "chain of evidence" ever surfaced after he accepted them. In an affidavit dated June 20, 1984, Ivory seemed to imply that he limited the examination of the items to himself. He wrote: "The boots I received on January 6, 1971, had no stains on them. I subsequently returned all the items upon request."[40]

When the human eye cannot always see the presence of blood on objects, sometimes chemicals such as phenolphthalien can detect its existence in difficult areas such as in the sole stitching of a boot. Yet no record of such an examination, or any other examination on the boots and clothing, has ever come to light.

On the day of the murders, the Fort Bragg CID agents and the provost marshal had claimed that no civilians were involved. If they were correct, and if Jeffrey MacDonald was lying, then something quite extraordinary had occurred. MacDonald described people of a certain mix of races and gender who were dressed a certain way—the rare combination of a white woman with floppy hat, blond hair, and boots in the company of a black man wearing an army field jacket, and in the company of two white males. By taking into account a blond wig, it is discovered that a group of Fayetteville drug users, specifically the Stoeckley group, included such a black-and-white pair fitting the description. These young people owned vehicles which matched those seen in the MacDonald neighborhood on the night in question. Their group included addicts, drug dealers, and self-styled cultists, many bent to violence. Three were convicted of kidnapping and conspiring to murder two of their own buddies over a drug dispute.

Other coincidences were reflected in the forensics: candle wax, a burnt match, long synthetic blond wig fibers, multiple bloody gloves, a bloody syringe, and other things. Also, bloody clothing belonging to one of the confessors had been turned over to the CID.

Still other evidence existed. Helena Stoeckley told Prince Beasley and Ted Gunderson that Greg Mitchell had been the man who had fought with Colette. Dr. Thomas Noguchi of Los Angeles County, and Dr. Ronald Wright of Broward County, Florida, both believed Colette's wounds were inflicted by a left-hander. Greg Mitchell was left-handed—MacDonald is right-handed. No Type B blood, Jeffrey MacDonald's type, was found on Colette's hands. But the CID laboratory analyses indicated the possibility of Type O blood on her hands. And Greg Mitchell had Type O blood. And a short brown hair, which wasn't MacDonald's, was found in Colette's hand. Greg Mitchell had brown hair, while MacDonald's hair was blond.

Even with all this evidence at their disposal, and even though many of Stoeckley's friends were prepared to testify that she said she was in the home that morning, prosecutor Jim Blackburn told the trial jury, "The only thing that links Helena Stoeckley to this crime scene is the fact that the defendant says that he saw a girl, and poor Helena doesn't know where she was between twelve o'clock and four-thirty in the morning."[41]

■

As Bost and I worked through the thousands of pages of army reports, we could not help but notice the CID penchant for holding back evidence that might challenge their claims. When we continued examining the records of the FBI and the prosecutors, we found similar practices. It seemed to us that the government's own documents reveal that this bias permeated the investigation, and tainted the case.

11

■

A Prosecutorial
Attitude

Soon after the discovery of the black wool fibers by the MacDonald defense team, Alan Dershowitz, Harvard professor and colorful defense attorney, visited an inmate at Terminal Island, the same prison in which MacDonald was being incarcerated. Dr. MacDonald, by chance, entered the visiting area of the prison. There he recognized the red-haired, bespectacled lawyer and called to him.

"Professor Dershowitz!"

"Dr. MacDonald!"

In the ensuing brief conversation, MacDonald brought Dershowitz up to date on his case, then added that they had just discovered that the government had suppressed the discovery of unmatched black wool fibers on the murder weapon and on Colette's body.

"The bastards!" Dershowitz exclaimed.

The defense team at that time was being temporarily headed up by Dennis Eisman, the attorney who had assisted Bernard Segal back at the army hearing in 1970. Eisman stepped aside in 1989, after the MacDonald-Dershowitz meeting, to give the field to Dershowitz and his sometime co-counsel, Harvey Silverglate. The two men had already proven themselves as successful "big-case" lawyers, and they were famous as no-holds-barred civil libertarians who eagerly challenged authorities. In 1985 the pair had succeeded in overturning the conviction of Claus Von Bulow, accused of trying to murder his wife.

Dershowitz was known for displaying flair within a courtroom, exceptional because courthouse histrionics were so foreign to his daily activities. A member of no legal firm, his primary focus was that of a long-tenured professor and mentor on the staid grounds of Harvard's School of Law at Cambridge, Massachusetts—a sanctuary he accepted at age twenty-five, following a humble background in Brooklyn. He was a slightly built man, with combed-back reddish hair matched by a mustache under rakish glasses. The ever-cluttered desk in his third-floor campus office was testimony to his wide interests and immense energy.

Harvey Silverglate provided the Boston legal firm through which Dershowitz worked his fervor in the courtrooms. Silverglate served not only as a second keen mind, but also as a counterbalance to the Dershowitz exuberance. The stocky Boston lawyer's carefully nurtured Vandyke beard advertised his orderliness. He demanded precision tasks of associates, tasks which left adversaries hard-pressed for room in which to maneuver.

Prior to the defense appeals of the mid-1980s Silverglate had coolly refused to get involved in the MacDonald case. He believed MacDonald hadn't gotten a fair trial, but he also felt that the defense evidence, as it then stood, would not convince a tough appellate court. Pressed by attorney friend Jane Wolf Eldridge[1] to look at the black wool and other new evidence after MacDonald had whetted Dershowitz's interest at Terminal Island, Silverglate now agreed not only that MacDonald was innocent, but that he actually had a chance to win in court. He decided to take the case on a pro bono basis. Dershowitz agreed to assist, also without pay.

Silverglate told others he had seen many miscarriages of justice, "but none so serious, so poignant, and so outrageous as this one."[2] Silverglate was only echoing what every other defense team attorney and investigator had said before him, including Ted Gunderson during my 1985 meetings with him.

Gunderson had assured me that when I began reading the case records in earnest I would find ample evidence that the case handlers "had it in for MacDonald." Given the emotional nature of the charges against him, "wife murderer and baby killer," Fred Bost and I would have been surprised not to have encountered some of this kind of prejudice. I, for one, must admit to having felt disgust toward Jeffrey MacDonald when in 1970 I first heard that he was accused of slaying his family. And then when I read *Fatal Vision* immediately after its publication in 1983, I was appalled that a man could be so externally and publicly attractive and yet so inwardly twisted. After my exposure to only a limited dose of the evidence, the government's side of it, I found it quite easy to believe that behind MacDonald's smiling face in photographs was the monster McGinniss described.

And, I must admit, when I first met MacDonald during a 1986 visit at Black Canyon Federal Correctional Institute in Arizona, I couldn't help wondering if those hands, those long, tapered, surgeon's fingers now busying themselves neatly stacking our vending machine quarters, had held the club and knives and ice pick that had sent his family into bloody oblivion. Sitting across an interview table from him, I felt a palpable, breathing prejudice toward him. After all, my government, my FBI, my Department of Justice, my Supreme Court, my America, and his friend, Joe McGinniss, had convicted him—he *must* be guilty, he *must* be lying. Could McGinniss have gotten by with his book if he had misrepresented the case as severely as MacDonald had claimed? Like one of the attorneys who would later examine our own book to see if we had collected sufficient documentation, I, too, didn't want to believe MacDonald was innocent, because to believe so would be to indict the entire system of holding back exculpatory evidence in order to convict him. Surely our system was fair. I ached to believe that the government had sound reasons for not revealing certain things to the jurors. Surely, I thought, those withheld items were somehow not what the defense team was trying to make them out to be.

After years of daily exposure to the boxes of source documents, Fred and I realized that it was impossible for many persons to have been familiar with the entire case. Most case handlers heard the views of army agent Ivory, or of former army lawyer Murtagh, and generally each case handler involved himself in only a single aspect of the investigation or prosecution. The case handler would submit his or her findings to an Ivory or to a Murtagh for inclusion in the overall discoveries. If MacDonald's lawyers are correct, it was at this point that certain facts were set aside. Therefore, the limited exposure of most "worker bees" in the case might not have been sufficient to displace the same kind of tangible anathema that I first felt toward MacDonald.

We knew that no government team would be less devoted to successfully convicting MacDonald than his defense team was to the purpose of freeing him. The presumption of a defendant's innocence by anyone but his mother is an ideal which is rarely ever fulfilled in the everyday courtroom. Like anyone else, case handlers are imbued with zeal, with team spirit, and they must guard against tunnel vision at every turn.

So, while we were prepared for some normal level of prosecutorial intent, what we actually found in the documents disturbed us like a train wreck in the night. Our efforts and discoveries were mirrored, later, by Silverglate's team, who delved into the same FOIA documents that had been previously examined by Brian O'Neill, and by Ellen Dannelly and her father, Ray Shedlick. All of us found, in essence, the same thing— that behind the file drawers of the army, the FBI, and the Department of Justice, a different case existed from that presented to the trial jurors in 1979.

Our discoveries caused us to ask who were these people, these case handlers who fought so hard to block Segal's attempts to get evidence in front of the jurors? What, specifically, did the government team know about evidence which the defense team and the jurors did not hear? And was there another reason, besides the legal statutes, that Judge Dupree had ruled against every one of Bernard Segal's twenty-eight motions? Bost and I also feel that our explorations in this one case might help answer a seminal question being asked of law enforcement and the justice system in general: Where are the weaknesses in the system? When evidence is withheld, how, exactly is it accomplished, and by whom?

Colonel Robert Kriwanek

As part of the army's 1970–1971 probe after the army hearing, which had resulted in MacDonald's exoneration and subsequent release from the army, Colonel Robert Kriwanek, the former Fort Bragg provost marshal, was temporarily recalled from Korea to Washington to be interviewed by the CID on the morning of December 18, 1970, ten months after the murders. At that time he conceded to his interviewer that "From the very beginning there was a strong presumption that Captain MacDonald murdered his wife and two children." Kriwanek made it known that he hadn't been just a man sitting on the sidelines. He told his questioner, "I took a close personal interest in this investigation from its very inception. . . . I was concerned that if a low ranking person was in charge, he would be likely to expend only limited resources. . . ."

But, as the man "in charge," apparently Kriwanek did what he could to block a fuller investigation by the FBI. He didn't inform the federal agents that Mica had seen a woman matching the description of the female MacDonald said he saw holding the light during the mayhem. And Kriwanek did nothing to see that the "presumed" murderer was informed of his rights, so on three successive days during that first week, MacDonald was questioned without ever knowing he had been singled out as the major suspect in the crime. In fact, MacDonald wasn't advised of his rights to maintain silence or to seek legal counsel until April 6, almost two months after the murders. Yet the possible need of legal counsel was publicly broached with Colonel Kriwanek early in the case. In a news story which appeared in the *Fayetteville Observer* two days after the crime, reporter Pat Reese wrote: "Asked if MacDonald has been assigned a military attorney, Kriwanek said that the doctor is being treated as a 'witness' in the investigation and indicated that there is no need for the counsel." This, by Kriwanek's own accounting, certainly was not the case. MacDonald was his "target" from the first moments, and, by any accounts in retrospect, sorely needed legal advice.

Despite this first assurance to the public that MacDonald was only a witness, Kriwanek, during his Washington interview later that year, detailed for his CID questioner some of the actions that were taken against MacDonald during his ten-day hospitalization. The colonel said Fort Bragg's public information officer was busy writing a news release that would one day inform the public of the doctor's arrest. "It was decided that a group of lawyers would be available to be used if MacDonald didn't ask for anyone by name," Kriwanek told his interviewer. Then he added, "The type of restriction he would undergo when he became a suspect was discussed during this period."

The CID

Kriwanek wasn't the only army official who seemed to have an "agenda." As already noted, William Ivory never accomplished a number of duties routinely expected of an unbiased investigator. These failures can hardly be disputed in the light of his own statements under oath, so the question must turn to why.

That there was a prosecutorial attitude seems apparent. But the "why" of it is far from being solved. Ted Gunderson, the former FBI bureau chief, theorized it was because of a continuous flow of drugs into Bragg from Southeast Asia, drugs the authorities knew about but couldn't stop. Gunderson conjectured that the CID had to "get" MacDonald or risk serious investigation into the drug scene on post. A CID agent who was a narcotics investigator working with Prince Beasley and Helena Stoeckley[3] on the Inter-Agency Narcotics Bureau insisted that someone was indeed dirty upstairs. He said that anytime he seemed to be getting close to a big bust, orders would move him on to another case. When asked whether these orders came from his boss Joe Grebner, the agent said, "No. Joe was a good man. It had to have come from somewhere higher than Joe." Green Beret physician Dr. Jerry Hughes said, "Drugs were everywhere on post. Everybody knew the stuff was coming in, and coming in big, but who was dirty and who wasn't we didn't know." Captain Jim Williams, who worked with MacDonald, complained that every experienced officer at Bragg knew better than to confront these addicts because they were armed and they were unbalanced. Only MacDonald, new and inexperienced, didn't seem to understand what he was getting into. Williams believed that MacDonald placed himself in between the kids and their drug supply, and got hurt.

These MacDonald supporters suggest that the real reason the CID pinned MacDonald for the murders and overlooked so much contrary evidence was that if they pressured the Stoeckley group, these drug dealers might point a finger back at the CID. This, they say, is why Ivory didn't file a report after interviewing Stoeckley even though she had no alibi, was on drugs that night, wore a blond wig and boots, was into candles and witchcraft, and traveled with a black man who also wore a field jacket. Was this why a bloody syringe apparently disappeared? Or why wig hair and other items found at the crime scene were never entered in the official reports? So many of these lapses occurred that only two reasons seem possible: Either the investigators were grossly incompetent or the information was deliberately withheld.

That the CID laboratory harbored an "attitude" against MacDonald is corroborated even in small things. Consider a CID laboratory note, written while incoming evidence was still being cataloged. It stated: "E-50— crushed hair in bathroom sink—if Colette's or Kim's, its one of his hand washings." This note reflects no presumption of innocence. This attitude was also revealed by Dillard Browning when he testified later at the trial. He told the court, "Well, if a vial contained fifteen or twenty fibers, I would select two or three at random and compare those two or three with the known pajama jacket."[4] This was still another example of the CID attitude that MacDonald had done the crime, so they succumbed to a tendency to ignore any fiber that didn't match the pajama top. Since only the pajama top fibers mattered in the CID's MacDonald-centered view of the case, they were automatically neglecting any possible fibers from outside assailants.

It was precisely the fibers from outside the house, brought in by possible outside assailants, that were most central to the defense case—yet, by case design since only MacDonald was being targeted, all such fibers were ignored by the army investigators. Consider, for example, a mystery acrylic fiber[5] and the foreign hair found in Colette's hand. They didn't fit the CID's target so they were set aside, as were the piece of skin from her fingernail and the unidentified fingerprint on the glass in the living room.

This CID attitude changed little with the second investigation against MacDonald which began in January 1971. This investigation itself was unlawful inasmuch as it breached the federal Posse Comitatus Act.[6,7] That congressional act forbids military personnel from being used to enforce civil law except when called upon by the president during emergencies. A 1955 Supreme Court interpretation of this act also made it illegal for military law enforcers to pursue civilians who were not threatening the military establishment, or to pursue a military lawbreaker into civilian life when the crime allegedly committed was such that it could be tried by a civilian court—as in the MacDonald case.

MacDonald had been honorably discharged from the service and therefore was no longer subject to the jurisdiction of the CID. But in late 1970 when the FBI refused to accept the case,[8] leaders in the CID pursued MacDonald into civilian life, spying on him, on his family, on his friends, and even on his attorney, Bernard Segal, all in violation of the Posse Comitatus Act.

To set up surveillances upon MacDonald's family and friends on Long Island, New York, the CID recruited sympathetic members of the Suffolk County Police Department's narcotics squad to do the job. A "confidential" report dated January 6, 1971, was submitted to the CID by a Suffolk County squad member, who had arranged to hear a conversation between Mrs. William Reich and MacDonald's brother-in-law, Robert Stevenson. As to surveillance against Bernard Segal, an entry made in the CID case progress file by agent Richard Mahon on April 6, 1971, mentions the secret file activated on the attorney. These clandestine activities by the army were taking place during a public outcry against just such actions, an outcry which resulted in a two-month hearing by the Senate Subcommittee on Constitutional Rights,[9] and which, supposedly, led to a cessation of spying on civilians.

At least one of the CID investigators recognized that repercussions might result from such infringements, so he took steps to conceal the most blatant offenses. Peter Kearns, the agent in charge of the reinvestigation, had a spy in the First Citizens Bank at Fort Bragg watching MacDonald's small but still active account there. On March 16, 1971, MacDonald wrote the bank, supplying the address and account number of a New York firm where he wanted his money transferred. The spy immediately made a machine copy of MacDonald's request and furnished the copy to Kearns. The agent didn't place this illegally acquired document in the case file, but instead kept it in a "safe file" away from routine documents. On it he wrote and signed this curt message: "Not releasable in any form!!"[10]

The attitude of investigators remained constant even after the FBI agreed to accept the case in 1974. In the same manner in which the CID had breached the Posse Comitatus Act, the FBI laboratory breached a long-standing policy in order to pursue MacDonald.

As with city, county, and state laboratories, the FBI laboratory has a stringent policy not to accept any evidence for evaluation if it has been previously examined in the same manner by another government laboratory. Two reasons exist for this policy: First, the second laboratory would have no way of knowing to what extent the initial laboratory had altered or contaminated the evidence during processing; second, if the two laboratories were to publish opposite findings, it would flaw any further court use of the evidence by the government.

Paul Stombaugh

At first, the FBI adhered to this laboratory policy in the MacDonald case. In 1971 the CID requested that Paul Stombaugh at the FBI laboratory examine the pajama top and determine the directionality of the tiny fibers in the puncture holes. Records prove that the FBI honored this request only because the CID agents claimed in writing that they hadn't made that type of examination.[11] But we know this claim was untrue, for a CID laboratory note dated March 23, 1970, contains a sketch of the back panel of the pajama top showing the position of nine ice pick punctures and indicating that two of these punctures were made from the inside and two from the outside.[12] In addition to this, on April 6, 1970, agent Robert Shaw told MacDonald, "We've taken this thing. We have examined it under laboratory conditions. We know what it's made of. We know what kind of fibers are in it, what kind of threads are in it. We know it's old, it's been around a long time. We know it hasn't been repaired to the extent that there are foreign threads in it."[13]

In 1974, however, this historic FBI laboratory policy was deliberately ignored. With the grand jury investigation under way, the FBI assigned Stombaugh the task of deciding whether the FBI would take investigative responsibility for the case.[14] Stombaugh was sent to Fort Bragg on October 23, 1974, to examine the crime scene personally and to study the evidence the CID had collected. Following his trip, he not only recommended accepting the case, he recommended the FBI laboratory temporarily set aside its policy of refusing to examine evidence that had already been examined by another laboratory. A Justice Department memo dated November 6, 1974, was the first indication of the policy breach. It stated, "Approximately 120 items of evidence that had previously been examined by the Army Laboratory were reexamined. . . ."[15]

But the government soon found itself struggling with the very dilemma that the policy was designed to prevent. Prosecutors soon were faced with the dire situation of government experts contradicting one another. To cite just two of scores of such examples: In 1970 Dillard Browning of the CID found pink "nylon" fibers in the sheet taken from the master bedroom floor, fibers which James Frier of the FBI secretly called "cotton" in 1979 before the trial. And Browning said that two fibers which were found where MacDonald claimed to have lain unconscious were identical to fibers in the blue pajama top, while Stombaugh later insisted that one was *not* from the pajama top.

These contradictions were not only kept hidden from the defense and the jury, but Stombaugh was groomed as the prosecution's ultimate expert. The CID's Browning and the FBI's Frier would be downgraded, leaving the key role to Stombaugh, and this reduced the chance of the laboratory contradictions being discovered at trial.

David Hardison

Stombaugh had many champions in the crowded courtroom during that summer of 1979. Chief among them was David Hardison, the jury foreman who pushed Stombaugh's claims in the jury room. Years after trial, however, an accumulation of evidence surfaced which evoked a question whether the jury foreman was highly enthusiastic about Stombaugh's work or whether he went to the trial purposely to convict MacDonald.

This allegation first surfaced in 1987, eight years after the trial.[16] Harnett County resident Raymond Klein told private detective Ray Shedlick that he had met Hardison upon retiring from the army in 1972. Hardison, a former highway patrolman, was a deacon in the local church, and for a while Hardison and Klein saw each other regularly. Klein alleged that on one of these occasions in the early 1970s Hardison told him that if he, Hardison, ever had a chance to see justice done, he would see that MacDonald was punished for killing his family. A year after Klein's disclosure, a similar story surfaced. When interviewed on September 9, 1988, Earl Black, owner and operator of an automotive repair shop not far from Hardison's home,[17] told of an afternoon in early July 1979 when Hardison came to his store very excited about being called to federal jury duty. Black said he asked his friend what he would do if he were to get the MacDonald case. According to Black, Hardison responded, "I'll convict the hell out of him if I do." Two other Hardison acquaintances also signed declarations that Hardison had so revealed his prejudice and intent.[18]

Despite these statements from Hardison's friends indicating that he may have been biased from the beginning, most of the trial jurors, when questioned in the late 1980s, recalled Hardison as having acted both fairly and competently as their foreman. They described him as a clearheaded man, as a just man, and even as a compassionate man. Only juror Eddie Parker complained that Hardison had been overbearing while arguing for MacDonald's conviction.

Before trial, as a normal part of the jury selection process, Hardison was asked under oath whether he was in any way prejudiced. Segal knew, of course, that Hardison had been a law enforcement officer. Hardison, answering voir dire questions in the crowded courtroom, insisted that he bore no prejudice. So Segal had left Hardison on the jury, overriding objections from Jeffrey MacDonald, co-counsel Wade Smith, and others of the defense team. Segal believed a former lawman would be incensed at the way the evidence had been handled by the CID, but his assumption proved to be grossly naive.

The FBI

MacDonald's defense attorneys complained in the latter years of their reinvestigation of the case that they'd found evidence that certain FBI affidavits were untrue. They referred, specifically, to affidavits filed by FBI agents which Murtagh used during the 1984–1985 appeal to discredit defense witnesses. The most flagrant of these, the defense team says, was the claim by an FBI agent that a medical examiner had retracted findings that cast doubt on the government theory of MacDonald's guilt.

In early 1984 lead defense counsel Brian O'Neill was writing the appeal on the Stoeckley confessions, the suppressed bloody syringe, the piece of skin, and his discoveries that Dr. Brussel had been in the employ of the CID on the MacDonald case for eight years. O'Neill believed his case was won, but he wanted to strengthen his claims if possible. To that end, he asked Dr. Ronald Wright, medical examiner of Broward County, Florida, to study the government investigators' recently released crime-scene reports and autopsy photographs. "The blow," Wright reported, "which fractured Colette MacDonald's skull was struck with a club that was swung in a left-handed swing by a person facing Mrs. MacDonald at the time she was standing. As the blow was very forceful I have concluded that it is consistent with someone who was left-handed." MacDonald is right handed. Greg Mitchell was left-handed.

In addition to this, Wright found evidence of another previously undiscovered weapon. In photos of Colette's and Kristen's bodies he found a number of double wounds, somewhat like snake bites. These, he reported, "are not knife wounds and are consistent with scissors."[19]

Dr. Wright also confirmed a peculiar "S" pattern of puncture wounds in Kristen's chest, a fact that had been specifically detailed in the autopsy report and mentioned by the army autopsy pathologist, Dr. William Hancock, Jr., at the grand jury hearing.[20] This group of ice pick wounds was separate from the other wounds, leading to an assumption that it was designed by intent. Helena Stoeckley added fuel to this suspicion when she told Ted Gunderson the stab wounds in the baby were purposely made in an "S" pattern, because they were meant to stand for "Satan."

O'Neill included Dr. Wright's affidavit in his appeal papers in 1984, but at oral arguments, he discovered via prosecution claims that an FBI agent had visited Dr. Wright. This agent, James M. Reed,[21] had written an affidavit saying that Dr. Wright had "retracted" his statement.

This was a devastating blow to O'Neill's efforts, but he apparently believed that Dr. Wright must have, as the agent said, reconsidered his bold statements about the wounds. O'Neill did not learn until five years later that Dr. Wright had never retracted his findings as the government said. In a declaration signed October 14, 1989, Wright emphatically stated, "At no time and to no one, including Special Agent of the FBI, James M. Reed, have I ever recanted my declaration of February 15, 1984." Wright stood by his conclusions that the blow to Colette's skull was consistent with left-handedness and that the double puncture wounds were consistent with scissors.

This deduction excited MacDonald's defense team, for unknown to Dr. Wright, scissors as a weapon had been mentioned in the case during the previous summer. At that time MacDonald's attorneys were attempting to salvage anything possible from the misfortune of Helena Stoeckley's death. They asked her husband, Ernie Davis, to put into writing everything he could remember her saying about the murders. In his affidavit signed July 25, 1983, he included these words: "Helena told me that everybody was scared and wanted to get out of there, and they all left in a hurry, leaving all the weapons behind, except for some scissors. Then they went to the donut shop and cleaned up."

Wright's claims corroborate later opinions formed by Dr. Thomas Noguchi, a medical examiner for Los Angeles County, when he examined the same photos and documents. Further, Noguchi insisted that it would have been "impossible" for Jeffrey MacDonald to have murdered his family in the way the government claimed because one man could not have used and controlled the number of weapons found at the scene and indicated by the forensic photographs.

In a similar vein, an FBI affidavit challenged the claim of Norma Lane, who with her husband had befriended Greg Mitchell during the years prior to his death. She had told defense investigator Ray Shedlick that Mitchell had confessed to serious crimes which occurred at Fort Bragg. After a subsequent interview by an FBI agent, the agent submitted an affidavit stating that Mrs. Lane was not certain whether Mitchell had been referring to something that had happened at Fort Bragg or in Vietnam. When Norma Lane later heard of this FBI affidavit, she charged that the agent had been untruthful, that she had never wavered in her statement that Mitchell spoke of crimes at Fort Bragg.

Another FBI challenge to defense claims was the government's presentation of a statement, signed by Homer Young, a former FBI agent and former Gunderson employee, claiming that the Stoeckley confession was elicited from her under duress from Ted Gunderson. Young later said that the statement was untrue, and he signed it because he believed that if he had not done so, the agents who prepared it would simply have filed a false affidavit saying that Young had made the claim anyway. Young also said he had hoped to go to the appeal hearing and take the stand to tell Judge Dupree that the FBI had engaged in wrongdoing and had lied about the issue.

But Young didn't get to do this because O'Neill agreed during the appeal hearing to let Judge Dupree weigh the affidavits without "in-person" testimony. O'Neill believed Dupree would give more weight to affidavits actually signed by Dr. Wright and Norma Lane than to affidavits about their statements signed by FBI agents who might have changed the words of the defense claimants. But O'Neill was wrong. Dupree gave more credence to the FBI agents' words about the defense witnesses' claims than to the signed and sworn witness statements themselves.

Brian Murtagh

The defense team, using the heretofore hidden documents which evoked further defense investigation, has found many bogeymen, but few of them garner more invective than Brian Murtagh. By 1989 MacDonald's defenders had thoroughly researched prosecutor Murtagh's history in the MacDonald affair, a history graphically exposed by documents acquired through the Freedom of Information Act. Defense attorneys now recognized an additional reason why Murtagh had fought so adamantly through the years to prevent FOIA access.

The defense lawyers learned that Murtagh had first entered the case in December 1971, shortly after being commissioned in the army as a captain fresh out of Georgetown University School of Law. Not yet twenty-five years of age, he was unseasoned as attorney, investigator, or army officer. The Judge Advocate General's office assigned him to duty at CID headquarters in Washington, D.C., where he was made the legal adviser to the MacDonald case.

By the time Murtagh came on the scene, MacDonald had been released by the army and had been working as a civilian physician for a year, yet the doctor was still being steadfastly and illegally stalked by the CID. His bank records were being examined, his mail was being watched, his telephone contacts were being listed, and his friends were being spied upon.[22] Even though his wife, Colette, had been dead for twenty-two months, MacDonald's social dates were being cataloged and each relationship secretly investigated to see whether a "love triangle" might have been a motive for killing his family.

This was the knowledge that was placed in Murtagh's hands when he was assigned to the case. Even a neophyte lawyer should have recognized that this secret army surveillance was a criminal breach of the federal Posse Comitatus Act; yet Murtagh, an army man himself, cooperated with the continuing investigation and quickly became a major part of it.

The new attorney familiarized himself with the evidence so well that within three months, on February 18, 1972, he shared the spotlight with chief investigator Kearns in a presentation aimed at getting the Justice Department to indict MacDonald. The effort failed because of a stated "lack of evidence," but Murtagh's demonstrated knowledge of the case resulted in his being invited to later meetings held by Justice Department members and by the U.S. Attorney for the Eastern District of North Carolina.

Thus, the young Murtagh found himself in the center of the case with a seat among the heavy decision-makers. But the spotlight suddenly went dark when, in March 1974, Alfred Kassab took things into his own hands and pushed the Justice Department for a grand jury proceeding. The CID, content to be finally free of the case, welcomed Kassab's move, and ignored requests by the Justice Department, not eager to prosecute MacDonald, to help them thwart the pressure from Kassab.

Major Steven Chucala, Murtagh's immediate boss, passed one of Kassab's requests to Murtagh for filing. A cover note informed the young lawyer that the CID commander, Colonel Tufts, had seen the Justice Department suggestion, but that Chucala had "reaffirmed that CID has completed its investigation. No further action."[23]

With the CID now out of the celebrated case, so, apparently, was Captain Murtagh. By his own admission, after learning that Victor Woerheide of the Justice Department would take the case before a grand jury, he called Woerheide in early June 1974 and begged a job.

He convinced Woerheide that he alone knew the evidence in its entirety, and Woerheide agreed to get him placed on special duty as a prosecution adviser.

Soldiers, by army policy, are required to seek job changes only through the chain of command, and it is seldom that an army commander looks kindly upon a subordinate who attempts to do otherwise. But Woerheide successfully concealed Murtagh's brash telephone call by arranging for the transfer through his own boss, Henry E. Petersen in the Department of Justice.[24]

The forced reassignment didn't sit well with Murtagh's superiors at CID headquarters.[25] Despite that, he shared the spoils of victory when the grand jury indicted MacDonald in January 1975. Two months later the young lawyer accepted an offer to resign his army commission and take a Justice Department job assisting Woerheide in the prosecution. Shortly afterward, Woerheide's sudden death of a heart attack in October 1975 created a void that promised to make Murtagh's services even more important.

Time and circumstances, however, started things downhill for him once again. Defense appeals and court wrangling forced years to pass with no trial possible. In the meantime the evidence was thoroughly sorted, cataloged, and studied. The day finally came when Jack Keeney of the Justice Department convinced his colleagues that the department itself need not participate in the trial. He said that evidence in the case was sufficiently laid out. Justice Department leaders agreed; the job was to fall to the U. S. Attorney's office in Raleigh alone, except for distant supervision.[26] Again, Murtagh was being squeezed from the picture.

And, again, he ignored the decision of his bosses, as he had done with Woerheide in 1974. This time he contacted George Anderson, the newly appointed U.S. Attorney for the Eastern District of North Carolina. Murtagh convinced Anderson that if allowed to share the prosecutor's table, he would assure a conviction.[27] As a result, Anderson arranged for Murtagh to assist James Blackburn, the Assistant U. S. Attorney in Raleigh. Blackburn would be in charge of the case for the office, and Murtagh would be his co-counsel at trial.

Murtagh's manner of circumventing superiors marked his general behavior throughout the case. For example, while he was in the army, even before his call to Woerheide in early June 1974, the Justice Department had once more secretly refused to indict Jeffrey MacDonald, citing, incredibly, the "exculpatory character of some of the evidence."[28] Murtagh at that time took it upon himself to prepare an angry draft response intended for the signature of his commander, an unusual move for a young captain who was far junior to the staff officers in the CID headquarters. In his uncool response, Murtagh argued that no exculpatory evidence existed. As part of his proposed official letter, he added an untruthful smear of the Kalin family, MacDonald's neighbors, by remarking, "We suspect that the intransigence of the Kalins stems from a desire to shield the [two Kalin] daughters from being linked sexually to Jeffrey MacDonald."[29] The attorney's reckless and unsubstantiated harangue was never sent to the Justice Department. His commander, Colonel Tufts, returned it with a rebuff indicating that a more experienced lawyer from the army's general counsel would be called upon to make an appropriate reply.[30] Again, Murtagh was "out of the loop."

In similar fashion, when Captain Murtagh was attached to Woerheide's office for the limited purpose of advising about evidence collected by the army, he ended up in the center of activity. When the bodies of Colette MacDonald and her children were about to be exhumed on September 9, 1974, Murtagh ordered New York FBI agents to obtain hair samples from the bodies. The agents were affronted, wondering why an army captain was giving them orders. They notified Bureau headquarters of the captain's demand and requested instructions "whether or not this should be done."[31] Paul Stombaugh was then dispatched to handle the matter. After all, a prosecuting attorney normally is not directly involved in evidence collection, which was Stombaugh's basic function.

On a later occasion, when a trial seemed imminent in 1975, some unknown army official was frustrating Bernard Segal's attempts to locate and contact potential army witnesses. Army authorities were rebuffing Segal, insisting that it was impossible to have mail forwarded to the soldiers. In desperation, MacDonald requested help from his district congressman, Representative Mark Hannaford. On MacDonald's behalf, Hannaford delivered seven letters to the army requesting that they be properly forwarded. His request was immediately granted.

Hannaford's act angered Murtagh. Teddi Phillips, an aide in Congressman Hannaford's office, took two calls from Murtagh in mid-July during which the brand-new Justice Department attorney "threatened to subpoena Hannaford before a federal grand jury to answer questions about his involvement in the MacDonald case." Phillips recalled the calls as blustery and obviously intended to prevent the congressman from aiding in the search for witnesses.

But Hannaford wasn't intimidated.[32] He told newsmen that he would forward yet another letter to a soldier on behalf of MacDonald, and that he also intended to write a letter to the House Judiciary Committee to determine the propriety of Brian Murtagh's phone calls. Hannaford's complaints went for naught. Murtagh was cleared of any wrongdoing by Richard Thornburgh, who would later become attorney general in the Bush administration.

Later in that year of 1975, Segal requested other witnesses' addresses from Murtagh himself as part of normal prescribed pre-trial requirements. When the addresses weren't given to him, Segal broached Murtagh's lack of ethics before the federal appeals court. In arguing against the complaint on October 8, Murtagh told Judge John D. Butzner, "There is no basis for Mr. Segal's complaint, your honor. We are still in the process of getting the present addresses of the witnesses—" But the judge cut him off in mid-sentence.

Butzner knew that the government had pushed hard for a trial two months previously, so all general pre-trial preparations such as sharing witness addresses should have already been accomplished. The judge asked, "Have you given the defendant the addresses?"

"No," admitted Murtagh.

Butzner threw up a hand in exasperation. "When were you going to give it to them," he asked, "the day before trial?"[33]

Four years later, when the trial jury in 1979 found MacDonald guilty, the verdict was overturned by the Fourth Circuit Court of Appeals after MacDonald had spent a year in prison. The Fourth Circuit ruled that MacDonald had been denied a speedy trial. However, on March 31, 1982, the U. S. Supreme Court voted 6 to 3 to reverse the lower court decision. In the past, the speedy-trial "clock" for any defendant began running when the defendant was charged with a crime. But the Supreme Court set that precedent aside. They now decided that, for MacDonald, the years between 1971 and 1974 didn't count on his speedy-trial clock because MacDonald wasn't under indictment until 1975.

Once this reversal occurred, formalities required that an arrest warrant be issued by Judge Francis Murnaghan, Jr., a justice of the appeals court which had earlier freed MacDonald on the speedy-trial issue. Before Murnaghan was advised of the Supreme Court decree, however, MacDonald was already in chains. Murtagh again had ignored protocol and had made an advance arrangement with Judge Dupree for a quick arrest. Murtagh excused the unusual arrangement by telling newsmen that fast action was needed to prevent MacDonald's "flight," even though for twelve years MacDonald had made every court appearance required, and even though, technically, Judge Dupree was not the proper judge to issue a rearrest warrant.

Records show that others suffered from Murtagh's slights, including fellow attorneys in the Justice Department and his bosses. A memo written by attorney Brandon Alvey demonstrates the extent to which Murtagh ignored office obligations. A new section chief had been assigned, and protocol required that each subordinate attorney write a memorandum which would familiarize the new superior with work in progress. Murtagh ignored the requirement. On Monday, July 16, 1979, the opening day of the MacDonald trial, Alvey hastily wrote a memorandum in Murtagh's stead.

The final paragraph of Alvey's memo informed the new boss that "Despite having been requested by your predecessor on several occasions to advise us as to the status of the case and to keep us posted on all matters, the attorney [Murtagh] has failed to do so. We learned of the trial date late Friday afternoon only as a result of a misdirected telephone call. Thus, while we are supposed to supervise this case, we cannot do so due to a lack of information."[34]

At the very least, this described a breach of conduct by Murtagh. Perhaps he simply didn't want to share the information with his boss; or perhaps he was too busy to write a memo containing enough detail to teach a new superior the MacDonald case. But there was another aspect to consider. That memo required by his boss would have forced Murtagh to detail his case, and to list documents and items of evidence he was *or was not* surrendering to the opposition. Such a written record would work against him if he intended to withhold crucial items, the very charge he would one day face at the hands of the MacDonald defense attorneys when suppressed documents eventually came to light.

A number of documented facts seem to support this. Records show that on December 5, 1978, when Murtagh was anticipating that the U.S. Supreme Court would defeat Segal's last attempt to prevent a trial, the prosecutor held a meeting of FBI laboratory technicians to discuss the physical evidence. Nine days later he wrote a letter to Morris S. Clark, the assistant section chief of the FBI laboratory's Scientific Analysis Section.[35] In his letter Murtagh listed specific laboratory comparisons he wanted redone.

In 1990, after the momentous defense discovery of the black wool fibers on the murder club, the defense researchers found Murtagh's requests for lab tests interesting, not only because the defense wanted to examine Murtagh's possible culpability in the alleged suppression of the lab notes, but they wanted to find out, specifically, what the laboratory had found in those exhibits. One of the things Murtagh wanted the FBI to recheck in 1978, according to his letter to the lab's assistant section chief, was a blue acrylic fiber that had been found among debris in Colette MacDonald's right hand. Splinters from the attack club had been found within her hand's grasp, placing her in fatal proximity to the wielder of the club, so this fiber of unknown source tended to show that an outside attacker, not MacDonald, could well have used that club on her. Murtagh wrote, "I am greatly concerned that the source of this fiber be identified. . . ."

Section chief Clark put the job in the hands of FBI laboratory technician James C. Frier and his assistant, Kathy Bond. Although the pair were methodical, they were unable to find a source for the blue acrylic fiber. That wasn't the worst of it, though. As a result of their wide-ranging probes, they challenged some prior findings made by Dillard Browning in the CID lab nine years earlier.

Browning had found three fibers among the debris from near Colette MacDonald's battered mouth, one of which he claimed matched Jeffrey MacDonald's pajama top (although the CID laboratory report was written in such a manner as to make it seem that all three fibers matched that pajama top). But when Frier actually examined these three fibers, he found no such match. Instead, he discovered in the debris taken from Colette's mouth area two black wool fibers of unknown source. In another instance CID lab tech Browning had labeled three fibers taken from Colette's body near her right bicep as "nylon." But Frier found them to be a rayon fiber, a white wool fiber, and a black wool fiber. On the lab note, next to the listing of the black wool fiber, Kathy Bond wrote the word "Source?", indicating that the FBI lab had not matched it to any known fabric samples taken from the house.

Frier's discoveries were obviously important to the prosecution, for a subsequent lab note shows that the technicians spent more than five hours on February 9, 1979, in the FBI's Room 3931M going over the lab findings for Murtagh. The attorney then instructed them to reexamine other exhibits, including the debris from the murder club. That reexamination led to the discovery of the unmatched black wool on the murder club.

By law, according to the rules of discovery, the results of these findings should have been shared with Segal.[36] For this reason, we think Murtagh faced an unenviable situation. First, he was in possession of information which showed his experts at odds with each other on a crucial exhibit, a murder weapon. Since his entire case was based on interpretations of circumstantial physical evidence, if it became known that the government's own experts disagreed among themselves about that evidence, the case could well disintegrate. Equally negative to his purposes as prosecutor, Murtagh now possessed evidence suggesting Colette MacDonald may have been attacked by a person (or persons) wearing black wool and blue acrylic, someone other than her husband, for the black wool and blue acrylic fibers would not be matched to anything MacDonald wore that night, and they would not be matched to any other fiber products found in the house. In addition, of course, the mystery hair in her left hand wasn't MacDonald's either.

That this knowledge, which might have destroyed Murtagh's case, was never given to the defense before or during trial is a matter of history. How that history unfolded during the hectic months preceding trial was eventually pieced together years later through the documents released by the Freedom of Information Act. On March 1, 1979, for example, Murtagh asked CID headquarters to furnish him with two copies of each CID lab note in its files, stating, "One copy will be for eventual release to defense counsel." But despite this written promise, at no time did he make an effort to give any of these notes to the defense either before, during, or after the trial. In fact, when asked for them repeatedly and officially, he refused to turn them over and was protected by Dupree's failure to rule that he share them with the defense.

At this pre-trial juncture Murtagh was well aware that Bernard Segal had increased his efforts to learn something of the evidence facing him. Under the Freedom of Information Act, on January 4, 1979, Segal had requested the FBI to make available to him virtually everything the FBI had in its files concerning the case, to include "all laboratory notes, bench notes, and technician's notes."[37] For some reason yet unknown, Segal's request was eventually shunted to the army CID by the FBI.

Meanwhile, the new FBI lab findings had to be handled within the official records process. This presented another danger to this closely held information. The FBI laboratory requires not only that all incoming requests for examinations be documented, but that FBI outgoing responses also be in writing. Yet on March 14, 1979, when Clark and Frier published the official response to Murtagh's letter of request, they failed to mention in their report the discrepancies between their findings and earlier findings by the CID. They also failed to mention the black wool found on the murder weapon and on the victim's mouth where she was struck with that club. In fact, they failed to mention anything which might be helpful to the defense. For example, although they had been specifically requested by Murtagh to identify the source of the blue acrylic fiber taken from Colette MacDonald's hand, and although they had failed to find a match, they made no mention of that fiber or their failure to match it. Instead, they wrote, incredibly, "No other fibers of apparent comparison significance could be associated with the items specifically requested in the referenced letter." Thus, a third party reading the official report would have no idea that no match was made on a fiber in a murder victim's hand, and that other, still-withheld reports existed.

Despite the evasive wording of the official report, Murtagh may not have trusted its transmission to him through normal channels. On March 15 he personally picked up not only the report itself but also the outbound carbon copy.[38] In addition, he personally carried away in his own station wagon the physical items that had been examined. Thus, while he was vigorously opposing Segal's requests to lab-test the evidence and Segal's demands for the laboratory notes, Murtagh managed to keep secret not only the vague report but also the fact that the examinations had even been made.

Segal would eventually be told, at the time when Murtagh requested him to agree to a stipulation of Frier's findings, that the FBI had retested the club fibers. But Judge Dupree's refusal to support Segal's motion for laboratory documents kept Frier's written notes secret, and Segal had no way of knowing the explosive information contained within them.

In later years Murtagh would claim he had given a copy of Frier's report to the assistant defense attorney, Wade Smith, sometime during the trial. The defense attorneys, on the other hand, insist they were never furnished the report. They point out that if such had been the case, they would have sought testimony about the reasons behind the FBI's sudden extensive laboratory efforts. The defense says that this report first came into their hands through the Freedom of Information Act after MacDonald had already served three years in prison.

Shortly after the FBI lab gave Murtagh this carefully worded official report, the CID received Segal's FOIA request from the Justice Department, the request which had been originally sent to the FBI. On March 23,

1979, a puzzled CID representative wrote Murtagh for guidance on what to do with it. Murtagh responded on March 30, ordering the CID not to release any of the requested materials, saying the items in question had already been denied to the defense attorney by the court.[39] This explanation, in effect, contradicted his internal letter of March 1 in which he stated an intention to surrender copies of the defense-desired CID lab notes, an intention never carried out.

Segal had kept pressing for information, however, and not long afterward, Murtagh's trial boss, U.S. Attorney George Anderson, denied Segal's latest plea to allow examination of physical items. In his letter of April 24, 1979, Anderson added, ". . . we are aware of attempts by defense counsel to obtain access to laboratory notes and investigative files of this case by using the Freedom of Information Act. . . ." Anderson's final paragraph stated, "In summary, it is very simply the position of the United States Government that the time for discovery is over and the time for trial of the case is present." Anderson's response astounded Segal. The U.S. Attorney was acknowledging that Segal wanted the lab notes and investigative files, and had even applied for them through FOIA, but his requests, which had gone on for four years, were too late. Anderson clearly intended to send Blackburn and Murtagh to trial with Segal blind to the facts still hidden in those notes.

Apparently, Anderson's letter stonewalling Segal didn't satisfy Murtagh's concerns about the evidence. On June 7, 1979, the prosecutor personally spent the day searching the murder apartment, which had been kept padlocked by the army for nine years. Years later Murtagh would tell the court that he had been looking for the source of the blue acrylic fiber found in Colette MacDonald's hand, and he had forwarded to the FBI laboratory for examination that day a blue sleeveless sweater knitted by Eve Freeman, Colette's aunt, as indicated by the knitter's name on the label. In forwarding the sweater, Murtagh ignored the FBI requirement that comparison requests be detailed in writing. Instead, he cited his desires via the telephone. In responding with the results of the lab examination two weeks later on June 21, the FBI was equally restrained in revealing what had been desired. The laboratory report contained a single sentence: "The Q130 sweater is composed of wool."

BRIAN MURTAGH AND THE PURETZ MEMO

Even more ominously, FOIA records reveal that sometime during this period before the trial, Murtagh had one of his young law clerks, Jeffrey

S. Puretz, research certain questions concerning a prosecutor's "discovery" obligations.

In short, Murtagh asked Puretz when must a prosecutor reveal the discovery of material that might suggest that the defendant isn't guilty.[40] One question by Murtagh read this way: "Need the detailed data of a lab report, as distinguished from the conclusions of the report, be disclosed, where such conclusions have been disclosed and are nonexculpatory?" This question apparently went to the argument about the lab notes, about the "detailed data" they contained, and about Segal's insistence that he was legally entitled to the data. Why else would Murtagh concern himself about turning over "detailed data" underlying a report surrendered to the defense, unless the excluded detailed data somehow failed to substantiate the report's conclusion that the defendant was guilty?

Another question that Murtagh put to Puretz read this way: "At what point in time must exculpatory materials be disclosed to the defense in a criminal proceeding?" This raises its own question: What right does a prosecutor have to withhold "exculpatory materials" even for a moment?

Despite these queries by Murtagh, it turned out that the key disclosure in Puretz's memo lay in still another critical area. The young law student indicated how the prosecution could avoid a penalty in cases where evidence is expected to be challenged as exculpatory and as having been withheld. In plain language, the secret he revealed was this: If the prosecution proves the defense had "opportunity" to examine the evidence, then the defense loses its right to charge the prosecution with suppressing that evidence.

When this memo was read by Harvey Silverglate twelve years after it was written, this point did not go unnoticed. Back when the memo was produced, Bernard Segal had already fought bitterly for four years to get permission to examine the physical evidence. Therefore on July 6, 1979, ten days before the opening day of the trial, it came as an unnerving surprise to Segal when Murtagh personally petitioned the court to allow the defense to "microscopically examine fibers that are connected with the physical evidence in this case." This move, just before trial, had shocked Segal because Murtagh previously had fought so hard against any exposure of the evidence to the defense.

Silverglate and Segal came to believe that by the letter of the law, as interpreted by Puretz in his memo to Murtagh, Murtagh was giving the defense a kind of qualified right to examine the evidence. But, hindered by restrictions against lab-testing any of the evidence boxed and stacked in that holding cell, the "right to examine" was tendered in a way that would render Segal unlikely to discover anything which would damage the prosecution's case. Perhaps Murtagh had adhered to the "letter of the law." It seems evident, however, that the move was in violation of the "spirit of the law," for the intent of the discovery laws is to protect the rights of citizens against government excesses. To that end, it was intended that a defendant have access to information he might use in his defense.

Did Murtagh trespass against fairness, for instance, when, even after allowing Segal into the holding cell with the boxes of evidence, he still wouldn't allow Segal to conduct chemical testing or full testing in a lab? Silverglate and Segal point out that the permission to enter the evidence cell and "eyeball only" the evidence came significantly too late to allow a true study of the hundreds of exhibits containing secrets still unrevealed. Had Murtagh held to the generous spirit of the law, the defense team later complained, he would have shared access to the information in all the typed lab notes, the handwritten bench notes, and the physical evidence itself.

In essence, a bitter Segal lamented after seeing the Puretz memo years later, "Murtagh held evidence of intruders in his closed hand, brought it near my face, then he opened his hand in a flash and cleverly closed it again. Then Murtagh turned to Judge Dupree in our post-trial writ and reminded the judge that the defense *did* have an opportunity to find the evidence during that fleeting glimpse. Judge Dupree nods his head in agreement, bangs his gavel, and says, in effect, 'Case closed.'"

BRIAN MURTAGH AND THE WITNESSES

Failing to conduct lab tests, Segal had only one way left to learn of test results: through cross-examination at trial of the government experts who had completed such tests. But here, too, Segal's attempts to learn the facts were blocked, for the law requires that cross-examination be limited to the matters brought up in the witness's direct examination— no "fishing expeditions" are allowed.

Two of Murtagh's witnesses knew things about the evidence that might scuttle the case if learned by Segal. One of these was CID lab tech Janice Glisson. Murtagh had to know from the CID lab notes he had obtained, and from his longtime familiarity with the case evidence, that some of Glisson's laboratory conclusions about the pajama top and about hair were highly damaging to the prosecution. For instance, she knew that the unidentified brown hair in Colette's hand hadn't matched MacDonald's. She also had found that the stains in his pajama top did not continue across the rip as Stombaugh would claim under oath. Glisson knew about the blond synthetic fibers in the hairbrush, and she knew that Stombaugh's directionality conclusions had prevented her from successfully performing the pajama top folding experiment. What if Segal, during cross-examination about hair and fibers, came across Glisson's knowledge about these items that hadn't been revealed to Segal?

That wouldn't become a problem for the prosecution, because when Murtagh brought Glisson to the witness stand he qualified her only as an expert in blood analyses, and questioned her only about blood. Legally, she could not address the comparisons she made with the foreign hair taken from Colette MacDonald's hand even if Segal had somehow come across knowledge of it through other means. Nor, as an expert qualified in blood analyses only, would she be required to reveal her failure to successfully fold the pajama top over Colette's wounds, or her discovery of blond wig hairs. Thus, Segal was blocked from learning, from Glisson's mouth, information that would strengthen his case and vastly weaken Murtagh's position were it to be discovered by the defense and jury.

Segal also might have discovered that FBI lab tech James Frier, also on the docket to testify as a government witness, had found black wool on the murder club. Unlike Glisson, however, Frier could be qualified as an expert in fibers only, which might put the black wool finding in danger of discovery by the defense should Frier be cross-examined.

But, as Fred Bost and I learned when we were reading the trial transcript, Segal didn't cross-examine Frier. Murtagh told Judge Dupree that the lab tech wasn't going to talk about anything of importance, some yarns from a rug which matched some yarns on a nightstand, and some fibers on the club which matched fibers in the master bedroom throw rug. Murtagh suggested they not waste the time to put him on the stand.

Murtagh spoke with a degree of detail which suggests that he had actually read Frier's notes. And why wouldn't he have read them? He, himself, had ordered Frier's tests, which resulted in the discovery of black wool fibers on the club, on Colette's mouth area, and on her pajamas. These could hardly be called insignificant locations—a murder club, and the body of the clubbed victim. This is the information Frier might have yielded to the defense had he been called to testify.

What's more troubling is that Frier's lab notes about the fiber debris found on the club listed *no pajama fibers*. So, if this were discovered by

Segal, or if Frier were to let this slip when he was called as an expert witness, Murtagh faced still another momentous challenge, because his own co-counsel, James Blackburn, considered the pajama fibers on the murder club to be the key proof of MacDonald's guilt. And Frier's failure to list pajama fibers on the club apparently contradicts the earlier findings of the problem-plagued CID laboratory.

Thus, whether by malfeasance, as is charged by the MacDonald defense team, or by gross confusion, Brian Murtagh's summation of Frier's laboratory findings was woefully incomplete. But it was beneficial for Murtagh that Frier be kept off the stand, for he was capable of telling much more than Murtagh was stipulating; and Segal, with no hint of this, accepted the stipulation as honest and correct. Upon hearing only part of the truth about Frier's lab studies, Judge Dupree excused Frier from testifying.[41]

It would be a full decade before Murtagh's activities were pieced together by the defense, to become the grounds for charging the prosecutor with deception. Writing about Brian Murtagh's "Kafkaesque" presentation of the physical evidence in the case, defense attorney Harvey Silverglate said in 1992, "The most prevalent pattern to emerge is the demonstrable way in which forensic science has been continually manipulated and distorted for the purpose of maintaining the fiction that MacDonald murdered his family."

Silverglate felt that the jurors accepted the government's "pseudo-science" as proof of MacDonald's guilt because of a common public misconception about the methods of criminal investigation. "Since the scientific and deductive methods of Sherlock Holmes captured the public imagination," Silverglate said, "the belief has been that with a close enough eye to ordinary detail, and a belief in the objectivity of forensic science, the mysterious will become clear." But Silverglate holds that "the opposite has been true in the MacDonald case, where science has been used to obfuscate rather than to enlighten."

"Too often in modern forensics," Silverglate says, "a desired conclusion is reached first, and science is given the task of interpreting the facts in such a way as to validate this conclusion, even in defiance of common sense."[42]

There is no doubt that either Glisson or Frier, if allowed to testify in all the areas of their work in the case, could have revealed facts about the pajama top folding experiment, about stains across rips in that garment, about the discovery of long blond wig hairs, and about unmatched black wool fibers on the murder club and on Colette's body—facts which would have seriously damaged the government's case. In fact, at one time or another these two lab techs had examined most of the key government exhibits in the case. And it is clear that moves by Murtagh eliminated any chance of damaging truths coming from the mouths of these two, the very lab techs who made discoveries seen as pivotal by the defense.

But as much as MacDonald's defense attorneys castigate the tactics of Brian Murtagh, they reserve a special, bitter condemnation for the man who allowed Murtagh to tie Segal's hands at trial, Judge Franklin Dupree.

Judge Franklin T. Dupree, Jr., and James C. Proctor

For want of a nail, an old story goes, a shoe was lost, which lamed the horse, which lost the battle, which lost the war, which lost the kingdom. MacDonald's defense attorneys register a similar litany of grievances, beginning with the denial of lab testing and the refusal to force Murtagh to turn over the handwritten lab notes. And Judge Franklin Dupree, they point out, could have stopped the escalation of errors at any single moment had he simply ordered Murtagh to turn over those notes at any of the various times Segal requested them over a period of four years.

Some persons suggest that such failures prove that the judge was prejudiced against Jeffrey MacDonald from the very beginning. Gunderson had told me that Dupree was the father-in-law of the first Justice Department prosecutor in charge of the MacDonald case. Was Gunderson's statement accurate? What does the record show?

Having been born in 1913, Dupree was fifty-seven years old when President Nixon appointed him to the federal bench in December 1970. At the time that he requested the MacDonald case, he had acquired less than four years of experience as a judge. By then, Judge Algernon Butler had acceded to Alfred Kassab's efforts and had maneuvered the reluctant Justice Department into preparing for a 1974–1975 grand jury investigation. Both sides in the legal battle assumed that the highly experienced Butler himself would supervise all aspects of the widely publicized, intricate multiple-murder case.

Victor Woerheide, who was to conduct the grand jury investigation, traveled to North Carolina on Tuesday, July 16, 1974, to coordinate with Judge Butler on how they would handle the case agenda. When the attorney arrived in Raleigh, however, he was told that a subordinate federal judge had requested and was granted permission to take charge.[43] As a result, when the grand jury later indicted Jeffrey MacDonald, Dupree became the judge who not only would arraign him, but would supervise the doctor's legal destiny through the following decades.

Unknown to the defense at the time, Judge Dupree was in a close relationship with a man named James C. Proctor. Proctor had been an associate in Dupree's private law firm from 1967 through 1969.[44] He regarded Dupree as a mentor, married one of Dupree's two daughters, and sired Dupree's first grandchild. He left the firm to take a post as an assistant U.S. Attorney in the Eastern District of North Carolina. As the federal government's resident Assistant U.S. Attorney in Fayetteville at the time of the MacDonald murders, he cheered the Fort Bragg CID agents' efforts to convict MacDonald.

JAMES PROCTOR AND THE ARMY HEARING

Proctor's own participation in the case began in an oblique manner while the Article 32 hearing was being held during the summer of 1970. When the army moved to take hair samples from MacDonald, Segal submitted a petition in the local federal court for legal relief from the order to take MacDonald's hair samples.

When the hearing on the matter was called in Clinton, North Carolina, Proctor himself went before Judge Butler to explain the government's stand, and he argued well. He told the judge that failure to get MacDonald's hair "would withhold from the Article 32 investigative authorities possible valuable and material evidence which could serve to exonerate the plaintiff as well as implicate him." On Friday, July 17, 1970, while the Article 32 hearing neared the end of its second week at Fort Bragg, Judge Butler evaluated the arguments and ruled that the civilian federal court exercised no jurisdiction in the hair matter. The army was free to do as it pleased.

Happy with his court victory over the hair issue, Proctor further inserted himself into the Article 32 proceedings at the first opportunity. That occasion presented itself five days later, on July 22, 1970, when FBI agent Robert Caverly was called as a witness at the closed-door army hearing. Proctor had been adamant that the FBI agent would not be allowed to participate without personal legal representation, and Proctor insisted that the representative would be himself.

The closer Proctor got to the case, the more he discussed it with the CID investigators, and the more he was convinced MacDonald was guilty. It came as a shock, then, when on October 23, 1970, he learned that

Colonel Rock ruled in MacDonald's favor and that General Flanagan was dropping all charges.

PROCTOR PRESSES THE JUSTICE DEPARTMENT TO PROSECUTE MACDONALD

The hair samples of MacDonald's which had gotten Proctor into the case, of course, turned out to be not similar to the questionable hair in Colette's hand. Nevertheless, Proctor himself immediately went into action against MacDonald following Rock's exoneration. Without authorization from his boss, who was on vacation, Proctor attempted to wrest control from the military. On that very day he tried to convince the army to refuse MacDonald any items from his old quarters and to have the quarters remain locked and guarded. When Bragg officials couldn't give Proctor a guarantee that they would carry out his wishes, he next requested guards be detailed from the U.S. marshal's office. When he was turned down there, he requested that chief FBI agent Robert Murphy in Charlotte furnish guards. Murphy informed him that the FBI could not comply with his request.[45]

Proctor then had an attorney friend at the Justice Department intercede with the army CID. The friend, James Robinson, called CID headquarters in Washington, D.C., on October 30, 1970, to request that the CID give "investigative support" to Proctor personally, pointing out that the FBI refused to do so and that a "killer was going free." Robinson told Lieutenant Colonel Malcolm R. Smith, the CID deputy commander, that Proctor felt he had "a triable case," and "with a little further investigative effort" would be able to take the case before a grand jury. Robinson, perhaps concerned with the ramifications of the Posse Comitatus Act, made it clear, however, that he was calling strictly on behalf of Proctor and was not making any type of formal request on behalf of the Department of Justice. Smith assured Robinson that the CID would cooperate with Proctor.[46]

Meanwhile, Proctor had been working hard to win over his boss, Warren Coolidge, the United States Attorney for the Eastern Division of North Carolina, who was still on vacation in Colorado. Proctor repeated things told him by Fort Bragg CID agents, and convinced Coolidge to support him in an effort to prosecute Jeffrey MacDonald in federal court.

On October 31, 1970, with Jeffrey MacDonald free from Article 32 charges, but still a serviceman under the legal jurisdiction of the army, Coolidge telephoned chief FBI agent Murphy in Charlotte to say he intended to bring MacDonald before a grand jury within ten days.[47] But Murphy, with J. Edgar Hoover's support, refused to do the bidding of the U.S. Attorney. Incensed at this attitude, Coolidge and Proctor made a trip to Washington, D.C., with the express purpose of having the Justice Department force the FBI into action. The trip was wasted effort, however, for Hoover won the argument. The CID investigation had been poorly handled, Hoover claimed, and he wanted no part of it. Coolidge was specifically ordered "to request no further investigation in this case."[48] In a telephone conversation with Murphy on November 18, Proctor admitted that he and Coolidge were told explicitly that an FBI investigation would never be requested by the Justice Department unless a substantial lead in the case was developed.[49]

Such was the outward situation when Jeffrey MacDonald was honorably discharged from the army on December 4, 1970. But behind the scenes Proctor was still seeking to indict him. On Wednesday afternoon, December 30, CID agents Richard Mahon and Robert Bidwell were called to a mysterious meeting at the Fayetteville FBI office of Lacy Walthall. When they arrived, Walthall introduced them to Proctor and they learned that the meeting had been secretly arranged by Proctor to keep the hierarchy in the FBI and Justice Department from knowing about it.[50]

Proctor knew that Bidwell and Mahon were Washington-based CID agents working under Peter Kearns. Supposedly the CID group was in Fayetteville to investigate charges brought by Mike Malley and Freddie Kassab against certain of the Fort Bragg investigators, but in actuality the group was beginning the probe promised to Proctor in the October 30 phone conversation between his friend James Robinson and Lieutenant Colonel Smith. Proctor told Bidwell and Mahon that he had arranged the secret meeting because he had tired of waiting for them to get in touch with him, and that he himself didn't dare call them. He explained that he had studied and prepared the MacDonald case for trial, and was therefore in possession of helpful documentation. Proctor insisted that if his boss, Coolidge, wouldn't furnish the papers to the CID for their use in the new probe, Proctor would furnish them himself.

Before the two-hour meeting broke up Proctor told the CID agents that earlier, while preparing a criminal trial against Captain MacDonald, he had collected all members of Coolidge's legal staff in Raleigh to brainstorm the issue. Captain Clifford Somers, the military lawyer who had unsuccessfully prosecuted the army hearing, had addressed the group, briefing them on the difficulties he had encountered. Proctor boasted to the CID agents that he himself would already be prosecuting MacDonald at that very moment if the effort hadn't been sidetracked by Washington. He told them that things were temporarily stalled because the Department of Justice wouldn't allow Coolidge to arrest MacDonald, but he said such an arrest was only a matter of time. In describing details to be used against MacDonald, he said that "the package is already wrapped up," with nothing needed except the final bow.

About five weeks after this meeting a staff officer at CID headquarters in Washington wrote an official memorandum to Peter Kearns instructing him to maintain close liaison with the Office of the U.S. Attorney for the Eastern District of North Carolina. In explaining this requirement, Major David B. Reed wrote that Warren Coolidge "has exclusive jurisdiction to prosecute this case before a federal court. Mr. Coolidge has assigned Mr. James Proctor, assistant U.S. attorney, to monitor investigative activity and to prepare for possible prosecution."

The most significant part of this secret directive is the date—February 4, 1971. The memo indicates that Proctor on that date was still involved in preparing a case against MacDonald and was staying in touch with all of the facts by monitoring "investigative activity." In effect, Proctor was the prosecutor in charge of the Justice Department's efforts against Jeffrey MacDonald at a time when he was still married to Dupree's daughter, and thus still in close contact with Dupree. Dupree himself had been a federal judge on the bench for almost two months, having been appointed on December 12, 1970, one week after MacDonald's honorable discharge from the U.S. Army.

PROCTOR'S FORMER FATHER-IN-LAW BECOMES JUDGE OF RECORD

The government record goes on to show that at some point during the 1974–1975 grand jury investigation the prosecutors suddenly sought to put the case into the hands of another judge even though Judge Dupree had not been uncooperative to the prosecution. This puzzling objective was disclosed in an internal FBI telegram to J. Edgar Hoover on February 14, 1975. Murphy, who sent the telegram, told Hoover that prosecutor Jay Stroud, who had assisted Victor Woerheide at grand jury, had indicated that a trial date would not be set until a new judge being sought was assigned.[51] Was it the relationship between Dupree and Proctor that had brought about the desire for change? In retrospect, the defense lawyers now believe that the prosecution had suddenly realized the Dupree-

Proctor relationship, and feared that if it were ever discovered, it might wreck the government's efforts.

Whatever the reason, despite the effort to remove him, Judge Dupree remained with the case. Less than two weeks after Murphy's telegram went to Hoover, Dupree secretly wrote Stroud instructing him to seek certain stipulations from Bernard Segal concerning deadlines for filing motions. As if in reprimand for the attempt to replace him, the judge informed Stroud, "For the convenience of all concerned the case should be tried in Raleigh and not in Fayetteville."[52] These nuances remained secret from MacDonald's defense team for many years. In fact, the team didn't even learn of Proctor's relationship to Judge Dupree until well after the doctor was convicted at the 1979 trial.

The newly hired private detective, Ted Gunderson, and his associate, Homer Young (also a retired FBI agent), uncovered the kinship in 1981, although by this time Dupree's daughter had divorced Proctor. When MacDonald finally won his battle forcing the release of documents under the Freedom of Information Act in 1983, Proctor's role in the case and his kinship to Dupree were confirmed.[53] Then later, as the NBC "docudrama" *Fatal Vision* aired in November 1984, more information surfaced concerning Proctor's role. The source was Proctor himself, who began bragging as a result of coattail publicity surrounding the TV movie.[54]

He had been interviewed on November 25, 1984, by a reporter for the *Independent*, a small daily newspaper servicing Fuquay-Varina, North Carolina, Judge Dupree's hometown. During the long telephone interview, Proctor told about being the federal prosecutor in Fayetteville at the time of the murders, saying that Jeffrey MacDonald had been a prime suspect "within hours" of the crime. He told the reporter, "Any gumshoe cop could have figured out he did it."

The reporter wrote: "Proctor was deeply involved with the investigation of the MacDonald case from the beginning. . . . For a time, Proctor said, he was going to Washington every two or three weeks, taking new evidence. He talked to Victor Woerheide, Justice Department prosecutor, and convinced him that he had a case against MacDonald."

During this reporter's interview, not only had Proctor confirmed his early interest in the case and where his bias lay, he also gave indications of how long he had been involved. It's known that Woerheide did not come into the case until 1974, so Proctor apparently remained committed for more than four years. Also during the telephone interview, Proctor detailed for the reporter the frustration he had felt during the period when the Justice Department refused to indict MacDonald, saying that he had "begged, pleaded, even threatened to resign" if MacDonald wasn't prosecuted. In giving the reporter an excuse for such rash conduct, he said, "I was young then."

So the surface facts, at least, seem clear: Judge Dupree's son-in-law was an impetuous young lawyer who held a passion to convict Jeffrey MacDonald. This emotional young man had attempted to usurp control of personnel in other agencies; he had held a clandestine meeting in direct disobedience of the Justice Department; he had doggedly attempted through the years to indict MacDonald; and, by his own admission, he had threatened to resign if he didn't have his way.

THE ISSUE OF JUDICIAL RECUSAL
A typical judge would automatically remove himself from a case the moment he recognized that a close relative had been active with either the prosecution or the defense, despite when or how that recognition came to pass. But Judge Dupree insisted upon retaining the MacDonald case even after his relationship to Proctor was publicly exposed. In the 1984 proceedings the defense team revealed those things learned about Proctor, and they requested that Dupree step down. But Dupree claimed on September 9, 1984, that he'd never talked with his son-in-law about the MacDonald case. The higher courts accepted this as true, claiming to believe that during those four years when Dupree's son-in-law was clamoring for MacDonald's indictment in the biggest case of his career, he had never talked with Dupree about it. Dupree remained the judge of record.

The relationship between the two men is well documented, as is Proctor's adamant pursuit of MacDonald, but did Proctor's zeal somehow affect Dupree's handling of the case?

JUDGE DUPREE AT GRAND JURY
Bernard Segal first came up against Judge Dupree on the opening day of the grand jury investigation in August of 1974. As a matter of grand jury procedure, Dupree had not allowed Segal to witness MacDonald's interrogation. During the first recess, MacDonald came out of the hearing room to a nearby anteroom where Segal waited. MacDonald told Segal that the prosecutor, Victor Woerheide, had demanded knowledge about his payments to lawyers, and he also wanted to know about things Segal had said to him in confidence. Astounded and angry, Segal called for an

immediate hearing with Judge Dupree. Away from the grand jurors, Segal protested to Dupree that such questions were clearly unethical and violated the client-lawyer privilege.

Woerheide didn't deny that the information he sought was protected by the client-lawyer privilege, but he cleverly pointed out that the privilege was with the client, not the lawyer. He told the judge that nothing prevented MacDonald from refusing to answer such a question. Woerheide insisted that "there is no prohibition with respect to asking the question" and he therefore intended to keep asking such questions.

Woerheide thus made it obvious that he was indeed encouraging MacDonald to refuse to answer questions. Segal objected to this tactic because he well knew that when a witness refuses to answer questions, it usually alienates the jury. The prosecutor might then use that alienation as a wedge between the jury and the defendant, possibly securing an unfair indictment.

The disgusted Segal asked the judge to put a stop to the obvious ploy. He reminded Dupree that MacDonald was testifying without benefit of counsel, and asked the judge "to advise the government to not play games with fundamental rights. They have no business going into legal advice and saying, 'Well, the lay person, he can decide to waive that.'" But the argument proved useless. When the judge refused to bridle Woerheide in the matter,[55] Segal wrote a letter to the jury foreman on August 13, 1974, advising him to "direct the government attorneys (and it's your absolute right to do so) to refrain from any direct or indirect attempt to question Dr. MacDonald about his discussions with his attorneys. . . ."

At the next instance of Woerheide asking a question which MacDonald felt was inappropriate, MacDonald reminded Woerheide of his lawyer's advice to the grand jury foreman. Woerheide, already incensed at Segal's letter, told MacDonald, "I might say, Dr. MacDonald, that you may inform your attorneys that as of this time they are not witnesses before the grand jury and it is not their function to advise, or give legal advice to the grand jury."

JUDGE DUPREE, JURY SELECTION, TRIAL

After MacDonald was indicted by the grand jury, Judge Dupree sought a quick trial. And when Segal presented preliminary motions, Dupree rejected them virtually out of hand, and set a trial date of August 18, 1975. But the circuit appeals court, upon receiving the motions, made a rapid appraisal and immediately saw that at least two of the motions held considerable merit. As a result, the U.S. Fourth Circuit Court of Appeals on August 15 ruled against Judge Dupree and ordered an immediate and indefinite stay of the trial until it heard arguments on all of the defense appeals.[56]

In the years that followed, the judge's decisions continued to frustrate Segal, even into the trial itself. As an example, during jury selection in 1979 Segal had spotted two prospective jurors he especially wanted to seat because of their apparently independent natures. One was a man with a doctorate in psychology. The other was an alert young woman who happened to be black.

When the prosecution challenged the psychologist, Dupree himself dismissed the man. The judge explained that since the defense wasn't pleading insanity and the prosecutors were not going to use psychiatry to show that MacDonald was the type who could kill his family, it would be unfair to seat a juror with special knowledge in psychology.

Then Dupree himself personally challenged the young black woman Segal had wanted to seat. Judge Dupree suggested that instead of serving on a jury, her time might be better spent helping her father on the farm.[57] The woman proudly disagreed, saying that she was not needed at home, that she had arranged her affairs for the occasion. Dupree asked her a few more questions, then disqualified her, excusing her with the remark that she could now go help her father harvest tobacco. The defense had lost a desired juror without the prosecution applying a valuable peremptory challenge.

Not long into the trial a sense of camaraderie between the judge and prosecutors became apparent to others, as did open antagonism between Dupree and Segal. At sixty-five years of age, the still vital and youthful Franklin Dupree had a reputation as a longtime, unbending anti-liberal, the exact political opposite of the defense attorney. Bernard Segal was a small, Jewish man who had pled civil rights cases for black people and who had flaunted a full head of long graying hair at a time when such a lack of tonsorial conformity was considered by many in the South to be in bad taste.

Judge Dupree's facial expressions and comments telegraphed his dislike for Segal, yet he "played" with the prosecution lawyers and even some witnesses as if they were old friends. On one occasion, after a lunch recess, Judge Dupree lightly instructed prosecutor Jim Blackburn that he could proceed to ask the witness, William Ivory, "one or two questions."

"Judge," Blackburn said, taking on the role of straight man, "I hope Your Honor will interpret the 'one or two questions' liberally."

Dupree delivered the anticipated punch line. "I will apply the usual rule and multiply it by a hundred," he said, winning some muffled laughter from the spectators, and easing William Ivory's transition to the witness chair.

Later, when Ivory had finished his testimony and was stepping down from the stand, Judge Dupree in friendly fashion asked the detective to buy him some German tennis shoes upon his return to Europe. The jury witnessed this friendly interchange between the judge and a key prosecution witness.

The judge's attitude toward the defense, on the other hand, was one of sternness. While star prosecution witness Paul Stombaugh was on the witness stand, Segal attempted to challenge the laboratory technician's credibility by revealing that Segal had discovered that the man had received little formal university training in the sciences, and minimal formal FBI instruction in the fields for which the prosecution was presenting him as an expert.

Although such a tactic of impeaching a witness is acceptable practice in a courtroom, Judge Dupree cut Segal short and rebuked the defense attorney for the direction he was taking. Dupree, who at one time had declined to censure Woerheide for deliberately asking questions regarding client-attorney privileges, now castigated Segal for attempting to bring up Stombaugh's school record which, according to Segal, seemed to speak directly to a matter of inflated credentials.

Although Segal, when cross-examining witnesses, was made to toe a strict line by Judge Dupree, the defense attorney complained bitterly that the judge seemed to allow the prosecutors much more leeway. Segal still recalls how Judge Dupree instructed Blackburn about asking hypothetical questions, in effect forcing the defendant to prove his innocence. When Judge Dupree failed to sustain repeated objections from Segal about this, Segal could do nothing but ineffectively request the judge to remind the jury that the burden of proof always remains with the government.

Dupree allowed Blackburn to continue the same technique even during the final arguments, impressing the jury obliquely with the fact that Jeffrey MacDonald could not prove his innocence. "Ladies and gentlemen," Blackburn told the jury, "I am not about to suggest that the burden of proof ever shifts to the defendant, because it doesn't. It stays with us."

Having made that statement, Blackburn then ignored it by beginning his turnabout system of judicial approach. "But you have to recall on cross-examination," Blackburn continued, "that we asked the defendant a lot of questions—that if the jury should find this and that, did he have an explanation. And you recall essentially his testimony: 'It would be pure conjecture.'

"Perhaps he does not have to explain, but think for a moment—if you were on trial for your life and the only thing that made your story perhaps not believable was its inconsistency with the physical evidence"—Blackburn paused for effect—"don't you think if you *could* explain it, you *would*?"

Then Blackburn went over each of the major items of evidence laid out by the prosecution. And again, each time, the reemphasis: "Don't you know that if he *could* have explained it, he *would* have?"

Having allowed the jury to be exposed to this technique, Dupree seemed to give a stamp of approval when he prepared the jury for making their judgment. In his final instructions before they left for the jury room, Dupree told them that if they chose to disbelieve Jeffrey MacDonald's testimony, they had every right to conclude that the doctor had murdered his family.[58] Not long afterward the jury looked at the blood chart to match the army's physical data against MacDonald's story. Their subsequent vote shows that the jury took Dupree's instructions to heart.

JUDGE DUPREE AND CONFIDENTIAL MEMORANDA TO THE PROSECUTORS

After MacDonald's conviction, nearly ten years passed before the defense team discovered that Judge Dupree had on at least three different occasions written to the case prosecutors without sharing that information with the defense lawyers.

One of these instances particularly troubled the defense team when the communications were discovered in FOIA material. After Dr. Brussel's unflattering assessment of MacDonald's psyche had been put into report form during trial by Brussel's psychologist, Dr. Silverman, Segal took steps to prevent MacDonald from being further injured by the probability of the Brussel-Silverman report going public. Upon learning that Dupree wouldn't allow any psychiatric testimony at all, Segal immediately prepared a motion to have the Brussel-Silverman report removed from the record. Segal had, after all, struck an agreement with Brussel and Silverman not to share that report with anyone unless Judge Dupree ruled to allow psychiatric testimony; and that agreement had been ignored when Murtagh gave it to Dupree. Now that report, which Segal considered bogus, was going to become a part of the public record which the prosecution could use at will to point to MacDonald's "homicidal" nature. That report, which contained opinions contrary to the reports of examinations of MacDonald by five other psychiatrists, would be the only official psychiatric report in the trial record, placed there by Dupree as part of his response to MacDonald's plea to be freed on bail pending appeals.

Dupree responded to Segal's motion to strike the report by writing a memorandum not to Segal and the prosecutors, but to prosecutor Jim Blackburn alone. And he marked the memo "CONFIDENTIAL." He told Blackburn he had just read Segal's motion. "I understand you will respond to this." Then the judge wrote, "Just what effect any agreement between the doctors and Segal would have on you," Dupree wrote, "I am not aware. . . . I would observe that the court did not rule that the defendant might not offer psychiatric evidence in support of his defense but simply limited such evidence to that tending to show defendant's character traits of peacefulness, etc."

This confidential memorandum, besides incorrectly stating Dupree's actual ruling,[59] was a one-sided secret communication with the prosecutor, which offered the judge's own views, thereby revealing to Blackburn how he might successfully argue. It is not difficult to understand why the discovery of this memorandum in the FOIA receipts angered Bernard Segal when he learned about it years later.

Nor was this memo the first ex-parte communication between Dupree and the prosecution. Pre-trial, on May 14, 1979, Dupree had written the prosecution, saying, "Let me know immediately when Segal responds to your letter of May 11 and I will be prepared to rule on his motion."

And in an earlier letter from Dupree to then Assistant U.S. Attorney Jay Stroud, February 26, 1975, Dupree had advised Stroud on what he "should do" to proceed toward the MacDonald trial.

MEDIA OBSERVATIONS OF JUDGE DUPREE'S ATTITUDE AT TRIAL

Even author Joe McGinniss commented upon Dupree's judicial attitude. In his book, *Fatal Vision*, which so thoroughly condemned and denigrated MacDonald, the author nevertheless pointed out how the judge's body language and tone of voice had been clearly negative toward the defense, and how it seemed to McGinniss to be a signal to the jury regarding the judge's own feelings about the case. "Judge Dupree," McGinniss wrote, ". . . was possessed of an unusually mobile, expressive face, and from the earliest days of the trial the expression most often seen upon it as Bernie Segal conducted cross-examination was one of distaste.

"Obviously alert, attentive, and sometimes even taking notes during Jim Blackburn's direct examination. . . ."

But McGinniss pointed out that when Segal was repetitively questioning a prosecution witness, ". . . the judge would lean back in his chair with his eyes closed, grimacing in exasperation or rubbing his temples as if his head ached. . . .

"With even casual spectators openly remarking on the judge's expression," McGinniss wrote, "it seemed only logical to assume that it would, to some degree, indicate to the jurors where his sympathies (or lack of sympathy) lay, and possibly even suggest to some where their own belonged."[60]

Immediately following the trial, a number of people critical of the way Dupree had acted on the bench wrote letters to the *Fayetteville Times* protesting his judicial conduct. As a consequence, reporter Wat Hopkins interviewed the judge.[61] When Hopkins asked about the judge's clowning, Dupree said it was to "put the jury at ease." Hopkins wanted to know about the irritation Dupree had displayed toward defense attorneys. Dupree responded, "I think impatient is a better word." When the reporter pointed out that the judge had a habit of using facial expressions that could obviously influence a jury—things like acting surprised, dismayed, irritated, or disbelieving—Dupree shrugged this away by saying, "I instruct the jury not to infer from anything I've said or done that I have any opinions in the case."

But Bernard Segal angrily retorts that such actions can't be so easily ignored; just as they were noted by those who wrote letters to newspapers, there is little doubt, Segal believes, that they were noted by the jury.

Judge Dupree and the MacDonald Appeals

On March 1, 1985, during a habeas petition to gain a new trial, the judge once again denied all defense motions. While setting aside as meaningless such things as Helena Stoeckley's confession, the then recently discovered bloody syringe, the missing piece of skin, and the destroyed fingerprints, Dupree ruled that nothing offered by the defense was of consequence because "No direct evidence of the alleged intruders was found to support MacDonald's version . . . of the murders."[62] In other words, it seems that Dupree ruled against MacDonald's appeal because no laboratory evidence had been presented that indicated the presence of outside assailants.

Back during the trial, when the issue of laboratory notes was discussed for the last time at a bench conference on August 21, 1979, Judge Dupree could have settled the matter by ordering Murtagh to relinquish the documents. Instead, after specifically refusing to rule that Murtagh surrender them, Dupree voiced a promise to Segal: "If the government has anything that classifies as *Brady* material and they do not give it to you, they are certainly going to get reversal. . . . That's their risk."[63]

When Harvey Silverglate filed his 1990 writ, he was appealing to the judge of record, that very same Franklin Dupree. The defense team discovery of the contents of the suppressed lab notes now offered Dupree an opportunity to keep the promise made at trial years earlier. In the 1990 brief, Silverglate focused on a simple argument. Those suppressed notes mentioned unmatched black wool and the unmatched blond wig hair, items which Segal could have used as corroboration for MacDonald's story. Now, Silverglate applied for the relief Judge Dupree had promised that MacDonald would "certainly" get.

But Murtagh had other ideas. In his response brief he claimed that since some of these lab notes were turned over to the defense via the FOIA in 1983, they should have been used in the petition made soon afterward, the so-called Stoeckley appeal of 1984–1985. Now, Murtagh and the government lawyers charged, it was too late to claim this information as new evidence. It was now inadmissible. Dupree was to view the case as if this evidence never existed.

Furthermore, Brian Murtagh claimed, he had done no wrong. He said he never knew about the black wool or the synthetic blond hair.[64] He claimed that neither of the lab techs, Frier nor Glisson, had informed him verbally or in writing of these items.[65] As to the crucial lab notes regarding the discovery of the black wool, Murtagh stated, "I cannot recall, after eleven years' time, whether or not I actually received them. . . . I can, however, state unequivocally that if I did have Frier's laboratory notes, I never reviewed their contents, until allegations were first made by Ted Gunderson late in December 1988."[66]

However, Harvey Silverglate believed that Murtagh *did* know, for the defense team's work on the documents released by FOIA led them to a lab note that reveals that Murtagh held a *five-hour meeting* with laboratory technicians in the FBI's Room 3931M on February 9, 1979, following his request for tests to identify an unmatched blue acrylic fiber found among debris in Colette MacDonald's right hand. Among other debris retested at that time, the lab technicians discovered the unmatched black wool fibers. And records show that Murtagh had called a *three-day meeting* in March 1979 to review the physical evidence, a meeting attended by those who actually had handled, tested, and analyzed each piece of the evidence. Considering that Murtagh used three full days to thoroughly review the nuances of the case evidence,[67] Silverglate thought it hardly reasonable to expect that Murtagh ignored or refused to evaluate what Glisson and Frier had to offer concerning hair and fiber findings. After all, their offerings might have included something Murtagh could have used to prosecute MacDonald.

Simply put, Silverglate believed that a Department of Justice prosecutor does not go into a major murder trial without learning what each evidence exhibit holds. He would be especially aware of foreign material on such exhibits as a murder weapon and the bodies of the victims. Is it reasonable, Silverglate asks, to believe that the investigators and prosecutors all failed to see, either in the notes or in the physical exhibits, the black wool fibers and blond wig hair?

If Brian Murtagh had no interest in *everything*, as he later claimed, why then, on March 1, three weeks after his five-hour meeting, did he write to the CID and specifically request copies of *every* laboratory note they had in their files?[68]

And, defense lawyers later pointed out, if Murtagh hadn't known about the exculpatory information in those notes, why hadn't he simply avoided four years of legal warfare with Segal? Why didn't he just turn over the notes Segal was begging for? Also, if Murtagh hadn't known what was in the notes, how could he honestly have assured Segal and Judge Dupree at trial that there was no exculpatory information in them?

MacDonald's defense lawyers insist that, according to the law, it doesn't matter whether Murtagh knew or didn't know about these exculpatory *Brady* items. They existed, and they weren't turned over when specifically requested, and they weren't turned over until congressional pressure brought them forward in 1983. But Silverglate believes he found something that proves Murtagh not only knew about the black wool, but also knew about the wig hair. Silverglate thinks Murtagh took steps to ensure that Bernard Segal would never find the wig hair in that jail cell in Raleigh in 1979. During the oral argument before Judge Dupree in the 1990 habeas effort at the federal district court level, Silverglate pointed out that in that evidence holding cell in which Segal and Thornton were finally allowed to "eyeball" the evidence pre-trial, Murtagh had kept the blond wig hairs in a closed box. But that significant box was not labeled "Blond Wig Hairs." It was labeled "Black and Grey Synthetic Hairs."

Confronted with this during the appeal, Murtagh denied any culpability and argued that Thornton nevertheless had opportunity to find these blond strands in that holding cell even in a mismarked box, if he had only looked harder. Murtagh argued that because Thornton had been given this chance to examine all the evidence that day in the jail cell, the defense had no right to claim such things were withheld even though Murtagh had held back the requested lab notes which would have signaled the existence of these crucial items. With an admirable example of circular reasoning, Murtagh argued that his withholding of laboratory notes now couldn't be an issue because Thornton had been given an opportunity back then to discover in that jail cell any physical item that might have been mentioned in those notes Murtagh had barred Segal from reading.

And this was the source of Silverglate's "needle in a haystack" complaint. Murtagh essentially claimed that the government graciously let Segal into the room stacked full of the evidence and then said, so sorry, you didn't find the salient pieces.

But Silverglate was not finished with Murtagh. In his habeas brief he also gave Judge Dupree what Silverglate believed was the actual game plan for the "suppression" of evidence, the intriguing Puretz memo. Silverglate reminded Dupree about Murtagh's uncharacteristic request to allow Thornton at the last minute to examine the physical evidence in that jail cell. Silverglate argued that, given the now-known events of the time, the Puretz memo, which clued Murtagh to the notion that if he gives Segal access to the evidence itself, that is, in boxes in the jail cell, he is not required to give up the source documents about that evidence.

Consequently, since Murtagh agreed only at the last minute to allow Segal in the jail cell with the stacks and stacks of evidence, and never really allowed lab testing, Silverglate charged the Puretz memo was an effort by Murtagh to circumvent justice and was a blueprint for the very arguments now being offered by the government prosecutor.

But Murtagh told Dupree that he had asked for the Puretz effort merely as a safeguard because he felt that Segal had considered any and all information as being exculpatory.

The defense considered this argument to be totally unresponsive. If Murtagh at trial had disclosed foreign fibers on the murder club, and foreign fibers on Colette's body, he would have been hard-put in devaluing these things in front of a jury. Now in 1990, with no jury to be concerned about, Murtagh freely admitted the existence of such fibers, but he called them "household debris," nothing but inconsequential rubbish from the rugs. He claimed that if this household debris had been made known to the trial jury, it would have had no effect whatsoever on their verdict.

Silverglate saw this as a lame offering. He pointed out that there was no matching black wool—debris, clothing, or otherwise—found anywhere at the murder scene; just as no doll with long blond tresses was ever found to match the mystery wig hairs.

JUDGE DUPREE'S RULING

After the oral arguments before Judge Dupree in Raleigh, the defense attorneys awaited his decision. In presenting his argument, Silverglate had recounted the physical items of evidence which favored MacDonald, but he focused his major argument on the fact that Brian Murtagh had withheld the lab notes which held exculpatory information, notes that had been expressly requested during the trial. Silverglate reminded Dupree of the promise the judge had made at trial, that if the prosecution was withholding exculpatory materials, the government would certainly get reversal.

The defense team soon learned in a crushing manner that the promise had been an empty one. Judge Dupree rendered his decision on July 8, 1991, only thirteen days after the oral hearing. The judge agreed that the laboratory notes held exculpatory information, and he agreed that the information had been withheld. Nevertheless, Dupree said, the defense had been given an opportunity to examine the physical evidence itself in that jail cell and thus discover the items written about in those withheld notes. This factor nullified the importance of the notes themselves, the judge claimed.

Further, Dupree decreed, although the wig hair and black wool were only now being mentioned in court proceedings, they must be ruled out as new evidence because they easily could have been presented in the 1983–1984 petition. Dupree ruled that Brian O'Neill at that time, since he was in possession of the lab notes in question, should have ferreted out the information and presented it. The judge deemed O'Neill as lacking "due diligence" in failing to make such a presentation, and thus the wig hair and black wool in effect became "old" evidence at that moment.

Judge Dupree had moved quickly and efficiently in presenting his ruling. On each count the scale of justice dipped low in Brian Murtagh's favor.

Like Bernard Segal before him, Harvey Silverglate complained bitterly. "Murtagh hides the magic needle in the haystack. He doesn't even tell you it's in the haystack. Then when you don't find it in timely fashion, the judge rules that since you didn't find it the government is absolved of responsibility."

Nevertheless, Dupree was the judge of record, and he had spoken. Silverglate swallowed his resentment and started back to work with his fellow defense lawyers and aides. Still working without pay, they planned the brief for the next appellate level.

12

■

A Fatal Vision

Immediately after the murders, the CID investigators puzzled over the incongruity of the chief suspect's "golden boy" image. By 1983, however, the pendulum had fully reversed; in the public eye MacDonald had become an unfeeling freak of nature, coolly denying a hideous crime for which he showed neither remorse nor regret. He was a flesh-and-blood Mr. Hyde, as it were, hulking behind Dr. Jekyll's mask of respectability.

This metamorphosis (or unmasking, as claimed by the government) began as early as 1970 when CID agents, angry with Colonel Rock's exoneration of MacDonald, pressed their superiors with the opinion that MacDonald was a murderer hiding behind the face of a caring physician. Others, such as Judge Dupree's son-in-law, James Proctor, and General Flanagan's legal adviser, Major Pedar Wold, had been convinced by the selected evidence shown them by CID agents, and they embraced the CID cause. Other things also influenced opinions and damaged MacDonald's public image, such as Alfred Kassab's switch in loyalties, and the brief psychiatric examination in 1979 by Dr. James Brussel, the former army psychiatrist who as early as 1971 had voiced his conviction that MacDonald was guilty after hearing only Ivory's truncated rendition of the investigation and the forensic evidence. Even Brian Murtagh would get himself reassigned by the army and then hand-carry evidence to the FBI, the record now showing much of that evidence to have changed. All these people contributed to the public's altered perception of MacDonald. But the chief standard bearer in the effort to bring the "real" Jeffrey MacDonald into public view was author Joe McGinniss.

Due to the riveting dramatic strength of his book *Fatal Vision*, and a book-adapted TV movie, both of which were presented as a tour into the mind of a family murderer, the public began to regard MacDonald as a wild-eyed animal who had clubbed and slashed his loving family to death, and who then concocted lie after lie in an attempt to avoid punishment.

When asked about the book, McGinniss repeatedly told reporters that this criminal was the MacDonald he knew, and that *Fatal Vision* was the true story, meticulously researched. But records of the McGinniss-MacDonald relationship, and admissions by Joe McGinniss under oath, reveal another, even stranger story than that told by McGinniss himself.

Back before the 1979 trial Segal had handed MacDonald his fee schedule and repeated a long-standing suggestion that MacDonald find a writer who could tell the public what was going on behind the scenes in the case. Also, a best-seller would help pay the bills. A short while later Joe McGinniss found MacDonald while researching a newspaper article, and MacDonald, in time, offered the project to him.

McGinniss was a tall, long-faced man with an empathetic smile and a quick Irish wit. By any standards he was a talented young writer, and he already had experienced a measure of success. In *The Selling of the President*, published in 1968, he dramatized himself as a young Democrat, stealthily working his way into the heart of the Nixon campaign organization to expose what he viewed as slick Madison Avenue techniques. By the time MacDonald met McGinniss in 1979, MacDonald himself had long since abandoned the idealism with which he had begun his brief and ill-starred army career. To a beleaguered Jeffrey MacDonald, McGinniss's political cynicism seemed refreshingly appropriate.

Besides a mutual sense of disillusionment with established authority, the writer and the accused, to an uncanny degree, held other things in common. The two men were the same age. They grew up in middle-class families within seventy-five miles of each other. McGinniss's two daughters were the same ages that MacDonald's daughters would have been. His son was the same age that MacDonald's unborn son would have been. The two men had rooted for the same sports teams. Both men were accomplished in their respective fields. Both were serious joggers; both enjoyed a good story over a cold beer; and both had suffered serious recent personal defeats, defeats that came to MacDonald via the court ruling to bring him to trial, and to McGinniss through the disappointing sales of his last several books. Both men were looking for a big win.

MacDonald welcomed the developing friendship, and discounted the claims of disgruntled Republicans still bristling over McGinniss's best-seller of a decade ago and similar cries of Democrats angry with a subsequent book, *Heroes*, which featured ugly personal attacks on several prominent persons. The theme of *Heroes* was that all those who might have been McGinniss's heroes were not heroes at all, because they held secret sins. McGinniss, on the other hand, in his own words in the book, revealed his own secret sins, which he detailed as drunkenness, unfaithfulness in marriage, his violence toward his girlfriend, his lack of concern for his daughter's illness, his emotional weakness as a child, and his own dreams, even prior to entering the MacDonald project, of the destruction of his own children. The underlying theme of that book seems to have been that since McGinniss honestly and openly admitted his regrettable but human failings, he was now somehow elevated. In the manner of a fighting, drinking, whoring but coolly honest Hemingway, McGinniss now was braver, more penetrating, more cruelly objective than others.

If McGinniss was anything, he was shameless, and MacDonald believed this writer, especially, would understand MacDonald's own marital infidelity, which MacDonald held as unimportant to the criminal case. McGinniss swore he would tell the truth in his proposed book. Although he made no promise to depict MacDonald as innocent, he continued right up to the date of publication to give that impression. MacDonald was satisfied enough with what the writer told him that he opened his files, his home, his very life to him. With the trial fast approaching, and believing he had found a champion and a kindred spirit, MacDonald also agreed to give McGinniss access to any document the writer wanted. But because McGinniss also asked to attend defense team meetings during the trial and wanted to receive copies of all documents, co-counsel Michael Malley openly and adamantly opposed the agreement.

Lead attorney Bernard Segal met Malley's objections by installing McGinniss as an official member of the defense team, thus obligating the writer, under law, not to reveal defense secrets until the court proceedings ended. Malley was still uneasy about the arrangement, reminding Mac-Donald that they were trusting a great deal to McGinniss's honor.

Malley grew even more uneasy when McGinniss insisted on a clause in the book contract which prohibited MacDonald from ever suing the author for what he might write. So Segal, realizing that McGinniss's sharp pen had skewered Eugene McCarthy, George McGovern, and William Styron, added a phrase which said that MacDonald would not sue McGinniss for whatever he might write, "provided that the essential integrity of my life story is maintained."[1] McGinniss readily agreed to this change, then signed the employment agreement making himself an official member of the defense team. With this agreement in hand, McGinniss arranged a publishing contract with Dell-Delacorte. The book's initial title, *Acid and Rain*, apparently came from the words of the female intruder in MacDonald's account of that rainy murder morning.[2]

At trial McGinniss became valuable in a personal way to both MacDonald and his mother. Because of a lack of physical evidence pointing to MacDonald's alleged intruders, and because Judge Dupree was continually denying every Segal motion, a palpable tenseness pervaded the university fraternity house where the defense team lived during the trial. During breaks in the proceedings, MacDonald and McGinniss took hard runs together which helped quell the mounting frustrations and anxieties. McGinniss continued to encourage MacDonald and his mother, and assured them that even if the jury were not getting the truth, their book, at least, would tell all. McGinniss and the power of the press were seen as the cavalry forming in the hills, pending disaster at trial.

It isn't surprising, then, that when the jury brought in three guilty verdicts in August of 1979, the McGinniss book became MacDonald's supreme hope in life. The day after his conviction MacDonald stood in the solitary unit at Butner Federal Correctional Institution. A forty-watt bulb cast a dim pallor over a lidless toilet and a narrow, naked bunk. His life had come apart again. He asked a guard for a pen and paper, then he wrote a first fateful letter to Joe McGinniss.[3]

I've got to write you so I won't go crazy. I am standing in my cell only because they don't allow chairs in solitary. I'm trying to fathom—trying to figure out what the fuck happened? The fucking walls are closing in. Every once in a while a warden or a shrink comes around and asks how I am. Someone in my voice answers "OK— just taking it one day at a time." What I mean is that "I'm going crazy—I'm trying to hold on one *second* at a time."

. . . Last night was the longest ever. The guard looked in my window with a flashlight every 15 minutes for 12 hours (suicide watch). The few times I fell asleep a flashlight would immediately penetrate my eyeballs. I couldn't figure out what the fuck I'm supposed to kill myself with. They only allow plastic spoons with the meal, the guard sits *right* outside my cell.

. . . the verdict stands there, screaming, "You are guilty of the murder of your family!!" And I don't know what to say to you except it is not true, and I hope you know that, and feel it, and that you are my friend.

So began one of the most bizarre correspondences in American legal and literary history. After the 1979 conviction, MacDonald began his second day in jail by writing McGinniss a letter which openly expressed his gratitude to the author. "My story will be told, and in time, I can hold up my head again."[4]

Earlier that afternoon Joe McGinniss visited MacDonald in prison and assured the new convict that he would tell the world the true story behind the convictions. Unable to contain his normally well controlled emotions, MacDonald wept openly. He later testified that McGinniss, also weeping, had hugged MacDonald as he left the visitor area.[5]

Bernard Segal had immediately filed a post-trial motion for bail to get MacDonald released while an appeal was filed. But the Bureau of Prisons was transferring MacDonald three thousand miles across the continent via a caged bus when Judge Dupree ruled against Segal's bail motion. Dupree wrote in his official decision that he didn't believe MacDonald's upcoming speedy-trial claims were valid. He also did not believe MacDonald had suffered great anxiety due to the nine-year delay of his trial, and Dupree therefore was denying MacDonald's request for bail pending the appeals court disposition of his bid for a new trial.[6]

The McGinniss Letters

On October 4, 1979, after more than a month's trip cross-country, staying in a different prison compound at each evening's stop, Jeffrey MacDonald sat in the bus as it entered San Pedro, California, and approached his new home, the barbed wire and stark chain-link fences of Terminal Island, the Federal Correctional Institution in San Pedro.

Awaiting him was his first letter from Joe McGinniss. In small, thready script McGinniss wrote, "Total strangers can recognize within five minutes that you did not receive a fair trial." On Segal's trial tactics, McGinniss wrote, ". . . in the face of such confidence from your entire team it did not seem my place to draw Bernie aside and say, 'Hey, are you sure this physical evidence sounds as hokey to a jury hearing it for the first time—presented by *The Government*—as it does to you who have known for 9 years that it was bullshit?'"

A second letter, dated September 28, arrived soon. McGinniss told MacDonald that the jury foreman, David Hardison, should have been

> . . . excused for cause the moment his former connection with the state police became known. The theory that as an ex-cop he would be indignant at the bungling of the crime scene just did not begin to offset the natural inclination of an ex-cop to side with the prosecution, especially when the prosecutor and Judge are good old boys and the defense attorney is an arrogant, abrasive . . . Jew. Amazing. . . . What the fuck were those people thinking of? How could 12 people not only agree to believe such a horrendous proposition, but agree, with a man's life at stake, that they believed it beyond a reasonable doubt? In six and a half hours? . . . It's a goddam good thing I'm writing a book; otherwise I don't know how I would cope with all these reactions I have.

McGinniss's letter indicated he was the champion MacDonald sorely needed, and for the next three years MacDonald cooperated fully with the writer. MacDonald offered McGinniss his own condo not far from the prison, and gave him access to his case records filed there. He also sent McGinniss the results of a continuing investigation by private detectives into the case. McGinniss also pressed MacDonald for audiotapes of Mac-Donald's memories, saying he needed them to get a sense of MacDonald; he needed to know everything about Jeff and Colette, even the intimate details of their sexual relations. He wasn't going to share the information with anybody, he promised in writing, and MacDonald could trust him not to misuse it. McGinniss wrote, "I'm not planning to juggle any facts. . . ."

Thus persuaded, MacDonald opened up to McGinniss in early 1980, secretly voicing tapes in his cell after midnight to conceal his illegal tape recorder. "This is Jeff MacDonald making the first two tapes for Joe McGinniss. . . .I'm having a little difficulty to sort of get into the swing of it." He stopped when he heard a guard's footsteps, and waited till the steps died away. He later arranged to have the tapes smuggled out and mailed to the writer.

McGinniss soon wrote back calling the first tapes a good beginning, but only a "useful sort of general overview." He insisted MacDonald dig deeper. "Remember, you are talking to me and only me, and anything you say will be placed in the context of the overall book; you don't have to worry about sensational newspaper headlines. . . . Cheers, Joe."[7]

McGinniss soon thanked MacDonald for the "very good tapes," adding that he knew how painful the process was for MacDonald. But, ". . . as in therapy," McGinniss wrote, "the more it hurts the more good it does." He told MacDonald the tapes were the one contribution he could make to the book "and I appreciate your putting up with the pain. . . .Please keep going. . . . Don't be bashful. I am the only one who hears these tapes, and beneath this cynical exterior beats a sentimental, gullible, Irish heart. Cheers, Joe."[8]

Having assured MacDonald that such recollections were not for public consumption, but only for the author's background material, McGinniss now primed the well of MacDonald's memory by admitting that he himself had married young and had gotten his own wife pregnant three times. The writer shamelessly confided that, to avoid family pressures and responsibilities, he had traveled a lot and he, also, had slept "with others whenever possible away from home." He, too, had enjoyed affairs around the world, "in Vietnam, Washington, D.C., and San Francisco and Paris and London and Miami, oh, well," McGinniss had quipped in his letter, "I better not think too much or I'll lose my train of thought here."

But still MacDonald refused to share details of his sexual moments with Colette, even though he did continue to provide tapes about other details of his life. McGinniss continually assured MacDonald that he was assisting in the book that would finally tell the "full and true story."

In the summer of 1982 McGinniss changed publishers. He wrote MacDonald it was because his editor at Dell-Delacorte had quit and that Delacorte was losing money. He thought the book could be better published by another house, but "the bastards at Dell" wanted the writer to give them back the $300,000 advance. His agent, Sterling Lord, approached G. P. Putnam's Sons and made a deal which garnered sufficient funds to free McGinniss from the Delacorte contract.[9] McGinniss continued working on the book.

At McGinniss's request, Brian O'Neill, now MacDonald's defense attorney, sent him the new appeal motions on the Stoeckley information. Ray and Cindy Shea, MacDonald's outside liaison team, shipped McGinniss the voluminous results of investigations by private detectives Ted L. Gunderson and Raymond Shedlick, Jr. Their queries by that time had produced more than twenty new witnesses who claimed that either the night before or the morning after they saw a suspicious woman and a group of men who appeared to match the descriptions MacDonald had given. Included among the witnesses were several who had heard admissions of guilt from Helena Stoeckley and Greg Mitchell, her boyfriend.

The Mike Wallace Interview

On June 1, 1983, MacDonald submitted to an interview with Mike Wallace of *60 Minutes*. MacDonald believed the purpose of the interview was to discuss the exculpatory aspects of the Stoeckley confessions and the newly discovered forensic items which the government had not revealed at trial. He was excited that he could now talk on national television about the missing piece of skin, the missing bloody syringe, the destroyed unmatched fingerprints the defense team had discovered up to that time, and the new Stoeckley findings.

But Wallace's on-camera questions in the warden's conference room in the Federal Correctional Institution in Bastrop, Texas, soon revealed that Joe McGinniss had portrayed MacDonald as guilty of the crimes. MacDonald said he felt his heart pound in his chest and couldn't get his breath in the swirling room as he fought to recover from the shock. He had trusted McGinniss for three years and had given him everything he wanted, fully believing McGinniss held for his innocence as he so often had said. And Wallace, it turned out, wasn't really interested in any new evidence.

MacDonald later said that his first inclination was to ask for time, to get away from the camera and regain his balance, but he knew that this would be seen as a sign of weakness and perhaps, by many, as a sure sign of guilt. Also, he realized that he had the eye of one of the most powerful programs in the country, so for the next ninety minutes Wallace queried a devastated MacDonald on camera about various McGinniss allegations which not only challenged MacDonald's character but his very sanity. Wallace appeared to be especially fascinated by McGinniss's soon-to-be-famous theory that MacDonald had murdered his family during a psychotic break caused by a deep-seated pathological hatred for females, a lack of sleep, and an overdose of diet pills.

MacDonald got through the interview by defending, as well as he could, claims he had never heard before. Wallace said that McGinniss's book revealed, among other charges, that MacDonald had carried on an illicit, secret affair with an old girlfriend; that he had seduced a sixteen-year-old girl while traveling cross-country with her; and that he had physically abused and threatened the life of a ten-year-old boy.

When the *60 Minutes* interview was over, the stunned MacDonald raced to his living quarters to phone Brian O'Neill, all too well aware of the harm this book could do to his approaching day in court. He cursed his naive trust of Joe McGinniss, realizing that the author had given no hint of his direction. Not once had Joe broached these damning subjects, not once had he offered an opportunity to explain or deny the accusations.

Brian O'Neill, as alarmed as MacDonald, began his own investigation of the charges McGinniss was making. He quickly wrote a letter to Mike Wallace advising that *60 Minutes* do the same before airing its show. He told Wallace that he had just taped an interview with the young woman McGinniss wrote about and she said she had never told the author about an affair with MacDonald, that McGinniss had never asked her about such an affair, and that it had never happened.

In response to another of the accusations, O'Neill admitted that Mac-Donald actually had, as McGinniss claimed, driven across country with a sixteen-year-old girl. But, O'Neill explained, it was in the company of the girl's mother and another sibling, and the family dog. In this case, too, the mother of the girl claimed that nothing resembling McGinniss's claims ever happened.

The mother of the ten-year-old boy MacDonald supposedly threatened stated "that Dr. MacDonald and her son, Danny, had 'rough-housed' together and at one time when Danny had acted up Dr. MacDonald had kiddingly threatened to throw him overboard or to hit his head against a bulkhead. She added that her son liked Jeff a great deal, that they kept in touch, that MacDonald advised the boy on his choice of colleges, and at a later time her son sent a long letter to Jeff thanking him for the positive influence Jeff had provided him in his life." This didn't sound like abuse to Brian O'Neill.

In closing his letter, O'Neill told Wallace, "I would hope that neither you nor *60 Minutes* would willingly be a part of the frustration of substantial rights in the criminal justice system merely to make sensational, but in the long-run, insignificant, allegations about a man's life. For these reasons, I strongly urge you to check the accuracy of Mr. McGinniss' representations."[10]

CBS aired the *60 Minutes* segment on September 30, 1983. Seven of the eight McGinniss claims contested by O'Neill had been scrapped. The lie MacDonald admittedly told Kassab, about finding and killing one of the assailants, remained. And *60 Minutes* included that part of the Mike Wallace interview which reiterated McGinniss's seminal theory that Mac-Donald had overdosed on diet pills, and suffered a psychotic break which caused him to explode and murder his family.

The Book

Its title now changed from *Acid and Rain* to *Fatal Vision*, McGinniss's book was published on September 16, 1983. Because the public and the media naturally perceived it as a true account of McGinniss's insider investigation into the case, it threatened to scuttle the efforts of the defense team in the appeals process. The team found many passages in which, they say, McGinniss erred factually, and they found almost nothing of the supportive evidence the defense lawyers had furnished him during his writing of the book to refute the government's case. McGinniss had not informed his readers about the scientific problems with Stombaugh's pajama top folding experiment, problems which Segal's expert had pointed out in trial, which even Stombaugh had admitted to, and which McGinniss himself had alluded to in a letter to MacDonald. Segal called the book a "horrible lie." His co-counsel at the army hearing, Dennis Eisman, said it was "a cruel book." Michael Malley termed it "fiction."

While *Fatal Vision* soon hit the best-seller lists nationwide, MacDonald's lawyers and private investigators compiled lists of key items which they considered errors in the book. For instance, to establish his viewpoint that MacDonald was a habitual liar, McGinniss claimed that MacDonald had lied about being offered a residency at Yale. Yet had the author asked MacDonald about the issue, MacDonald would have shown him a letter from Yale's Dr. Wayne Southwick, the chief of orthopedic surgery, mentioning his "considerable pride in the fact that you were planning to come here to train with me."[11]

McGinniss said throughout the book that MacDonald had lied to Co-lette about being offered a trip to Russia to serve as physician on the army boxing team. Yet McGinniss had failed to interview Sherriedale Morgan, the Fort Bragg boxing coach, to check on the issue, even when the author and the coach appeared together during a court hearing. Morgan later verified that MacDonald had not lied.

"These were small things," Segal said, "but they were important things. They set the stage for large things." An even more gross error was McGinniss's unresearched claim that MacDonald had refused to take the sodium amytal examination during the grand jury hearing in 1975.

When *Fatal Vision* was published, many, many people wrote MacDonald asking why, if he wasn't guilty, did he refuse to take the sodium amytal examination when the grand jury asked him to? The true story, which was ignored by McGinniss, was that when MacDonald agreed to take the exam prosecutor Woerheide misrepresented to the jurors the words of MacDonald's psychiatrist and pushed through a vote for indictment even while arrangements were being made for the "truth serum" examination to take place. McGinniss didn't report this prosecution chicanery. Without researching what really happened, he chose to report, erroneously, that MacDonald refused to submit to a sodium amytal session, thus leading millions of readers to believe MacDonald had feared the truths which might be exposed.[12]

Having reported that MacDonald had refused the "truth serum" test, McGinniss faced an easier task in convincing his readers that MacDonald was an inveterate liar. MacDonald admitted he had, indeed, told one lie. He had foolishly told Kassab that he had found one of the intruders and had murdered him. "Then," MacDonald complained, "McGinniss was able to use that one lie to make credible his claim of other lies, statements which I never made."

Segal complained after reading *Fatal Vision* that McGinniss also did not fully report the conditions under which MacDonald told his lie to his father-in-law, and that one side of the story is that MacDonald had lied to alleviate the Kassabs' pressure on him to hunt down the killers and torture them, and, hopefully, to let the Kassabs get on with their lives. "By telling only part of the story," Segal said, "McGinniss convinced readers that MacDonald might not be such a sterling character after all. This, in time, helped McGinniss sell his story about MacDonald flipping out on diet pills and slaughtering his family. Yet his portrayal was false."

Many people, hearing MacDonald's complaints, questioned why he didn't sue McGinniss if the book had so misrepresented the truth. MacDonald's chagrined attorneys, including Bernard Segal, admitted that McGinniss apparently had protected himself well from just such a lawsuit by insisting, as he had in 1979, that MacDonald sign the agreement never to sue him. Even Segal's addendum to the contract, demanding that

McGinniss maintain the integrity of MacDonald's life, didn't seem to have any real value following the much-publicized conviction. After all, in a libel suit one has to prove damages, and what further damage could accrue to the reputation of someone sentenced to three consecutive life terms for murdering his pregnant wife and two little daughters?

But MacDonald argued with his attorneys that McGinniss had agreed to portray the "essential integrity" of his life. How could the author claim to have done that when he failed to emphasize the scores of witnesses to his love for his family, his relationship with Colette and the children, and his life's work in emergency medicine, which was, after all, saving lives, not taking them? Nevertheless, MacDonald's attorneys remained convinced that the courts would refuse to honor such arguments from a man who stood convicted of slaughtering his family.

While MacDonald was pressuring the attorneys to find a way to sue McGinniss, an event occurred which belied the author's claims that Jeffrey MacDonald was an unfeeling monster. The day before NBC aired the first segment of the *Fatal Vision* docudrama (and on the very day that Cathy Perry was telephoning the FBI seeking to confess), MacDonald was summoned by inmates to the prison cell of a man who had stopped breathing. With his hand, MacDonald wiped the vomit off the man's mouth, put his own mouth to the man, and breathed life back into him while also doing closed-chest massage to restart his heart. MacDonald ran alongside the gurney and continued his resuscitation efforts while attendants and guards carried the inmate one hundred yards to the infirmary where MacDonald advised a young medic about an injection, which stabilized the patient.[13,14]

On the following night, MacDonald's attorney, Brian O'Neill, was sitting at home in Los Angeles watching the first segment of *Fatal Vision* on television. At 10 P.M. a newsflash announced that "*Fatal Vision* killer," Dr. Jeffrey MacDonald, had saved a life in prison. O'Neill said the announcement had a bizarre, disorienting effect on him. Still, O'Neill assured his angry client that he could not sue.

MacDonald's Polygraph Examination

MacDonald thought he knew a way to show the public, however, if not the courts, that McGinniss's book and the court conviction might be in error. Famed defense attorney F. Lee Bailey and private investigator Ted Gunderson suggested he take a polygraph exam for Bailey's then-new television show.

MacDonald approached his attorneys about it. At the very crux of Joe McGinniss's claims against MacDonald's veracity was McGinniss's allegation in the book, oft repeated on the talk show circuit, that MacDonald had failed a polygraph test in 1970, an assertion MacDonald adamantly denied. MacDonald said that he had *begun* a polygraph examination in 1970, but the examiner began asking him "crazy" questions, such as had he had sex with animals, and had he had sex with his daughters. MacDonald says he cut the exam short and walked out, disgusted with an "obviously bent examiner." Bernard Segal, in whose offices the event had occurred, corroborated MacDonald's claim that this had happened, that the polygraph exam had begun but was not completed. However, during the closed-door grand jury hearings of 1975, Brian Murtagh had hinted about this polygraph incident, for which Murtagh had no records, and claimed then, and later in court, that MacDonald had "failed" a lie detector test.[15]

MacDonald's lawyers, busy preparing appeals about new evidence, saw no legal benefit in accepting F. Lee Bailey's offer. A polygraph would do them no good in court, so the lawyers initially ignored the idea.

The matter was reopened when Dr. Jeffrey Elliot interviewed MacDonald in 1985 for *Playboy* magazine. Elliot told MacDonald that *Playboy* would feel better if he would submit to a polygraph. This time MacDonald insisted his lawyers make an appointment with the best polygrapher they could find.

On March 18, 1986, MacDonald finally sat for a polygraph examination by Dr. David C. Raskin, a psychology professor at the University of Utah. Dr. Raskin had conducted examinations in some of the leading criminal cases in the country, including the recently completed John DeLorean case, and had also worked for branches of the U.S. government in security matters. This was the reason the defense team chose him. They hoped his work with the government would neutralize any future claims that he wasn't a competent polygrapher.

Dr. Raskin performed the examination in Black Canyon Federal Correctional Institution near Phoenix where MacDonald was then housed. MacDonald was hooked up to the machine, awaiting the questions. He later said he remembered that April day, long ago, when he had agreed to take a polygraph for CID chief Grebner that afternoon, then learned that Grebner didn't have a man ready, as he has claimed. And he recalled the truncated exam in which the examiner asked him about sex with animals. MacDonald says he couldn't help being nervous. The prior aspects of polygraphy hadn't been kind to him.

With the machine's electrodes attached to MacDonald, Dr. Raskin asked many questions, always returning to those that were key to the issue.

"Did you inflict injuries on your wife and children?"

MacDonald answered, "No."

"Did you directly cause their deaths?"

"No."

"Did you arrange to cause their deaths?" Raskin asked.

"No."

After the test, Dr. Raskin analyzed the data and concluded that Mac-Donald's answers indicated no deception.[16] In a second "blind" evaluation, MacDonald's name was masked and the polygraph data tapes given to an examiner in another state. That examiner, too, concluded that the polygraph subject, although unknown to him, was being "truthful."[17]

Raskin's press release and the article in *Playboy* gave MacDonald hope that if he generated enough public support, his attorneys might be able to convince an appeals court to take a serious look at his evidentiary claims. One way to get that support, MacDonald believed, was somehow to press Joe McGinniss into civil court and onto a witness stand, under oath, to examine McGinniss's misrepresentation of his own beliefs, and to challenge the detrimental material in *Fatal Vision*.

MacDonald v. McGinniss

While MacDonald's attorneys continued to discourage efforts to sue McGinniss, MacDonald corresponded with Donna Bruce Koch, a law student who had visited another inmate at Terminal Island Federal Correctional Institution when MacDonald had first been incarcerated there in 1979 after the conviction. She soon became intrigued by what appeared to her as a "classic inequity."

She had no way of judging whether the attorneys' lists of errors in the book[18] were actually errors, nor had she formed an opinion whether

MacDonald was, in fact, guilty of the murders. Taking another tack, the small, intense brunette delved instead into contract law. "A contract," she said, "is an agreement. Did McGinniss break his agreement . . . to treat MacDonald fairly, and if so, can MacDonald sue him for damages?"[19]

After weeks of study she said she believed that McGinniss was linked in "a fiduciary relationship" with his subject. As such, she wrote, he was required to act in good faith. "Since Joe wrote the one-sided contractual agreement, and did not interview relevant people when given a clear opportunity to do so, by half-truths and innuendo distorted the truth to Jeff's damage, and concealed the book from Jeff until after publication, Jeff can probably use a claim of misrepresentation for recovery against McGinniss. . . . in a fiduciary relationship there is a duty to disclose material facts." She told MacDonald that he probably could sue McGinniss—not for libel or slander, but for fraud. Her approach was unique, innovative, and risky, but MacDonald and his defense attorney, Brian O'Neill, liked it.

O'Neill agreed that McGinniss's book and the subsequent movie, seen by the public as truth, had probably hampered the court appeals, for judges also read books and watch television. But the lawyer warned MacDonald that the civil endeavor, though highly worthwhile, would be expensive, in both time and money. He steered MacDonald to Santa Monica civil attorney Gary L. Bostwick, a robust and straightforward former Peace Corps volunteer who had grown up on a Wyoming ranch. Bostwick had successfully represented such clients as Steve and Cindy Garvey against *Newsweek* subsidiary *Inside Sport*,[20] and also Tehran hostage Jerry Plotkin and Mark Goldstein in a suit against *Playboy*.

On August 31, 1984, Bostwick filed a fraud and breach-of-contract suit against Joe McGinniss claiming $15,000,000 in damages.

The MacDonald Tapes

During pre-trial preparations for the civil lawsuit McGinniss was required to surrender the tape recordings MacDonald had made for him years earlier. Bostwick compared the tapes with those segments in *Fatal Vision* which purported to be "The Voice of Jeffrey MacDonald." He satisfied himself that, as MacDonald claimed, McGinniss had skillfully edited passages to make it seem in many of the book segments as though MacDonald had taped glib, nonstop soliloquies of self-adoration. But nowhere in McGinniss's book were MacDonald's taped words of concern about the tragic deaths of Colette and the children. The writer had placed MacDonald's doctored thoughts between ongoing revelations of the government's claims, not bothering to challenge the government claims with any of the relevant defense evidence that had been put at his disposal, not bothering to express in the book his own expressions of disdain which he had written to MacDonald. The results, Bostwick charged, were fictional and the book could not be legitimatized as nonfiction.

One section in *Fatal Vision* involved the audiotapes MacDonald made about a 1972 vacation MacDonald took to Tahiti with a woman McGinniss called "Joy."[21] McGinniss's presentation creates an image of MacDonald only enjoying himself sexually, with no thoughts of his murdered family intruding into the tropical setting.

However, in a tape section which McGinniss deleted in the book's presentation of the Tahiti trip, MacDonald says, "[I] had this strange ambivalence that has never really gone away, although it's lightened up considerably, about feeling bad every time I had a decent time. I noticed that after some months with Joy that every once in a while there'd be a day when I really didn't spend a lot of time brooding about Kim and Kris and Colette; and I had this paradoxical feeling of loneliness and sort of unhappiness and a little guilt every time that occurred. . . ." McGinniss ignored these words, which depicted a man suffering normal grief. Instead, McGinniss used MacDonald's comment about enjoying a "nonstop" sexual relationship with Joy on this vacation trip.

Another such section of "The Voice of Jeffrey MacDonald" occurs on pages 649 through 653 (Signet paperback edition) to end *Fatal Vision*. That segment begins:

> What's the sense of all this? It's crazy. John Lennon gets shot. It's—it's— I mean there's no sense. I don't pray to "another god [*sic*]." Umm, you know, to a—a god in another world is what I mean.
>
> I—I just believe in life here. Uhh, I—we make our bed and we must lie in it, basically, and um, I think that, you know, man has the ability to create his own environment with, uh—heh!—certain mitigating features, uhh, natural and unnatural disasters.
>
> But there's just gotta be something else. It can't be that life is made up of a series of tragedies and travesties and, and, insanities.

The quoted segment goes on for five pages, as if it were an uninterrupted musing by MacDonald. It is not. The piecing together can be best appreciated by considering McGinniss's own typewritten transcript of the tapes. Some of the first paragraph exists on page 344,[22] but there is no mention of John Lennon getting shot in this segment of the tapes. McGinniss didn't tell his readers that his third paragraph comes from page 523, 179 pages later, or that he soon returns to page 344. He failed to let anyone know that he skipped a section about MacDonald talking about his family, lamenting "my lack of attention to Colette and the kids. I wish I had been with them a little bit more, one more time, said I love you once more, um, and also to my father, I feel the same way about my father."

Perhaps as important, the broader context of the taped words about religion is missing. In this particular instance MacDonald was remembering his religious training, noting a current inability, under the circumstances, to believe it, yet recognizing that he still had faith that life must mean something.

Had McGinniss shown his readers the full quote they would have seen Jeffrey MacDonald, whether guilty or innocent, as a man struggling for life's meaning. However, as the reassembled "quotation" is presented in the book, positioned next to the claim of MacDonald's guilt, the readers see a hollow, vain man who had murdered his wife and children and who is now lamenting an early career move.

In putting together the final segment of MacDonald's words in the book, McGinniss jumped from location to location in the tapes ten times, sometimes linking speech excerpts from a hundred transcript pages apart, a linkage where weeks had actually passed between the speaking of the words on the prison tapes. Yet McGinniss presented it as a single run-on quote. A study of the nine taped areas quoted in this misleading segment shows that five major deletions and many smaller deletions were made—all without the use of ellipses, punctuation required to show that words were skipped.

In fact, in order to justify the book's title, McGinniss seems to have deliberately changed a word in a MacDonald quote. The actual quote McGinniss took from his transcript on page 192 reads, ". . . I still think of her as the epitomy [sic] of womanhood." But McGinniss changed the quote to read, "I still see her as the epitome of womanhood." This is not a major change and, under normal circumstances, probably wouldn't deserve an objection. But in the context of McGinniss's use of the quotes to paint an ugly MacDonald, it may seem particularly callous. Making this change in the quote allowed McGinniss to employ it artfully in the closing of his book, using the implications of his now conveniently embedded verb *see* to suggest that what MacDonald "saw" was "a fatal vision."

McGinniss's Offers

While preparing for the civil trial, MacDonald's attorney, Gary Bostwick, became equally troubled by McGinniss's failure to reveal, either in the narrative of the book or in "The Voice of Jeffrey MacDonald," the information that was being uncovered by MacDonald's lawyers and private investigators even while McGinniss wrote the book. Consequently, in *Fatal Vision*, McGinniss had largely ignored any problems about the government's physical evidence, problems which McGinniss's letters to MacDonald had acknowledged to be significant, chief among them being the pajama top folding experiment.

Bostwick said that the letters McGinniss wrote to MacDonald while they worked on their book project together were as revealing as the tape recordings. "McGinniss had misled MacDonald into thinking that the writer believed in his innocence. That untruth," Bostwick said, "was how he got MacDonald to cooperate with him for three years; and that misrepresentation was, in my opinion, fraudulent."

In early July 1987, only days before the civil trial was to begin in Los Angeles, McGinniss offered MacDonald $200,000 if he would settle out of court. MacDonald told Bostwick that was the final insult. Bostwick, in turn, told McGinniss's lawyers to prepare for trial. At his request, MacDonald had been moved from Black Canyon Federal Correctional Institution in Arizona to the FCI at Terminal Island near Los Angeles, but only upon his agreement to accept solitary confinement in lieu of being among the general prison population. A cell in the solitary confinement unit would become his home for nearly four years following the McGinniss trial because MacDonald wanted to stay near his mother who was terminally ill and couldn't visit him in Arizona. Thus, the Bureau of Prisons allowed him to stay at Terminal Island near his mother's home, but only under the condition that he remain in solitary confinement. No reason was ever given for this action. After his mother passed away, he was transferred to the FCI at Sheridan, Oregon.

Every trial morning for about six weeks MacDonald arose hours before dawn to dress, eat, and board the prison bus for the hour-long ride to the federal courthouse. He would exit the bus and allow himself to be attached to a long chain with twenty to twenty-five other prisoners scheduled for trial or hearings, and then he was led to his courtroom. There, finally, he would sit only a few feet away from Joe McGinniss and challenge the author's treatment of him in a court of law.

Civil Trial

Judge William J. Rea, a trim, square-shouldered man of sixty-seven years, presided over the civil proceedings. In a quiet but no-nonsense manner, he insisted at the outset that the attorneys address the six-person civil jury from a podium in the center of the room about twenty feet in front of him.

To open the McGinniss trial, Gary Bostwick, in a characteristically calm, even voice, explained that the charges against the writer were fraud, breach of contract, intentional infliction of emotional distress, and that McGinniss had kept money that belonged to MacDonald. Bostwick, wearing a dark pin-striped suit, presented the plaintiff's view of the legal issues. "McGinniss's letters had promised Jeffrey MacDonald his love, support, belief, credibility." Then, Bostwick declared in an even quieter voice, "he betrayed a friend." Bostwick's purpose was to establish that McGinniss had misled MacDonald. While showing this, he hoped to show that the author also had misrepresented MacDonald's character in the book.

Jeffrey MacDonald was by now completely gray-haired after serving six years in high-security prisons, yet, largely because of his regimen of running and exercise, he was as tanned and trim as a lifeguard. In wing-tipped shoes, dark blue suit, and new yellow tie, he appeared the well-to-do, forty-four-year-old practicing physician he might have been.

Bostwick arranged for his attractive co-counsel, Joann Horn, a tall, well-dressed brunette, to sit next to MacDonald, no doubt to dispel concerns by jurors about MacDonald's "boundless rage" against females.

On the opposite side of the courtroom, Daniel J. Kornstein, a New York lawyer assisted by local counsel Mark Platt, represented Joe McGinniss. Kornstein, a small, brown-haired man, was fashionably attired in a dark brown suit. Kornstein was no stranger to the publishing world, having authored two books on the law.

For his opening statement, Kornstein walked quickly to the rail of the jury box, leaned toward the jurors, and told them that MacDonald had been convicted of clubbing and slashing to death his wife and two little daughters. As Kornstein's face suddenly twisted in anger, he wheeled and pointed back to MacDonald, shouting, "*Now he wants two more victims— Joe McGinniss and the truth!*"

His startling onslaught following Bostwick's gentle delivery brought gasps from the jury box and the gallery of spectators. Darting back toward the podium, Kornstein whirled again and informed the jury that he didn't think McGinniss had done anything wrong, because the author had a duty to get close to his subject; the author needed to understand his subject, and live with him. "The subject knows that," Kornstein said, "the author knows that." It was MacDonald, not McGinniss, who had perpetrated a "continuing fraud on the public."

As the lawyer thrust himself away from the podium and again charged toward the jurors, Judge Rea's soft, cold voice stopped him. He turned and looked up at the judge.

"Mr. Kornstein," Judge Rea said, "you will remain at the podium, as we agreed."

Kornstein nodded his head quickly, apologized, and returned to his station at the podium, gripping its sides with both hands as if he feared he might cast himself again toward the jurors. He rocked to his toes, then back down, only to lift up again, still holding on as if without warning he might launch bodily into the air, so great was his anger at the wrongs Jeffrey MacDonald had done Joe McGinniss. A few of the jurors now looked at each other and smiled nervously. Gary Bostwick stopped shuffling papers, looked over his glasses at Kornstein, then turned and grinned at MacDonald. Several visitors in the gallery sniggered, drawing a sharp glance from Judge Rea.

Kornstein's foray to the jury box wasn't the only rule he had broken. He also had called Jeffrey MacDonald a "murderer." Judge Rea already had forewarned both sides not to address whether MacDonald was guilty or innocent of the murders. The result of the criminal trial in 1979 was to hold no sway in the issue before the court, the question of whether McGinniss had defrauded Jeffrey MacDonald.

Not only had Kornstein's opening remarks defied the judge's instructions, they also refuted Kornstein's own pre-trial arguments. Kornstein, during bitterly fought pre-trial motions, had argued against allowing admittance of the criminal issue; for Bostwick had come to believe, from the record itself, that MacDonald wasn't guilty of the murders, and Bostwick had early on expressed his desire to enjoin McGinniss in discussions of MacDonald's factual innocence. It was Kornstein who had said he wanted nothing discussed except McGinniss's First Amendment rights to write and say what he believed.

Consequently, Kornstein's open accusation of MacDonald as a murderer, "clubbing and slashing," angered and surprised Bostwick. For the next six weeks Judge Rea would find himself constantly refereeing attempts by a dogged Bostwick now determined to present evidence that the verdict of the criminal court in 1979 was a mistake. A harried Judge Rea continued to impress upon the two warring attorneys that the issue before the court here was not a question of MacDonald's guilt, but that of McGinniss. In this court, the issue wasn't murder, but fraud, and therefore the only legitimate subject at hand was the behavior of Joe McGinniss during the writing of the book over a period of four years, 1979 to 1983.

Before McGinniss was called to testify in his own behalf, he once again offered to settle out of court. And again, MacDonald refused, insisting that he wanted McGinniss's responses under oath, and in a court record.

THE MCGINNISS TESTIMONY—ON FINANCIAL AFFAIRS

The author began his five days on the stand seemingly confident, answering boldly, looking out at his supporters in the gallery, smiling often. But as the testimony wore on, day after day, he appeared increasingly nervous, responding more quietly, his eyes often on his hands. Gary Bostwick asked him about his publisher problems and the financial troubles he had suffered during the writing of the book. McGinniss had bought a new house, and Delacorte had threatened to sue him for the return of the nearly $300,000 they had given him in advance money. During the examination by Bostwick, McGinniss often brought a hand up to push his straight brown hair out of his eyes. Sometimes he nervously "whooshed" his breath out from between ballooned cheeks.

Bostwick queried him about interfering with the payments of royalties to MacDonald. In a pre-trial deposition, Sterling Lord, McGinniss's agent, had already told Bostwick that McGinniss had written him a letter ordering MacDonald's royalty payments to be diverted from MacDonald. The money was to be sent to McGinniss's own lawyer. Lord had complied with the request and had stopped the checks to MacDonald. Accounting figures verified that at least $90,000 had been diverted.

A huge projection screen hung against the north wall of the courtroom, used by Bostwick to show documents to the jury. With the actual royalty records displayed on the screen, Bostwick asked McGinniss to explain why he had stopped MacDonald's royalty payments. McGinniss said that MacDonald's money was being held in an escrow account pending disposition of the lawsuit, that he had ordered his agent to withhold the money because MacDonald had broken his agreement not to sue him. The subpoenaed records projected upon the screen, however, showed that the money in question had been diverted even before MacDonald brought the suit against the author. Thus, McGinniss's motive in the fund diversion now seemed open to question.

THE MCGINNISS TESTIMONY—ON MISLEADING MACDONALD

Bostwick also considered it important that the jury learn when McGinniss had changed his views about MacDonald's innocence. In *Fatal Vision* McGinniss had depicted himself as conducting his lengthy research and becoming gradually and reluctantly convinced of MacDonald's guilt. He made the same claim to Bostwick from the witness stand. If this version of when he believed MacDonald guilty were true, then at the time of McGinniss's supportive letters he either still believed in MacDonald's innocence or was only then beginning to have doubts. Bostwick asked McGinniss whether he had told reporters that he already believed in McDonald's guilt at the time the jury's verdict was read in 1979.

McGinniss said he hadn't done this, but Bostwick immediately played a recording of the author being interviewed by radio host George Putnam in Los Angeles, taped on September 28, 1983. On the tape McGinniss said, ". . . my mind was made up the same day the jury's mind was made up—at the conclusion of the trial in 1979. I think at that time—I know at that time—I was convinced beyond a reasonable doubt that he had done this."[23] These words put the lie to McGinniss's claims in the book, and his claims to Bostwick, under oath, only moments earlier.

McGinniss listened to the words echoing through the courtroom. When the machine was turned off, he told Bostwick he couldn't be sure that was his voice.

Judge Rea turned suddenly toward McGinniss and said, "Well, surely you recognized your own voice."

McGinniss grinned, then lost his hold on the grin and looked at his hands.

Joe McGinniss's wife, Nancy, provided still a third story when she testified on the issue of when her husband had decided MacDonald was guilty. Under oath, she said that her husband had not been truthful when he told reporters he first believed MacDonald was guilty when the verdict came in. She said she told Joe not to tell that story because "it wasn't true." Bostwick asked her when Joe McGinniss, in her opinion, actually had changed his mind about MacDonald.

Joe had visited Alfred Kassab in the spring of 1981, she said. After that visit, she told Bostwick, her husband believed MacDonald was guilty.

The George Putnam recording was proof that McGinniss had told at least two different stories about when he believed MacDonald guilty, one story in his book, one on the radio show with George Putnam. But Bostwick wanted McGinniss himself to admit in open court, under oath, that he had knowingly lied to MacDonald, his contractual partner in the book project. Then, Bostwick reasoned, the jury would have to find McGinniss guilty of fraud in a legal contract. But, even in the face of his wife's story and his own admissions on the Putnam tape, McGinniss at first stubbornly resisted Bostwick's naked attempts to pry such an admission out of him.

The author told Bostwick that MacDonald's expectation of a positive book was nothing but self-deception. So Bostwick referred McGinniss to the letters themselves, projecting each one on the large screen as it was discussed. Bostwick insisted that through the letters McGinniss himself had led MacDonald to think the author believed in him. The lawyer pointed out such entries as, "Total strangers can recognize within five minutes that you did not receive a fair trial."

Soon McGinniss began softening his previous denials, at one point saying, "I believe I was encouraging him not to discourage me from finishing the book. . . ."

But Bostwick wanted McGinniss to say it plainly. In *Fatal Vision*, the author had argued MacDonald's guilt by relying on the government's view of the evidence, without introducing opposing information. This was particularly true of the way he characterized the experiment of "stabbing through the pajama top." Knowing this, Bostwick projected a letter from McGinniss to MacDonald, mailed on March 3, 1981, nearly two years into the writing of the book. In the letter, McGinniss told how a friend of his, a scientist, was both "angered and offended" by the government's methodology in the pajama top demonstration. McGinniss wrote, ". . . you got screwed by lousy, lazy pseudo-science. . . ."

Still on the attack, Bostwick then displayed for the courtroom the next letter, written by McGinniss to literary agent Sterling Lord on the same day of his letter to MacDonald about the "pseudo-science."

"The irony of all this," McGinniss wrote to his agent, "is that so far

MacDonald has not even seen the book and still has no idea how mad he's really going to be. But the more he hears ahead of time about how mad he *should* be, the more time he has to work on his strategy to discredit me and my findings. . . ."

Then Bostwick projected a third letter which had also been written on that same day, this one from McGinniss to his editor regarding MacDonald's questions about the book. "The ice is getting thinner," McGinniss wrote, "and I'm still a long way from shore." Thus Bostwick had succeeded in showing that, on the same day, McGinniss had written a pro-MacDonald letter to MacDonald, and anti-MacDonald letters to his editor and agent.

In attempting to explain these variations, McGinniss replied to a question by saying he had led MacDonald on because "the man had killed before. I didn't know what he was going to do to my wife or my kid. He wasn't in prison at that time."[24] This accusatory answer elicited a quick, sideways glance at the author by a solemn-faced Judge Rea, while a chorus of groans arose from a crowd of MacDonald supporters in the courtroom.

But Bostwick continued, pushing for an outright admission that McGinniss had lied to MacDonald. He kept showing the jurors McGinniss's letters, one after another, each one containing solemn assurances of fidelity. Finally, McGinniss admitted that the reason he had misled MacDonald was because he "just didn't want to get him all agitated and doing the kinds of things that would prevent me from moving forward with the book." When Bostwick received that admission, complete with self-confessed motive, he moved on.

His next line of questioning centered on whether McGinniss had misrepresented MacDonald to his readers. This was a topic especially important to MacDonald himself; and it was one of the main reasons he had instituted the lawsuit against McGinniss. To this end, Bostwick projected for the jurors a letter from Phyllis E. Grann, McGinniss's editor at Putnam.[25] In the letter Grann asked McGinniss, "Is Mildred [Kassab] trying to railroad Jeff? Should reader get that impression? Would you want to add some explanation for the change in [her] testimony? Reader is certainly left with the impression that Mildred will lie to get Jeff convicted. Wouldn't it be better to close this chapter with some comment of your own?"

Regarding another section of the manuscript, Grann wrote, "All this does make the reader wonder if Jeff might be innocent.[26] Would you want to add a few paragraphs of your own to lessen the impact?"

THE MCGINNISS TESTIMONY—THE DRUG PSYCHOSIS THEORY

Bostwick next sought to convince the jury that, to make his book "better," McGinniss had deliberately contrived some of the more damaging portions of the story. In a pre-trial deposition, McGinniss had admitted to Bostwick that he had developed the book's psychological theories and the drug-ingestion theory to give his readers something more than merely the 1979 trial results. Because of this admission, before bringing McGinniss to trial Bostwick told MacDonald he suspected that editorial requests for "dramatic shaping" had induced McGinniss to develop his own "drug-psychosis" theory, which actually became a central theme. By developing such a theory, McGinniss was able to satisfy the most vexing problem in the government case, the question that was never answered, that of MacDonald's alleged motive. How does a man change from gentle father to slashing maniac in one terrible moment? McGinniss offered an ingenious explanation.

Like the fictional Dr. Jekyll who ingested a sinister potion to unleash the beast inside, McGinniss painted MacDonald as another inwardly tortured physician. MacDonald supposedly took drugs which ripped away his veneer of respectability to reveal the twisted creature he really was. McGinniss shows himself privy to MacDonald's secret diary and, indeed, his very thoughts through the tape recordings. The author used clues from these imprints of MacDonald's psyche to track down a motive for the murders, a motive which nine years of investigation by several very determined government agents had not revealed.

The so-called "diary" had been requested by Bernard Segal when he had first taken the murder case back in 1970. He immediately had asked Jeffrey MacDonald to write down everything he had done through the weeks preceding the murders and for some time afterward. MacDonald had freely furnished that set of notes to McGinniss for his book research. In *Fatal Vision* McGinniss wrote that he had become intrigued after discovering that MacDonald's diary had addressed the subject of diet pills.

McGinniss, while writing his book, sought out the CID lab reports on the analyses of MacDonald's blood and urine, just as Bernard Segal had done many years before him. And, as Segal had learned earlier, McGinniss discovered that the CID lab tests revealed no dangerous drugs. But unlike Segal, McGinniss tracked down Joseph J. Barbato, the young CID laboratory technician who had run the tests on MacDonald's fluids after the murders. Barbato told McGinniss that the machine he had used was capable of detecting only lethal levels of amphetamine. This left open a possibility that if MacDonald actually had taken large, but nonlethal, doses of amphetamine it might have remained undetected.

Had he taken large doses?

All that McGinniss could point to was a single diary entry made by MacDonald about diet pills. When Bernard Segal asked MacDonald to write the diary in April of 1970, he asked MacDonald to write down anything and everything he could remember about his activities preceding the murders. The notation that sparked McGinniss's imagination was worded this way:

> It is possible I had 1 diet pill at this time. I do not remember, but it is possible. I had been running a weight control program for my unit and I put my name at the top of the program to encourage participation. I had lost 12–15 lbs. in the prior 3–4 weeks, in the process using 3–5 capsules of Eskatrol Spansule (15 mg. Dextroamphetamine[,] "speed") and 7.5 mg. Prochlorperazine (Compazine) to counteract the excitability of the speed.

Three to five diet pills over the entire three- to four-week period should not have caused the violent, psychotic reaction McGinniss envisioned, and which the crime scene indicated. McGinniss, however, chose not to read the paragraph that way. He surmised in *Fatal Vision* that to have attained a psychotic state wherein MacDonald succumbed to a boundless rage, MacDonald must have taken not three to five capsules in nearly a month's time, but three to five capsules a *day*—perhaps 90 to 150 such capsules!

McGinniss never attempted to answer a most obvious question about MacDonald's note about diet pills. MacDonald was a trained physician actually working as a drug abuse counselor. If he had, indeed, overdosed on amphetamines, he would have known it. Would he then have called attention to it in a diary? At the time, Segal hadn't decided MacDonald was innocent, and he himself was looking for a motive for the murders. He didn't find a motive. Joe McGinniss, on the other hand, said there was one.

The motive for murder, McGinniss surmised, existed deep in MacDonald's psyche. He suggested that MacDonald suffered from a kind of "narcissism," pathological in nature, and that he harbored a secret, "boundless rage" against females, a hatred toward women never before exhibited, a hatred kept precariously in check while living with three females. This secretly sick MacDonald, clandestinely insane, fatigued from overwork, and burdened with family pressures, supposedly ingested enough pills, McGinniss guessed, to evoke a serious, uncontrollable drug psychosis that finally pushed him over the edge.

McGinniss put it this way:

> Might it be too much to surmise that since early childhood he had been suffering also from the effects of the strain required to repress the "boundless rage" which psychological maladjustment had caused him to feel toward "child or woman, wife or mother . . . the female sex?"
>
> And that on this night—this raw and somber military-base February Monday night—finally, with the amphetamines swelling the rage to flood tide, and with Colette, pregnant Colette, perhaps seeking to communicate to him some of her new insights into personality structure and behavioral patterns—indeed, possibly even attempting to *explain* him to himself—his defense mechanism, for the first and last time, proved insufficient?
>
> Would it be too much to suggest that in that one instant—whatever its forever unknowable proximate cause might have been—a critical mass had been achieved, a fission had taken place, and that by 3:40 A.M. on February 17, 1970, the ensuing explosion of rage had destroyed not only Jeffrey MacDonald's wife and daughters, but all that he had sought to make of his life?[27]

McGinniss thus left his readers believing that he had uncovered the mechanism which caused MacDonald suddenly to turn into the raging maniac the government prosecutors had described at trial. According to McGinniss's theory, MacDonald killed Colette and Kimberly during a psychotic snap, then came to his senses and deliberately murdered baby Kristen to silence the only witness.

McGinniss quoted important medical books to support his musings of drug use and psychopathic patterns. He wrote that the fatigued MacDonald had worked all night "every night" with little sleep, another factor which contributed to his supposed psychosis. He also assured his readers that neighbors had observed signs of MacDonald's drug psychosis, citing changes in behavior even before the murders. He told his readers that doctors had observed symptoms of drug use after the murders.

Now, in 1987, with McGinniss on the witness stand, Bostwick sought to show that each of the items upon which McGinniss had based his theory was erroneous, speculative, or completely contrived. He sought to show that McGinniss, like John Steinbeck in his novel *East of*

Eden, had created a monstrous character, albeit fictional, out of whole cloth.

For instance, McGinniss told his readers that the statement about diet pills was the very first entry in MacDonald's diary following the murders and thus suggested a guilt complex. But it wasn't the first entry. The diet pill notation was recorded among notes for February 16. It was where it should have been given Segal's instructions to him. The note appeared a full 54 single-spaced typed lines into the entry.

Bostwick reminded the jurors that MacDonald had written in his diary that he *might* have taken a total of three to five pills, and that McGinniss had only *theorized* he had taken what would have amounted to thirty to fifty times as many.

In *Fatal Vision* McGinniss had quoted two medical books as authorities for his idea that MacDonald must have ingested more amphetamine than he had admitted in the diary. Bostwick later said he had encountered so many instances of McGinniss "making things fit his own needs" that he suspected McGinniss might have misquoted the medical books. So Bostwick's staff located copies of the 1977 *Physicians' Desk Reference* and the 1980 edition of *Goodman and Gilman's Pharmacological Basis of Therapeutics*, whose quotes McGinniss had cited.[28]

In *Fatal Vision* McGinniss had quoted from *Goodman and Gilman*, about amphetamine tolerance, using these words: "Tolerance does not develop to certain of the toxic effects of amphetamines on the central nervous system, and a toxic psychosis may occur after periods of weeks." With a copy of *Fatal Vision* in his hand, Bostwick read this quote aloud to McGinniss, then he asked the writer, "Didn't you cut off part of the sentence?"

"Well, generally if I cut off part of a sentence I'll use ellipses."

"Well, that's what I thought," Bostwick deadpanned. "Doesn't the sentence really say that it would occur after periods of weeks *to months of continuous use?*" The lawyer had the text of *Goodman and Gilman* in hand to prove his point. Thus, he was able to point out to the jury that McGinniss had left out part of the book's words, leading the reader to believe that amphetamine psychosis might occur more quickly than the medical literature really said.

Bostwick did not believe that this truncation of a sentence was of grave importance, except that it was the forerunner for another more serious misuse of a second medical reference book.

Another medical quote contained two misleading errors. In *Fatal Vision*

McGinniss inferred that a passage in the 1977 edition of *Physicians' Desk Reference*, commonly called the *PDR*, supported his drug-psychosis theory. On the stand the writer assured Bostwick that he had, as Bostwick suggested, intended the quote to bolster his idea that MacDonald must have ingested three to five pills a *day*.

After this admission Bostwick handed McGinniss the *PDR* and asked him to find the section in the medical book which supported his theory, as indicated to *Fatal Vision* readers. McGinniss, sitting in the witness seat in front of the jurors, looked through the *PDR*, but eventually, and with embarrassment, had to admit he could find no such section.

Bostwick then demonstrated the second *PDR* error. In *Fatal Vision*, McGinniss had quoted the medical reference book concerning the signs of chronic amphetamine intoxication. Bostwick projected this *Fatal Vision* quote onto the screen, then asked the author, who was holding the *PDR*, to read from the actual text he claimed to have quoted. McGinniss read aloud, "Marked insomnia, irritability, hyperactivity and personality changes."

But McGinniss's words written in *Fatal Vision*, the words purportedly quoted from the *PDR*, went further than that. McGinniss had added something to the quotation. In *Fatal Vision* he had written: "'marked insomnia, tenseness, and irritability, hyperactivity, confusion, assaultiveness, hallucinations, panic states,' and 'the most severe . . . psychosis.'"

Bostwick called McGinniss's attention to the differences in the wording, specifically to the manufactured words "assaultiveness, . . . panic states, . . . psychosis." He suggested the author deliberately fabricated the quote in order to justify a shaky theory and to shape the readers opinions of Jeffrey MacDonald.

Bostwick continued chipping away at McGinniss's theory of drug psychosis. McGinniss had suggested in his book that MacDonald had become fatigued and had been taking an excess of diet pills because he was working at his hospital job "every night" after his army job and was getting little sleep. Had McGinniss looked into the issue more closely, he might have discovered that an FBI agent reported on the very day of the murders that MacDonald's moonlighting work at Cape Fear Valley Hospital was limited to eight duty sessions. These occurred on December 28, 1969; January 15, 17, 21, 25, and 31; and February 6 and 12. His work at the Hamlet Hospital was limited to his opening duty, February 15.

Bostwick's own investigation about MacDonald's work schedule corroborated that FBI report, that MacDonald had worked only one or two nights a week. Bostwick asked Joe McGinniss where he had gotten his erroneous information that MacDonald had been working all night for many nights and was fatigued. McGinniss said he thought it was from the investigation of CID agents Pruett and Kearns. Bostwick handed McGinniss the Pruett-Kearns report. It made no such claim. Bostwick then asked McGinniss if he had spoken with anyone who could verify his claim. He said he had not. He had also failed to include his own knowledge, from MacDonald's tapes to him, that MacDonald had stated that his case load had been light the night before the murders and that he had, in fact, gotten almost a full night's sleep in the absence of emergency cases.[29] The fatigue factor, so well employed by McGinniss in his drug-use theory, was not based upon facts.

But McGinniss had gone even further to establish his theory. He also had claimed in his book that neighbors had noted MacDonald's "pallor, fatigue, and changed personality" in the weeks preceding the murders. But neither Bostwick nor MacDonald's criminal defense lawyers had found any evidence of this in the statements and testimonies of MacDonald's friends, neighbors, or fellow workers, so Bostwick asked McGinniss if he had ever talked with anyone "that told you that Dr. MacDonald manifested symptoms of overuse of Eskatrol in the weeks before February 17th, 1970?" McGinniss finally admitted that he had actually talked with no one about it.

In *Fatal Vision* McGinniss even had claimed that MacDonald had exhibited signs of drug psychosis *after* the murders. Again, Bostwick's own investigations had discovered no one who saw such signs. He asked McGinniss if he had really talked with anyone who had seen signs of amphetamine psychosis after the murders. McGinniss said that the doctor who had treated MacDonald in the emergency room of Womack Army Hospital had said that after the murders that morning MacDonald displayed symptoms of "fatigue and mental depression."

Speaking in a low tone, and with his temper barely contained beneath his tremulous voice, Bostwick asked, "Mr. McGinniss, did it ever occur to you that someone who had just watched his family being murdered would manifest symptoms such as extreme fatigue and mental depression?"

"He didn't see them murdered!" McGinniss retorted.

Judge Rea's white head jerked toward McGinniss, and the entire courtroom fell suddenly silent, for this was exactly what MacDonald himself had maintained for seventeen years. He *hadn't* seen the murders. When his family was killed, he was in the living room fighting with intruders. Observers at the trial later commented that they asked themselves at this moment whether Joe McGinniss, in his heart of hearts, really ever believed the central tenet of his own book. Following the stunned reaction to his comment, McGinniss stammered, then said, "Well, he watched them being murdered as he murdered them," his voice now weak and much subdued. Bostwick let McGinniss's words hang in the air for a while before going on.

THE MCGINNISS TESTIMONY—NARCISSISM

The attorney brought up the author's theory that MacDonald possesses a suppressed rage toward the female sex. Bostwick quoted McGinniss's words from *Fatal Vision* that spoke of "the 'boundless rage' which psychological maladjustment had caused him to feel toward 'child or woman, wife or mother . . . the female sex.'" Bostwick then asked McGinniss, "Where is that phrase quoted from?"

McGinniss told him that the idea was from a book titled *The Culture of Narcissism*, by Christopher Lasch, a professor of history.

In that book, under a section entitled "The Castrating Women of Male Fantasy," were the words that had caught the attention of McGinniss. Professor Lasch had written: "The fear of women, closely associated with a fear of the consuming desires within, reveals itself not only as impotence but as a boundless rage against the female sex."[30]

Bostwick, seeking whether McGinniss had tried to substantiate whether MacDonald actually harbored a "boundless rage," asked the author if he'd ever talked about this supposed hatred toward women with MacDonald's mother or sister. McGinniss said he had not. Bostwick asked him, "Did you talk to *any* woman that had an acquaintance, a relationship, or a familiar connection with Dr. MacDonald to determine whether that woman felt that any [of MacDonald's] behavior had shown psychological maladjustment toward the female sex?"

McGinniss could only remember one such woman and he admitted that she "didn't phrase it quite that way, but I came away with that impression."

Bostwick didn't like the answer. "I'm asking if you suggested it to anyone else in order to check out your theory." McGinniss then answered that he had not. Bostwick asked him if he'd spoken with any of MacDonald's male acquaintances about MacDonald's supposed rage against women. McGinniss said he had not.

To support his suggestion that MacDonald suffered from a pathological form of narcissism, McGinniss also had quoted passages from Otto Kernberg's book, *Borderline Conditions and Pathological Narcissism*. Using Kernberg, McGinniss established in his book that people exist who seem to be normal, but have no real emotional depth. These people exhibit characteristics of "grandiosity, extreme self-centeredness, and a remarkable absence of interest and empathy for others. . . ." Kernberg wrote that these patients experience an "overriding necessity to feel great and important in order to cancel feelings of worthlessness and devaluation."

Bostwick asked McGinniss the obvious question, "Did you talk to any professional medical people or psychological people about pathological narcissism?"

"Yes," McGinniss said.

Bostwick stopped, cocked his head, and looked directly at McGinniss. "Now, that was not true, was it?"

"Well, pathological narcissism per se, as a subdivision of psychopathic personality, the answer is 'yes'."

Bostwick reminded McGinniss that he had been asked this exact question during a pre-trial deposition and that McGinniss had also answered the question in the affirmative at that time. Referring to the pretrial deposition question a year earlier, Bostwick now said, "You were not telling the truth; isn't that so?"

"Well, I wouldn't characterize it that way," McGinniss said, "but I would say that I spoke to professional psychiatric people about psychopathic personality, of which narcissism is a subdivision."

But Bostwick didn't let up. "Didn't you ask your attorney later to send a letter to us to tell our firm that you had not, in fact, spoken to anyone about pathological narcissism?"

"I believe," McGinniss said, "that [letter] regarded a question of journalistic privilege."

At this, Bostwick produced the letter in question, written by McGinniss's lawyer, Daniel Kornstein. In that letter Kornstein reminded Bostwick that McGinniss had claimed journalistic privilege in giving his answer during the deposition, meaning he was not required to name interviewees because it involved revealing a source. This, in fact, would be a matter of journalistic privilege, but Kornstein wrote that he now wished to withdraw objections to the question. The letter, which Bostwick read for the jury, revealed that there had been no need for journalistic privilege because McGinniss had no sources to protect. Kornstein had written that McGinniss now wished to "amend" his "yes" answer, to state that "Mr. McGinniss interviewed no one in connection with pathological narcissism." [31]

With that letter now part of the court record, Bostwick asked again, "Mr. McGinniss, did you talk to anyone that you can recall that you would say were friends, relatives, co-workers, or colleagues, to ask whether they had observed any behavior that could be termed pathological narcissism?"

This time McGinniss said, almost inaudibly, "No, I did not."

THE MCGINNISS TESTIMONY—LABORATORY INVESTIGATION

That left only two items in Bostwick's list of goals involving McGinniss's key drug theory: McGinniss's claim that the CID had not specifically asked the laboratory technician to test MacDonald's blood and urine for amphetamines, and McGinniss's claim that the technician had said that the army didn't consider amphetamines to be dangerous drugs.

On August 7, Bostwick addressed the issue with the lab technician, Joseph J. Barbato. Even though Barbato was called as a McGinniss witness, he stated from the stand that McGinniss had incorrectly quoted him, that he *was* asked to test for dangerous drugs in MacDonald's urine. He added that, contrary to McGinniss's claims in the book, he *did* know in 1970 that amphetamines were a restricted and dangerous drug.[32]

Bostwick then demonstrated, with McGinniss back on the stand, that the writer had ignored his own knowledge when he claimed in the book that the military hadn't considered amphetamines a dangerous drug. He admitted under Bostwick's questioning that Colette's body was *specifically* tested for amphetamines at Womack Army Hospital because CID agents thought the extreme violence of the crimes might be the result of amphetamine abuse by persons involved.

THE TESTIMONY OF DR. ROBERT SADOFF

With the completion of Barbato's testimony, Bostwick had undermined every basis for McGinniss's theory that MacDonald had suffered a drug psychosis. There remained only the question of whether a psychiatrist might agree with the layman's theories advanced by McGinniss. Bostwick called Dr. Robert Sadoff, who had examined Jeffrey MacDonald three times over a nine-year period.

Joe McGinniss had claimed in his book that during the grand jury hearing Sadoff "did not seem nearly so certain of his [earlier] opinion," which in 1970 had favored MacDonald. McGinniss also claimed that Sadoff, in response to questions by Victor Woerheide in 1975, had agreed that MacDonald might have lost control in a chaotic incident, resulting in the murder of his family. Bostwick wanted the issue of Sadoff's opinion cleared up once and for all. On the stand at the civil trial Dr. Sadoff insisted that his opinion had remained constant over the years, that he found no pathology in Dr. MacDonald and that he didn't think he was capable of murdering his family.

During Kornstein's cross-examination of Dr. Sadoff, the lawyer addressed the controversial passage in Fatal Vision. Victor Woerheide had asked the psychiatrist whether MacDonald could lose control. Sadoff had said he believed MacDonald, under certain conditions, could lose control. So in challenging the psychiatrist's testimony that his opinion had remained constant over the years, Kornstein made reference to that response. "When you were giving those statements," Kornstein asked Sadoff, "were you referring to Jeffrey MacDonald?"

Twelve years had passed since that grand jury hearing,[33] and, at first, Sadoff seemed not to remember the conditions of the conversation. After thinking about it, he said, "As a hypothetical, as a general possibility."

His memory, it turns out, was accurate. A review of the grand jury testimony in question reveals that the discussion was, in fact, couched purely as hypothesis. In a lengthy dialogue of give-and-take between Victor Woerheide and Dr. Sadoff, Woerheide suggested that if the government's evidence against MacDonald were factual, and that if MacDonald, indeed, possessed the negative, selfish characteristics Jeffrey MacDonald was being accused of having, and if MacDonald were an active, outwardly strong man who might have had an Achilles heel—a vulnerability involving his male ego—might he snap if he were overworked, and tired, and challenged in the area of his weakness? If that were to happen, Woerheide asked, could he lose control?

Sadoff had replied that he could, indeed. Woerheide then suggested that "chaos" would ensue. Sadoff had agreed that it might. All this, of course, based upon the hypothetical "if" in each instance. But McGinniss had completely excised the conjectural mood of the exchange.

In the civil trial in Los Angeles, Sadoff assured Daniel Kornstein that he still believed his earlier assessments of MacDonald to be valid. He made it clear that he did not believe Jeffrey MacDonald to be of a personality type to have murdered his family, and that he had found no psychiatric abnormalities in MacDonald.

A "NEW JOURNALISM" DEFENDED

During this civil trial, Kornstein defended McGinniss with the argument that MacDonald was merely attacking "freedom of speech." To aid in this effort, he introduced William F. Buckley, Jr., and Joseph Wambaugh, both celebrities of some note, and both friends and supporters of McGinniss. Through them Kornstein attempted to show that misleading a subject is merely a standard procedure used by authors to get at the truth.

He asked Buckley, "What is the scope of the author's discretion to encourage self-deception on the part of the subject?" With a grin Buckley responded that in his opinion it is appropriate to "feign agreement with the subject in order to encourage further conversation. . . ."

On cross-examination, Bostwick asked Buckley if it was all right to tell the subject "something you don't really believe, in order to get more information from him."

"Yes," Buckley said. "That is right, understood in context."

Bostwick asked author Joseph Wambaugh the same question. Wambaugh, in plainer language than Buckley had used, strongly defended McGinniss's actions. However, he said he didn't like to have the word "lie" applied to his own efforts to secure a subject's cooperation. He said he would tell "an untruth" to get the story.

To counter any favorable effect Buckley and Wambaugh might have had on the jurors, Bostwick introduced Dr. Jeffrey Elliot, a professor at North Carolina Central University. Elliot had published a number of books, most based upon interviews with political figures, including Fidel Castro. He had also interviewed MacDonald for *Playboy* magazine, and, at the time of the civil trial, planned to write a book on the MacDonald case.[34]

Elliot, a diminutive and dapper professor, assured Bostwick that lying to a subject is "unacceptable, extremely irregular, and unprofessional." Elliot claimed that a writer who misleads a subject will ultimately lose respect in the field and, in time, will likely be injured by his own deception.

THE JURORS

On Thursday, August 13, 1987, after six weeks of trial, Judge Rea read the six-person civil jury their instructions, asking them to specifically answer thirty-six questions toward resolution of the case. He advised them that he would be absent for a week while attending the Ninth Circuit Court's Judges Conference in Hawaii, and if they reached a verdict the federal magistrate would keep it sealed until his return.

In voting on the initial issue—whether MacDonald had fulfilled his contractual obligations to provide McGinniss with the information needed to write the book—the jurors stood 5 to 1 in MacDonald's favor. The disclaimer was juror Lucille Dillon, a small, prim, middle-aged woman. And because of Dillon, the decisions could go no further.

Some of the jurors later complained that Dillon, having read *Fatal Vision* as a court requirement, had decided that Jeffrey MacDonald was a cold-blooded murderer, and for that reason she would not discuss the case. Other jurors said she either retired to the bathroom to read the newspaper, or she sat by the window and refused to consider the evidence, or complained about the arguing giving her a headache. A male juror later said Dillon told him, "I don't believe any of MacDonald's witnesses were telling the truth, but all of Joe's witnesses were true."

Jurors later said that when pressed to discuss the letters McGinniss had written to MacDonald, Dillon refused, claiming that authors must have freedom.

By Monday, August 17, the jury realized something must be done. Jury foreperson Elizabeth Lane sent a note to the federal magistrate saying that Dillon had sided with McGinniss and wouldn't consider any of the issues. The magistrate placed a long-distance call to Judge Rea in Hawaii, and the judge ordered the jury to continue its deliberations.

When the judge returned to court on Friday, however, there had been no change in the situation. At a bench conference he suggested replacing Lucille Dillon with alternate juror Jackie Beria, but Kornstein opposed the move. The nature of the note to the magistrate had indicated things weren't going well for McGinniss in jury deliberations.

As the jury filed back into the courtroom, Lucille Dillon kept her attention on Joe McGinniss, smiling at the author as she walked across the front of the jury box toward her seat on the end of the first row. When she reached her place she smiled even more broadly at him and dipped her head and shoulders in a delicate curtsy before taking her seat.

Judge Rea polled the jurors and asked them whether they really believed they had reached an impasse. Each agreed they had. The judge voiced his regrets, but said he had no choice but to declare a mistrial. When he adjourned court, the jurors stood up and filed out. Lucille

Dillon looked toward McGinniss and smiled at him again. McGinniss nodded his head toward her and smiled back.

MacDonald immediately announced he would force McGinniss to face a new jury. Kornstein, in turn, filed a motion asking Judge Rea to throw MacDonald's case out of court, claiming that "McGinniss's book is a monument to the art of nonfiction journalism. The thoroughness of his research, the substantial truth of his assertions, and the soundness of his opinions were established beyond question at the trial." It is not clear whether Kornstein meant the criminal trial against MacDonald or the civil trial against McGinniss.

Nevertheless, Judge Rea ruled MacDonald had ample cause to sue McGinniss again. Upon this announcement, McGinniss again asked MacDonald to settle out of court, this time offering $325,000. Bostwick drove to the prison at Terminal Island to deliver the news of McGinniss's new offer. He told MacDonald that if he continued with the suit, they'd have to wait at least a year before the new trial could be scheduled; then, even if they won, he'd have to fight hard in the appeals courts for at least another year before receiving any funds. Bostwick advised him to accept McGinniss's offer. MacDonald, whose defense coffers were once again depleted, agreed.

On November 30, 1987, McGinniss's insurance company settled the case for the author for just under a third of a million dollars. McGinniss announced that he had paid the money not because he was admitting any wrongdoing, but because he wanted to get the "MacDonald mess" behind him once and for all.

After Judge Rea announced the mistrial, reporters interviewed the civil trial jurors. Most jurors said they had ignored any question of whether MacDonald was guilty or innocent of murder, but instead had focused on the matter of fraud, being particularly concerned about the content of McGinniss's letters to MacDonald. One juror said that in his own mind he had determined that McGinniss had, indeed, misled MacDonald and that MacDonald would have been due damages. Since the deliberations had not proceeded, he said, he had not thought far enough ahead to be concerned about the amount of damages. Another juror, on the other hand, had thought about it, and said she would have awarded MacDonald "millions of dollars to set an example for authors to show they can't tell an untruth" to their subjects.

One juror concluded that the MacDonald he had watched at the civil trial wasn't the same MacDonald the author had described in the book.

Alternate juror Jackie Beria, who sat through the entire trial, stated that while McGinniss presented MacDonald as a monster in his book, it "was clear that the monster in *Fatal Vision* really was Joe McGinniss. He was the character he tried to make his readers believe MacDonald was."

After the mistrial I encountered McGinniss standing in the hallway talking to a group of young journalism students. I hadn't seen most of these kids at the trial, so I wasn't surprised that they didn't take exception to McGinniss telling them that "This was a real victory for free speech."

I listened for a moment, then, against my better judgment, moved nearer the circle of youths surrounding him, and I said, "But, don't you think you shouldn't have misquoted the medical books?"

He turned quickly toward me and said, "I didn't."

"Joe, the judge asked you to read from the books you said you'd quoted, then they projected your words from *Fatal Vision* onto the screen. They had been changed in favor of your drug theory."

"In my mind," McGinniss said, "I didn't misquote."

"Joe, I was there."

"I don't want to talk to you," he said. He turned on his heel and stalked down the marbled hallway. His admirers turned angry faces on me, then, in a flurry, charged away to seek him out again.

Janet Malcolm

At the end of the civil trial in Los Angeles, both sides had announced victory. McGinniss claimed he had stood up for First Amendment rights; MacDonald said that McGinniss's admissions on the stand proved the author had committed fraud. McGinniss went back home, while MacDonald returned to prison.

Back on the East Coast, McGinniss and his lawyer, Kornstein, began a publicity effort to turn the tables on MacDonald. They attempted to present McGinniss as a victim of a false lawsuit, inviting various journalists to write on the subject. Apparently, only one journalist, Janet Malcolm, a writer for the *New Yorker*, accepted the invitation.

She interviewed both McGinniss and MacDonald over many months in addition to studying the court record and exhibits. The result was a lengthy two-part magazine article in the *New Yorker* which she later published as a book.[35] Malcolm's work sent shock waves through the media industry, not so much because of her findings about the McGinniss trial itself, but because of her bold claim that every person interviewed by a writer ends up being victimized. Malcolm used the relationship that developed between Jeffrey MacDonald and Joe McGinniss as the case in point, severely criticizing the author's behavior in that relationship. Although she declined to explore the issue of MacDonald's guilt or innocence, she made it clear that McGinniss had spread a blight that would never dissolve, a pestilence that would continue to feed like cancer on the character of Jeffrey MacDonald. "Should MacDonald actually get a new trial, and even turn out to be innocent," she wrote, "he will be able to rebuild his life, but he will not be able to efface McGinniss's story."[36]

The Kassab Suit

Even though the six-week civil trial had revealed a markedly different story than the one published in *Fatal Vision*, Alfred and Mildred Kassab refused to accept the thought that Jeffrey MacDonald was to gain from the outcome. So Mildred Kassab sued MacDonald under California state statutes for the amount of the McGinniss settlement, claiming that MacDonald had no right to profit from his crime.[37] In deference to MacDonald and his attorney Gary Bostwick, Judge Edward Ross convened civil court in January 1989 in the warden's conference room at Terminal Island Federal Correctional Institution in San Pedro, south of Los Angeles.

To MacDonald's satisfaction, the name of Joe McGinniss, rather than his own, was at the center of the four-day affair. "It's a shame that McGinniss isn't here," Judge Ross remarked. He told the gathering that, according to his reading of the case records, McGinniss had not only defrauded MacDonald but also had lied to the Kassabs while trying to gain their cooperation against MacDonald. Ross likened McGinniss's conduct to that of "a thief in the night," then he corrected himself, saying, "I guess a thief in the night wouldn't see you. He is more of a con man than he is a thief." Judge Ross told the court that "the action by MacDonald against McGinniss was proper, it was not a sham, it was based on clearly discernible evidence, and should have proceeded."

The remainder of the brief trial consisted of the arguments about who was entitled to the nearly one-third million dollars MacDonald recently had been awarded from McGinniss. After listening to both sides, Judge Ross evoked shades of Solomon and apportioned the money in such amounts that neither party would benefit from an expensive appeal. As grandmothers of the slain children, Mildred Kassab and Dorothy MacDonald were awarded shares, the MacDonald lawyers were then paid their fees, and Jeffrey MacDonald was allowed to keep the rest. Neither side filed an appeal.

With the civil trial against him ended, and despite his condemnation by Judge Ross in the Kassab action, McGinniss continued his insistence that he had been a victim of MacDonald's vengeance. In 1989, Signet published a new paperback edition of *Fatal Vision*. In the book's new epilogue, McGinniss again made his claim that the civil trial had been an attack on his First Amendment rights, and that Judge Rea just hadn't been smart enough to understand that this was a First Amendment case. McGinniss told his readers that during the civil trial Judge Rea had allowed inquiry into the alleged falsehoods in the book, but, McGinniss wrote, "none was found."

McGinniss's Admission

The motive for Joe McGinniss's conclusions in the new epilogue is difficult to assess in light of a statement the author had made during preparations for MacDonald's suit against him. McGinniss's flagship theory, of course, had been his personal "discovery" that MacDonald had taken too many diet pills and had thus suffered a psychotic break which resulted in the murders. In a pre-trial deposition, Bostwick had queried McGinniss about these drug-psychosis claims. McGinniss explained to Bostwick that it had been just a theory, that he had to give his readers more than just the "rehash" of the trial. Then Bostwick asked him a curious question. He asked Joe McGinniss if he personally believed his own theory.

The writer said that he wasn't there, he didn't witness the murders.

Bostwick asked the question again. "Are you personally convinced that the explanation that you suggested with respect to the diet pills and the psychotic snap actually happened?"

Since this was the dramatic backbone of McGinniss's book, the answer Bostwick received was monumental. Joe McGinniss finally replied, "I'm not convinced that it actually happened."[38]

PART
FOUR

The Great Writ

13

Appeal

Even as Harvey Silverglate wrote the brief for the Court of Appeals for the Fourth Circuit, the appeals process itself was being transformed in a fundamental way. And it worried him.

For many years the legal system had attempted to protect innocent people, via the writ of habeas corpus, against incarceration and execution. These same protections were extended to anyone, innocent or guilty, who had been convicted by illegal means. The philosophy behind protecting the due-process rights of even the guilty is driven by the concern that if a government can lie and cheat to convict people they "think" are guilty, that government also possesses the unfettered power to employ lies and false evidence against anyone they want to "get." Due-process rights, then, are fundamental to simple political freedom.

But, as might be expected, criminal defendants sometimes abused the writ. For example, a prisoner condemned to the gallows might file an appeal on only a single issue, deliberately holding back a second item to be used later. This ploy served to keep the hangman at bay. To prevent this, legal architects gradually redefined the habeas writ early in the twentieth century to require a prisoner to demonstrate that he filed his appeal as soon as possible after he found the new evidence and hadn't held it back to thwart justice.

But there were abuses of the system by the police authorities, too, and in the 1950s a more liberal Supreme Court felt it necessary to broaden due-process rights for defendants. Zealous police in various parts of the country were being accused of ignoring the rights of citizenry to make convictions. For instance, black or Jewish defendants sometimes found themselves at the mercy of "old-boy" justice. So the high court enacted strict rules to discourage coerced confessions, and to prevent an accused person from being questioned against his will without legal protections due him through an attorney advocate. It also strengthened search-and-seizure laws, which forced police to follow policies restricting their interference in private lives.

To some, these rules seemed good. They attempted to keep police and eager prosecutors from violating basic rights. But other people felt that the burden on the police and the courts, especially during a time when the crime rate was rising, was too much. Under those revised rules, if a convicted person could prove in a habeas writ that an officer or prosecutor had violated a procedural rule, the courts held that the prisoner was due immediate relief from his criminal sentence, this without any question about his actual innocence or guilt.

Not surprisingly, these new "rights" were unpopular among some policemen, prosecutors, and judges, who complained that their hands were being tied and the system was becoming "soft on criminals." In short, under the new rules, they could not convict some people they "knew" were guilty.

The arguments over the habeas appeal writ heated up during a time that rights violations and procedural error led to more and more cases being overturned because of prosecutorial error or outright cheating by the authorities. On April 17, 1991, Linda Greenhouse reported in the *New York Times* that "40% of all death penalties [in state courts] are overturned as a result of a Federal judge finding constitutional error in the conviction or a sentence." This angered conservatives, who saw these reversals as a fundamental hindrance to law enforcement's efforts to execute murderers. The Supreme Court's insistence that police adhere to these strict procedures was being regarded by some powerful people, including some Supreme Court justices, as an undeserved sanctuary for the guilty. Drug dealers, for example, with the money to pay clever lawyers, might beat the system even though they might be guilty of the charge brought against them. The Supreme Court majority nevertheless remained steadfast, throughout the fifties, sixties, and seventies, still interpreting these procedural requirements as a protection of basic freedoms. They considered it better that some criminals go free than an innocent person be punished wrongly. In the parlance of the day, as some saw it, the legal pendulum had swung to the left.

But critics of the high court grew more numerous, and Presidents Nixon, Reagan, and Bush appointed conservative justices to fill vacancies in the Supreme Court. This new Court, on balance, exhibited a hard attitude toward appeals. While Supreme Court decisions were not strictly split along political lines, certain trends did appear, and defendants and their lawyers saw some procedural rights taken away as the judicial mood began to swing back to the right.

At one time, for example, it had been illegal for a police officer to stop and search a vehicle unless he could prove that he had reason to suspect wrongdoing. A policeman could not, for instance, stop only long-haired teenagers to search their cars, indiscriminately and without cause, simply because they belong to a group that policemen might consider suspect. In 1990 the high court altered this requirement while reviewing a Michigan case involving random roadblocks designed to locate, identify, and arrest intoxicated motorists.[1] Liberal jurists immediately complained, unfruitfully, that this decision damages the Fourth Amendment prohibition against illegal search and seizure. The great pendulum of justice moved further right, and kept moving.

The Supreme Court ruled in 1990, in an opinion that shocked many, that coerced confessions are not necessarily inadmissible in court.[2] Still another conservative decision allows prosecutors to withhold from grand juries evidence which might show the defendant to be truly innocent, for grand juries are now seen by the Court as investigative, not judicial, bodies. Conservatives applauded the change, arguing that prosecutors need this power to fight the war on drugs and related crime. So the system moved still further to the right.

The conservative majority on the Court, having become a formidable power by the end of the eighties, made an effort to put a stop to what it considered frivolous appeals, which included, in their opinions, most second appeals. Chief Justice William Rehnquist, tired of cases being overturned, had appointed a committee of judges to prepare the Powell report, which recommended to Congress that the 1990 crime bill include vigorous new legislation which would virtually eliminate second habeas appeals. But a Democratic Congress would have no part of the plan, fearing that under such a rule, once someone is convicted, new forensic and witness evidence, or evidence of government wrongdoing, would not earn a new trial even for a defendant who might actually be innocent. Many liberal congressman had bitter memories of police stopping "hippies," or blacks, or teens, and planting evidence such as marijuana or weapons and getting convictions for long jail terms. Under the Rehnquist-Powell plan, those defendants would have little chance of righting the wrongs against them.

A majority of Congress, voicing concerns that the Rehnquist-Powell effort represented a thrust at the heart of judicial fairness, felt it would destroy protections erected over centuries of judicial and legislative progress. They tossed out the entire package.

McCleskey v. Zant

Rehnquist struck back, as prophesied by some, at the next available opportunity. In the Supreme Court decision *McCleskey v. Zant*, on April 16, 1991, the Court executed a hard right turn, and proved that it could create new law—without Congress. In *McCleskey* the justices made it almost impossible for claimants to receive a second appeal hearing even if they had discovered new evidence, or had found proof that the government had withheld evidence, or otherwise had violated their procedural rights.

In this decision, which hit liberal circles like a declaration of ideological war, the Supreme Court ruled 6–3 to deny the petition of Warren McCleskey, a black man who had been convicted in 1978 of killing a police officer during a robbery. An inmate in an adjacent cell had testified in McCleskey's trial that McCleskey had bragged to him about killing the policeman. The judge allowed the informant's evidence and it led to McCleskey's conviction.

McCleskey's first habeas petition had been denied, and he remained on Georgia's death row. Before his execution date, however, his attorney discovered that the prosecution had set him up, using another suspected lawbreaker as a stooge. The authorities had purposely shifted this helpful inmate to the cell next to McCleskey, with instructions that he report anything self-incriminating he might hear McCleskey say. Obviously, in such arrangements, something is usually offered in return for a good report. But at trial the authorities failed to reveal their plan to the jurors, and the planted inmate gave devastating testimony condemning

McCleskey as if he hadn't been placed there precisely for that purpose, and as if he were reporting his information out of desire to do right.

After McCleskey's attorney learned about this secret and, at that time, illegal plot between the snitch and the government authorities, he filed a new appeal based upon this withheld information which had come from a compromised witness. The defense lawyer could now claim that the snitch's testimony might have been a lie told to gain favors for himself. Also, at the time of this appeal, by the rules of the game then, an unfair prosecution had occurred. The appeal showed that an alleged lawbreaker gained favors from officials by agreeing to spy on a man they were trying to convict, knowing precisely the type of information the officials were seeking, and then subsequently earning his favors by supplying that information. The rules have held that if testimony is acquired in this manner, the jury must be told about it so as to decide if it is trustworthy.

To McCleskey's lawyer, the important factor was that the charade finally had been discovered, and that this violation of McCleskey's constitutional rights would stave off the execution and gain him a new and now fairer trial. To the ruling faction of the Supreme Court, however, the violation itself was considered inconsequential, as was the possibility that the snitch could be lying. To the Court the *timing* of the defense discovery of the ploy was the issue of importance. The Supreme Court ruled that McCleskey's lawyer should have worked harder to unmask the violation sooner, in time to include it with his earlier habeas petition; and since he failed to do so, McCleskey now must pay the price decided by the jury at trial even though those jurors never heard that the damning testimony was bought, and they never had an opportunity to determine whether that bought testimony could be trusted. The Court decided McCleskey's death sentence must be carried out, and the operable principle wasn't that the prosecutor hadn't done wrong, but that the defense hadn't discovered it in time. Law, in this new philosophy, wasn't made for man; man, to paraphrase a borrowed sentiment, was now considered made for the law.

This new Supreme Court precedent worried Harvey Silverglate because, as in *McCleskey*, this was Dr. MacDonald's second habeas appeal. The new rule hadn't even existed when McCleskey went to trial, of course, yet McCleskey would die without a full hearing because of the rule. And that new principle hadn't even been in effect when McCleskey, or MacDonald for that matter, made their first appeals. Yet the "Johnny come lately" rule now left McCleskey awaiting execution on death row, condemned by what may well have been another person's lie. The Supreme Court ruling had disintegrated a crucial protection from government shenanigans, and Silverglate feared MacDonald might also fall victim to this new roadblock to justice.

When the details about *McCleskey* were published, many people, including some judges, registered bitter complaints. In a newspaper editorial[3] Judge Stephen Reinhardt,[4] himself a court of appeals judge, denounced the decision as an attack on basic human rights, rights that had been wrested from the totalitarian state over centuries of effort. Others complained that, in making this new "law," the Court had usurped legislative power that had been reserved specifically for Congress. But the loudest cry Chief Justice Rehnquist would hear came from no less than a fellow justice of the Supreme Court.

Justice Thurgood Marshall, one of the three Supreme Court justices who had disagreed with the majority in *McCleskey*, wrote a blistering dissent, focusing in part on the questionable reliability of the government's informer against Warren McCleskey. Justice Marshall pointed out that since the informing inmate's testimony against McCleskey was arranged for and, arguably, paid for, that McCleskey might not have said what the inmate claimed he said, and he might, in fact, be innocent of the killing. Justice Marshall had other reasons for believing McCleskey might not have committed the crime. Marshall reminded the court that McCleskey had denied being the person who shot the policeman, and, even though McCleskey did own a pearl-handled handgun whose caliber matched the fatal bullet, another member of the robbery gang admitted that he himself had carried the gun "for weeks at a time." Still another witness had testified to seeing *only* this second man carrying the gun, not McCleskey. Justice Marshall feared that the McCleskey ruling against second habeas appeals might have been decided, ironically and incredibly, in the case of a man who was actually innocent.

Marshall especially was angered that the Court ruled McCleskey's attorneys should have found out sooner that the state had secretly arranged for the snitch's testimony. Regarding this lack of "due diligence" on the part of McCleskey's attorneys, Justice Marshall reminded the court that the lawyers *had*, in fact, "interviewed the assistant district attorney, various jailers, and other government officials responsible" for placing the cooperative inmate next to McCleskey's cell, and, during these interviews, all of these authorities, claiming to speak truth, denied any knowledge of an agreement between the inmate and the state. In short, Justice Marshall pointed out that these authorities had lied to secure a conviction. That, under the earlier rules, would not have been deemed fair unless disclosed to the jury.

"Against this background of deceit," Marshall wrote, the state's withholding the facts of the matter "assumes critical importance." Since McCleskey's lawyers didn't try hard enough to "pierce the State's veil of deception," Marshall continued, the courts' decision "creates an incentive for state officials to engage in this very type of misconduct."

Justices John Paul Stevens and Harry A. Blackmun joined Marshall in his written dissent, that *McCleskey v. Zant* "departs drastically" from precedents laid down over past centuries and that it is "an unjustifiable assault on the Great Writ." Marshall added, "Ironically, the majority seeks to defend its doctrinal innovation on the ground that it will promote respect for the 'rule of law.' Obviously, respect for the rule of law must start with those who are responsible for pronouncing the law."

Marshall closed by saying that the *McCleskey* ruling actually "rewards state misconduct and deceit. Whatever 'abuse of the writ' today's decision is designed to avert pales in comparison with the majority's own abuse of the norms that inform the proper judicial function. I dissent."

Warren McCleskey, whether guilty or not, was executed on September 25, 1991.

Even though *McCleskey* struck fear into the MacDonald defense team, they were, at first, cautiously hopeful about one thing. The Supreme Court had promised an exception to this prohibition against second appeals. Even if the defendant failed to include the evidentiary claim in his first appeal, the federal court is allowed to entertain the second habeas petition if, and only if, in the court's view, the new evidence shows that the defendant is actually innocent of the crime and that a miscarriage of justice has occurred. On that provision, Silverglate surmised, MacDonald might win, for in Silverglate's opinion, the government's theory of MacDonald's guilt was manufactured by a malicious interpretation of the crime scene, by an exclusion of much evidence in MacDonald's favor, by withholding knowledge that the CID and FBI lab tests reported different findings on the same evidence, and by clever manipulation of physical items.

The Supreme Court soon encountered an opportunity to prove that their *McCleskey* promise had been made in good faith, that evidence of innocence, whenever it was found, would gain a claimant a hearing. The lawyers of a Virginia coal miner, Ronald Coleman, found new evidence that death row inmate Coleman had been somewhere else at the time of his sister-in-law's murder. They learned that another person had been heard talking about committing the murder. And they learned that a semen sample of a second party may have been collected from the victim's body. These things contradicted the prosecution's theory of the case, and the government's in court. Therefore, the defense attorneys, banking on the Supreme Court's new promise in *McCleskey*, filed an appeal to have this new evidence considered—but they filed thirty-three days after the judge signed the conviction order. That proved disastrous, for under Virginia law such a document must be filed within thirty days of the judge's order. The lawyers were three days late. Ronald Coleman, like Warren McCleskey, was executed without an evidentiary hearing to examine possibly exculpatory new findings. Predictably, conservatives shed few tears, and liberals howled in dissent.

The Court faced another opportunity to prove that new evidence of innocence really mattered under the new habeas system. Lionel Herrera was convicted of murdering a Texas policeman in 1981. His lawyers found strong evidence that the policeman may have been killed by Herrera's brother, Raul, who had since died. They filed a habeas petition and faced government lawyers who argued, straight-faced, that it would not be unconstitutional for the state to execute a person who was actually innocent. This statement, which was emblazoned in headlines across the country, echoed the sentiments of Justice Sandra Day O'Connor in her comments about *McCleskey*, that these were state's-rights issues and the federal government, including the Supreme Court, has no business looking over the state judge's shoulders.

The United States Supreme Court turned down Herrera. Even without an evidentiary hearing to explore the factuality of his claims the majority decided out of hand that the new evidence was no good. Like the claims of McCleskey and Coleman, the courts ruled that this information should have been presented earlier. The Supreme Court, in turn, found that it was the place of the governor of the state to grant clemency in state cases, that the federal government had no business in such affairs. Historic protections had been removed. Herrera was left to await execution while the Supreme Court simply stepped out of the picture to rest on a new doctrine which allowed the states to continue executions in spite of the procedural transgressions of prosecutors, errors which had overturned 40 percent of the recent capital cases.

Many saw this as sloppy justice, as an abrogation by the Court of the solemn promise they'd made in their *McCleskey* ruling, a promise to hear the second appeal of someone who might actually be innocent. How would the Court know one might be innocent, critics asked, unless they granted a hearing into the factuality of the new evidence? A refusal to grant such a hearing was viewed by many defense attorneys as a clear signal from the now powerful conservative Court to the state judicial systems that they no longer had to worry so much about procedural errors. The guarantee to hear second habeas petitions in cases where factual innocence might be indicated was seen by many legal observers as a hollow promise offered more for the public than as an actual standard for the system.

In short, many believed that the Supreme Court had become the protector of an errant state court system, and it had abdicated its historical role as a defender of the rights of the individual against clearly demonstrated excesses of the state. Justice Harry Blackmun was so troubled by the *Herrera* decision that he read his dissent publicly before the Court, and, shockingly, pronounced the majority decision as "perilously close to murder." Blackmun, for one, had had enough.

Apparently others felt the same way. We saw a Mike Luckovich political cartoon in the January 28, 1993, edition of the *San Francisco Chronicle* following the *Herrera* decision. It depicted a man strapped into an electric chair. Nearby stood a robed judge with his eager hand on the switch. The condemned man, face twisted, beads of sweat on his brow, holds in his hand a document labeled, "Late Evidence That Proves My Innocence."

The judge pulls the switch anyway, saying "Show it to God."

Harvey Silverglate claimed that this "so-called provision to consider cases in which evidence might point towards innocence so far seems nothing more than the Supreme Court's media package to put a humane face on a grotesque ruling. They used the promise to get the votes to condemn McCleskey and establish the new precedent. Their real concern was to clear the dockets and to stop appeals which embarrassed the system and lessened its power." Silverglate further explained that to do this the Court must assume, without full review, that *all* the cases affected by *McCleskey*, both state and federal, are about guilty defendants, which clearly cannot be the case since mistakes can be made and are made in the system. "Due process has been cast to the wind," Silverglate said. "We simply cannot turn our backs on habeas petitions." He called the Court's claimed concern about actual innocence "a cruel joke."

"In the past," Silverglate commented as he prepared his appeals arguments, "after finding such explosive suppressed evidence as the unmatched black wool on a victim and on the murder weapon, and after finding the unmatched wig hair, also suppressed, not to mention the foreign hair in Colette's hand, and the other things, we would have been assured of a new trial, no matter when we found it, either before or after the first appeal, if we could show that we didn't hold it back just to harass the court or to ward off punishment. But not after *McCleskey*," Silverglate points out. "Now, we'll be fighting very hard just to get the habeas court to let us have an evidentiary hearing to put Murtagh and the lab techs on the stand under oath to ask them what happened here and why they didn't allow the jurors to see evidence of this nature."

Silverglate indeed faced an uncertain battle, for now an appealing defendant must prove to a very resistant judge, before he ever reaches a jury of peers, that he is actually innocent. And he might have to prove it without the power to bring his evidence and witnesses into an evidentiary hearing, and without the ability to cross-examine them under oath, as he would be allowed to do in a trial by jury. Without guarantee of a hearing or a trial by jury, the defense lawyer may now only write his claims in a habeas writ, then make a short, possibly only a thirty-minute, presentation to the judges. The defense attorney's fear is that a judge might simply say that he is not personally convinced by the new or subsequently withheld evidence, then, untroubled by the prosecution's misbehavior as in the McCleskey cover-up, arbitrarily refuse a hearing to examine the issue further. That judge will simply deny the habeas petition.

Arguments before the Fourth Circuit

As the defense team neared the date for oral arguments on their brief in front of the Fourth Circuit justices in Richmond, after having been denied by Judge Dupree in Raleigh the summer before, they were painfully aware that the principles inherent in *McCleskey* had already bitten MacDonald once. Judge Dupree, ironically the very judge who refused to rule that Murtagh turn over those critical lab notes during trial, now allowed Murtagh's *McCleskey* argument to carry, that MacDonald should have found out about the black wool and the wig hair sooner, no matter that it hadn't been given Segal at trial, no matter that Silverglate now saw the items as corroboration of the stories of MacDonald, Stoeckley, Mitchell, and Perry.

So, if the conviction wasn't reversible because Murtagh didn't turn over the lab notes, the defense team would have to prove to these judges that MacDonald was factually innocent. Therefore, Silverglate had designed his brief in an attempt to destroy what he called the "myth" of the evidence of MacDonald's guilt. In this brief he reminded the three-judge panel in Richmond of the confessions of the Stoeckley group. He also called their attention to the scientific problems with much of the government's evidence, such as the pajama top folding experiment performed at the expense of earlier laboratory findings. He reminded them of the lost piece of skin, the lost bloody syringe, the foreign brown hair in Colette's hand, the unmatched black wool fibers, and the unmatched blond wig hairs. These things and others, Silverglate hoped, should cause the court to wonder whether MacDonald might be innocent after all.

In this new brief, Silverglate also gave considerable attention to the "Puretz memo," which he insisted was nothing less than a blueprint for the cover-up. This telltale memo, he said, actually presented Brian Murtagh with an "out" from the dangers of withholding exculpatory evidence. It was evident that this plan went into action, Silverglate argued in his appeal brief, when only days before trial Murtagh suddenly allowed Segal and Thornton into the jail cell with the boxes. Silverglate charged that after Murtagh had fought hard for years to keep Segal away from the evidence, now it suddenly seemed important to Murtagh, just before trial, that "the defense at least get into the same cell as the evidence. Why this sudden change of heart?" After all, Judge Dupree had continually ruled with Murtagh on this issue. Why did Murtagh switch after having won his point? If it was out of fairness, why didn't he just turn over the lab notes, point at their mention of the black wool on the murder club, show Segal where Glisson had noted the finding of blond wig hair, take Segal down to the jail cell and get the box out of the stack, open it and say, "Does this speak to your client's claims?"

That, of course, didn't happen. And Silverglate charged that Murtagh's real purpose was not disclosure, but to get Segal into the cell with the evidence boxes only to satisfy the letter of the law, only to say later, "He was in the cell with the evidence; it's his fault if he didn't find it." In essence, if the defense ever got its hands on the lab notes and learned about the black wool, the wig hair, and other things, Murtagh could claim that even though he had refused to turn over the handwritten notes that mentioned these things, he didn't really suppress evidence, for it had been in those boxes in the jail cell. And even though the official published laboratory reports excluded the exculpatory evidence that had appeared in the handwritten bench notes, Murtagh still hadn't suppressed anything for he had, after all, given Segal an opportunity to find the physical evidence itself that day in that jail cell—which is exactly what Murtagh had claimed in the government's written response to the habeas petition before Judge Dupree. And, Silverglate pointed out in his brief at the Fourth Circuit Court, this is what the pre-trial Puretz memo had advised Murtagh he could do.

Knowing the government lawyers would press their points at the upcoming oral arguments before the Fourth Circuit, and understanding the current mood of the now heavily conservative system, Silverglate felt his only chance was to fight very hard for an evidentiary hearing, during which he would have the right, finally, to lab-test the evidence, and employ subpoena power. That power would allow him to call Murtagh and Blackburn and all the lab techs to the stand and examine them about each item they had handled and ask why they eliminated from the published reports most of the evidence in the handwritten notes which would have been welcomed by Segal at trial, evidence which supported MacDonald's account of events.

To that purpose, Harvey Silverglate and Alan Dershowitz proceeded to Richmond to plead their claims in oral argument. Because they felt the *McCleskey* decision had destroyed the very soul of habeas procedure, they approached the appeals court with fear and trembling. As they entered the court to advocate Jeffrey MacDonald's innocence and to ask for an evidentiary hearing, they felt they were walking into a lions' den, and the lions had just eaten God.

On Wednesday, February 5, 1992, Harvey Silverglate, Alan Dershowitz, Phil Cormier, and a small army of attorneys and paralegal assistants carried a half-dozen evidence cases three blocks from their hotel to a federal courtroom in downtown Richmond, Virginia. The morning marked a cool and crisp winter workday in the bustling city, yet eager spectators filled the courtroom and spilled over into the hall. They were bullied to silence by bailiffs, who were, in turn, eyed coldly by the three judges, Francis O. Murnaghan, Jr., John D. Butzner, Jr., and David Russell.

Brian Murtagh appeared cheerful as he sat silently at the prosecutor's table. He was there only to observe the government's presentation. This alone was a radical change from those arguments held the previous June before Judge Dupree where Murtagh took an active part. Appearing on Murtagh's behalf this day was the Justice Department attorney, John F. DePue, who had shared this task with him throughout the various post-trial MacDonald appeal arguments.

Inasmuch as the habeas appeal was imposed by the defense, Harvey Silverglate, a balding, bearded man with sad, gentle eyes, was first to address the court, informing it of the manner in which his side planned to use its allotted time. He would argue the merits of the case, that Jeffrey MacDonald's constitutional rights were violated by Murtagh's suppression of exculpatory evidence which, had it been presented to the jury, likely "would have gained him an acquittal."

Silverglate claimed Murtagh should have turned over the specific exculpatory evidence when he received it, not hide it, then sit back and let Segal try to find it after Judge Dupree's ruling effectively prohibited lab testing and specifically kept Segal from seeing the lab notes. For Murtagh to now claim that Segal's trip to the jail cell constituted legal discovery is "a cruel cop-out."

Silverglate gave a short summary of past court actions in the case before addressing the subject of the blond wig hair and the way lab notes concerning the hair had been withheld. "What is critical to us," he told the court, "is that the exculpatory evidence from our point of view was not the physical exhibits, it was the government's examination report of what that exhibit was."[5]

But Judge Russell preferred to focus on the physical material itself, not on the fact that Murtagh did not turn over the handwritten notes which finally revealed the wig hair, black wool, and other things. Silverglate found this troublesome because the government had never claimed that they had made these notes available at trial. The government's failure to provide the exculpatory notes *was* the issue, not the actual physical items which the defense still had never lab-tested in twenty-one years of litigation. But Judge Russell, instead, asked whether the prosecution had given the defense an opportunity to examine the blond synthetic hair—which, of course, touched on the Segal visit to the boxes of evidence in the jail cell.

Silverglate conceded to Judge Russell that an opportunity "of sorts" had been provided, an opportunity that required the defense first to find the item, which had not been offered through normal discovery channels as it should have been. He explained the situation hypothetically, saying, "Had I been trial counsel, and had the expert found this needle in the haystack, I'm sure I would have asked him to examine it." Silverglate went back to his original viewpoint. "But bear in mind that the really powerful exculpatory evidence here was the government's own concession [in the withheld lab note] that this was a wig."

He pointed out that the government, even at this late date, was trying to "disown" Janice Glisson's exculpatory lab note about wig hair. Even though she specifically called the long, blond, synthetic fibers wig hair, the government was attempting to persuade the court, now that the defense had found the lab note, that the hair could only have come from a doll or a mannequin.

Judge Russell started back over it, saying, ". . . they've got an expert that said it is a piece of material and it well could have been something that came from a doll."

Silverglate acknowledged that the government expert had so claimed. Russell went on, "Your expert said it came from probably, came from a wig."

Silverglate shook his head. "No, not what our expert said—but it's what *their other* expert said." For two government experts, Janice Glisson and Michael Malone, two people on the same side, had indeed contradicted each other's conclusions. Both said the fibers were synthetic blond hair, but army lab tech Glisson said it came from a wig. The government's next expert, *after* MacDonald's people finally found out about the blond fiber, said, after the government team had come under fire, that it couldn't have come from a wig, it must be doll's hair.

But again Judge Russell missed the point. "Whoever it was," he said, "this is a battle of experts." It seemed that Russell had now dismissed Silverglate's central suppression issue as inconsequential, or impossible to understand.

So, Silverglate tried again, attempting to make the judge realize how important Janice Glisson would have been as a witness brought to the stand during trial in 1979 to explain her note about wig hair. The MacDonald defense "would have been in terrific shape," Silverglate said, "because we would have had a *government* forensic expert saying what we wanted to hear, rather than a *defense* expert." The jurors would have known that the government's own expert had said that blond wig hair existed at the scene of a murder for which a woman wearing a blond wig had confessed.

All of this, of course, had been explained in detail in the written brief presented to this appellate court on October 3, 1991, yet Russell challenged Silverglate as if the judge had no knowledge of the matter. Judge

Russell said, "She [Glisson] was there at the trial, you could've questioned her about this blond hair." This statement told Silverglate that the judge still hadn't understood that the defense hadn't been given the lab notes at trial.

"No, that's not true, Your Honor," Silverglate gasped, correcting the judge again.[6] He then explained how the prosecutors had qualified Glisson at trial only as an expert in blood work, and how the prosecutors had asked her nothing about her examination of hairs or fibers, as if she had not examined scores of hairs and fibers in this very case. Silverglate pointed out that by doing this, the prosecution escaped the requirement of turning over her notes on hairs and fibers to accompany her testimony.[7]

Russell asked, "Did you try to challenge her on the notes?" Russell, incredibly, *still* hadn't understood, or acted as if he hadn't yet heard, that the notes had been withheld.

"No," Silverglate said patiently, "because we had no idea that she had done fiber examinations, Your Honor. They put her on [the stand] only as an expert on blood, we now know that it was blood. If they had—"

"When did you find out that she had made an examination of the hair or whatever it was?"

Silverglate replied, "We found out in the 1983–1984 period that she had done this. This is long after the trial. We had no idea—"

Russell interrupted to ask a most uncomfortable question, "How long before you had your first habeas petition filed?"

"Not long before—about the same time."

The dreaded *McCleskey* decision had reared its head.

After a brief discussion as to whether the defense had sufficient knowledge of the synthetic hair to have used it during the first habeas corpus petition, Judge Russell came back to the point that he still hadn't grasped. He asked, "Well, were her notes not made available to you at the trial?"

"No, Your Honor," Silverglate said, his voice finally cracking in exasperation. "Not only were the notes not available at trial, but we had no idea that she even had done work in this area. That was the problem, she was qualified very narrowly. We now know why, because if she had been qualified more broadly—"

Russell interrupted again, this time to point out that a prosecutor would be expected to qualify an expert witness only to the degree needed for presentation of evidence. "They called her to do the blood work. What would they have called her for otherwise?" he asked. And again Silverglate tried to explain that the government lawyers called her to testify about something that wouldn't hurt their case, and they failed to qualify her in the area of fibers, which might have hurt them had Segal found out from her about the wig hair.

But by now, Silverglate's repeated attempts to explain the blond wig hair argument to Judge Russell had cost him most of his valuable time. Silverglate had done little more on the blond wig hair than get his arguments on record. With the clock ticking, he switched the focus to the black wool, and to its importance in pointing toward a suspect. "MacDonald we know was wearing pajamas," Silverglate said. "Stoeckley testified that she always wore black or dark purple clothing. So the evidence in the record is a lot closer to linking Stoeckley than it is to linking MacDonald, who didn't wear and wasn't wearing black at all."

Silverglate further suggested to the court that the existence of the laboratory notes evoked three questions. The first was, "Was the evidence suppressed? We know it wasn't turned over," Silverglate said, "there's no question about it. Judge Dupree so found; the government concedes."

Silverglate presented his second question. "Was the evidence exculpatory? Judge Dupree found it was exculpatory."

And, third, "Would it have influenced the jury? . . . obviously," Silverglate claimed, "had MacDonald possessed these lab notes at the time of trial, the case would have been an entirely different case. Just about any standard applicable to this powerful exculpatory evidence might have led to a different result."

Then Silverglate's time was up.

When Alan Dershowitz stood to address the court, he announced that he would press two points—that the government had abused the law, and that the abuse was reaching the courts at this late date because it had only recently been recognized, not because of a lack of diligence by defense attorneys in 1984. In offering this, Dershowitz defended the diligence of defense attorney Brian O'Neill, for the prosecution's strongest claim, under *McCleskey*, was that, even though Murtagh hadn't shared the information at trial, O'Neill should have found the black wool and wig hair sooner, and he should have made the current charges while attempting to gain a new trial back in 1984. Dershowitz told the court, "With all due respect, Your Honors, put yourself in a situation of having received ten thousand pages of handwritten or Xeroxed material, in which the government whether deliberately or inadvertently deflects the attention of the defendants from one hay stack to another, wherein the defendant was trying to find a needle."

Dershowitz then spoke of the wig hair about which Silverglate had struggled without visible success with Judge Russell. Dershowitz made it clear that O'Neill himself had never seen Janice Glisson's first laboratory note concerning the synthetic wig hair, that this note was reviewed by a paralegal assistant who failed to bring it to O'Neill's attention at the time, perhaps because the note was somewhat cryptic in that even Glisson in this first note seemed uncertain that it was wig hair. (She even placed a question mark in her notes after writing down her discovery.) Had O'Neill used this note in the 1984 appeal, the prosecution could easily have dismissed it by saying that the question mark indicated a guess, and the fiber had turned out not to be wig hair after all. The prosecution had employed this tactic with the piece of skin, and with the hair in Colette's hand. So, the first Glisson note was, in effect, nonconfirmatory, and would have been easily dismissed by the prosecution.

Dershowitz explained that since the blond wig hair itself was well hidden in that jail cell in a box labeled "Black and Grey Synthetic Hairs," and since only the nonconfirmatory note had been revealed in the 1983 FOIA, the real miracle occurred in 1990 when paralegal John Murphy[8] during a search of CID files in Baltimore CID headquarters stumbled upon the second note by Glisson which substantiated the existence of the wig hair.

Even after years of FOIA requests, this important lab note, one which left no doubt that Glisson had decided this was wig hair, still hadn't been turned over. This was the crucial *confirmatory* find, Dershowitz claimed, that resulted in the current defense challenge. And that find came years after the last appeal and should be considered new evidence.

Dershowitz next linked the synthetic blond hair to the wig-wearing Helena Stoeckley, rather than to the small, short-haired dolls owned by the MacDonald children. Dershowitz then turned quickly to the discovery of the black wool on Colette MacDonald and on the murder club and the failure of the prosecution to reveal those critical finds.

"The issue in this case, Your Honor," Dershowitz said, "is that the government came up with a new theory in 1990." Dershowitz was speaking now about the "transfer theory of locard," an argument the government never voiced in the case until the current appeal was filed in 1990. This theory, in essence, supposes that foreign items on an exhibit, such as clothing fibers on a dead body, might have gotten there not by direct contact with the initial source, in this example the wearer of the clothing, but through contact with an intermediating object, such as a shag rug. The clothing wearer visits the apartment and sheds clothing fibers; the fibers get caught up in the rug; and later the dying person rolls across the rug and the fibers adhere to the body. Under these circumstances there has been no direct contact between the clothing wearer and the dead person, despite the fact that the location of the fibers, to the uninformed, would imply such contact.

In Dershowitz's view there was a serious problem with the government's application of the transfer theory of locard to the black wool fibers and the wig hairs in the MacDonald case. The government knew that MacDonald's lawyers were trying to establish the existence of strangers at the murder scene, and therefore the presence of foreign black wool fibers on the murder weapon and on the victim of that weapon, and nowhere else in the home, was critical. If such fibers were found in these key places and on nothing else, therefore being foreign fibers, this would have been extremely useful to Segal at trial. And it would have been useful, since Stoeckley wore a blond wig, to have fibers that the CID lab tech Glisson called blond wig hairs. To Dershowitz it seemed self-serving for the government, when the wig hair and black wool, suppressed for years, were finally discovered via FOIA releases, to *now* claim that these fibers were transferred inadvertently from somewhere else, not from outside murderers, especially when no blond wig and no black wool clothing were found in the house by army and government investigators.

Dershowitz asked the three judges to analyze what the government seemed to be admitting by voicing this transfer theory of locard. "What they're saying is that they were only looking for evidence connecting *MacDonald* to the crime, and they were discarding evidence which could *not* be connected to MacDonald, *which was the crucial evidence of his innocence!*"

Fred Bost and I, observing Dershowitz's argument before the Fourth Circuit Court, saw no softening in the faces of the old justices, no lenient nodding in understanding, in fact, not one sign that they believed the government was wrong in claiming that anything foreign to MacDonald in the home had to be considered inconsequential to the case. Yet, to Bost and me, it seemed especially cruel to assume that MacDonald was guilty because nothing was found in the home to support his story of intruders or Stoeckley's story that they were there, when anything that supported these claims had been systematically removed from the typed reports, from the view of the defense lawyers, from the trial judge, and from the jurors.

Dershowitz moved on to the government's claims that Brian Murtagh at the time of trial knew nothing of the blond wig hair or the discovery that the black wool existed. The defense had traversed this ground extensively since the discovery of the fibers. They had learned that on February 9, 1979, while preparing for trial, Murtagh had requested more examinations, specifically an examination of debris from the wooden club. Murtagh subsequently denied before Judge Dupree in 1991 that he was ever informed of the results of his requests, results which showed the existence of black wool in these exhibits.[9]

Dershowitz offered that, on this issue, a double standard was being applied by the court. The government lawyers, he explained, were supposedly familiar with the evidence they controlled, yet they claimed they were totally unaware at trial of the existence of the blond wig hair and the black wool fibers on Colette's body and on the murder club, which had been revealed as a result of their own specific requests for lab testing. Yet despite this failure to know their own evidence, the courts continued to regard these *government* lawyers as being diligent. On the other hand, he pointed out, *defense* attorneys were now being accused by the courts of lacking required diligence because they, at trial, failed to dig out these very same government handwritten bench notes the contents of which the prosecutors now claimed ignorance—bench notes which the government lawyers adamantly refused to turn over to the defense attorneys before trial, during trial, and long after trial.

As Dershowitz pressed the issue of the prosecutors' knowledge of the lab notes on these exhibits, Judge Russell said, "They weren't trying to lie to anybody, I don't think. Were they?"

Dershowitz, seizing an opportunity to assist Silverglate's request for an evidentiary hearing on exactly this issue, responded, "We haven't had a hearing on it, Your Honor."

Russell said, "The only information—"

But this time it was Dershowitz who interrupted. He told how Judge Dupree during the hearing the summer before had summarily refused to allow any testimony of witnesses on any of the issues claimed by the defense, issues now being argued today. "We haven't had a hearing on that. We sought a hearing on Mr. Murtagh's good faith. The court [Judge Dupree] had said, 'I know Mr. Murtagh and he's been before me before. I make a finding of good faith.'" Dershowitz shook his head in disgust. "That's not the way a good-faith determination is made."

"Remember, your honor," Dershowitz said, "this case has been decided [at the district court level] without an evidentiary hearing. So you can't make a finding that there wasn't diligence—"

Now Russell interrupted. "You don't mean to say you're charging that Mr. Murtagh told a lie, are you?" he demanded.

"We are charging, and we have charged in our papers, that Mr. Murtagh engaged in a conspiracy to deflect attention away from this material," Dershowitz retorted angrily.

Judge Russell tossed up a hand in apparent anger, rolled his eyes, and threw his head back in an expression of disgust. As Dershowitz continued to argue this charge, the judge held his angry gaze steadfastly on the ceiling. Justice Russell refused to look at the fiery defense attorney as he breezed through the occurrences which he believed cast suspicion on Murtagh—the untrue stipulation, during the trial, about what lab tech Frier would be able to testify about, even though Frier was the man who found the black wool. Dershowitz recalled that Murtagh limited Glisson as a blood expert when she, also, knew a great deal about fibers and foreign hairs. He decried the Puretz memorandum, and he reminded the judges that Murtagh's team had placed the highly crucial blond wig hair in a mislabeled box.

Russell finally turned his gaze from the ceiling, and as he looked at Dershowitz, the judge's eyes were hostile and his voice was harsh. "You found out the *conspiracy* and you're going to indict the man now, is that your theory?"

"Your Honor, all we know is that—"

"You were diligent enough to do that," Russell retorted angrily, "but you were not diligent enough to find anything about this material?"

The damning spirit of the *McCleskey* decision hovered near, but Dershowitz stood his ground. "It's interesting that the court is willing to accuse [MacDonald's] lawyers of lack of diligence," he pointed out, "but is unwilling to have a hearing on whether or not that quote 'lack of diligence' was in some way generated by deliberate misconduct on the part of the government. . . ."

But Judge Russell had had enough. He cut Dershowitz off sharply. "Thank you very much," the judge barked. "Your time has expired."

The lead government lawyer, John DePue, a thin, blond, energetic man, summed up the prosecution's viewpoint. He told the judges, "The government's position both with respect to '*Brady*' and the 'abuse of the writ' issue can be summarized in a few short words—that defendants

either had, or had access to, each and every item of exculpatory information here at issue today, and elected not to take advantage of those
opportunities that were afforded them by the government."

As the defense lawyers saw things, this was exactly the legal move
uncovered for Murtagh by the pre-trial Puretz memo twelve years earlier.
DePue now addressed the "Catch-22" of that issue, telling the three appellate judges, "On June 19, 1979, the defense forensic expert, Dr. John
Thornton, was provided unfettered access to the government's evidence
repository for the purpose of selecting exhibits for his own forensic
analysis. It's also undisputed that within that evidence repository was
each and every item of exculpatory evidence that is at issue here."

DePue's statement ignored Segal's four-year battle to lab-test the evidence, and it ignored Dupree's ruling that all forensic testing had to be
completed in a matter of a few days. And he denied that the label on the
box containing the synthetic hair was meant to be misleading. He told
the court that if Thornton had opened that box, which Dershowitz had
pointed out was labeled "dark synthetic fibers," he would have found
inside it a mailer labeled "synthetic hair blond." These words were an
open appeal to the *McCleskey* decision again, that the defense lawyers
weren't diligent. DePue pressed *McCleskey* harder, arguing that it was
now too late to use the evidence in appeal. In short, it should have been
used in 1984, during the first habeas petition.

Sitting in the gallery listening to DePue's arguments, I looked over at
Fred. He shook his head, for Fred and I knew that these discoveries
couldn't have been used in the 1984 appeal because they were made
years after 1984. We knew this because Fred had been in on the discovery
of the handwritten Glisson note confirming the existence of the wig hairs.
I well remembered the memo from Ellen Dannelly after she found the
words "black wool" in the handwritten notes; and I was in the same room
with my wife when she established that these black wool fibers which
Dannelly had discovered might have been the same two fibers the army
had called blue cotton pajama fibers, the two fibers prosecutor Blackburn
had called the most important proof of MacDonald's guilt. So Fred and
I asked ourselves, how could MacDonald have presented evidence in
1984 that really wasn't discovered until five or six years later?

And, we thought, even if MacDonald's lawyers had been less than
diligent that day in the jail cell with the evidence, should MacDonald
die in prison for that? I was brought back from my musings as I heard

John DePue claim that this evidence didn't matter anyway because the black wool and the blond synthetic fibers were merely "garbage . . . nothing more than household debris."

"And, incidentally," DePue said, "this evidence, even if it suggests the presence of intruders in the MacDonald household, simply had no bearing on the government's theory of prosecution . . . if all the hippies in Fayetteville would have been in the house, including Helena Stoeckley, they would not have accounted for, or impugned in the least, that forensic evidence. There is no other explanation for it other than that Jeffrey MacDonald committed the murders."

DePue attacked the idea that the twenty-two-inch-long synthetic blond hair and two other shorter synthetic hairs found in the hairbrush had been used in a wig even though lab tech Glisson had identified them as wig hairs, unequivocally, in her confirmatory lab note after examining them a second time. In response to the current appeal petition, the FBI laboratory in 1990 had determined that these three fibers were made of saran. DePue told the court that such a fiber "simply is not suitable for the manufacture of wigs because of its physical appearance and because of the way it's manufactured. Instead, it's used for things like doll hair, mannequin hair, outdoor furniture. Now unless the defendant wants to maintain that Ken and Barbie did it, I don't see how this hair helps them very much today."

Turning to the question of the black wool, DePue told the court that these wool fibers didn't match one another, implying that they could not have come from the same person. This was hardly a valid argument considering that Jeffrey MacDonald's pajama top itself consisted of four different kinds of fibers. To DePue, the locations where the dark fibers were found—on the murder club, on Colette's mouth, on her pajama top—were not strategic as Silverglate claimed, merely accidental. He suggested the black wool was debris from the rug in the master bedroom where Colette MacDonald's body, and perhaps the wooden club, had once rested. DePue made this claim even though the official report of the CID analysis of the debris collected from this rug showed absolutely no black wool, a fact which might have, in other times, invalidated the facile transfer theory of locard. "We know that the MacDonald family owned wool clothing," DePue said, "we have pictures of them, we have testimony from the father-in-law saying that they did." He suggested that the wool from this clothing at some time or other fell to the rug and later attached itself "to the club and the woman's body."[10]

DePue pointed out that, under recent federal court rulings currently in effect, meaning, of course, the *McCleskey* decision, the evidence in question must point to no less than "probable innocence" of the defendant. He told the judges that they must ask themselves if the synthetic fibers and black wool, if they had become known to the jury, would have resulted in MacDonald's acquittal. "And I don't think that any reasonable fact-finder, or any reasonable appellate court, would come to any such decision," DePue said.

When it came time for the defense's rebuttal, Dershowitz rose to ask the court to allow an evidentiary hearing in which sworn question-and-answer testimony would settle the matter. As proof of the need, he pointed to the ongoing argument of whether saran fibers were used in human wigs in 1970. According to DePue, the FBI had conducted an exhaustive investigation and had determined that saran fibers were never used in wigs. But Dershowitz stood in the center of the courtroom and waved a book over his head, telling the court loudly, "We have, Your Honor, three standard textbooks, not cited by the government, all of which indicate that wigs *are* made of saran. It is in the record that we sought a hearing."

Judge Russell called upon DePue to respond to these remarks. DePue denied that any textbooks suggested that saran fibers were used in "human cosmetic wigs." As to the need for a hearing, DePue told the court that "Judge Dupree decided that an evidentiary hearing wasn't necessary, it was sufficient in our brief."

At this, an outraged Dershowitz shot to his feet. He lifted the textbook high and offered to show the judges the exact quotes which cited that saran was used in wigs, quotes DePue had left out of his brief. Judge Russell, just as quickly, told Dershowitz curtly that it wouldn't be necessary.[11]

In the defense's final argument, Silverglate pointed out that, contrary to the government's attempt to focus on raw material, the key factor in the appeal was the suppression of the laboratory notes.[12] The notes revealed wig hair, and confessor Helena Stoeckley was known to have worn a wig on the murder night. The notes had revealed unmatched black wool on a weapon and on a corpse. It was this written information that the defense hadn't been allowed to see. That was what mattered, according to Silverglate.

He paused, looked up at Justice Murnaghan, and reminded him that Murnaghan himself had written in an earlier appeal in this case that had

Murnaghan been the trial judge, he would have allowed the jurors to hear the Stoeckley witnesses tell about Stoeckley's confessions. Murnaghan had stated that if the jurors had heard about the confessions, the damage to the government's case would have been "incalculably great." Now, Silverglate said, had these lab notes been turned over to the defense, they would have provided the hard forensic evidence of intruders that Judge Dupree had required before he let the Stoeckley confessions in. But Murtagh absolutely had refused to supply this evidence even when pressed for it. Silverglate insisted that if these lab notes had been turned over, as required, Judge Dupree would have had no choice but to allow the Stoeckley witnesses to tell the jurors that she had confessed to being involved in the murders. The trial record clearly reveals that Dupree himself had stated officially that without corroboration he wouldn't allow the testimony about her confessions. And if the jurors had heard those confessions, which supported MacDonald's story, Silverglate now told Murnaghan, the damage to the government's case would have been, as Murnaghan had earlier assessed, "incalculably great." In essence, Silverglate argued that if the lab notes had been turned over, MacDonald's conviction never would have occurred.

■

On the Richmond sidewalk outside the Fourth Circuit Court of Appeals following the arguments that morning, a reporter asked attorney Alan Dershowitz how long the defense team was prepared to fight for MacDonald. Dershowitz pushed his chin into the reporter's face and said, "Forever." He opened a textbook to a certain page and showed the reporter where it said that saran *was* used for wigs, despite government claims to the contrary. "Can you get your camera on that?" Dershowitz asked, holding the book closer. "Can you see that? Well, so could the prosecutor. He lied to the judge moments ago. He lied to me. He lied to you." Dershowitz stabbed the book for emphasis. "Jeffrey MacDonald is innocent. He will never quit, and I will never quit until we get this evidence before a jury."

Over lunch after the oral arguments, a subdued Silverglate complained, "The judges never let us get to the merits of the evidence," he said. "Somehow we've got to get to the merits. They keep throwing up *McCleskey*. They keep throwing up procedure. No one seems to care that we've now got evidence that MacDonald didn't do this thing."

After lunch, I walked with the defense attorneys to a hotel room where they awaited rides to the airport. Dershowitz talked a few minutes, then left in a car with one of the younger members of the team. Silverglate wouldn't sit down. He walked the room slowly, as if he were stalking a cure for misery, his head down, his shell-shocked eyes focused somewhere about three floors below. Some of the other lawyers and aides were off to the side, going over the arguments, trying to get their own heads wrapped around what had just happened. Silverglate, still in his overcoat, stopped in the middle of the floor and looked at me. His eyes might have been those of an army officer who had just seen his entire company wiped out. "Things aren't good here," he said softly. "This is very bad."

"Do you think these judges might think about what you and Alan said today," I asked, "and finally let you have an evidentiary hearing?"

"They're not looking for proof of MacDonald's innocence, they're looking for excuses not to look at the proof. So, no, they won't give us a hearing."

The Fourth Circuit Decision

They didn't. On June 2, 1992, the three Fourth Circuit judges denied MacDonald's appeal because of "procedural default," stopping at that. It was strikingly simple. They found that MacDonald should have presented his claims in the 1984–1985 appeal. He was now too late. The decision went no further. Their written decision stated that the appellate judges declined "to reach the merits of [MacDonald's] petition." This was lawyer language for saying that they never got far enough to consider the value of the black wool and wig fibers. They chose not to delve into the question whether these items were, as DePue had claimed, "household debris." And they didn't reconsider MacDonald's innocence. Their ruling that the evidence was tardy precluded such an argument whose actual validity would have to have been made during an evidentiary hearing, and such a hearing, contrary to the now doubtful promise in *McCleskey* to make exceptions in cases of innocence, was not being allowed.

In this official opinion, written by Judge Russell and joined by Murnaghan and Butzner, the appeals court applied the "abuse of the writ" doctrine. Justice Russell pointed out in the opinion, "Courts have developed the abuse of the writ doctrine in order to curtail endless filings of successive habeas petitions . . . While we are keenly aware of MacDonald's insistence as to his innocence, at some point we must accept this case as final. Every habeas appeal MacDonald brings consumes untold government and judicial resources."

In the court's view, MacDonald had held back these items from his 1984 appeal and had waited until 1990 to present them. To Harvey Silverglate, the claim that "Jeff would hold back such information, and choose to rot in prison seven more years before using it to get out of prison is ridiculous."

Since MacDonald's attorney Brian O'Neill hadn't immediately figured out the new evidence when he received approximately 10,000 pages of FOIA in 1983, at a time when he was convinced the Stoeckley confessions would turn the tables for MacDonald, it seemed to me that Silverglate might now file a new petition based upon a claimed lack of diligence by O'Neill. Hadn't the justices left MacDonald that opening? But Fred Bost directed my attention to a statement in Justice Russell's written decision which seemed to be blocking that possibility. In this passage, Russell had written, "Although such decision by [defense counsel O'Neill] may in retrospect be deemed attorney error, erroneous strategic decisions do not amount to cause."

So, in a bizarre twist, it seems that O'Neill's failure to dig out this evidence is sufficient cause under *McCleskey* to deny MacDonald a new trial, but it *isn't* sufficient cause under the doctrine of attorney incompetence to now *get* him a new trial. The greater sin, then, is not Murtagh's sin of concealment. It is that MacDonald's tardiness delivers hardship to the crowded courts.

My closer reading of the appellate turndown revealed something else that didn't seem fair, at least to my layman's sense of justice. The appellate court refused to consider that Murtagh had assured Segal and Dupree during trial that there was no *Brady* material in the lab notes. About that issue Russell wrote, "While MacDonald may have an argument for cause at trial, the argument is inappropriate here. Counsel's possession of the relevant documents prior to the first habeas petition negated any concealment claim." The court's position was the same as Murtagh's, which was: Even if Murtagh had held back information, the key legal point under the new rules was that MacDonald had found it too late. Silverglate believed that the decision represents the justice system's new habeas corpus position, and seems to justify Thurgood Marshall's angry assessment of *McCleskey*, that it "rewards state misconduct and deceit."

In effect, Silverglate had played his very best card, saying to Murtagh, "You cheated. You held back lab notes that contained information that would have freed MacDonald." And, in darkest irony, Murtagh, with the supportive Rehnquist Court looming large behind him, played a card that said, simply, "You should have found it sooner. You lose."

MacDonald began his twelfth year in prison as Silverglate, without hope, prepared his brief to the same Supreme Court that had authored *McCleskey*.

The practical effects of *McCleskey* in this case and others didn't go unnoticed across the country. Judge Stephen Reinhardt wrote of the current habeas situation in a May 7, 1991, *Los Angeles Times* op-ed article: "Whatever the term may be, the judicial and political ideology that drives the current Supreme Court does not portend well for individual rights or fundamental freedoms in these United States." The *Los Angeles Daily Journal*, for June 22, 1992, ran a cartoon depicting five robed justices with huge bodies and very small heads. They stand over a fallen female figure labeled "Habeas Corpus." Her hands are lifted in self-defense as the justices rain blows upon her with long clubs. In an article on the habeas argument in that same edition, Elisabeth Semel wrote, "In plain English this means that freedom may never come for the wrongfully convicted and the unjustly sentenced."[13]

Jeffrey MacDonald

After the Fourth Circuit justices refused him an evidentiary hearing, I made arrangements to visit Jeffrey MacDonald at the Sheridan Federal Correctional Institution in western Oregon. I cleared the four security gates and followed a guard through the visiting room where scores of inmates sat with their families. I had been there so many times that I had learned how not to hurt so bad when I saw a little child sitting on the lap of a father who would be locked up for as long as it took his child to graduate from high school. I simply avoided eye contact and headed toward the tiny interview cubicle where I would meet with MacDonald.

In prison they call him "Doc," because he has saved several lives in cases of heart attack or drug overdose, and the intramural athletes come to him with their twisted knees, sprained ankles, and aching shoulders—even though this is considered improper due to Bureau of Prison guidelines prohibiting inmates from practicing their civilian careers.

I waited a long time for MacDonald that day. This was not unusual, for my journalist's paperwork at prisons was often lost in the control office. Sometimes the warden's people even forgot to take the release form to MacDonald's cell, then later said, "Sorry, MacDonald didn't sign for you to interview him." This required some scrambling on my part, phoning an assistant warden, or someone else with whom I had chatted on earlier visits.

Finally, fifty minutes late, MacDonald came in, smiling. He shook my hand and accepted the coffee I had gotten for him in the vending machine, black, no sugar. He hadn't changed much from the time I had met him. He still looked strong, lean, and fit. But his hair was fully white now and he had dark circles under his eyes. Sometimes when we visited we talked about advances in medicine—he still subscribes to his medical journals and reads new editions of books in emergency medicine and orthopedics. He seems to believe he'll be a licensed doctor again. He keeps preparing for his board examinations, but, year after year, it has a way of not happening for him.

To keep his sanity in the face of failure, he meditates every day, lifts weights, and runs five to six miles around and around inside a small cage. He listens to classical music and learns about the composers, and he reads the books he never had time for when he was doctoring. He once sent me a copy of Edith Wharton's *Ethan Frome*, with a note that said, "I sometimes forget how rich and wonderful some of these old classics can be. Enjoy." Another time he phoned me and told me to pick up a tape of Max Bruch's "Violin Concerto in D." MacDonald said that Itzhak Perlman's recording, which he had just listened to on a Portland station, was the best piece of music he'd ever heard in his life.

This was unlike the MacDonald McGinniss described, yet, in reading the transcripts of the tapes MacDonald made for McGinniss, he was the same caring person toward McGinniss that he now seemed to be toward me. Everyone I had ever met who had known MacDonald before the conviction had expressed the same admiration for him. When I had interviewed those doctors and nurses who once served with him, they assured me he was a warm person and a "great" doctor. One physician who had worked closely with MacDonald in the trauma center for years told me MacDonald's diagnostic ability was so accurate as to be "uncanny." David Yarnell, a movie producer in Southern California, told me that his stepdaughter had lost part of a finger in an accident. All doctors who saw her immediately after it occurred advised that the severed part couldn't be reattached. Not Dr. MacDonald. He performed the surgery and saved the finger. Yarnell's brother had been in and out of hospitals with symptoms for which no physicians had found a cause. Yarnell was married to a woman who had decorated MacDonald's condominium years earlier. She suggested Yarnell send the man's medical records to MacDonald in prison. MacDonald looked at the information and diagnosed a dangerous tumor in the brain. The man immediately entered the hospital, and further tests detected the tumor in the brain formation where MacDonald said it would be.

Dr. Jerry Hughes, a former Green Beret physician who had served at Fort Bragg at the same time as MacDonald, offered him the job at Long Beach, in part because Hughes witnessed Dr. MacDonald's very first tracheostomy on a bucking, fighting patient. Against great odds, Hughes said, MacDonald pulled the operation off and saved the man's life. "He's got great hands and he can think on his feet. That's why he's a good emergency physician. He really listens to his patients, too," Hughes said, after relaying several examples. "That's what makes him a great doctor."

I was to hear many, many more stories about his lifesaving efforts. The Long Beach Police Department made him a lifetime honorary officer for performance "beyond the call" when he saved the life of an officer wounded in a shoot-out. A retired nurse told me, "As handsome as Jeff was, and as much attention as the young nurses paid to him, he always went out of his way to make me feel good about myself. I'm not pretty, never was, but with Jeff I felt pretty." She told me, during the civil trial in Los Angeles, that she would forfeit the remainder of her days if she could only get him back into the trauma center again. "No one was ever better there," she said.

Even Alfred Kassab said he had charisma. The CID said that six months after his wife's death MacDonald had bedded down one of the army's civilian secretaries at his BOQ. That is true. What the army investigators didn't reveal is that, when they interviewed her, the woman insisted that it was she who approached MacDonald, and the affair was her idea. And when they asked her how often it had happened, she replied, proudly, "As often as possible."

Talking with MacDonald, observing his ability to bounce back from defeat after defeat, it is easy to understand Kassab's warning about his charisma, and the secretary's claims, and the nurse's lament. I came to believe there is a depth to him that a superficial relationship doesn't reveal. He asks about Fred Bost, or Gail and Bob Boyce, who for many years had manned an office for his defense efforts in California, or about Donna Bruce Koch who worked on the McGinniss trial. He remarks that

Barbara Gallagher, his secretary at St. Mary, is doing well; he speaks warmly of Lucia Bartoli, a close friend and defense team member researching saran fibers in wig hairs manufactured in the sixties; or MacDonald wonders if I've seen Gunderson and has Gunderson lost weight like he had promised after that little scare with his heart.

But there's also a refreshingly boyish side still there, too, for after MacDonald has bored you with stories about the great composers, or spent a half hour explaining the medical reasons for a baseball pitcher's arm to fail, he lets go on football. He's an avid fan, and keeps detailed files on college players as if he were a pro coach considering them for the NFL draft each summer. His team is the New York Giants. But MacDonald wasn't winning football games, or much of anything these days. The Fourth Circuit had just turned him down when I went to see him.

"Now, what?" I asked.

"Supreme Court," he said, "but don't expect anything from them. After all, they are the ones who wrote *McCleskey* that let them kill me in Richmond."

"If the Supreme Court won't give you a hearing, then what?"

"I'll just stay here in my little concrete condo," he said, but his eyes showed pain. "Hah!" he said, pushing it away. "How's the book?"

"Soon," I said. "What's Silverglate got up his sleeve?"

"Congress. That's the next step. They should have written a decent habeas law in the first place. One that works, one that lets the bullshit appeals be heard quickly, then really looks hard at those appeals where real evidence has been found, *especially* when the government hasn't turned over evidence we asked for."

"So you think it's going to take an act of Congress?"

"You tell me," he said. "Nothing else has helped. Think about it. You want me to explain it all again?"

I told him to go ahead. He had it down by heart by now, but sometimes during my interviews he'd get started and flash on another dark irony, which always pleased him.

"That morning," MacDonald said, "I awoke to my wife and daughter's screams and I saw a black man wearing a field jacket with E-6 stripes on it, and two drugged-out white guys and a white woman with blond hair. I saw a light flickering on the woman's face. I thought it was a candle. Then, lo and behold, an MP actually sees a woman with a floppy hat at what ungodly hour?"

"3:55 A.M., I believe."

"Yeah, just moments after I phoned. And, hey, she's standing on a street corner, where? You got it, three blocks away. And then we find a woman who actually has a black friend wearing a field jacket with E-6 stripes. What a coincidence! The guy's *real*. And we learn later that the son-of-a-bitch walks around with what? A God damn baseball bat. Ah, but we then learn that the young woman has other friends in the drug trade and some of them had actually kidnapped and attempted to murder a fellow user-dealer who snitched on them. And, what do you know, the young woman just happens to have a cheap blond wig which she wore that very night, and a floppy hat which she wore that night, and boots which she wore that night. And she had no alibi for, guess what, just those few hours in question—hey, *big* surprise. And, poor thing, she even thinks she was in my house that night, watching Colette struggling with Greg Mitchell, and Mitchell's a, guess what? A brown-haired, left-handed guy and the experts say Colette was killed by a left-handed guy. And Stoeckley's neighbor sees her arrive home that morning in, guess what, a blue Mustang like the one Prince Beasley saw her in the night before, and like the Mustang my neighbor saw drive by my house the night of the murders. And when this Helena Stoeckley's neighbor presses her she says she didn't kill anybody, hey, she loves children, but she might have held the light while someone else murdered them. *Jesus!*

"Then they find fresh candle wax, and not just anywhere, mind you. They find it where? On the coffee table, and in Kimmie's room. And, guess what else? Another one of my neighbors saw people carrying candles toward my house. Candles! A guy at Dunkin' Donuts sees a woman and a black man come in to wash blood off their hands that very morning. A newspaper woman sees a young woman she identified as Stoeckley in the company of a black man in a grocery store across the street from a trailer where Prince Beasley would find drugs later that day. And guess who told Beasley the drugs would be in the trailer? Yeah, Stoeckley.

"Also that morning a carhop at a drive-in restaurant sees someone dressed like Stoeckley, with, guess who, a black man and a white guy, and the woman tells the carhop MacDonald's family are dead and he's hurt and in the hospital. And Stoeckley's friends, who aren't questioned for a year, mind you, have no alibis either. But Stoeckley doesn't just admit her involvement to her neighbor, Mr. Posey. She also tells a cop, Prince Beasley, who calls the CID. Ah, but they don't come get her and her friends and break the case. Too busy. But they *do* go get her, secretly, mind you, and Ivory talks to her. Then instead of bringing her in when she professes no alibi, and admits she wore a blond wig, boots, and a floppy hat that night, or instead of going after her murderous God damn friends, they fail even to make a report about her, or even take notes about the interview with her. Then they give her, or *somebody* gives her to the FBI under an alias without telling the FBI that the CID agents themselves, *and* a city cop, think she's the woman I saw, and the FBI use her as an informant to give them names of people who Stoeckley absolutely *knows* weren't there that night. Now, the army lab techs find a bloody syringe, a piece of skin on Colette's fingernail, *four* bloody gloves, blond wig hair, all kinds of unmatched fingerprints, and a hair in Colette's hand that isn't mine, hey a brown hair, by the way, and I'm blond, but they cover all this up, tell the MP to keep his mouth shut about seeing the woman in the floppy hat, then the army CID agent makes up this bullshit staged-scene theory and accuses me, but Colonel Rock sees through it when they change the report about the brown hair in Colette's hand."

At this point MacDonald, who had already done twelve years in prison over this, started laughing. "Jesus, this *isn't* funny," he said, "but the assholes were so *bad!*" MacDonald abruptly stopped laughing, and said, "Wait. It gets *worse!*"

"I know, but it's not—"

"No, wait, listen, it gets really bizarre."

Tired of it after nearly eight years in this myself, I let him go anyway, knowing it's the stuff his faith is built upon. Someday, he always says, people are going to know.

He continued his litany of horrors. "While the army CID is under fire for screwing up the investigation and covering up Stoeckley, guess what happens? That's right! An *army* lawyer, mind you, working for the CID who screwed me in 1970, this weird little guy named Murtagh, takes this box of jimmied evidence to the Justice Department. *Now*, guess what? There's a head hair from Colette, wrapped around a what? A pajama fiber! It's brand new, wasn't there when the CID looked at it time and time again. How creative! And the foreign hair they found in Colette's hand, the one thing that clobbered them in the army hearing, has now become nothing. Somebody had cut it till it's too small to test. Who did that? Somebody did it, but who? The CID had even written notes on how different it looked from other hairs they checked. But now, *surprise, surprise*, not only is it too little to lab-test anymore, they hide the fact that this was the hair they tested against me so Segal can't challenge them at trial! Say, bye bye to still another piece of evidence. Wonder who set that up? Wonder who carried the evidence up to Stombaugh? You got it, Murtagh himself."

"But you can't prove Murtagh changed the evidence."

"Can't prove anything until you can get your hands on it, and get him on the stand in an evidentiary hearing, which they aren't going to let me have.

"So," MacDonald says, his eyes tearful, "now they get a grand jury hearing, then an indictment, then a trial in which we can't lab-test the evidence, can't even see the damned lab notes. And Dupree won't allow the Rock report, or psychiatric evidence, or the seven Stoeckley confession witnesses. I'm convicted because the jurors, who *still* don't believe I did it, ask to see the blood chart, and, what did Murtagh arrange? The chart he gives the jurors shows no blood in the hallway. Hey, MacDonald must be lying, these twelve people say. *Murtagh* couldn't be lying; he's the God damn *government*." MacDonald's voice cracks, and I realize there really is no fun in this for him.

"So I'm convicted," he says, softly. "Then four years after trial we finally get the FOIA material, but we were all excited about Stoeckley's confessions then, thinking she would send me home, and we didn't take time to figure it all out and analyze every line in the lab notes until *after* we had filed the Stoeckley appeal. That Stoeckley appeal was turned down because we had 'no corroboration' at the crime scene, corroboration they had actually lost or destroyed or just kept quiet about! And now, by the new *McCleskey* rule, it's too late to use it in court, even though by this time we've found four people who heard Mitchell confess, and Cathy Perry confessed, and we now learn that Stoeckley even confessed to the FBI and to Murtagh himself." MacDonald let out a hollow laugh. "And do you know the most macabre irony in the entire case?"

"Go ahead."

"Murtagh said we should have known about the black wool and wig hair sooner."

"Yeah."

"*We're* supposed to have known about it, then he claims that *he* didn't even know about it. So I go back to jail—go directly to jail, do not collect the hundred dollars. Think about that. How am I supposed to know about something, under penalty of spending my life in here, when he says he didn't even know about it, and when it's locked away in his own files! *Good God!* Is that insane?"

"Why do you think the courts continue to rule against you?"

"Joe McGinniss convinced the world that I'm not only guilty, but I'm nuts, like some hideous monster. I loved my wife and children. I did not kill them. But the power of the printed word, in the form of *Fatal Vision*, appears to legitimize my conviction, and in so doing, I believe, legitimizes the court's refusal to allow an evidentiary hearing. I find it horribly humorous, macabre, in fact, that the only way Joe could convince the world that I was guilty, even with the conviction, was to convince them that I was on drugs and committed the mayhem and overkill that only a drug-wasted mind could have committed. He totally ignored Stoeckley, Colonel Rock's request to investigate her, and all her murderous friends. Then, to convince his readers that I was on drugs he went to ridiculous lengths, made up doctors' opinions, misquoted medical books, and, in short, invented a theory which he finally admitted, under oath, mind you, that he didn't even believe himself. Kafka would have had a field day with this."

"So next stop Congress," I said.

"The courts won't listen, so, hell yes, it's going to take an act of Congress."

"But the Supreme Court isn't made up totally of conservatives. There's still a chance."

"Forget that," MacDonald said, "they're the ones who *wrote* the *McCleskey* decision in the first place."

"You have absolutely no hope in the Supreme Court?"

"None."

MacDonald was right. On November 30, 1992, the Supreme Court released a statement that it wouldn't review the case. They turned him down, without comment.

Epilogue

Eight Decembers had come and gone since I met Ted Gunderson on that strange, foggy night in Chinatown. He still calls from time to time to learn what we've found. Each time, the congenial old detective reminds me, "You said I was crazy, didn't you?"

"I admit it. I did."

"Well, MacDonald didn't do it, you have to admit that now, don't you?"

"It doesn't matter," I said. "Until the courts give him a hearing, he's still locked up."

"They will," Gunderson said. "Time's are changing."

And they were. For one thing, many members of the prosecution team had, one by one, succumbed to serious questions about the quality of their characters. Warren Coolidge, who as U.S. Attorney in North Carolina had sought to indict MacDonald in federal court, proved to be an embezzler. After leaving federal service for private practice, he admitted to taking funds from his firm and was disbarred. In like manner, Woerheide's methods used at the grand jury investigation had been criticized by legal colleagues, and his partner in that venture, Jay Stroud, later bribed a key witness in the "Wilmington Ten" case. This act, when revealed, caused a reversal of the conviction in that notable case. And lead prosecutor James Blackburn ended up crossing the criminal line in an incredible manner.[1]

Blackburn had ridden on his fame in the MacDonald case to the job of U.S. Attorney of the Eastern District of North Carolina. Then, like Coolidge before him, he entered private practice and proceeded to engage in the kinds of criminal acts he once might have prosecuted. Shortly after joining the prestigious firm of Smith, Helms, Mulliss, and Moore in 1987 he was made a full partner. Partners in a law firm are bound by contract to handle clients only through the firm, but within two years Blackburn was recruiting secret clients. A later investigation by authorities disclosed that in subsequent years he solicited some fifteen to twenty such cases, allowing him to pocket $140,000 in hidden fees. During this period he remodeled his lush west Raleigh home at a cost of $80,000, paid $20,000 initiation to an exclusive social club, and purchased a second luxury car, a BMW convertible.

His workload was extensive and clients grew impatient for progress. To prevent any of this impatience from exposing his illicit activity, he manufactured seventeen felonious court documents, even forging two federal court judges' signatures, using this paperwork to fictionally advance or close cases. The monetary awards of the court from these fictional endings were provided to clients from funds he embezzled from his firm.

The subterfuge fell apart on January 12, 1993, when a routine audit disclosed shortages in an account, causing the firm to notify the North Carolina State Bar. Within two days Blackburn admitted some of his wrongdoing and resigned his position. But the firm continued its probe and discovered even more discrepancies. On January 25, the state bar obtained an injunction temporarily denying Blackburn the ability to practice law. At the urging of his attorneys, he entered the psychiatric facility at Duke Hospital in Durham for a week.

On July 13, 1993, a Wake County grand jury indicted him. Instead of facing a jury, he placed himself at the mercy of a local judge. On November 29 he pleaded guilty to twelve counts of forgery, fraud, and embezzlement of $234,000, claiming he had no memory of the crimes. On December 6, Wake County Superior Court Judge Henry Wight determined the punishment, but only after listening to Blackburn's two psychiatrists state that their client had suffered from "psychotic delusional depression." In contrast, Wake County District Attorney C. Colon Willoughby pointed out that Blackburn's business colleagues and clients noticed no changes in him during that period. Willoughby reminded the judge that Blackburn had no difficulty in recalling what sums of money he took from the firm at various times.

Judge Wight waived the testimony and sentenced Blackburn to three years in prison and another ten years suspended upon good behavior. He ordered Blackburn to repay the $234,000 to his firm, continue psychiatric treatment, and give 100 hours community service to society. Wight told the court he was recommending immediate work release from prison and that Blackburn would not have to report to prison until after the Christmas holiday.

Blackburn entered prison on January 3, 1994, and on January 14 he began a work release program of former U.S. senator Robert Morgan, working every day except Sunday, spending his nights behind bars. He was paroled on April 26, 1994, and is now a free man, having served a total of 113 days in prison for his crimes, 87 of which were part-time incarceration.

The irony is that it was Blackburn in conjunction with Brian Murtagh who convinced Judge Dupree to regard psychiatric offerings as nothing but "character testimony." Yet when Blackburn found himself in trouble, he didn't hesitate to seek psychiatric backing. None of this promised any legal help to MacDonald; instead, he drew hope from other quarters.

In January 1993 Bill Clinton became president and promised ethics reforms throughout the government. In March 1993 he appointed Janet Reno as head of the Justice Department. Reno had been lauded as a strong-minded advocate of due process and judicial fairness. She immediately announced that she wouldn't allow prosecutors to "hang the scalps of innocent defendants on their belts." She ordered the Justice Department to seek ways to release FOIA information, virtually canceling the policies of previous administrations which allowed officials to withhold documents on the slimmest of reasons. And Reno announced that she was eager to look at any new evidence in any case. All these things encouraged the defense team as they prepared another habeas writ based upon further prosecutorial misconduct and other new evidence.

Perhaps equally as promising to MacDonald's attempts to get a new trial or at least an evidentiary hearing, conservative Supreme Court justice Byron White promised to vacate his office in favor of retirement even while battle lines over the writ of habeas corpus were being drawn in Congress. Perhaps another justice would not vote to eliminate second habeas appeals in cases where exculpatory material had been withheld by prosecutors. Most defense team members believe it's a fair bet that *McCleskey* isn't a "done deal," and that the far-right pendulum may swing away again.

And the star government apologist, Joe McGinniss, began to suffer setbacks. In the summer of 1993 Simon and Schuster published Joe McGinniss's book *The Last Brother*, supposedly a biography of Senator Edward M. "Ted" Kennedy. The author immediately came under blistering criticism for inventing entire conversations between members of the Kennedy family. By his own admission, McGinniss had never interviewed these persons on the issues at question. In replying to the scathing rebukes from Kennedy experts, historians, book reviewers, and other writers, McGinniss defended himself by classifying his new work as "interpretive biography" based upon his research and others' writings. This writer, who was widely praised in 1983 for his investigative reporting for *Fatal Vision*, was finally, in 1993, seeing his methods being questioned by the very people who had originally championed him.

A few days after the McGinniss-Kennedy skirmish began, even while Jeffrey MacDonald and Harvey Silverglate lamented the Supreme Court's refusal to hear the case, the defense team was encouraged by a surprising Court ruling that a prosecutor now may be sued for monetary damages if he knowingly misrepresented to the media, to the grand jury, or to trial jurors the facts of a case, especially if that prosecutor had entered the field as an investigator in the case in question. Not surprisingly, this 5–4 decision sent Silverglate scurrying back to the MacDonald files to locate those instances in which Murtagh's public statements might not have matched the information he had in his files.

Something else brought even greater encouragement, actually avid excitement. At this writing, defense team researcher Lucia Bartoli had found a manufacturer who had made wigs of saran in the late 1960s. The manufacturer tracked down and sent to her one of those old wigs. Laboratory examinations proved it to be made of the same material as the blond wig fibers found in the hairbrush in the MacDonald home. One of the key government arguments at the appeals hearing was that human wigs had never been made of saran. With such a wig actually in hand, Silverglate felt he might possibly be able to force his way back into court.

■

In the beginning, Fred Bost and I envisioned wrapping this enigmatic case into a neat package, telling our readers, in effect, "Here's what happened, and here's why." In retrospect we see that we were only partially successful. That isn't to say we are displeased, of course, with our achieve-

ments in researching, confirming, and exposing information—particularly
concerning those crucial facts withheld from the defense and from the
public. We feel good about that. But we both realize now that the question
of "why" these things were held back will forever be denied us. So, we
can only speculate.

In kicking the question around, Fred and I came up with four possible
motives for a cover-up. Perhaps the perpetrators, collectively or individually, were so sure that Jeffrey MacDonald was guilty that they chose to hide
evidence to keep from confusing others. Perhaps they felt a requirement to
win their issue, at all costs, regardless of ethics. Perhaps they were protecting something they were hiding, something that might be revealed if
the case expanded in other directions. Or perhaps we ourselves were
seeing something imaginary, misreading bungling and incompetence for
something more sinister.

A failure to penetrate this mystery, however, should not detract from
the information revealed here. The fact is that, regardless of the reason,
certain things were denied the jury in the MacDonald murder case. Only
the reader can decide how much weight to give those things. As for Fred
and me, if we were jurors in a new trial, if we were shown the facts now
known about this case, we would find Jeffrey MacDonald wrongly accused
of murder.

The army said the crime scene was well protected. It was not. They
said it was competently searched. It was not. They said they could prove
the scene was staged by MacDonald. They did not. They said neighbors
saw and heard nothing that night. Not true. The army and the government
said nothing was found to support the presence of intruders at the crime
scene. That was false. And, now that we know about the hair in Colette's
hand, the bloody syringe, the multiple bloody gloves, the piece of skin,
the wig hair, and the black wool fibers, this was the cruelest lie of all.

Like Colonel Warren Rock in 1970, we would rule the government's
charges to be "not true." Like Colonel Rock, we would further suggest a
reinvestigation of the murders, with authorities specifically probing the
related activities of Helena Stoeckley and her troubled young friends.

Notes

1. The Murders on Castle Drive

1. The narrative action described in this prologue is from testimony at the army Article 32 hearing in 1970 by persons involved: Carolyn Landen, William A. Boulware, Kenneth C. Mica, Richard Tevere, and Jeffrey MacDonald.
2. Landen worked for the Carolina Telephone Company, which serviced some of the housing units on Fort Bragg, ten miles northwest of Fayetteville.
3. While describing this at the Article 32 hearing, Mica failed to fully identify Williams. Two military police with that surname were at the scene—Edward J. Williams and Donald R. Williams, Jr.
4. These are sergeant chevrons for pay grade E-6, appearing as three inverted V's with a single "rocker" at the bottom. These cloth stripes on the sleeves were seldom seen at the time because they were being discontinued by the army, to be replaced by metal collar insignia, and would be illegal to wear following June 30, 1970.
5. MacDonald's claim of having the story molded by investigators is substantiated in at least one instance by the transcript of an interrogation on April 6, 1970, when he was questioned by CID agents. Until that moment MacDonald had told others that the black man was striking him with a "baseball bat." Agent Robert Shaw wanted to believe that the only bludgeon involved in the murders was the splintery shaft found in the backyard. Consequently, Shaw posed a question by saying, "We think that this club that you originally thought was

399

a baseball bat or something might have come from around the house or something like that." When MacDonald didn't argue about this switch, the CID subsequently used it against MacDonald by citing a lack of splinters from the club in the living room where he said he had been attacked.

2. The Crime Scene

1. William Ivory's own version has him arriving a few minutes earlier, when MacDonald was still in the house, but the investigator for the provost marshal, Hagan Rossi, has stated that he and Ivory got there together and that MacDonald was being put into the ambulance. Also, Ivory said he had no memory of anything happening in the hallway where multiple witnesses saw MacDonald struggle off the gurney to get to his baby's room, and curse the MPs who helped pull him back onto the gurney. In addition, statements by military police do not corroborate that Ivory was in the house at that time.

2. Ivory's movements through the house, and his concerns, are taken from his own statements and testimony at the army hearing, the grand jury hearing, and the trial.

3. The following day Ivory began a series of repetitive tests whereby he and others took turns kicking the coffee table to see if it would remain on edge. He says it never did.

4. An army provost marshal on a military post is equivalent to a police chief in a civilian community. The CID and the provost marshal are two different army law enforcement groups, with neither having jurisdiction over the other. While the provost marshal reports to the base commander, the CID is responsible to its headquarters in Washington, D.C. This arrangement supposedly provides an independent investigative agency over which a base commander can exercise no control in matters that might embarrass his command.

5. Alfred Kassab overheard part of this argument from an outer office and reported it to Jeffrey MacDonald and other family members and friends at the hospital that Friday night, according to statements made by both MacDonald and his mother.

6. Testimony of Hilyard Medlin at the army's Article 32 hearing.

7. The fibers at this location are discussed in greater detail later in the chapter.

8. In the government's response to MacDonald's first appeal after his conviction, the prosecutors summarized the strength of their position and Ivory's methods unequivocally: "The government's case from the outset has consisted almost exclusively of physical evidence culled from the crime scene, the testimony of scientific experts interpreting that evidence, and the logical inferences to

be drawn from it." (Taken from the government's appellate brief filed December 29, 1979; Docket No. 79–5253, p. 84.)

9. Telephone interview of Janice Pendlyshok with author Fred Bost, June 21, 1988.

10. DA Form 2823, Witness Statement, James Warner Paulsen, 29 Dec 70, 1135 hours, oath administered by Harold C. Peterson, witness Peter E. Kearns, 2 pages, statement under oath.

11. Even after this error was discovered, no effort was made to follow the truck and retrieve the garbage.

12. Sworn statement of Franz J. Grebner, defense deposition, pre-Article 32 hearing, p. 58.

13. Paulsen made it sound easy, saying he had been allowed to move about without question. "I went into all three bedrooms to look at the bodies," he said. "I walked through the kitchen with either an MP or a CID agent and walked into the backyard. I just looked around and did not notice anything. I just turned around and came back into the house through the rear door. I picked up the wallet and put it in my pocket and took it outside and put it in the ambulance." He said he was back in the house about fifteen minutes later when he heard the CID agents talking about the wallet being missing from the desk, "and I was searched and they checked the ambulance."

14. The wallet was found alongside the road near the hospital by a passing soldier on the day of the murders. Grebner didn't tell MacDonald it was lost until MacDonald was released from the hospital.

"Can you explain why the MPs searched the ambulance and did not find the wallet?" Paulsen was asked.

"Yes, they searched carelessly. They just looked inside and under the seats and opened my medical bag. The search was not very thorough." Paulsen explained that he had hidden the billfold on a ledge above the driver's sun visor.

15. MacDonald mentioned the existence of that bottle of amphetamine diet pills when he first testified before the grand jury. He had been assigned a weight reduction program for the troops and used *Eskatrol* in that effort. Dr. William P. Neal, who came to the house to examine the bodies and make an official pronouncement of death, had spotted the bottle, whose contents could draw about $3,000 on the street. In a taped interview two months after the crimes, Dr. Neal happened to mention seeing the *Eskatrol* bottle. (The interview was tape-recorded for the prosecution by a consultant, Dr. Russell Fisher, the Maryland medical examiner, on April 14, 1970.)

The doctor said he noticed the bottle while being escorted by a CID agent whom he didn't identify. William Ivory was apparently that man, for he gave sworn testimony on three occasions (at the Article 32 hearing, before the grand jury, and at the 1979 trial) that he personally escorted Neal throughout the apartment that morning. Ivory himself corroborated the existence of the bottle when he testified before the grand jury and said under oath that amphetamines were found in the closet (testimony of William Ivory before the grand jury, August 20, 1974, p. 108). Yet a photograph of the closet's contents made on the day of the murders fails to show the *Eskatrol* bottle. And when the supplies in the closet were inventoried on February 27, ten days after the murders, the *Eskatrol* tablets were not there.

16. When MacDonald left the hospital, his in-laws, the Kassabs, asked him for two of Colette's rings to possess as keepsakes. On March 9 MacDonald passed the request to the CID, who went to the house to find them and learned that those particular rings were missing. MacDonald kept pressing for the return of the rings and finally a thorough, but unsuccessful, search of the murder quarters was conducted by Shaw and the army prosecutor, Clifford Somers, on June 19.

Michael Malley, a MacDonald defense attorney, complained to the government later that year that the crime scene had been poorly handled, and he used the loss of the rings as partial justification for the complaints. During the internal probe to answer the Malley charges, a CID agent had asked Colonel Warren V. Rock, the Article 32 hearing officer, "Did CID agents fail to inventory the crime scene?"

"Yes," Rock said, pointing out that such an inventory, to be later checked with Captain MacDonald, would have been a logical procedure.

17. DA Form 19–31, Military Police Receipt for Property, as required by Army Regulation 190–22.

18. Statements of Chaplain Kenneth Edwards and Rosalie Edwards to private investigator Raymond Shedlick, Jr., June 5, 1984; supplemented by an interview with author Fred Bost, May 11, 1988.

19. DA Form 2820, Statement by Accused or Suspect Person, Robert Bolden Shaw, Jr., 16 Dec 70, 2025 hours, interrogator Peter E. Kearns, witness Lyle B. Smith, 21 pages, statement under oath.

20. Grand jury transcript, Richard Tevere, Oct 23, 1974, pp. 20–21.

21. FBI Report, interview of Donald Kalin 2/18/70, dictated 2/24/70, typed February 25, 1970.

22. Letter from Jim Williams to Dr. Jeffrey MacDonald, dated March 31, 1988.

23. Trial testimony of Dr. William Neal.

24. Major Joe Parson, the assistant provost marshal, was questioned about the matter on December 20, 1970. He said he saw not one, but two strangers in blue jeans in the living room. (DA Form 2823, Witness Statement, Joe W. Parson, 20 Dec 70, 1400 hours, oath administered by Robert R. Bidwell, no witness, 10 pages, statement under oath.)

Neither of Parson's descriptions matched that given by Mica. Mica's statement and Parson's statement were both at odds with that of Fort Bragg's CID chief, Franz Joseph Grebner, who reported that he saw a man in blue jeans and white jacket in the living room. (DA Form 2820, Statement by Accused or Suspect Person, Franz Joseph Grebner, 20 Dec 70, 1800 hours, interrogator Peter E. Kearns, witness Lyle B. Smith, 3 pages, statement under oath.)

When asked to explain the existence of the unidentified people in jeans, CID agents Grebner, Ivory, and Shaw said they were medics from four different ambulances. Nothing in the eyewitness statements supports the idea that there were four ambulances.

Even though Grebner, Shaw, and Ivory all said the man was a medic, they admitted they didn't determine that themselves, they were told it by someone whose identity they couldn't recall.

Only one medic, Private James Paulsen, was ever questioned on the subject. During the reinvestigation following MacDonald's discharge, Paulsen was interviewed by CID agents Harold Peterson and Peter Kearns (Witness Statement, Franz Grebner, December 29, 1970). Paulsen told them there had been only two ambulances at the scene and that no off-duty medics had been called in to help. Paulsen, not known for his truthfulness, nevertheless presented a story which might explain why others later might have thought there were more than two ambulances. At the call for aid that morning, Paulsen said, all four medics responded in two ambulance vehicles, the two being a line ambulance and a "cracker box," which is a field ambulance designed for rough terrain. One ambulance with three attendants took Mac-Donald to the hospital and a while later was recalled to the scene, manned by only one person, Jeffery, because detectives determined two ambulances would be needed to remove the corpses. The two ambulances remained parked at the residence until about 5:30 A.M. At that time, roughly an hour and a half after the arrival of the first military police, MacDonald's wallet was found missing from its position in the living room. Medics Paulsen and Jeffery were searched, their ambulances were searched, then their frustrated superiors ordered them to drive their ambulances back to the hospital and await a call. When at about 8 A.M. the CID decided it was finally time to move the bodies, the two medics and their ambulances were recalled for the final time to the murder scene.

Agents Kearns and Petersen did not question or discount Paulsen's "two-ambulance" explanation. They went on to ask him about the medics' clothing that morning. They were still trying to learn the identity of the mystery man in jeans, the man who allegedly moved the flowerpot and sat on the furniture. Paulsen told the investigators that he and the other three medics involved—Juan Castelan, John Nuchereno, and Donald Jeffery—had reported to the hospital at 4 P.M. on the afternoon before the murders and had completed their full shift without interruption. The other three medics wore hospital whites for that tour of duty, he said, but his own whites were dirty, so he had worn the conventional army fatigue uniform consisting of a green field jacket and green fatigue trousers. Under the field jacket he had worn a dark navy blue shirt.

Kearns asked Paulsen, "Do you recall seeing anything in the house moved or touched by anyone prior to the time that the photographer started taking pictures?"

"I seem to recall someone saying something about a flowerpot, but I don't know what."

"Could that comment have been directed to you?"

"It was not directed to me," Paulsen said.

No further effort was made to invalidate Paulsen's statement.

About this person, confusion continued to reign. Grebner, Ivory, and Shaw each admitted that they themselves had never established that the man supposedly seen in blue jeans had been an army medic as they had reported when their crime-scene control was under fire. In fact, each detective had been told by someone else that the man was a medic, but in each case they couldn't remember who had told them so. Agent Shaw, for example, said he had gotten the idea from an MP, but he didn't know who and didn't check it out himself because it wasn't his duty to do so. (Interrogator Peter E. Kearns, witness Lyle B. Smith, 21 pages, statement under oath.)

Despite the contrary indications in the witness statements, the CID announced that the "unknown civilian" was Private James Paulsen, saying he had been set apart from the others on the scene because of the blue shirt he was wearing under his field jacket. (Memorandum for the Army General Counsel from the U.S. Army CID Agency, subject: The Kassab and Malley Allegations; the Senator Ervin Inquiry; 5 Jan 71.) Other sightings by several people of a man in jeans were officially ignored. This conclusion was repeated by the Secretary of the Army's legal office in a report to Representative Emanuel Celler on April 6, 1971, thus assuring the congressman that no one on the premises had worn blue jeans. (Letter to Honorable Emanuel Celler, House of Representatives, from Office of the Secretary of the Army, Chief of Legislative Liaison, 8 Apr 71.)

25. For example, one of MacDonald's slippers was found resting on the leg of the overturned coffee table, giving investigators another item to point to in their "staged-scene" theory. Yet the action of the mystery man voided such a presumption, for while moving to sit at the couch he could have accidentally kicked the slipper against the table. The whole purpose of protecting a crime scene is to prevent such possible compromises of evidence.

26. Witness Statement, William Paul Neal, February 27, 1971, 9 A.M., oath administered by John W. Reynolds.

27. A few ridgelines of a fingerprint were found on the blade near the handle, showing not only that the knife would accept prints, but that it had been wiped clean.

28. Grand jury transcript, Richard Tevere, Oct. 23, 1974, pp. 54, 56.

29. This minuscule quantity of blood, a tiny fleck at the tip of the blade, could be identified only inconclusively as either Type A or Type O (Colette's or Kristen's type, respectively). Neither of these possible blood types supported the prosecution's theory that Colette used the knife to wound her husband. In fact, Type A blood on the knife tends to support MacDonald's story that he pulled the knife from her chest.

30. To further bolster the prosecution's theory, Paul Stombaugh, the FBI technician, testified at the trial that in his expert opinion this bent, dull Geneva Forge knife had made none of the cuts in Colette MacDonald's pajama top, and therefore he did not believe she had been stabbed with that knife. However, the first military policemen on the scene all agreed that the woman's pajamas were in such disarray that one of her breasts was exposed, so it isn't necessarily true that all knife thrusts found in her chest must have gone through her pajamas.

    If it is accepted that the knife did not have to go through Colette's pajamas, then one of the prosecution's own expert witnesses made MacDonald's account possible. Dr. Russell Fisher had made a comparison of the Old Hickory knife and the Geneva Forge knife. Fisher, the chief medical examiner and pathologist for the state of Maryland, had been hired by the CID in 1970 as a private consultant in the case. He told the grand jury on December 11, 1974, that "either of these two knives, in my judgment, or both, may have been used in inflicting stab wounds upon these three people. . . . I think they [the wounds] could have been done with the less rigid and somewhat duller knife if sufficient force were used in inflicting the wounds." (Testimony of Dr. Russell S. Fisher before the grand jury, p. 27.) Having given the grand jury this opinion, which was contrary to the government theory, Fisher was not called upon by the government to testify at the trial.

31. Tevere had handled the phone in such a manner that would have left fingerprints (he had demonstrated at the army hearing how he had picked up the handset at the grip using two fingers and a thumb, the normal way). His attempt was observed by others.

32. Photographs of the master bedroom also show the telephone in an entirely different position from that in which Tevere claimed he left it. Tevere, the MP who had actually handled the phone, was asked by Bernard Segal during the army hearing if he had allowed the phone to dangle as shown in the photo ("No, I didn't"), and Segal then asked him if he ever saw the phone dangling in that position ("No, I didn't"). Still later Tevere, looking at the photograph again, stated emphatically, "I didn't leave the phone this way."

(Testimony of Richard Tevere at the Article 32 hearing, pp. 192–193, 196–199.)

33. Sworn statement of Robert B. Shaw, defense deposition, pre-Article 32 hearing, p. 85.

34. These were medic Donald Jeffery at the murder site, and medics Johnny Yeager and Michael Newman at the hospital emergency room. See the CID statements of all three men and the Article 32 testimony of Michael D. Newman.

35. In his grand jury testimony on August 21, 1974, (pp. 4–10), Robert Shaw swore that he discovered the weapons in the backyard during those twilight moments before the 7 A.M. dawn. But in an unsigned, undated prosecution paper released to the defense through the Freedom of Information Act, Grebner revealed that when he first arrived at the murder apartment shortly before 5 A.M., Shaw was already busy conducting a search of the yard. Also, during a sworn, transcribed statement given prior to the Article 32 hearing, Grebner told how he had entered the apartment, completed a rapid circuit inside, and returned to the living room at which time Shaw sought him out. He said Shaw led him to the backyard to show him weapons that had just been discovered. Grebner added that it was dark and raining and he ordered the weapons to be covered. Given the stated chronology, this backyard discussion would have taken place at about the time Dr. Neal was busy examining the corpses inside the apartment, precluding Shaw being inside watching Neal examine the bodies. Three military policemen also told about finding the weapons during the hours of darkness. Also, Peter Kearns, the narrator in the film put together by the CID for the benefit of the Justice Department, presented a photograph of wooden stakes in the ground, and said they marked the murder club's location. Kearns then said, "During a previous search made during the hours of darkness, the stick was removed to protect it from the falling rain." If Shaw wasn't in the house with Dr. Neal, it follows that the integrated testimony of his fellow CID agents also becomes suspect.

36. In a sworn statement given to CID agent Robert Bidwell on December 20, 1970, Parson stated: "Between the time that I arrived at the MacDonald residence and until the crime scene was turned over to a group of investigators from the CID laboratory for processing, nothing was disturbed in that house to the best of my knowledge other than a medical doctor turning over the bodies to check them."

37. Dr. Neal testified at the army hearing that while certifying the deaths that morning, he took the pajama top off Colette MacDonald's chest and rolled her body over to a face-down position in order to examine her back. No additional photographs were made after his examination, so no confirmation exists that he repositioned the corpse exactly as it had been found. Since the

investigator's chalk line was drawn after Neal departed, the drawn line represents the position in which Neal left the body, not necessarily the position in which he found it. This means that if he moved the body as he described, he may have repositioned it onto fibers.

A CID laboratory report tends to support Neal's story that he moved Colette's body. Colette MacDonald's bloody face at some time had made contact with a dirt-laden rug (as might have occurred upon the doctor's rolling her as he described); debris taken from her face included "matted yellow paper fibers, particles of nut meats, small round dots of colored paper material, and dust." (See the CID Consolidated Laboratory Report, Exhibit E-3 [debris from mouth area of Colette MacDonald]; findings in Paragraph 62b, p. C-7.)

38. Article 32 testimony of Dr. William P. Neal.

39. Nuchereno revealed this move when he was questioned by the prosecution in 1974 for the grand jury investigation.

40. See Autopsy Report of Colette MacDonald as written by George Gammel, February 17, 1970.

41. In 1973 the U.S. Attorney for the Eastern District of North Carolina, Thomas P. McNamara, requested an investigation into the loss of the skin fragment. As a consequence, in early March of that year, William Ivory submitted a sworn statement identifying himself as the last person admitting to having seen it. According to his statement, Ivory had hand-carried a load of items from Fort Bragg to the CID laboratory at Fort Gordon on Wednesday, February, 25, 1970, the week after the murders. Instead of returning to Fort Bragg the following day, he spent a couple of days observing "the procedures used by the lab technicians in the handling of the evidence in this investigation." On Saturday morning one of the lab technicians was working with material in plastic containers. Ivory wrote, "I went to the microscope and held each container under the lens and observed the contents. . . . In the container marked fingernail scrapings of Colette MacDonald I observed a substance which appeared to me to be a small piece of skin. I could see that the tissue was still oily, that is, not dried out."

Ivory said he verified it with a lab technician, Dillard Browning. "I later learned that when questioned about the piece of skin," Ivory wrote, "the laboratory technicians denied seeing it." (Witness Statement, William Francis Ivory, March 2, 1973, oath administered by B. J. Grotts.) This is the only information the army or the government has released explaining the loss of the skin.

Laboratory records show that when the technicians tested the debris scraped from the victim's fingernails, the skin was not in the exhibit. It was never, officially, seen again.

42. When the army opened a second investigation in 1971, they secretly consid-

ered the loss of the skin as a weakness in their case. It was then that CID agent Paul Connolly submitted a delayed witness report on the matter on March 19, 1971. In this new report on his visit to MacDonald in the hospital thirteen months earlier, he told of seeing a fingernail scratch down MacDonald's chest. (Witness Statement, Paul Augustine Connolly, March 19, 1971, 0850 hours, 3 pages, oath administered by Darrell J. Bennett.) But Connolly had already submitted a written report of that visit shortly after the visit was made, and nowhere in his first report, in 1970, had he mentioned any scratch on MacDonald's chest.

43. Interview of Dr. Severt Jacobson with Fred Bost and Jerry Potter in Pinehurst, North Carolina, Saturday, July 15, 1989.

44. At trial, CID lab technician Hilyard Medlin said he compared the print on the glass with the many control prints taken from investigators, family, friends, and from MacDonald himself and he found no match. The print was adult sized, so the MacDonald children could be ruled out. Colette's prints, taken at the hospital, were usable enough to rule her out, too.

45. Two pubic or body hairs were taken from the sheet that remained on the master bed; two hairs were found among the debris taken from the bloody bedspread; and a body hair was found among the debris taken from the end of the hallway where MacDonald claimed he had lain unconscious. The hairs from the bedding are still unidentified, never matched to any person. And according to a note written by CID lab technician Dillard Browning on March 10, 1970, the hair in the hallway was simply ignored.

   Other government documents show that hairs from the murder club were also either lost or discarded. The club, after being found in the backyard, had been placed, at some point, in a plastic bag by Shaw. At the laboratory, the emptied bag was dropped into a trash can until someone happened to think that debris might have fallen from the club in transit. Browning examined the bag's debris on March 6, 1970, and found "three pubic or body hairs" of which he, again, made "no comparison due to lack of knowns or controls." When an FBI technician examined this same debris in 1979, he listed no hairs. Apparently, they had vanished.

46. In comparing the hair to three sample hairs, she described it on paper as "Probably a body hair or short head hair and slightly tapered worn end and other end slanted (broken). Small amount fragmented medulla (above worn end); granular pigmentation. Med. brown. Parts striated [unreadable] pigmentation and gross color quite similar to K(a) J(a) and E-35(a)." Exhibits K, J, and E refer to three hairbrushes. The (a) refers to hairs from those brushes. While they appeared "similar," they were found not to match.

47. The hairbrush and hair fibers were ignored for another year and examined only when the CID was forced to reinvestigate the case.

48. This burnt match was listed on DA Form 19–31, Military Police Receipt for Property, collected on February 20, 1970, by SP4 Walter F. Rowe.
49. FBI Report CE-70–3668 (undated), made by Special Agent Warren H. Tool and released to Dr. Jeffrey MacDonald by the Freedom of Information Act in July 1983.
50. When questioned about the syringe later, the CID authorities said that it never existed, that the FBI man imagined hearing Medlin mention a syringe during his address to the Fort Bragg officials.
51. These gloves, three cloth and two rubber, are listed in the CID Consolidated Laboratory Report of July 1972 as exhibit D34K (p. 9), with findings listed in paragraphs 26 and 27.

3. The Woman in the Floppy Hat

1. The paper was dated Monday, November 17, 1969.
2. This robbery occurred on Wednesday evening, September 30, 1970.
3. Witness Statement, John William Reynolds, March 1, 1971, at CID headquarters in Washington, D.C., 2 pages, with oath administered by agent Benjamin D. Ferraro, Jr.
4. More about Milne's sighting later.
5. From an interview with a CID agent who asked that his name not be used.
6. This drug amnesty program was first publicized in the Fort Bragg newspaper, the *Paraglide*, on June 11, 1970. It was described in the March 1971 issue of *Army* magazine by author Fred Bost.
7. The Operation Awareness halfway house was opened on June 7, 1970.
8. Visitors to Fort Bragg on August 27–28, 1970, were Senator Harold Hughes, D-Iowa; Senator Richard S. Schweiker, R-Pennsylvania; and Senator Peter H. Dominick, R-Colorado.
9. The *Fayetteville Observer*, September 25, 1970.
10. The murder of Albert Chavis.
11. The park riots occurred on August 29 and 30, 1970.
12. Medical records show that Helena Stoeckley was admitted to North Carolina Memorial Hospital at age fifteen for heroin addiction.
13. Beasley said this was the arrest of Allen Mazerolle, a dapper little dealer, who, on Helena Stoeckley's lead, was detained and booked for possession of LSD.
14. Interview of William Archbell by Prince Beasley, March 31, 1983.
15. FBI Investigative Report dated February 27, 1970.
16. While this event is documented in the FBI report cited above, the black drug dealer's name wasn't included. In an attempt to learn the dealer's name,

Fred Bost made queries at the Fayetteville Police Department, but the record apparently had disappeared, and no mention of the arrest appeared in the local newspapers.

17. Green Beret Captain Jim Williams had served as one of MacDonald's escort officers during his house arrest during the Article 32 proceedings. He had been the officer who blocked the CID's first attempt to take hair samples from MacDonald. Disgusted with McGinniss's book, *Fatal Vision*, and still chary of the press, Williams was reluctant to be interviewed by us. He agreed, however, to write a letter to Jeffrey MacDonald, who was free to share it with us. In that letter Williams recalled the key events of that period. He was very concerned that the army had placed MacDonald, a green and idealistic young doctor, into the position of dealing with hardened troops addicted to heroin, and then had made it mandatory that MacDonald turn in the names of heroin users who had come to him for counseling. From a letter by Lt. Colonel Jim Williams, U.S. Army (Retired), to Dr. Jeffrey R. MacDonald, and a copy to Jerry Potter, March 31, 1988.

18. This agent requested to remain anonymous in this book.

19. In his December 15, 1970, statement, CID chief Grebner said that the CID knew Helena Stoeckley even before the murders and knew that she was a drug user.

20. This information is based on a 1989 interview with the former Fort Bragg agent conducted by BBC producer Ted Landreth, and a subsequent interview by Jerry Potter on May 9, 1990.

21. Jeffrey MacDonald claimed that the black man who attacked him was wielding a club that was smooth and felt to him like a baseball bat.

22. Mrs. Averitt's account comes from her sworn witness testimony in federal court, Raleigh, on September 19, 1984, as part of Jeffery MacDonald's bid for a new trial.

23. Dorothy Averitt would later testify for the defense in Raleigh on September 19, 1984, during Jeffrey MacDonald's bid for a new trial based, largely, upon Helena Stoeckley's confessions.

24. Signed and sworn statement of Joan Green Sonderson, September 21, 1983.

25. This drug raid and the participants are substantiated by both police and court reports, as well as a newspaper story published the following day, February 18, 1970, in the *Fayetteville Observer*, p. 2. The drugs confiscated were marijuana, hashish, and LSD.

26. The manager of the trailer court confirmed this in a 1979 interview, saying she had no trouble recalling it because it was the first time she had ever rented a trailer to persons of mixed race.

27. Guin first told his story to Fred Bost during an interview on July 23, 1979.

28. Guin said he hadn't bothered reporting his sighting of the young people. He

knew the trailer had been raided that afternoon, and assumed the raid had been motivated by authorities seeking the tenants as murder suspects.

29. The government claimed that Mrs. Boushey's story is contradicted by Elizabeth Ramage, who was driven home from night school by Colette MacDonald. In a 1984 statement responding to questions from government agents, Ramage did not recall being separated from Colette MacDonald that night and didn't see the scene Mrs. Boushey describes. (Affidavit of Elizabeth Ann Ramage, May 17, 1984, City of Victoria, Province of British Columbia, Canada. Witnessed by Robert Mulligan, Commissioner for Taking Affidavits, Province of British Columbia.) However, in a 1992 interview, Mrs. Ramage was asked whether, after class, she went to the restroom. She remarked that she'd never even thought about it, but that she and Colette were both pregnant, Colette due in May, Mrs. Ramage in June. She agreed that she must have gone to the washroom after the two-hour class. She also allowed that she and Colette might have been separated for a few moments at this time. (Telephone interview of Elizabeth Ann Ramage by Jerry Potter, September 13, 1992.) The women's restroom in that building was on the second floor. Colette was allegedly seen by Mrs. Boushey, halted by the surrounding young people near the first-floor landing, en route from the second floor to the building's exit.

If Colette had gone to the restroom and then made her way down the steps before Ramage had exited the restroom, there is room for a scenario in which Colette would have been alone, on her way down to the first floor, when Boushey saw her.

30. A businesswoman, Eleanor Danson (not her real name), stopped at Dunkin' Donuts on Bragg Boulevard in Fayetteville. At about midnight four "hippies" came in, a white female and three males, two white, one black. One of the males was holding on to the young woman. The four stood and waited for a booth to open. The woman wore a large, light-colored floppy hat and a light-colored jacket. She carried a large shoulder bag and held it tightly. She had blond hair and appeared to be high on drugs.

31. A field jacket, which is a heavy coat soldiers use in the field, is not the same as a fatigue jacket, which is actually a shirt, the top part of "fatigues," which are, in essence, army work clothes. Many non-military people, however, confuse the names of the two garments.

32. Sworn statement of Marion L. Campbell to private investigator Raymond Shedlick, Jr., June 24, 1983.

33. See the Article 32 transcript, testimony of Mrs. Winnie Casper, pp. 1033–1045, and testimony of Edwin George Casper II, pp. 1601–1607.

34. Affidavit by Rita B. Shortill, signed and notarized on June 13, 1991.

35. Kenneth Lamb made this statement to private investigator John Dolan Myers, August 6, 1979.

36. The details mentioned here were given in a statement to private investigator Ted L. Gunderson, former FBI bureau chief, Los Angeles Bureau, by Mrs. Jan Snyder, on December 13, 1980. Her original statements to neighbors, made on the day of the murders, telling of seeing the group, were corroborated by one of those neighbors, John Chester, who appeared as a witness at the Article 32 hearing, 1970. Mrs. Snyder herself appeared later at the hearing and denied seeing anyone. In her 1980 statement to Gunderson, she said she so testified because she was fearful of her life.

37. Declaration of private investigator Raymond R. Shedlick, February 24, 1984, following his interview of Carlos Torres.

38. Real name withheld by request.

39. FBI Witness Statement of Janice Pendlyshok, February 18, 1970. CID Witness Statement by Agent John William Reynolds, March 1, 1971. Telephone interview with Fred Bost, June 21, 1988.

40. Article 32 testimony of Pamela Kalin.

41. James Douthat and Michael Malley, army lawyers on the defense team, investigated claims during the army hearing. The claim of the night man at Dunkin' Donuts was among these. All that now exists of this report is a note in MacDonald's diary. Malley and Douthat remember it, but don't remember the man's name, and the notes they took have apparently been lost.

42. Article 32 testimony of William Posey.

43. Account of Beasley's encounter with Helena and the group is taken from Fred Bost's interviews with Beasley and from Beasley's statements to former FBI bureau chief Ted Gunderson. In contrast, Beasley had signed a four-page statement for the CID on March 1, 1971, in which he referred briefly to this encounter by writing, "At this time she did not state to me that she could not remember what happened that night. I don't believe the question came up." Beasley would later say that the document was prepared by the CID and he gave it only a cursory reading before signing it.

44. Faddis Davis, the police dispatcher on duty that night, is deceased. Corroboration of Beasley's call for the CID that night is from a statement by former deputy sheriff Blaine O'Brien who was on duty and monitored the call. A CID agent who worked on the Inter-Agency Narcotics Bureau with Beasley also corroborated Beasley's concern that the CID pick Stoeckley up for questioning. Sheriff's detective John DeCarter also told Fred Bost that Prince Beasley, on the week of the murders, told him about Helena's admissions of involvement in the crimes.

45. Detective Beasley's notes were filed at the police station. Years later when he tried to retrieve them, he learned that they, and all other records of members of the Stoeckley group, seemed to have disappeared. (From an interview by Fred Bost and Jerry Potter with Prince Beasley, July 1989.)

46. Prince Beasley has described this event to numerous persons, testified to it at the trial, and told of it during various television interviews.

47. It would be incredible that Ivory, the lead investigator in this highly visible case, would not have been told about a call from Beasley, a fellow member of the Inter-Agency Narcotics Bureau, especially since that call was about detaining possible suspects in the MacDonald murder case. On May 9, 1990, Jerry Potter and Prebble Potter, Jerry's wife, interviewed a CID agent who had worked with Ivory in response to that call. The agent, now retired, didn't want his name used in the book. He implied that Ivory indeed had learned of Beasley's call. "Because of Beasley," the agent said, he and Ivory picked up Helena Stoeckley at a two-story drug rehabilitation center and took her to a safehouse. The agent remembered this happening two days after the murders.

48. In his army hearing testimony Ivory told Colonel Rock he knew her friends well enough to know they would kill her if they found out she had informed. In his grand jury testimony William Ivory described her life-style in a manner which could only have come from someone who knew her well, or was attempting to be seen as someone who knew her well. He also said that even before the murders he had "field-interrogated" Helena a couple of times. Beasley also said he had seen William Ivory, Helena Stoeckley, and Beasley's boss, Rudy Studer, together in a car. To our knowledge no one in the CID has gone on record to deny that Stoeckley was their informant, as well as Beasley's.

49. The CID agent and May 9, 1990, interview referred to in Note 47.

50. In his December 15, 1970, statement, Ivory's boss, Joe Grebner, said that Helena had been talked to within the first few days following the murders, and also interviewed on several occasions by other agencies. Also in that statement, Grebner stated that Helena was interviewed even prior to the army hearings, months earlier, then interviewed again during the hearings. Also during the hearings Ivory himself admitted that it was he who had interviewed her twice. He also told the hearing officer that she had no alibi.

51. The report was made in 1971 to Congressman Emanuel Celler in response to demands by Celler for explanations of alleged irregularities in the CID investigation.

52. An FBI interoffice teletype was sent from Charlotte to Washington, D.C., on February 18, 1970, the day after the murders, stating in part: "All known drug addicts in area of Fort Bragg and Fayetteville, N.C., being questioned and all informants of all law enforcement agencies being contacted."

53. Report to Honorable Emanuel Celler, House of Representatives, by Colonel Philo A. Hutcheson, in response to the Michael Malley allegations of CID misconduct, p. 43, response to allegation number 20, that the CID failed

to pursue leads about Helena Stoeckley. "She was questioned early in the investigation by members of the Fayetteville Police Department and FBI agents—not as a suspect, but because of her knowledge of the local 'hippie' community."

54. Retired Fayetteville police sergeant Charlie House is one of those persons who recalled this order. He made it known to Fred Bost during an interview in August 1989.

55. These actions by the FBI have been confirmed by numerous former residents of the area, some of whom were photographed and tape-recorded. Also, William Ivory alluded to such FBI activity during his second testimony at the Article 32 hearing in 1970.

56. This report was typed on February 27, 1970, FBI File Number CE-70–3668.

57. On May 7, 1990, Fred Bost, while reading documents in the army CID Records Holding Facility in Baltimore, Maryland, found the report on the hospital arrest with names intact.

58. See the CID Case Progress File, dated April 7, 1971, comment by Mahon.

59. Greg Mitchell's interview with William Ivory, May 25, 1971, in which Mitchell says that Cook was a heroin addict. Mitchell adds, "I met him at Operation Awareness on Fort Bragg."

60. The Hickory Trailer Court was located at 3840 Murchison Road; Matthews Foreign Car Service was located at 4410 Murchison Road.

61. This revelation was taped by Fred Bost during an interview conducted on February 6, 1981.

62. Fred Bost found a reference to this May 11, 1970, arrest when he visited the U.S. Army records depository in early May 1990.

63. CID agent Robert Shaw alluded to such an incident during his pre-Article 32 hearing deposition with MacDonald's lawyers.

64. Citing the Privacy Act, the FBI declines to divulge the names of the men in the report, and they only describe the black man without naming him. The black man thus far remains unidentified because the local newspaper failed to publish the arrest, and the local arrest records for the period have since been lost or destroyed.

4. The Army Hearing

1. MacDonald's wounds, substantiated by hospital records and doctors' statements, are discussed in detail in a later chapter.

2. The conversation between Jeffrey MacDonald and CID agents Grebner, Ivory, and Shaw is from transcripts of the CID recording of the April 6, 1970, interview at CID headquarters, Fort Bragg, North Carolina.

3. The clothing placed on the sofa is yet another indication of poor investigative

techniques. Investigators knew that the sofa was the scene of an alleged struggle, and possibly could yield minute evidence of that struggle if kept protected. Yet the clothing was placed on it three hours before the lab technicians arrived at the scene.

4. Preliminary CID Laboratory Report, April 6, 1970, p. 13, regarding exhibits F-1 and F-2 (urine and blood samples from Jeffrey MacDonald), says that the exhibits "did not reveal the presence of any dangerous drugs or narcotics. Further examinations of Exhibit F-2 by the USAH [U.S. Army Hospital] at Fort Gordon, GA. showed same to contain 0.150 mg/ml of ethyl alcohol—this generally means that the subject was not under the influence of alcohol."

The above lab report was based, in part, upon the more complete handwritten lab notes, marked "P-C-FP-82–70, 24 Feb 70, JJB"; JJB are the initials of CID laboratory technician Joseph John Barbato. The notes read in full: "Received from Chamberlain on 24 Feb 70 one test tube containing blood sample and urine sample both taken from MacDonald. Examinations—the blood sample was examined for dangerous drugs by following set separation scheme and finally running acid absorption curve which did not indicate the presence of dangerous drugs. Examinations of the urine sample followed the set procedures set forth in our notes and our final results did not reveal the presence of any dangerous drugs. Examinations of the liquid contents of the jar did not reveal the presence of any narcotics or restricted drugs."

5. Article 32 testimony of Alfred Kassab.

6. *Fayetteville Observer*, July 20, 1970.

7. A military hospital is authorized to accept a civilian patient only when injuries are so grievous that movement to a civilian hospital would further endanger the person's health.

8. "Comparative examinations of the hairs (found in Mrs. MacDonald's hand) revealed same to be dissimilar to the hairs (removed from Capt. MacDonald's body)."

See the CID Laboratory Report, written by Dillard O. Browning at Fort Gordon, Georgia, July 29, 1970.

9. Amended Hair Report from Fort Gordon Army CID Laboratory, September 2, 1970, signed by Janice Glisson.

10. May 9. 1990, interview by Jerry and Prebble Potter with a retired CID agent who didn't want his name used. He stated that "because of Beasley" he and Ivory picked Helena up at a two-story drug rehabilitation center and took her to a safehouse.

11. Kenneth Mica, telephone interview with Jerry Potter, October 21, 1991.

12. This was approximately 22 minutes after MacDonald's phone call for help.

13. Posey had not learned the correct spelling of this last name, and those involved in the hearing assumed it was spelled "Stokely," which is the way it was spelled in the transcript and in Colonel Rock's report.

14. A man later identified as Helena's boyfriend, Greg Mitchell, called himself "Jim" when checking into a drug rehabilitation home.
15. See Note 10.
16. Cumberland County Court Cases 70cr11492 and 70cr11504.
17. Terry Ingland was convicted on September 22, 1970, of conspiracy to murder Richard Fortner. He was sentenced to ten years in prison.
18. From *Report and Proceedings under Article 32 Uniform Code of Military Justice*, by Colonel Warren V. Rock, October 13, 1970, p. A24.
19. The subject of Helena Stoeckley is covered in detail in later chapters.
20. From Jeffrey MacDonald's typed report for Bernard Segal, October 14, 1970, of Captain Hammond Beale's meeting with MacDonald to bring the defense up to date on the hearing results. The essential tone of the meeting was corroborated by Beale in a telephone conversation with Jerry Potter on February 23, 1990. Although Beale said he could not remember, after twenty years, the details of the actual conversations, Beale said, upon reading the typed notes, that he was "certain they are correct."
21. See Note 10.
22. Wold cited the subsequent federal conviction of MacDonald as justification for his belief in 1970 that MacDonald would eventually be brought to justice.
23. Telephone interview with Colonel Pedar C. Wold at Schofield Barracks, Hawaii, July 1989.
24. FBI Teletype, J. Edgar Hoover to Robert M. Murphy, October 28, 1970.

5. Reversals

1. Dr. Hughes, a former Green Beret physician, had given MacDonald the moonlighting emergency medicine position at Fayetteville's Cape Fear Valley Medical Center in late 1969.
2. FBI Teletype, Robert M. Murphy to J. Edgar Hoover, November 2, 1970.
3. FBI Teletype, Robert M. Murphy to J. Edgar Hoover, November 18, 1970, and FBI General Investigative Division Memorandum, November 19, 1970.
4. Posse Comitatus—that is, "power of the county"—is the traditional law which allows peacekeepers to deputize other citizens. In early history, a U.S. marshal would commonly deputize soldiers, leaving their commander frustrated. To end this practice, the U.S. Congress, on June 18, 1878, made it illegal to use military members for civil law enforcement except when called upon by the president during emergencies.

   Then in 1955 a Supreme Court decision made it additionally illegal under this Posse Comitatus Act for military law enforcers to pursue a military lawbreaker into civilian life when the crime allegedly committed was such that it could be tried by a civilian court. Since federal statutes sufficiently covered murder on a government reservation, the 1955 court decision made it illegal for the army to investigate Jeffrey MacDonald once he was released from uniform.

5. Proof that the CID's reinvestigation of Jeffrey MacDonald was in conflict with the Posse Comitatus Act is found in a letter to CID headquarters from the army general counsel (Subject: USACIDC Investigation of the McDonald [sic] Murder Case; April 7, 1978; signed by Jill Wine-Volner, general counsel).

6. Letter, First Lieutenant Michael J. Malley to Lieutenant General John J. Tolson, December 6, 1970; letter, Alfred G. Kassab to R. Kenly Webster, army deputy general counsel, December 5, 1970; letter, Rep. Allard K. Lowenstein to J. Edgar Hoover, December 8, 1970.

7. Memorandum to U.S. Army general counsel, December 10, 1970.

8. Affidavit of Peter E. Kearns—United States District Court for the Eastern District of North Carolina, June 30, 1984, paragraph 2.

9. DA Form 2823, Witness Statement, Warren V. Rock, 5 Jan 71, 1000 hours, oath administered by Peter E. Kearns, no witness, 8 pages, statement under oath.

10. Memorandum for the Army General Counsel from the U.S. Army CID Agency, Subject: The Kassab and Malley Allegations; the Senator Ervin Inquiry; 5 Jan 71.

11. In one instance Mike Malley had written a simple, straightforward accusation, an accusation denied by Tufts. "MPs on the scene could have supplied much information," complained Malley, "yet they were never interviewed in depth." This was a serious charge because grave decisions depended upon the positioning of physical evidence. It was critical that all persons early on the scene be interrogated and placed on record regarding whether they had seen anything moved.

When Kearns asked Grebner on December 15, 1970, why the case files held only four MP statements, Grebner said he had ordered statements obtained and "assumed that statements had been taken." (See DA Form 2820, Statement by Accused or Suspect Person, Franz Joseph Grebner, 15 Dec 70, 1402 hours, interrogator Peter E. Kearns, witness Lyle B. Smith, 22 pages, statement under oath.) Malley's charge, therefore, was true. Grebner had failed to confirm that his orders were carried out.

In another instance, Malley and Kassab had charged that investigators allowed an unknown civilian wearing jeans to wander through the crime scene. Colonel Tufts' response denied such a person had been seen.

Yet military policeman Kenneth Mica swore he had seen a person wearing blue jeans pick up the overturned flowerpot in the living room. (See DA Form 2823, Witness Statement, Kenneth C. Mica, 21 Dec 70, 0945 hours, oath administered by Lyle B. Smith, no witness, 6 pages, statement under oath.) Major Joe Parson, the assistant provost marshal, questioned on December 20, 1970, said he saw not one but two strangers in the living room who were wearing jeans. (See DA Form 2823, Witness Statement, Joe W. Parson, 20 Dec 70, 1400 hours, oath administered by Robert R. Bidwell, no witness, 10 pages, statement under oath.) Grebner, too, during his interview with Kearns, also admitted to seeing a man there in jeans. (CID Witness Statement, Franz Joseph Grebner, December 15, 1970.)

12. CID Case Progress File, December 29, 1970, Bidwell.
13. CID Case Progress File, December 30, 1970, Bidwell.
14. CID Case Progress File, January 7, 1971, 0800 hours, Kearns.
15. CID Case Progress File, January 7, 1971, 1300–1540 hours, Kearns-Grebner.
16. The depicted events and conversations to and in Nashville, unless otherwise noted, are based on memory of the occasions as stated by Prince E. Beasley to Fred Bost on April 5, 1981, and November 7, 1988. Many events are given parallel substantiation by Mahon's entries in the CID Log for Feb. 27–28, 1971.
17. Ibid.
18. Statement signed by Prince E. Beasley, Nashville, Tennessee, March 1, 1971.
19. CID Case Progress File, 16 Apr. 71, Mahon.
20. CID Case Progress File, 21 Apr. 71, Mahon.
21. CID Case Progress File, 22 Apr. 71, Mahon.
22. Except where noted, the subsequent events depicted in Nashville are based upon entries in the CID Case Progress File, April 23 to April 30, 1971, as recorded by Mahon.
23. Witness Statement, Robert A. Brisentine, Jr., Fort Holabird, Md., April 26, 1971, oath administered by D. J. Presson.
24. Polygraph Examination Report, Helena Werle Stoeckley, April 23, 1971, administered by Robert A. Brisentine, Jr.
25. The interview conversations cited here are detailed in the following four documents: (1) Witness Statement, Kathy Ann Smith, May 5, 1971, 1315 hours, signed May 6, 1971, oath administered by William F. Ivory, witnessed by Richard J. Mahon; (2) Witness Statement, Diane Marie Cazares (née Hedden), May 7, 1971, 1345 hours, signed on May 7, 1971, oath administered by Richard J. Mahon, witnessed by William F. Ivory; (3) CID Case Log, 11 May 71, Mahon-Ivory: Statement of Accused or Suspect Person, Bruce Johnny Fowler, May 11, 1971, 1515 hours, oath administered by William F. Ivory, witnessed by Richard J. Mahon; and (4) Statement by Accused or Suspect Person, Gregory Howard Mitchell, May 25, 1971, oath administered by William F. Ivory, witnessed by David B. Reed III.
26. CID Report of Investigation, USACIDA, 3rd Progress, Period 26 May-29 Jun 71, dated June 30, 1971, signed by Peter E. Kearns and approved by David B. Reed III.

27. These statements are contained in a Justice Department memo from Williams to White, dated January 16, 1975.

28. The story which follows is taken from the grand jury transcript for the period January 21–24, 1975, specifically the testimony of Dr. Jeffrey R. MacDonald and Dr. Robert Sadoff. Also see the Mailgram from Bernard Segal to the grand jury, January 23, 1975. Also see the sworn affidavit by Michael Malley, April 25, 1975, notarized in the District of Columbia (the notary's signature is illegible in our copy). See also the sworn affidavit of Dr. Jeffrey R. MacDonald, notarized by Mary Congdon of Los Angeles County on April 24, 1975. See the motion, by Segal, to Dismiss Indictment for Defects in Grand Jury Proceedings and Prosecutorial Misconduct before the Grand Jury, submitted to John R. Whitty, clerk of the U.S. District Court of the Eastern District of North Carolina, on July 28, 1975.

29. More about Brian Murtagh and his history in the MacDonald case will be discussed in a later chapter.

30. Boston Attorney Phil Cormier, working with attorneys Harvey Silverglate and Alan Dershowitz, researched this issue in 1989 and 1990. He found that the case records confirmed that Bernard Segal had submitted an initial request for "discovery" on April 4, 1975, and that the government had responded on April 25, 1975, with a refusal to "furnish the lab notes, methodology, nature and name of physical examinations, scientific tests and experiments made in connection with this case." The government's refusal to furnish the requested laboratory data was based on its insistence that laboratory reports submitted to the defense contained all pertinent information. Cormier followed the paper trail through the following years, noting a continued pattern of a prosecution denying materials to the defense while at the same time affecting an appearance of cooperation. Cormier found a letter written to the army by Murtagh on March 1, 1979, just before the trial, requesting that the CID laboratory furnish him with two copies of all chemists' notes concerning each case report. Murtagh explained in his letter that the second copies "will be for eventual release to defense counsel." Although this letter was written four years after Segal's initial request for just such notes, Cormier established that Murtagh never surrendered the notes to the defense as he had promised to do. On August 20, 1979, after the prosecution had rested its case, and nine days before the trial's end, Segal had made a motion to dismiss the indictment on the very basis of the government's failure to disclose, through the years, requested "discovery" documents. That complaint, like the others before it, had been to no avail. Murtagh's refusal to provide the requested items was ignored by the court.

31. Order from F. T. Dupree, Jr., Chief United States District Judge, dated June 19, 1979.

6. The Evidence at Trial

1. At trial, Dillard Browning testified that the wax evidence "seemed brittle and dry, which would indicate to me that it was at least several weeks old when I received it." But on cross-examination, he admitted that he didn't receive and begin examinations of the wax until the middle of March, three weeks after the murders, which would have indicated that the wax was deposited in the apartment about the time of the murders. See trial transcript, pp. 3890 and 3899.

2. See trial transcript, arguments before the court on July 31, 1979, p. 3246(18).

3. Trial transcript, p. 4325.

4. Trial transcript, p. 4327.

5. Trial transcript, p. 4332.

6. In most cases, the experts involved were the precise government witnesses who had testified at the trial, but since the defense didn't have the lab notes for comparison at trial, they had no opportunity to inform the jurors of these contradictions among the government's own experts.

7. Stombaugh said that he had folded the pajama top in the exact way it was found at the murder scene, based on pictures made of Colette MacDonald's body. But the first military policemen on the scene say the photographs do not show the body as they found it. (Only one of the group of military policemen first through the doorway, Sergeant Robert Duffy, said the pajama top was on Colette MacDonald's chest at the time. The others, according to sworn testimony at the Article 32 hearing, did not recall seeing it on her at that time.) The photographs show the wounds and the woman's breasts covered by the pajama top. The chief investigator, William Ivory, testified on the subject at the trial. He stated, "I did not see [the pajama top] covering those punctures in the chest." And the military policemen who had earlier rushed into the room that morning remembered immediately seeing the exposed left breast "including the nipple on the breast." This quote is from a statement made by Kenneth Mica to Captain Brian Murtagh when Murtagh interviewed him prior to his grand jury appearance. (See FBI Witness Report, Kenneth Mica, interviewed 9/17/74, transcribed 9/27/74. The statement generally repeats testimony of Mica and other MPs at the army Article 32 hearing conducted earlier.)

In fact, during an interview with Captain Brian Murtagh on September 17, 1974, Kenneth Mica indicated MacDonald's pajama top might actually have been on the floor between the man and woman when he arrived. Mica told Murtagh he had moved between the pair and he remembered kneeling on the rug and being aware of a piece of clothing under his legs "which could have been a pajama top." (FBI Witness Report, Mica, 9/17/74.)

This tends to confirm Joseph Paulk's memory about the pajama top. During a 1989 interview Paulk was asked at what moment he had first noticed the garment. He replied, "I sort of recall MacDonald trying to put that over her because one of her breasts was exposed." (Tape-recorded interview of Joseph Paulk by Fred Bost, October 15, 1989.)

So, if multiple eyewitness statements and Stombaugh himself are to be believed, the photographs taken that morning do not depict the pajama top as it was first seen, and the photographs, therefore, become useless as validation for Murtagh's claim regarding Stombaugh's experiment.

8. In Stombaugh's experiment, for example, on three different thrusts the ice pick would have gone through five layers of cloth.

9. In fact, in June 1971 Stombaugh made a sketch of the ice pick in which he recorded the exact width of the blade at various distances from the tip. At an inch and a half (the deepest wound in Colette MacDonald), the blade was 0.120 inch wide. According to Stombaugh's measurements, the blade would have had to penetrate another inch and a half to reach its maximum width.

10. See the trial transcript for the bench conference held August 22, 1979.

11. A laboratory report sent to the CID by the FBI in 1971 cited the directionality of certain ice pick holes in Jeffrey MacDonald's pajama top (FBI Laboratory Report 70–51728-PC-F7279 JV, July 2, 1971). In collectively addressing all of the garments examined, the report stated that the apparent frequent handling of the victims' clothing caused the tiny yarns in most of the ice pick holes to return to their original positions. But in addressing MacDonald's pajama top alone, the report immediately goes on to say, "However, based upon a microscopic examination . . . , six holes in specimen Q12 had the general appearance of being 'entry' holes and five holes had the general appearance of being 'exit' holes." (An entry hole would be one puncturing from the outside of the garment inward; an exit hole would be from the skin side of the garment outward.) Stombaugh numbered the holes while making this examination. His sketch and notes made at the time indicate that the holes showing directionality from the outside to the inside were numbers 1, 5, 12, 16, 21, and 22. The holes showing directionality from the inside to the outside were numbers 3, 6, 9, 14, and 20.

12. The idea of stabbing through the pajama top had been kicked around from the very beginning. Clifford Somers, the army prosecutor at the Article 32 hearing, suggested it in his closing arguments. Glisson's failed experiment was disclosed in a CID laboratory note discovered by defense investigators at the CID Records Holding Facility in Baltimore, Maryland, on May 7,

1990. The CID evidence log gives additional support that this abandoned experiment occurred. The log shows that the pajama top was sent by mail from the evidence room at Fort Bragg to the CID laboratory on October 7, 1971, for additional analysis, supposedly for six days. The garment was returned to Fort Bragg on October 26, 1971, nineteen days later.

13. Stombaugh charted his experiment by assigning a number to each of the twenty-one wounds as positioned on Colette MacDonald's chest, placing the numbers 1 through 21 in a column. Next to each of these entries he then indicated the fabric hole (or holes) in the pajama top which he thought was (or were) related to that wound, using the identification number(s) written on the garment. Where he believed a thrust passed through more than one layer of cloth, he recorded the sequence starting with the hole number on the upper outside, followed by the number on the next layer, and so on, moving downward to the victim's chest. To point out one of several inconsistencies, one such listing (wound #1) was for a supposed thrust through three layers and involved holes 20, 21, and 22, in that sequence. This means that hole 20 went from the outside of the garment to the inside, then because of the fold the ice pick making hole 21 would go from the inside of the garment to the outside, then the final hole, 22, would be from the outside inward. In coming to this conclusion, Stombaugh ignored his 1971 findings in which he recorded hole 20 as being from the *inside* out, hole 21 being from the *outside* in, and hole 22 being from the outside in.

14. See the 1979 trial transcript, pp. 4571–4572.

15. Interview of Dr. Severt Jacobson with Fred Bost and Jerry Potter at Pinehurst, North Carolina, Saturday, July 15, 1989.

16. In fact, Dillard Browning testified to the grand jury, itemizing the pajama fibers and bloody hairs in this particular debris (transcript, Browning, p. 35). He found none entwined, and the bloody hair was not Colette's, according to him, but Kimberly's. He stated: "I found several of the cotton threads and one polyester thread. Also in this exhibit, I found hair from Colette and hair from Kimberly. Kimberly's hair was bloodstained."

17. This interview took place on February 19, 1970, two days after the murders.

18. Pam Kalin made the (alleged) statement on February 19; the Article 32 hearing began on July 6.

19. Grand jury transcript, Pamela Kalin, Aug. 27, 1974, pp. 22–26.

20. Ibid., pp. 35–40.

21. Pamela Kalin and members of her family earlier insisted that she had never, even in the beginning, identified any of the weapons as coming from MacDonald's house. When the CID had asked her in 1970 if a knife had come from MacDonald's kitchen she responded that she didn't know, that it might have. That hypothetical was used against MacDonald early on. The agents told

MacDonald on April 6 that someone had positively identified the knife as coming from his house, but that had not been true.

22. Statements of Chaplain Kenneth Edwards and Rosalie Edwards to private investigator Raymond Shedlick, Jr., June 5, 1984. Confirmed by statements to Fred Bost, May 11, 1988.

23. See CID Consolidated Laboratory Report, 1972, pp. 6 and C-2, paragraphs 11 and 14.

24. In a written confession in 1980, Helena Stoeckley told of seeing Colette MacDonald attacked on the bed. If her story is true, this would account for the blood on the bedspread.

25. The bedspread was cataloged by the FBI as Exhibit Q110. The resultant FBI laboratory report stated: "Q110 through Q115 and Q120 were examined for the presence of fabric and/or foot impressions. However, none were found." (FBI Laboratory Report dated November 5, 1974.)

26. The prosecution molded its theory that MacDonald had carried Colette in the sheet and had stepped upon the blood-soaked bedspread, in part, because photographs show the sheet and bloodied bedspread crumpled together near Colette MacDonald's body. But the government possessed information that the bedding was not in that location when the military police first arrived. Lieutenant Paulk, the officer in charge of the military police patrol, told the CID in 1970 that he felt certain that when he entered the room both the top sheet and bedspread were still on the bed, pushed toward the bottom. Paulk repeated this belief during a taped interview with author Fred Bost on October 15, 1989.

27. Witness Statement, William F. Ivory, December 17, 1971, oath administered by Peter E. Kearns, no witnesses.

28. One of the first such uses for ultraviolet light occurred in New Hampshire in 1934. Bloody footprints, details of which were not visible to the naked eye, were found and photographed, helping to solve a murder case. (See *State* v. *Thorp* 171A 633.86, N.H. 501 [1934].)

29. FBI Report, interview 2/18/70, dictated 2/24/70, typed February 25, 1970.

30. On July 11, 1990.

31. On July 25, 1990.

32. Laboratory note by Dillard Browning, Exhibit D-216, March 13, 1970.

33. See Article 32 transcript, p. 793. If the footprints had been made at the time the government envisioned, they should have been long dry by the time Shaw first viewed them.

34. James Blackburn was forced out of the practice of law in January 1993. See the Epilogue.

35. See Autopsy Report of Colette MacDonald as written by Dr. George Gammel, February 17, 1970. The skin is mentioned here.

36. In 1973 the U.S. Attorney for the Eastern District of North Carolina, Thomas P. McNamara, requested an investigation into the loss of the skin fragment. As a consequence, in early March of that year, William Ivory submitted a sworn statement identifying himself as the last person admitting to having seen it. According to his statement, Ivory had hand-carried a load of items from Fort Bragg to the CID laboratory at Fort Gordon on Wednesday, February 25, 1970, the week after the murders. Instead of returning to Fort Bragg the following day, he spent a couple of days observing "the procedures used by the lab technicians in the handling of the evidence in this investigation." On Saturday morning one of the lab technicians was working with material in plastic containers. Ivory wrote, "I went to the microscope and held each container under the lens and observed the contents. . . . In the container marked fingernail scrapings of Colette MacDonald I observed a substance which appeared to me to be a small piece of skin. I could see that the tissue was still oily, that is, not dried out."

    Ivory said he pointed it out to a lab technician, Dillard Browning. "I later learned that when questioned about the piece of skin," Ivory wrote, "the laboratory technicians denied seeing it." (Witness Statement, William Francis Ivory, March 2, 1973, oath administered by B. J. Grotts.)

    Laboratory records show that when the technicians tested the debris scraped from the victim's fingernails, the skin was not in the exhibit. It was never, officially, seen again.

37. When the army opened a second investigation in 1971, they secretly considered the loss of the skin as a weakness in their case. It was then that CID agent Paul Connolly submitted a delayed witness report on the matter on March 19, 1971. In this new report on his visit to MacDonald in the hospital thirteen months earlier, he told of seeing a fingernail scratch down MacDonald's chest. (Witness Statement, Paul Augustine Connolly, March 19, 1971, 0850 hours, 3 pages, oath administered by Darrell J. Bennett.) But Connolly had already submitted a written report of that visit shortly after the visit was made, and nowhere in his first report, in 1970, had he mentioned any scratch on MacDonald's chest.

38. During an interview of Dr. Severt Jacobson with Fred Bost and Jerry Potter at Pinehurst, North Carolina, Saturday, July 15, 1989, Dr. Jacobson said, "I made notes and I drew diagrams. There were no fingernail scratches on MacDonald."

7. Helena Stoeckley at Trial

1. From an interview with Bernard Segal by Jerry Potter; and an interview with Red Underhill by Chris Olgiati and Ted Landreth in their documentary on

the MacDonald case, *False Witness*, produced by the British Broadcasting Company, June 1989.

2. Telegram to FBI, SAC Charlotte from unknown agent, dated 11/3/78.

3. This documentary information was furnished by Dr. Peter Holland, the psychiatrist who treated Helena Stoeckley. Dr. Holland came forward with his information about Stoeckley's confessions to him and to others at the hospital after seeing a segment about the murder case on the ABC *Good Morning America* television newsmagazine, February 21, 1992. The newscast mentioned that Stoeckley's confessions were at issue, so Dr. Holland felt it was his public duty to tell what he knew.

4. He told private investigator John Myers that he had understood that the CID would come through the neighborhood to question everyone, but even though he lived across the street from the MacDonalds, he said he was never approached. He hadn't reported the incident because he was soon leaving the army, was entering college in another city, and wanted to get his family settled. He said he was relieved when MacDonald was cleared during the hearing in 1970, but when he heard MacDonald was going to be tried again in 1979, he decided to tell his story. (Interview with James Milne by John Myers, February 27, 1979. Follow-up interview by Wade M. Smith, July 28, 1979.)

5. Records show she was actually sixteen years old at the time of her high school graduation.

6. She named the books as *The Treasury of Witchcraft*.

7. According to Federal Rule of Evidence 804(b)(3), hearsay evidence may be admitted if the hearsay statement "was at the time of its making so far contrary to the declarant's pecuniary or propriety interest, or so far tended to subject him to civil authority or criminal liability. . . ."

8. Lynne M. Markstein told the MacDonald defense team that she had talked with Stoeckley, and Segal's private investigator, John Myers, took her statement at the time of the trial. Another statement from Markstein was taken by John Myers and Ted L. Gunderson on January 23, 1980.

9. See the 1979 trial transcript, p. 5792.

10. The report of April 20, 1971, said that the fibers in the brush were "similar in gross color, pigmentation and structure to the hair of Exhibit E-4 and could have had the same source of origin." (The debris of Exhibit E-4, taken from Colette MacDonald's right hand, contained, among other things, some head hairs that were later matched to her.)

11. See the 1979 trial transcript, p. 5698.

12. Hilyard Medlin said fingerprints failed to adhere to the wood because it was so weathered. Robert Shaw, the CID agent who recovered the weapon in the backyard on the morning of the murders, testified at the Article 32 hearing that it "had cracks in it running with the grain, similar to the kind of cracks

which appear in wood when exposed to long periods of wind, rain, and sun." (Article 32 transcript, Robert Shaw, p. 842.) And laboratory notes made by Dillard Browning specifically stated that the club was "exposed to the elements" more than those wooden items examined from inside the home. (See CID laboratory notes P-C-FP-82–70-R2 & 3, 19 Mar 70, DOB.) In fact, Browning had to cut the end of the murder club to make the growth rings visible in order to compare the rings to those in an indoor bed slat. The bed slat, which had been protected indoors, required no cutting because the growth rings were easily seen.

Also, a picture exists of Colette painting Kimberly's bed in the backyard. And documents prove that the government matched the paint on the board as the same as the paint on the bed.

13. See the 1979 trial transcript, p. 5807.
14. *U.S. v. MacDonald* (4th Circuit, 1982).
15. See the affidavit signed by James E. Friar, July 25, 1983.
16. Day 21 was August 17, 1979. This quote appears on p. 525 of *Fatal Vision*, 1989 Signet paperback edition.
17. Defense memo by Doug Widmann, January 16, 1991.
18. Trial transcript of arguments made before the court out of the jury's presence on July 31, 1979, p. 3246 (98).
19. *Brady v. Maryland*, 373 U.S. 83 (1963). The courts say of *Brady* material that if doubt exists about whether the evidence is of value to the defense, the benefit of the doubt is to be given the accused and the evidence must be made known to him. This must be done even if the defense has not made a request for the evidence. But the prosecutors' obligations go even further than that, for even if the defense does not know such evidence exists, and if the prosecution knows that the defense has no knowledge of it, the prosecution is still obliged by law to make the evidence known in sufficient time for the defense to make full use of it at trial.
20. FBI Report 70–3668–949–950.

8. The Psychiatric Issue at Trial

1. Interview of Bernard Segal by Jerry Potter, May 31, 1988.
2. Telephone interview of Dorothy "Perry" MacDonald by Jerry Potter, May 1, 1988. Testimony of Dorothy "Perry" MacDonald in *MacDonald v. McGinniss* civil trial, July 1987. That McGinniss made the statement about getting drunk is also corroborated by Bernard Segal.
3. The members of the defense team who accompanied MacDonald to Smith's office were attorneys Bernard Segal and Wade Smith, law clerk Sara Simmons, and Segal's assistant, Fran Fine. The interview occurred on August 13, 1979.

4. Memorandum prepared by Bernard L. Segal, August 13, 1979. "It is agreed that if the Court rules that the defendant Jeffrey R. MacDonald may not offer psychiatric evidence in support of his defense, that no part of any interview, test or evaluation made by either of you may be disclosed to any person whatsoever except upon the written consent of Dr. MacDonald. The said restriction applies to any and all information that either of you may obtain orally from Dr. MacDonald. If the court rules that the defendant may offer psychiatric evidence in support of his defense then this agreement does not preclude disclosure of information obtained by either of you in a manner consistent with professional standards for psychiatrists and psychologists."

5. This is from an interview on May 9, 1990, by Jerry and Prebble Potter of a former CID agent who requested his name not be used in the book.

6. This, too, was recalled by the above-mentioned former agent.

7. See CID Substantiation Report, File #71-CID011–00015, p. 99.

8. From a discussion with Jerry Potter in the federal court building in Los Angeles during the trial *MacDonald v. McGinniss*, July 1987.

9. Letter and summary of memories from Mike Malley to Jeff MacDonald, July 8, 1971, p. 55. It should be pointed out that this letter was written before any signs of a breach appeared between Kassab and MacDonald.

10. References concerning the memories of Helen Fell are taken from a letter she wrote to Jeffrey MacDonald, dated January 23, 1990, citing her memories of the 1970–1971 period.

11. Kassab was proud of the part he played in Canadian intelligence during World War II.

12. Kassab had tape-recorded the telephone conversation. He later destroyed the tape, but only after making a typewritten transcript. As MacDonald now claims, he had tried to get Kassab to see that even though he had "killed" one of the attackers "it's a very depressing type of thing, because nothing changes. I mean, I mean, it's still—Colette, Kimmie, and Kristy are gone." Kassab agreed, saying, "nothing will change anything."

Kassab surrendered the typed transcript to government prosecutor Brian Murtagh on December 4, 1978, more than eight years after the conversation had occurred. See telephone transcript under a page with a Xeroxed "Memo from Fred Kassab," and in Kassab's handwriting, to "Bryan," date "12/4/78," and the written notation, "Please excuse spelling," with the signature "F." This memo apparently signifies transference of the transcript from Kassab to Brian Murtagh on December 4, 1978. This transcript came to light under the Freedom of Information Act.

13. From statement by Jeffrey MacDonald; see corroboration of luncheon meetings in trial testimony of Mildred Kassab, p. 3312.

14. Department of Justice Routing Slip to Jim Robinson in Room 2110, dated 1/20 (1971).

15. CID Case Progress File, 27 Apr. 71, 1830–2115, Kearns/Pruett.

16. CID Case Progress File, 2 Apr. 71, 0800–1700, Kearns.

17. CID Case Progress File, 3 Apr. 71, Reed. And CID Case Progress File, 13 Apr. 71, Reed.

18. CID Case Progress File, 27 Apr. 71, Kearns-Pruett, 1930–2115.

19. See trial testimony of Helen Fell, p. 6120.

20. Mildred Kassab substantiated the occurrence of this dinner to a newspaper reporter during the 1979 trial, saying she prepared a lobster dinner for her son-in-law. Contrary to the story of Helen Fell, however, Mildred Kassab insisted she had only wished MacDonald "Godspeed and good luck." These statements were made to reporter Rick Thames of the *Fayetteville Observer* during an interview on August 23, 1979. When *Fatal Vision* was published in 1983, Mildred Kassab insisted that by mid-1971 she and Freddie knew that MacDonald had murdered her daughter Colette and her grandchildren. The written record, as well as her psychological makeup, challenges that later claim. By her own sworn words, Mildred Kassab was a woman willing to pluck out tongues. Would this kind of woman have prepared a lobster dinner for the "known killer" of her daughter and grandchildren and then have wished him "Godspeed and good luck"?

21. Letter to Commanding General [sic], U.S. Army CID Command, from Alfred G. Kassab, dated March 4, 1974.

22. Routing and Transmittal Slip to Colonel Glaser from Major Chucala containing a four-paragraph discussion of the situation, dated March 20, 1974.

23. Ibid.

24. Memorandum for Colonel Tufts, subject: MacDonald Murders—Inquiry, signed by Steven Chucala, dated 1 May 1974.

25. Letter to Attorney General William B. Saxbe from Judge Algernon L. Butler, May 1, 1974.

26. See the article "Gun-Carrying Doctors," *New York Times*, June 3, 1974. Brussel describes three incidents in which he had to use his .32 Iver Johnson handgun. He once discouraged a drug addict who wanted a methadone pill. He caused another "almost stoned" man to back off. And he dissuaded the unwelcome advances of three youths, one of whom had said, "Hold it, Whitey. We got something to say to you."

27. See paragraph 2, subparagraph 1, of a memorandum signed by Jack G. Pruett of the CID, dated February 23, 1971, indicating that a "background check" of Dr. Brussel was initiated on February 5, 1971.

28. Brussel, James A., and Hitch, K. S., "The Military Malingerer," *Military Surgeon*, 93:1, 33–44, July 1943.

29. Brussel, who died in October 1982, wrote numerous articles and eight books, including *Casebook of a Crime Psychiatrist*, published by Bernard Geis Associates, 1968; *An Introduction to Rorschach Psychodiagnostics in Psychiatry*, a

training manual which he co-authored with Kenneth S. Hitch, 1950, N.Y. State Hospitals Press; and *Instant Shrink*, co-authored with Theodore Irwin, published by Cowles Book Company, 1971.

30. *The Concise Guide to Somatic Therapies*, Lawrence B. Guttmacher, M.D., published by the American Psychiatric Press in 1988, states, on p. 88, that the early history of electroconvulsive therapy was a "period of indiscriminate overuse." Treatment in the United States today occurs three times a week. Six to twelve treatments are administered to depressed patients, while twelve to twenty episodes are indicated for schizophrenics (p. 93).

    Today, also, the treatment includes counseling, sedatives, and oxygenization to reduce the incidence of cardiac arrests, bone fractures, and undue trauma. (*Psychiatry for Medical Students*, Robert J. Waldinger, M.D., published by the American Psychiatric Press, Inc., 1984, pp. 388–394; *Textbook of Psychiatry*, John A. Talbott, M.D., published by the American Psychiatric Press, 1988, pp. 836–841).

31. In New York, Brussel published an article advocating a radical "intensive electric shock" program he and co-author Dr. Jacob Schneider had conceived. The treatment was nicknamed "The Blitz" (officially named B.E.S.T.). "The B.E.S.T. in the Treatment and Control of Chronically Disturbed Mental Patients—A Preliminary Report," James A. Brussel, M.D., and Jacob Schneider, M.D., *Psychiatric Quarterly*, 25; 55–64, 1951. The article had been read as a paper in May 1950 during a meeting of the Finger Lakes Neuropsychiatric Society in Willard, New York.

32. See "The Use of Methedrine in Psychiatric Practice," by James A. Brussell, M.D., David C. Wilson, Jr., M.D., and Lewis W. Shankel, M.D., *Psychiatric Journal*, Number 28: 381–394, 1954.

33. When Alan Dershowitz joined the MacDonald defense team and began reading the case record, he recalled a talk Dr. Brussel had given at Harvard Law School during which Brussel expressed pride at using his psychiatric training to assist the police in getting confessions.

34. Witness Statement, William F. Ivory, 7 Feb 71, sworn to and witnessed by Peter E. Kearns.

35. See *Drugs and the Brain*, Solomon H. Snyder, published by Scientific American Library, 1986, and *Textbook of Psychiatry*, John A. Talbott, M.D., published by the American Psychiatric Press, 1988.

36. *The Encyclopedia of Human Behavior: Psychology, Psychiatry and Mental Health*, Robert M. Goldenson, Ph.D., published by Dell, 1975. The first edition was published by Doubleday, 1970.

37. See After Action Report—The USACIDC Investigation of the MacDonald Murders, Fort Bragg, North Carolina, dated March 10, 1972, with 21 enclosures, signed by Lt. Col. Saunder Weinstein, director of the Investigative Directorate. According to this report some unnamed pathology and psychiatric

"professional advisory personnel" went on record as saying "that Doctor MacDonald was not truthful in his rendition of the events on 17 February 1970; and this, coupled with other evidence, identified MacDonald as the perpetrator of the murders." Dr. Brussel was the only psychiatrist furnishing reports on the case as a CID adviser.

38. See MacDonald's records from Dr. Bruce H. Bailey at Walter Reed Army Hospital; see the transcript of a meeting between CID agents Jack Pruett and Peter Kearns, and Bernard Segal and Jeffrey MacDonald. The transcript was prepared by Diane Scarangelli, court reporter; the meeting was held on the tenth floor of the Widener Building, Library of the Philadelphia Bar Association, downtown Philadelphia, Pennsylvania, Friday, 10:30 A.M., February 19, 1971. See Peter Kearns's entry in the CID Case Progress File, 2 Apr. 71, 0800–1700. See letters from Jack G. Pruett to Bernard L. Segal, Apr. 2, 1971. See CID Case Progress File, 3 Apr. 71, Reed. See CID Case Progress File, 5 Apr. 71, Pruett-Reed. See letter to Bernard L. Segal, Esquire, from Peter E. Kearns, dated May 17, 1971.

39. Transcript of Jeffrey MacDonald's tape-recorded report on his interview with Dr. James A. Brussel and Dr. Hirsch Lazar Silverman made upon MacDonald's return to quarters after the interview on August 13, 1979. That Dr. MacDonald reported the details of the interview immediately following the event is attested to by the sworn statement of Bernard L. Segal, February 28, 1984.

40. After the trial Bernard Segal filed a motion to have the Brussel-Silverman report removed from the record. He complained that he had effected an agreement with the two doctors that they were not to release the report to anyone unless Judge Dupree allowed psychiatric testimony. Dupree responded to Segal's motion to strike the report by writing a memorandum, not to Segal and the prosecutors, but to prosecutor Jim Blackburn alone. And he marked the memo "CONFIDENTIAL." He told Blackburn he had just read Segal's motion. "I understand you will respond to this." Then the judge wrote, "Just what effect any agreement between the doctors and Segal would have on you," Dupree wrote, "I am not aware. . . ." From this one might assume that James Blackburn furnished the report to Dupree, and Dupree was pointing out to Blackburn that he might retort that an agreement between the doctors and MacDonald certainly had no hold on Blackburn.

41. It should be noted that sixteen years have passed since Dr. Silverman wrote these words, yet Jeffrey MacDonald's "personal and social adjustment," despite major adverse occurrences, has been normal and has not required any "consistent psychotherapeutic intervention" or "psychiatric attention" as Silverman insisted would be necessary.

42. The tapes were made on June 22, 1979.

43. In May 1971 Segal had received a letter with Brussel's name mentioned in it as the doctor who would review MacDonald's psychiatric documents for the

CID, but since Segal hadn't intended to turn over the medical information, he ignored the letter and paid no attention to the name of the psychiatrist mentioned therein.

9. The Verdict

1. See the closing argument of James Blackburn at trial, August 28, 1979.
2. Trial transcript, Dr. Frank Gemma, p. 3006.
3. The CID agent who related this addition did not want his name used in the book. He stated in an interview on May 9, 1990, that he had understood from the investigating CID agents that MacDonald had "refused to cooperate and wouldn't answer any CID questions."
4. Another person who claimed to have seen MacDonald's puncture wounds at this time was his friend Ron Harrison. When interviewed under oath by Peter Kearns on June 14, 1971, long before the ice pick controversy, he told of visiting MacDonald at the hospital and described the various wounds he had seen. As part of this description, recorded and witnessed by A. J. Bennett, he said, "I also noticed numerous pinpoint wounds on his chest, arms, and abdomen. . . . As I recall there were one or two wounds in his neck, pin points of blood that may have been pick marks."
5. Study entitled *MacDonald Murders, Fort Bragg, North Carolina*, by CPT Brian Murtagh, JAGC, undated, four parts plus Appendix; received by the Justice Department on March 11, 1972.
6. Grand jury transcript, Severt H. Jacobson, p. 8.
7. Jacobson had particularly noted in MacDonald's left chest a pattern of wounds so in line and so close together that they could have been made by the tines of a fork. These injuries had intrigued him. He described these for the grand jurors as "a line of kind of puncture marks, very small punctures about the size of the end of a lead pencil." (See grand jury transcript, Dr. Severt Jacobson, pp. 10–11.) Jacobson had been much more expansive about this series of wounds earlier, and nearer in time to the actual event, at the army Article 32 hearing in 1970. Also, at the 1979 trial he included testimony of finding these "punctate wounds" on MacDonald's chest, saying that in his opinion they had been made by "a very sharp object—something that did not have a lot of width or breadth." (See trial transcript, Dr. Severt Jacobson, pp. 2858–2859.)
8. Interview of Dr. Severt Jacobson with Fred Bost and Jerry Potter at Pinehurst, North Carolina, Saturday, July 15, 1989.
9. Grand jury testimony, Jacobson, p. 12.
10. Grand jury transcript, Merrill Bronstein, Dec. 4, 1974, p. 11.
11. Grand jury testimony, Dr. Severt Jacobson, November 13, 1974, p. 22.

12. Grand jury transcript, Dr. Frank Gemma, pp. 9–10, p. 16, pp. 33–34, 37–41.

13. Trial transcript Dr. Severt Jacobson, pp. 2878–2880.

14. Dr. Severt Jacobson was interviewed on July 5, 1989, by Fred Bost and Jerry Potter at Pinehurst, North Carolina.

15. This blood spot will be discussed at length later in the chapter.

16. Joe Grebner, Shaw's boss, is on record saying that when he arrived shortly before 5 A.M. Shaw was in the front yard with others making a search of the grounds. Only minutes after that three military policemen, Robert Duffy, Raymond Jackson, and John Sellick, spotted the weapons in the backyard. Jackson ran around to the front to report the find. A CID agent came around the corner of the building and Sellick pointed out the location of the weapons to him. Grebner, who had been in the house only minutes, is on record under oath as saying he was then taken outside by Shaw to be shown the weapons and it was "dark and raining." And then an ambulance driver, James Paulsen, who was not at the scene later at the time Shaw claims he discovered the weapons, told of being shown a knife that was found in the backyard. It was in the "hands" of one of the law enforcement people. During the army hearing, MP Dennis Morris on the witness stand was shown the photographs made under Shaw's directions. He said the weapons were not in the position in which he had first seen them.

17. The former soldier who spoke with Ellen Dannelly didn't want his name released and wouldn't sign a formal statement.

18. The applicable quotes from the CID lab report of February 28, 1970, are: "two purple multi-strand cotton fibers, identical to the purple thread used to sew the seams of the pajama top" as well as "Numerous blue, green, yellow/green, single strand nylon mostly all are bloodstained. These fibers are identical to the fibers from the multicolored rug."

19. See the 1979 trial transcript, testimony of Dillard Browning, August 6, 1979, pp. 3784–3790.

20. A similar sloppiness occurred when Hilyard Medlin assured his bosses that a footprint which had fallen apart in his hands was MacDonald's, even though he admitted photographs failed to prove this. Discrepancies between subsequent tests of other items, both by the CID and the FBI, are numerous.

21. See the trial transcript, pp. 3877–3878.

22. FBI technicians James Frier and Kathy Bond cataloged a green woolen fiber, six rayon fibers (two green, three blue, and one gold), and nine white cotton fibers.

23. According to the handwritten laboratory notes.

24. Even though the formula of two dark fibers and other light fibers was found in all army and FBI listings of the fibers on the club, the defense team opted for caution in their 1990 appeal and still did not claim that only the black

wool fibers were found. The debris from the club had been presented to Frier and Bond in three forms: in a vial, in a pillbox, and on a slide. Apparently the two threads thought to be from the pajama top were residing in the pillbox, because Kathy Bond's initial inventory note, before any actual analyses took place, stated: "(2)Pillbox contains 2 short pc's sew thr (like blue PJ top)." An element that causes further confusion is her following notation, "(left as is)." Did this mean that Frier and Bond ignored the fibers in the pillbox, and never examined them, choosing only to examine the other materials? Perhaps. And if this is what happened, then the two "pajama" fibers were still in existence, still serving as thorns gouging the defense. But if this is true, a new question must be asked: How then did two additional *dark* fibers (the black wool) suddenly materialize among the lighter colors of the other fibers? Two dark fibers that were never before cataloged? Ultimately, the lawyers reasoned, it didn't matter, for no black wool was found in the MacDonald home and that meant that the black wool would have been claimed as foreign fiber by Bernard Segal had he known about it.

25. The prosecution activities which led to the discovery of the black wool, and the withholding of information about it, will be discussed in Chapter 11.

10. Post-Trial Admissions and Confessions

1. From a taped interview of Fred Thornhill conducted by Fred Bost on October 4, 1988.

2. From a taped interview of Gloria Hayes by Fred Bost on September 27, 1988.

3. Comments by Richard Embrey are from a taped interview by Fred Bost on October 12, 1988.

4. A news story circulated by the Associated Press on August 6, 1980, under the title "Foreman of MacDonald Jury Stands by Verdict," quotes David Hardison as saying, "We kept waiting for the defense to come up with something—anything—that could raise a reasonable doubt in our minds."

5. Comments made by Eddie Parker are from a taped interview by Fred Bost on November 1, 1988.

6. Prince Beasley showed a copy of the confession to Bost on December 22, 1980. The following day Bost's news article was published in the *Fayetteville Times*.

7. In addition to this interview on January 2, 1981, Bost interviewed Stoeckley again a month later on February 6. In both instances he found her to be a responsive, intelligent woman.

8. Either Stoeckley knew, from an earlier visit to the neighborhood, that the Pendlyshoks had such a dog, or this is one of Stoeckley's falsehoods. The

dog was indeed tan, but in a telephone interview with Fred Bost on June 21, 1988, Mrs. Pendlyshok said her dog was in her bedroom with her on the night of the murders, and it was her dog barking in the room with her that awoke her to the sounds of a woman and children screaming.

9. According to a note in the CID log made on December 29, 1970, as a result of questions put to Helena Stoeckley by CID agents Robert Bidwell and Richard Mahon on that date, Stoeckley said when she was in jail she was visited by a CID agent and a lawyer named Thompson. She does not name Ivory during her Bidwell-Mahon interview; however, Ivory was the CID agent who interviewed her in jail. He says so in the sworn written statement he made on December 15, 1970, when he was interviewed by Peter Kearns as a result of the Kassab-Malley charges.

Another CID log entry for February 23, 1971, confirms the arrest itself. This entry shows how Mahon checked arrest records of Helena Stoeckley and found that she had been arrested for trespassing on September 2, 1970.

10. This is reference to Fred Truitt, a Fayetteville police detective who was a friend of Helena Stoeckley's parents.

11. Helena Stoeckley's medical records show that she suffered liver problems throughout her adult life.

12. The story of the confession was published with limited circulation in the *Fayetteville Times* on December 23, 1980, followed by a personal interview story in the same paper on January 9, 1981, both by Fred Bost.

13. The agent's name is blacked out in the FOIA document.

14. These statements were made on November 17, 1982, and were recorded in an FBI report dated November 22, 1982; released to the defense through the Freedom of Information Act on June 4, 1993.

15. This letter was read in full before the court in Raleigh on September 19, 1984, during MacDonald's bid for a new trial.

16. The *60 Minutes* tape, filmed on May 21, 1982, was never aired by CBS; Jack Anderson's interview was aired on September 18–19, 1982.

17. All aspects of Mitchell's military history are based upon entries in his military personnel records.

18. From interviews of the Bishops by CID agent Richard Mahon on April 12–13, 1971.

19. Mitchell graduated from the drug rehabilitation program on September 15, 1970.

20. Mitchell arrived in Vietnam on November 14, 1970.

21. DD Form 214, Certificate of Release or Discharge from Active Duty, Gregory Howard Mitchell, Army RA, AR 635–212, signed by John V. Radoll, Maj. AGC, dated February 25, 1971, at Fort Lewis, Washington.

22. Mrs. Canady told Fred Bost in a February 11, 1994, interview that she didn't come forward during the trial because she believed that the local sheriff's

department had made a report about her seeing the words written on the farmhouse wall. She thought such a report would have been made a part of the trial evidence. When she learned, much later, that either the deputy had made no report or it had not been given to Segal, she discussed the matter further with her husband; they agreed that she should call Ray Shedlick, MacDonald's private investigator. Defense team efforts to locate the name of the deputy have been fruitless. Records were poorly kept, memories had faded, and many deputies worked the rural areas during the period in question and have since left the area.

23. Interview with Norma Lane by the authors and private investigator Ellen Dannelly, April 18, 1988. Mrs. Lane had made this statement in earlier interviews conducted by private investigator Ray Shedlick, Dannelly's father.

24. Greg Mitchell is mentioned in *Fatal Vision* on p. 234 and 639 (Signet paperback with 1989 epilogue).

25. Declaration given to Ray Shedlick, signed by Norma Lane, April 14, 1984.

26. See the transcript of oral arguments before Judge Franklin Dupree in the 1984–1985 appeal, January 14, 1985, vol. 1, pp. 159–160.

27. This statement and all others attributed to Bryant Lane are in his signed declaration of July 15, 1988. Mr. Lane repeated his story during a filmed interview by ABC's *20/20* TV crew at the Ramada Inn, Fayetteville, on Thursday, July 12, 1990.

28. Affidavit of Sam Lee, July 15, 1988. Notarized by Mary B. Gibson.

29. Cathy Perry had been a close friend of Helena Stoeckley at the time of the murders, as stated by a number of witnesses. Indeed, during a taped interview of Stoeckley on February 6, 1981, she gave Fred Bost a detailed description of Cathy Perry and the girl's mood swings in 1970.

30. Statement by Accused or Suspect Person, Jackie Don Wolverton, concerning his arrests and disciplinary actions, dated March 17, 1971, given to Daniel R. Wanken who administered the oath, witnessed by George D. Trogdon.

31. Gunderson found Wolverton in Charlotte, North Carolina, in 1983.

32. The Haymount area encompassed Candy's black-painted pad at 908 Hay Street where Helena Stoeckley told Beasley that cult meetings took place; it also encompassed the Stoeckley apartment at 1108 Clark Street, where William Posey claimed to have seen witchcraft meetings. Only a few blocks separated the two buildings.

33. CID Case Progress File, 1030–1730, January 6, 1971, Kearns.

34. Witness Statement, Darrell Jack Bennett, 5 Apr. 72, 1530 hours, oath administered by Peter E. Kearns.

35. This docudrama, aired on November 18 and 19, 1984, was based upon Joe McGinniss's book of the same name.

36. Private detective Ellen Dannelly, while studying government records, discovered these blood spots and recognized their possible significance.

37. Oral Arguments for New Trial, January 14, 1985, Vol. 1, p. 49.
38. Judge Dupree's denial of motions, March 1, 1985, pp. 38, 41.
39. *False Witness* aired in June 1989 on approximately 120 independent television stations nationwide.
40. Affidavit of William F. Ivory, June 20, 1984, p. 3.
41. See the 1979 trial transcript, pp. 7108–7109.

11. A Prosecutorial Attitude

1. Eldridge wrote Silverglate on September 29, 1989, saying, "Frankly, your and Alan's involvement could make an enormous difference in the outcome of a very distressing story and in this man's life."
2. Letter to writer Melinda Stephens from Harvey Silverglate, March 26, 1990.
3. This agent asked that his name not be used.
4. Trial transcript, Dillard Browning, p. 3811.
5. This fiber is discussed later in this chapter.
6. Posse Comitatus—that is, "power of the country"—is the traditional law which allows peacekeepers to deputize other citizens. In early history, a U.S. marshal would commonly deputize soldiers, leaving their commander frustrated. To end this practice, the U.S. Congress, on June 18, 1878, made it illegal to use military members for civil law enforcement except when called upon by the president during emergencies.

   Then in 1955 a Supreme Court decision made it additionally illegal under this Posse Comitatus Act for military law enforcers to pursue a military lawbreaker into civilian life when the crime allegedly committed was such that it could be tried by a civilian court. Since federal statutes sufficiently covered murder on a government reservation, the 1955 court decision made it illegal for the army to investigate Jeffrey MacDonald once he was released from uniform.
7. In a letter dated April 7, 1978, the army general counsel reprimanded the CID for violating the Posse Comitatus Act after the military discharge of Jeffrey MacDonald.
8. In a letter to the Justice Department on November 4, 1970, the chief FBI agent in North Carolina, Robert Murphy, made this position crystal clear when he complained about "the refusal of the Army authorities to cooperate with this bureau at the outset." (See letter to Assistant Attorney General, Criminal Division, and Director of the FBI, from Special Agent in Charge Robert M. Murphy, FBI Charlotte, North Carolina, November 4, 1970.)
9. The hearings were held during the months of February and March, 1971, under the chairmanship of Senator Sam J. Ervin, Jr., D-North Carolina. The

unauthorized and uncontrolled military surveillance of civilians was one of the main focuses of the meetings.

10. A copy of the illegally acquired document with Kearns's notation was among papers released to the defense in 1983 through the Freedom of Information Act.

11. This claim was made in the request letter to J. Edgar Hoover from Henry H. Tufts, June 7, 1971.

12. This lab note was released under the Freedom of Information Act in June 1990. It is the same lab note that indicates the bloodstains did not match across the tears in the pajama top, as would be later claimed by Stombaugh.

13. See the transcript of the interrogation of Jeffrey MacDonald, April 6, 1970, p. 23.

14. U.S. Government Memorandum from Washington to SAC, Charlotte, dated 10/22/74.

15. U.S. Government Memorandum to Mr. White from M. E. Williams, November 6, 1974.

16. See recorded deposition given to Raymond Shedlick by Raymond R. Klein on Monday, April 20, 1987; see also declaration of Raymond R. Klein given to Fred Bost on September 23, 1988.

17. See the signed declaration by Earl W. Black given to Fred Bost on September 9, 1988, following a taped interview.

18. This conversation hadn't been a quiet one, and others who were present admitted they heard the remark. Joseph Bowden, who was visiting the Blacks at the time, signed a declaration on September 7, 1988, and Richard James, a mechanic, signed a declaration on September 9, 1988.

19. Declaration of Broward County Chief Medical Examiner Dr. Ronald K. Wright, February 15, 1984.

20. Grand jury testimony of Dr. William Hancock, Jr., p. 15.

21. Affidavit of FBI Special Agent James M. Reed (App. Vol. I, Tab. Q), July 12, 1984.

22. See following four documents: (1) Case Progress Form of CID agent Young, 8 Dec. 71, listing Dr. MacDonald's calls from July 14 to November 4, 1971, including the length of each call by minutes; (2) Letter to Commander, Detachment E, 12th MP Group, Brooklyn, New York, from CID headquarters, Washington, dated December 14, 1971, subject: Request for Assistance, signed by Leigh P. Hopp, assistant operations officer; (3) Military Police Criminal Investigation Case Progress Form, Dec. 71, 1900–2230 hours, Young/Tillson; and (4) Witness Statement by William Charles Ward, 17 Jan. 72, 4 pages, oath administered by Walter L. Young, no witnesses.

23. Handwritten note to Brian from Maj. C, dated 22 Apr. 74.

24. Petersen wrote three letters on June 3, 1974; one to the Secretary of the

Army, one to the army's Judge Advocate General, and the third to the CID commander. Without specifically asking for Captain Murtagh, Petersen nevertheless made sure he would get Murtagh by requesting the services of a CID legal officer "thoroughly familiar with the case."

25. Memorandum for Record, subject: MacDonald Murders—Inquiry, signed by Steven Chucala, dated 11 Jul. 1974.

26. See the U.S. Government Memorandum to Lawrence Lippe from Brandon Alvey, dated July 16, 1979.

27. Ibid. This contact is mentioned in the Alvey memo, page 2.

28. Letter to Thomas P. McNamara from Carl W. Belcher, Dec. 21, 1973.

29. Draft letter (never delivered) to Mr. Henry E. Petersen, created for the signature of Henry H. Tufts, undated.

30. Memorandum for Judge Advocate, USACIDC, signed by Henry H. Tufts, CID commander, dated January 21, 1974.

31. U.S. Government Memorandum to SAC, Charlotte, from Supervisor [deleted], dated 9/10/74, p. 4.

32. See Raleigh News and Observer, July 30, 1975.

33. Transcript, oral arguments, U.S. Court of Appeals, Fourth Circuit, Oct. 8, 1975.

34. U.S. Government Memorandum to Lawrence Lippe from Brandon Alvey, dated July 16, 1979.

35. Letter to Morris S. Clark from Brian Murtagh, dated Dec. 14, 1978.

36. When a case goes to trial, both sides are supposed to have equal knowledge of the evidence on hand. The rule for prosecutors is simple and is sometimes referred to as the "Brady rule." Exculpatory evidence (that is, evidence which tends toward clearing a defendant) must be revealed. If there is doubt as to the evidence being of value, the benefit of the doubt should be given the accused and the evidence made known to the defense. The rule says that to do otherwise is to deny due process. The governing precedents are found in the court case of Brady v. Maryland, 373 U.S. (1963), and in further clarifications as found in United States v. Bagley, 473 U.S. (1985), and United States v. Agurs, 427 U.S. (1976). A clarification of Brady in the latter reference states that when a prosecutor has received a specific request for evidence relevant to the defense, his failure to respond to the request is "seldom, if ever, excusable." (Agurs, supra, 427 U.S. at 106, 96 S. Ct. at 2399, 49 L. Ed. 2d 342.)

Judge Dupree made reference to this principle when prosecutor Murtagh, claiming that certain oft-requested documents held nothing helpful to the defense team, refused to turn them over to Bernard Segal. Judge Dupree didn't force Murtagh to turn over the documents, but said that if they were later discovered to hold exculpatory material the case would "get reversal."

37. Letter, Freedom of Information Request, to the FBI director from Alan J. Gilman and Bernard J. [*sic*] Segal, dated January 4, 1979.
38. See the handwritten notation on the first page of the report: "Original and cc picked up by B.M. Murtagh on 3–15–79."
39. Letter to Lieutenant Colonel John F. Lynburner from Brian M. Murtagh, dated March 30, 1979.
40. We date this undated memo's production before trial because of information supplied by its author, Jeffrey S. Puretz. In an affidavit signed for the MacDonald defense team on October 15, 1990, attorney Anthony P. Bisceglie told of a telephone conversation on August 24, 1990, in which Jeffrey Puretz assured him that the memorandum researched at the request of Brian Murtagh was prepared in preparation for the MacDonald trial and was delivered to Murtagh sometime before the trial, although Puretz could not be certain of the date. The Bisceglie affidavit was made part of the 1990–1991 defense writ.
41. Frier's personal knowledge of the black wool would not surface for ten more years, when former FBI bureau chief Ted L. Gunderson, retired and working for the MacDonald defense, questioned Frier in Italy and elicited an admission that he had, indeed, found the black wool on the murder weapon.
42. "Junk Science," Phony Forensics, and Other Distortions of Reality in the Case of *U.S. v. MacDonald*. A memo on the case by Harvey Silverglate, September 1992.
43. See the following letters: to Thomas P. McNamara from Judge Algernon L. Butler, July 31, 1974 (and second informal letter, same addressee, same date); to Algernon L. Butler from Thomas P. McNamara, Aug. 5, 1974.
44. *Martindale-Hubble, North Carolina Edition*, 1967, 1968, 1969, for the law firm, Dupree, Weaver, Horton, Cockman & Alvis.
45. FBI Teletype, Robert M. Murphy to J. Edgar Hoover, 1258 hours, October 28, 1970.
46. Washington, D C., Subject: MacDonald Case, dated November 2, 1970; signed by Lieutenant Colonel Malcolm R. Smith, deputy commander.
47. See FBI Teletype, Robert M. Murphy to J. Edgar Hoover, November 2, 1970.
48. See two FBI teletypes from Robert M. Murphy to J. Edgar Hoover, the first dated November 2, 1970, the second dated November 18, 1970.
49. FBI Teletype, Robert M. Murphy to J. Edgar Hoover, November 18, 1970.
50. All information concerning the meeting depicted here comes from CID Memorandum: Telephone Conversation between Mr. Bidwell and Sergeant Wilson, CI Division, 31 December 1970.
51. See FBI Airtel from SAC, Charlotte, to Director, 2/14/75. The sentence of the telegram being referenced here (with editorial meanings added for abbreviations) reads as follows: "AUSA [Assistant United States Attorney] Stroud advised arrangements are currently being made to assign a USDJ

[United States District Judge] from outside the EDNC [Eastern District of North Carolina] to handle the trial of the subject and as soon as these arrangements are finalized, a date for trial will be set."

52. U.S. Government Memorandum to Jay Stroud from Judge Dupree, subject: MacDonald, date: February 26, 1975.

53. These particular FOIA documents were released on April 22, 1983.

54. The comments and quotes included here are derived from the news story "Proctor Says Movie Confirms His Memories of MacDonald Case," by Shirley Hayes, the *Independent*, Fuquay-Varina, North Carolina, Wednesday, November 28, 1984, p. 1.

55. See transcript of the grand jury investigation, Jeffrey MacDonald, first appearance, Vol. 1, pp. 9–30.

56. One motion was approved by the Fourth Circuit Court of Appeals twice, once before trial and once afterward. In eventually denying this motion concerning "speedy trial," the U.S. Supreme Court split its decision. Yet Judge Dupree in two decisions on the subject had seen no merit at all.

57. From transcript of the examinations of potential jurors.

58. From trial transcript, Charge, p. 10, A.137.

59. Judge Dupree actually had stated something quite different. He had said that he would not allow Segal to present psychiatric testimony regarding MacDonald's state of mind, his absence of malice toward his family, *or* his character.

60. See *Fatal Vision* by Joe McGinniss, Signet paperback with 1989 epilogue, pp. 492–493.

61. Hopkins's story was published on September 25, 1979.

62. 640 F. Supplement, 286 (E.D.N.C. 1985).

63. See trial transcript, August 21, 1979, p. 2053.

64. This affidavit was signed by Brian Murtagh on February 19, 1991.

65. See affidavit, p. 5.

66. See affidavit, pp. 6–7.

67. To understand how thoroughly the evidence was reviewed, it is only necessary to refer to the follow-up correspondence from the prosecutors to the attendees. Hilyard Medlin was asked to adjust discrepancies between his findings and those of Walter Page; and Shirley Green was told to reconfirm her statements with Paul Stombaugh.

68. See Brian Murtagh's written request to the CID, dated March 1, 1979.

12. A Fatal Vision

1. The contract was signed August 3, 1979.

2. McGinniss received an advance payment against future royalties of $250,000.

Of the first $150,000, McGinniss received 80 percent, MacDonald 20. On earnings over $150,000 McGinniss was to receive two-thirds and MacDonald one-third. See the contract with Dell-Delacorte, August 21, 1979, signed for Dell by Donald Braunstein, vice-president. The percentages to MacDonald and McGinniss are detailed in an agency agreement dated July 16, 1979, and signed by Bernard L. Segal and Sterling Lord, attorney in fact and agent for Joe McGinniss.

McGinniss would later apply for and receive an additional $50,000 advance from the publisher. He then told MacDonald he needed $20,000 "off the top" of that advance, before sharing it. He said he needed the money for photocopying the case records. MacDonald believed the amount was grossly exorbitant for photocopying, but he gave the writer the funds, and they split the remaining $30,000. (From an interview with Jeffrey MacDonald by Jerry Potter, October 6, 1990, Terminal Island Federal Correctional Institution, San Pedro, California. The figure is also verified by the case financial records presented at the civil trial *MacDonald v. McGinniss in Los Angeles.*)

3. Letter, Jeffrey MacDonald to Joe McGinniss, August 30, 1979.
4. August, 31, 1979, letter from Jeffrey MacDonald to Joe McGinniss, following McGinniss's visit.
5. MacDonald's tone of hope immediately following Joe McGinniss's visit is recorded in his letter to McGinniss written the same day, August 31, 1979.
6. Order of Judge Franklin T. Dupree, Jr., signed Sept. 7, 1979; filed Sept. 14, 1979.
7. Letter from Joe McGinniss to Jeffrey MacDonald, January 16, 1980.
8. Letter from Joe McGinniss to Jeffrey MacDonald, May 30, 1980.
9. July 16, 1982, letter from Joe McGinniss to Jeffrey MacDonald.
10. Letter from Brian J. O'Neill to Mike Wallace, June 14, 1983.
11. A letter from Dr. Wayne O. Southwick from the Department of Orthopaedic Surgery at Yale Medical School. Dr. Southwick wrote, "I am sorry that I have not written to you sooner regarding your decision to withdraw from the residency program. I am deeply sorry that you do not feel able to go ahead at this time. . . . I take considerable pride in the fact that you were planning to come here to train with me." The letter was drafted on July 7, 1971.
12. Upon the publication of *Fatal Vision* MacDonald received a great deal of hate mail from people who reacted strongly to MacDonald's continued claims of innocence in the face of McGinniss's research into MacDonald's personal life. The question about his refusal to take the sodium amytal examination when the grand jury asked him to was the question most asked of MacDonald.
13. The "Ira" lifesaving episode was corroborated during an interview of Father Bill Nadeau on November 18, 1989. Nadeau was a chaplain at Bastrop Federal Correctional Institute at the time of the incident.

14. Throughout his years in federal prisons, MacDonald has been forbidden to practice medicine.

15. During the civil trial of 1987, Clive Backster, the polygraph examiner in question, said he had lost his records of the MacDonald polygraph. MacDonald's defense attorney, Gary Bostwick, expressed surprise at this and asked him if he had any record of having been paid for the alleged examination. Backster couldn't produce a record of having been paid.

16. Letter from Dr. David C. Raskin to Brian O'Neill, May 17, 1986.

17. Dr. Raskin's procedure also involved a unique computer compilation of the technical data, which theoretically precludes subconscious human manipulation of the results, a sort of cross-check to the actual polygraph readings. Like Dr. Raskin, the computer, too, concluded that MacDonald was not deceptive when he said that he inflicted no injuries on his wife and children, that he did not directly cause their deaths, and that he had not arranged to cause their deaths.

18. The compilations of exceptions MacDonald's defense team members found in *Fatal Vision* finally fell into two groups: errors, or things McGinniss might have inadvertently written without knowing or without checking the record, and outright falsehoods, which the lawyers felt McGinniss knew, but stated incorrectly.

19. Donna Bruce Koch's opinions and interest in the MacDonald-McGinniss relationship were expressed to both of us in meetings and telephone conversations from approximately April 1986 to approximately October 1987. Also, on November 25, 1987, she made an audiotape for us which detailed her logical path through the arguments that finally resulted in her ten-page opinion quoted herein in part.

20. The Garveys' marriage had been represented unfavorably by *Inside Sport*. The case was settled out of court.

21. Two transcripts of the tapes exist. Joe McGinniss had a partial typescript made during his writing of the book, and Jeffrey MacDonald arranged for Christian Schuller to transcribe the complete tapes.

22. Using the numbering on McGinniss's typescript.

23. Transcript of "A Portion of a Radio Program on September 28, 1983—The George Putnam Show—on Radio KIEV AM (Los Angeles)."

24. On July 29, 1980, the Fourth Circuit Court of Appeals overturned MacDonald's conviction because his rights to a speedy trial had been violated. MacDonald was released on bail on August 22, 1980, after serving about a year in prison. On March 31, 1982, the Supreme Court, reviewing the MacDonald case, made a major change in the speedy-trial law. Under the change, the clock begins ticking not on the day a defendant is charged, but on the day he is indicted. With this change the high court reversed MacDonald's speedy-trial win, ruling that his speedy-trial started on January 24, 1975, when he

was indicted, not on May 1, 1970, when he was formally charged. He was returned to prison that day.

25. Phyllis E. Grann letter to Joe McGinniss, November 4, 1982.

26. Since manuscript page numbers do not translate to book page numbers, the authors were unable to establish with certainty the subject matter the editor was writing about here.

27. *Fatal Vision*, p. 610 (1989 Signet paperback edition).

28. For McGinniss on diet pills, see *Fatal Vision*, p. 611 (1989 Signet paperback edition). After Bostwick's assistants had made unsuccessful requests at dozens of medical libraries in Los Angeles, Alice Karasick, of USC's Norris Medical Library, located the editions of *Physicians' Desk Reference* and *Goodman and Gilman's Pharmacological Basis of Therapeutics* in a storage unit.

29. The FBI investigation corroborated that while moonlighting in the Hamlet Hospital on the night before the murders, Jeffrey MacDonald had slept a great deal of the time.

30. Page 205, *The Culture of Narcissism*, Christopher Lasch, published by W. W. Norton and Company, 1977.

31. Letter from Daniel J. Kornstein to Gary Bostwick, November 4, 1986.

32. MacDonald's defense team had researched the army's position on drugs during the time of the murders and learned that General John J. Tolson, commander of Fort Bragg at the time of the murders, testified before a seven-week congressional subcommittee hearing on drug abuse in the military in late 1970. (See *Report of a Special Subcommittee to Investigate Alleged Drug Abuse in the Armed Services of the Committee on Armed Services*, House of Representatives, Ninety-Second Congress, First Session, April 23, 1971, U.S. Government Printing Office, Washington, D.C.) During his congressional testimony General Tolson outlined the serious drug problems at Bragg, including amphetamine abuse. Another study compiled in 1970 by Bernard N. Nossiter and reported by the Washington Post–Los Angeles Times News Service supported Tolson's statements. Nossiter estimated that 2 to 3 percent of Fort Bragg's troops "are 'strung out' on heroin, amphetamines and other hard drugs. That means," Nossiter wrote, "800 to 1,000 addicts on this one post." Another study published in the *American Journal of Psychiatry* in October of 1970 listed amphetamines as second only to marijuana as the drug of choice among army users. In that study 5,482 men in 56 separate army posts were polled. Of these, 27 percent "admitted to the use of drugs; and of those admitting use, 83 percent had used marihuana, 26 percent LSD, 37 percent amphetamines, and 5 percent had used heroin."

33. Dr. Robert Sadoff didn't actually testify at the grand jury hearing. Because Sadoff was ill with influenza, Woerheide went to his home to interview him on January 22, 1975. Woerheide read from the transcript of the interview to the grand jury two days later, on January 24.

34. Dr. Jeffrey Elliot had approached MacDonald about doing a book on the case, and MacDonald had agreed to work with him. Elliot contracted Jerry Potter to share the writing duties. When Elliot, a black studies expert, bowed out of the project to accept an invitation to write a book in Africa, Potter continued the MacDonald book with Fred Bost.
35. *The Journalist and the Murderer*, Janet Malcolm, published by Knopf, 1990.
36. Ibid., p. 144.
37. The legal aspects of this lawsuit remain in question and would have been settled in appeals court; however, neither side appealed the judge's decision.
38. Transcript of Continued Deposition of Joe McGinniss by Gary L. Bostwick, October 30, 1986, pp. 130–133.

13. Appeal

1. See *Michigan v. Sitz*, 1990.
2. See *Arizona v. Fulminante*, 1990.
3. See the *Los Angeles Times*, May 7, 1991.
4. Judge Reinhardt sits on the Ninth Circuit in California.
5. All quotes concerning the appeal arguments are from the 55-page transcript of the proceedings.
6. This specific point was covered in the written appeal brief which had been submitted to the court.
7. According to a federal statute known as the "Jencks Act," verbatim statements in government files which are attributable to a trial witness on a subject upon which that witness will be questioned by the prosecution must be turned over to the defense. A summary or a "rehash" of what the witness said or wrote isn't covered. If the Jencks material agrees with what the witness says on the stand it isn't introduced at trial and it doesn't come to the jury's attention. If, however, the Jencks material, the verbatim statement, contradicts what the witness says on the stand, then defense counsel can use it to impeach the witness's testimony in court.
8. This discovery was made by John Murphy and Fred Bost when the two made the search together.
9. Murtagh's denial was despite the written records showing that he made an oral request on January 4, 1979, to "identify source of fibers" in the debris from the right biceps area of Colette MacDonald's pajama top, known as FBI Exhibit Q88, and then later, on February 9, requested more examinations, specifically requesting an examination of debris from the wooden club, Murtagh subsequently denied before Judge Dupree in 1991 that he was ever informed of the results of his requests—results which showed the existence of black wool in these exhibits.

10. This is a classic example of the transfer theory of locard, with a rug acting as the intermediary item. Wool goes from clothing to a rug then to a club, without the clothing ever being near the club.

11. Bost and I considered it unfair for the government, after hiding the existence of the synthetic blond hair at trial, to now impose the condition that it be proven to be of high-quality synthetic hair for a *human* wig. And we considered it counterproductive for the defense to attempt to prove the same. Stoeckley and her friends were inveterate night scavengers gathering things out of garbage cans, such as items of food, clothing, and the floral wreaths Stoeckley displayed in her yard on the day of the MacDonald funerals. Also, Stoeckley's wig was known to be of such poor quality that she wore it as a "joke." It might, indeed, have been a mannequin wig taken by Stoeckley or one of her friends from the trash dump of some store during one of their night haunts. To now insist that the defense prove that the wig was made for human wear is to beg the question, ignoring the fact that lab tech Janice Glisson's note said it was from a "wig," and that this note would have been helpful at trial, and that it was withheld at a time when the CID and, indeed, Brian Murtagh were well aware that Stoeckley had a wig and was wearing it the night of the murders.

12. Silverglate referred to a precedent, *Washington v. Murray*, in which the defense had a like claim, and in which the court sided with the defendant.

13. "Myths About Habeas Corpus," by Elisabeth Semel, *Los Angeles Daily Journal*, June 22, 1992.

Epilogue

1. James Blackburn was disbarred effective April 16, 1993. (*North Carolina Lawyers Weekly*, April 26, 1993, p. 1.)

Acknowledgments

The authors are especially grateful to everyone responsible for the Freedom of Information Act, without which the government documents upon which this book is based would have remained hidden. We owe a special debt to Prebble Potter for eight years of research, investigation, and document management. We also wish to thank our editor at W.W. Norton, Hilary Hinzmann, and our agent, Jane Dystel, who shared the vision necessary to nurture this project from idea to book over too many long years; Debra Makay, our incredibly talented manuscript editor at Norton; Lucia Bartoli, current information liaison person and brilliant researcher for Dr. MacDonald; Dr. Jane DiGiovanni, who shared her meticulous study of the bloody footprints in the hallway of the murder apartment; Jim Fraenkel, who shared his insightful university paper on the MacDonald case evidence; Debbie Ackert, for her research; Frank Armour, former Cumberland County records custodian, for information about the period of the murders; Alice Karasick, a librarian at Norris Medical Library of the University of Southern California, for her dogged and successful search for out-of-print medical reference books; Daisy Maxwell, a librarian at the *Fayetteville Observer-Times*, for assisting Fred Bost in the search for information; Gail and Robert Boyce, longtime MacDonald supporters, ever eager to share files with us; Elsa Dorfman, for help with the photographs; Marie Vitco, for providing her notes from the civil trial; Reg Henry, former city editor of the Monterey *Herald*, and Sue Chace, of the Ventura *Star-Free Press*, for kindnesses rendered; Phyllis Hughes Abatte, for long years of effort on many projects; Barbara Gallagher Mayotte, for her work in the case; author George Warren, for his kind support; criminalist Richard Fox, for his analysis of the crime-scene photos and for sharing his insights into the field of criminology; members of Dr. MacDonald's legal team, who readily provided all documents we requested—Jason Gull, Donna Bruce Koch, Michael Malley, Dennis Eisman, Bernard Segal, Harvey Silverglate, Alan Dershowitz, Brian O'Neill, Jim Douthat, Anthony Bisceglie, Roger Spaeder, David Hickerson, Norman Smith, John J.E. Markham, Philip Cormier, Thomas Viles, Andrew Good, John Murphy, Doug Widmann, Chauncey Wood, Jane Wolf Eldridge, Sandie Fennell, Audrey Stone, Barbara Weintraub, Bernadette Mirisola, Gia Barresi, Jennifer Pyle, Nestor Davidson, Jennifer DeMarrais, Jo Ann Citron, and Cynthia Rios; the people of J. A. Majors, Inc., for their constant and uncommon goodness during the writing of this book; and the officials at the Bureau of Prisons facilities at Black Canyon, AZ, at Terminal Island, CA, and at Sheridan, OR, for arranging for our interviews with Dr. MacDonald.

Index